MEDIEVAL ISLAMIC PRAGMATICS

Sunni Legal Theorists' Models of Textual Communication

MEDIEVAL ISLAMIC PRAGMATICS

Sunni Legal Theorists' Models of Textual Communication

Mohamed Mohamed Yunis Ali

Routledge
Taylor & Francis Group
LONDON AND NEW YORK

First Published in 2000
by Routledge
Richmond, Surrey

2 Park Square, Milton Park, Abingdon, Oxon, OX14 4RN
270 Madison Ave, New York NY 10016

Transferred to Digital Printing 2009

Typeset in Sabon by LaserScript Ltd, Mitcham, Surrey

British Library Cataloguing in Publication Data
A catalogue record of this book is available from the British Library

Library of Congress Cataloguing in Publication Data
A catalogue record for this book has been requested

ISBN10: 0–7007–1102–3 (hbk)
ISBN10: 0–415–56777–7 (hbk)

ISBN13: 978–0–7007–1102–4 (hbk)
ISBN13: 978–0–415–56777–0 (pbk)

Publisher's Note
The publisher has gone to great lengths to ensure the quality of this reprint but points out that some imperfections in the original may be apparent.

To my parents, my wife and my children

Contents

Acknowledgements x
Transliteration conventions xi
Abbreviations xii

Chapter One – Introduction 1
1.1. General background 1
1.2. The legal theorists' pragmatic approaches to communication 7
1.3. Aims and scope of the study 10
1.4. A note on terminology 12
1.5. The structure of the study 12

Chapter Two – *Waḍ*[c] and Use **15**
2.1. Introduction 15
2.2. *Waḍ*[c] 16
2.2.1. Universal and particular *Waḍ*[c] 18
2.2.2. General and specific *Waḍ*[c] 25
2.3. Use 29
2.3.1. Intention 30
2.3.2. Context 34

Chapter Three – Interpretation 41
3.1. Introduction 41
3.2. *Fiqh*, understanding and interpretation 44
3.3. Signifying by expressions and the signification of expressions 46
3.4. Context from the viewpoint of the addressee 52
3.4.1. Comprehensive sight of text 52
3.4.2. Context as a signifying element 53
3.4.3. Types of context 55
3.5. The mainstream interpretation model 58

3.5.1. The *uṣūl* (principles and bases) 63
3.5.1.1. The Principle of the Speaker's Disposition to Make his Intention Manifest 64
3.5.1.2. The Principle of the Speaker's Truthfulness 66
3.5.1.3. The Principle of *Iᶜmāl* 68
3.5.1.4. The Principle of Immediacy 69
3.5.1.5. The Principle of *Istiṣḥāb* 77

Chapter Four – Ibn Taymiyyah's Contextual Theory of Interpretation 87
4.1. Introduction 87
4.2. Call for a contextual approach 89
4.3. Philosophical background 90
4.3.1. Ibn Taymiyyah's ontological position 91
4.3.2. Ibn Taymiyyah's theory of cognitive relativism 94
4.3.3 Ibn Taymiyyah's contextual theory of definition 95
4.4. Ibn Taymiyyah's contextual view of language and meaningfulness 98
4.5. Ibn Taymiyyah's contextual view of the *waḍᶜ*-use distinction 100
4.6. Ibn Taymiyyah's contextual view of the meaning-intention distinction 101
4.7. Ibn Taymiyyah's contextual view of signification 103
4.8. Ibn Taymiyyah's critical review of *ḥaqīqah* and *majāz* dichotomy 105
4.8.1. The view of the adherents of *ḥaqīqah* and *majāz* dichotomy 106
4.8.1.1. Arguments in favour of the distinction between *ḥaqīqah* and *majāz* 108
4.8.2. Arguments against the distinction between *ḥaqīqah* and *majāz* 109
4.8.3. Ibn Taymiyyah's account of *majāz* 114
4.9. Ibn Taymiyyah's model of interpretation 125
4.9.1. *Taʾwīl* (diverting to non-apparent meaning) 127
4.9.1.1. The limitations of *taʾwīl* 130

Chapter Five – Ways of Signification 141
5.1. Introduction 141
5.2. The semiotic classification of signification 142
5.2.1. *Waḍᶜ*-based verbal signification 146
5.2.1.1. Types of *Waḍᶜ*-based verbal signification 149

5.2.1.2. Criticisms of the classification 154
5.3. The text-based classification of signification 158
5.3.1. The *Ḥanafī* method of dividing text-signification 159
5.3.1.1. The express meaning of text 159
5.3.1.2. The alluded meaning of text 161
5.3.1.3. The inferred meaning of text 166
5.3.1.4. The required meaning of text 170
5.3.2. The *Shāfiʿī* method of dividing text-signification 175
5.3.2.1. Al-Juwaynī's classification 176
5.3.2.2. Al-Ghazāli's classification 179
5.3.2.3. Al-Āmidī's classification 180
5.3.2.4. Ibn al-Ḥājib's classification 185
5.3.3. Implicature 187
5.3.3.1. Types of implicature 188
5.3.3.1.1. Congruent implicature 188
5.3.3.1.2. Counter implicature 192
5.3.3.1.2.1. The pillars of counter implicature 192
5.3.3.1.2.2. The validity of counter implicature 193
5.3.3.1.2.3. The bases for counter implicature 201
5.3.3.1.2.4. The conditions for the validity of counter implicature 206
5.3.3.1.2.5. Types of counter implicature 209

Conclusion 234

Bibliography 245
1. Arabic titles 245
1.1. Primary sources 245
1.2. Secondary sources 248
2. English titles 249
Index 253

Acknowledgements

I would like to express my sincere gratitude to Professor M.Y. Suleiman for the constructive criticism patiently provided throughout the course of writing this book. I am profoundly grateful to him for his valuable comments and corrections. My sincere thanks go also to Dr M.V. McDonald from Edinburgh University, Dr Farida Abu Haidar from the University of London, and Dr Adrian Gully from University of Exeter, who carefully read the final draft and made valuable remarks and corrections.

I am indebted to Dr Mohamed Hasan Grenat, Dr Moḥamed S. al-Seghayar, Mr Jamal Gieber and Mrs Eileen Broughton for their proof reading of one draft of the book.

Moreover, I should like to thank Miss I. Crawford the previous secretary of the department of Islamic and Middle Eastern Studies, and Miss Lesely Scobie the present secretary for their help.

My warmest thanks go to members of the academic staff and my colleagues at the department for their co-operation. I am also grateful to Dr Ronnie Cann and Professor J.R. Hurford from the Department of Linguistics for allowing me to attend some of their lectures.

Finally, I owe a debt of profound gratitude to my father for his continuous care and encouragement, to my wife Mrs M. Ṭayyār, who patiently made her best to make my stay in Edinburgh easy, and to my children ^{c}Abd al-Muhaymin, ^{c}Abd al-Raḥmān and Isrā', who very often missed me when I was supposed to be with them.

M.M.Y. Ali
Edinburgh

Transliteration Conventions

This study follows the transliteration system of the United States Library of Congress as outlined in The Cataloguing Service Bulletin No. 49, November 1958. However, the *tāʾ marbūṭah* at the end of a word is written as *t* when it is part of the *iḍāfah* construction and *h* when it is not.

Abbreviations

ʿAḍud = ʿAḍud al-Millah wa-l-Dīn, *Sharḥ Mukhtaṣar al-Muntahā l-Uṣūlī li-Ibn al-Ḥājib*, 2nd edn. (Beirut: Dār al-Kutub al-ʿIlmiyyah, 1983).

Ali's Translation of *THE HOLY QURʾĀN* = *Ali, A. Yusuf, THE HOLY QURʾAN: Text, Translation and Commentary (Brentwood, USA: Amana Corp, 1983).*

Al-Āmidī (1983) = Al-Āmidī, Sayf al-Dīn ʿAlī b. Muḥammad, *al-Iḥkām fī Uṣūl al-Aḥkām* (Beirut: Dār al-Kutub al-ʿIlmiyyah, 1983).

Al-Āmidī (1986) = Al-Āmidī, Sayf al-Dīn ʿAlī b. Muḥammad, *al-Iḥkām fī Uṣūl al-Aḥkām*, ed. Sayyid al-Jumaylī, 2nd edn. (Beirut: Dār al-Kitāb al-ʿArabī, 1986).

Al-Anṣārī = Al-Anṣārī, ʿAbd al-ʿAlī, *Fawātiḥ al-Raḥamūt bi-Sharḥ Musallam al-Thubūt*, 2nd edn. (Qum, Iran: Dār al-Dhakhāʾir, 1368).

Al-Asnawī = Al-Asnawī, Jamāl al-Dīn ʿAbd al-Raḥīm b. al-Ḥasan, *Nihāyat al-Sūl fī Sharḥ Minhāj al-Uṣūl*, (Beirut: ʿĀlam al-Kutub, n.d.).

Al-Bājī = Al-Bājī, Abū al-Walīd Sulaymān b. Khalaf, *Iḥkām al-Fuṣūl fī Aḥkām al-Uṣūl*, ed. ʿAbd Allāh Muḥammad al-Jabūrī (Beirut: Muʾassasat al-Risālah, 1989).

Al-Bannānī = Al-Bannānī, *Ḥāshiyah ʿalā Sharḥ al-Jalāl al-Maḥallī ʿalā Matn Jam ʿ al-Jawāmiʿ (Beirut: Dār al-Fikr, 1982).*

Al-Baṣrī = Al-Baṣrī, Abū l-Ḥusayn Muḥammad b. ʿAlī b. al-Ṭayyib, *al-Muʿtamad fī Uṣūl al-Fiqh*, ed. Khalīl al-Mays (Beirut: Dār al-Kutub al-ʿIlmiyyah, 1983).

Al-Bayḍāwī = Al-Bayḍāwī, Nāṣir al-Dīn ʿAbd Allāh b. ʿUmar, *Minhāj al-Uṣūl bi Sharḥ al-Asnawī* (Beirut: ʿĀlam al-Kutub).

Al-Bazdawī = Al-Bazdawī, Fakhr al-Islām, *Uṣūl al-Bazdawī* (bi-Kashf al-Asrār li-l-Bukhārī), 2nd edn. (Beirut: Dār al-Kitāb al-ʿArabī, 1994).

Al-Bukhāri = Al-Bukhārī, ʿAlāʾ al-Dīn ʿAbd al-ʿAzīz b. ʾAḥmad, *Kashf al-Asrār ʿan Uṣūl Fakhr al-Islām al-Bazdawī*, ed. Muḥammad al-Muʿtaṣim Bi-Allāh al-Baghdādī, 2nd edn. (Beirut: Dār al-Kitāb al-ʿArabī, 1994).

Al-Ghazālī, al-Mustaṣfā = Al-Ghazālī, Abū Ḥāmid, *al-Mustaṣfā min ʿIlm al-Uṣūl*, 2nd edn. (Qum, Iran: Dār al-Dhakhāʾir, 1368).

Grice (1975) = Grice, H.P., "Logic and Conversation" in Peter Cole and Jerry L. Morgan (eds.), *Syntax and Semantics, 3: Speech Acts* (New York: Academic Press, 1975), pp. 41–58.

Grice (1991) = Grice, H.P., "Logic and Conversation", in Steven Davis (ed.), *Pragmatics: A Reader* (New York: Oxford University Press, 1991), pp. 305–315.

Al-Harawī = Al-Harawī, Hasan, *Ḥāshiyah ʿalā Ḥāshiyat al-Sharīf al-Jurjānī ʿalā Sharḥ al-ʿAḍud*, 2nd edn. (Beirut: Dār al-Kutub al-ʿIlmiyyah, 1983).

Ibn al-Ḥājib = Ibn al-Ḥājib al-Mālikī, *Mukhtaṣar al-Muntahā l-Uṣūlī*, 2nd edn. (Beirut: Dār al-Kutub al- ʿIlmiyyah, 1983).

Ibn al-Ḥalabī = Ibn al-Ḥalabī, Raḍī al-Dīn Muḥammad b. Ibrāhim, *Ḥāshiyat Anwār al-Ḥuluk ʿalā Sharḥ al-Manār* (n.p. al-Maṭbaʿah al-ʿUthmāniyyah, 1319 A.H.).

Ibn al-Malik = Ibn al-Malik, Muʿizz al-Dīn ʿAbd al-Laṭīf b. ʿAbd al-ʿAzīz, *Sharḥ al-Manār* (n.p. al-Maṭbaʿah al-ʿUthmāniyyah, 1319 A.H.).

Ibn Taymiyyah, Fatāwā = Ibn Taymiyyah, Aḥmad, *Majmūʿ Fatāwā*, ed. ʿAbd al-Raḥmān b. Qāsim and Muḥammad ʿAbd al-Rahmān b. Wāsim (Rabāṭ: Maktabat al-Maʿārif, n.d.).

Ibn Taymiyyah, al-Imān = Ibn Taymiyyah, Aḥmad, *al-Imān*, ed. Muḥammad Nāṣir al-Dīn al-Albānī and Zuhayr al-Shāwīsh (Beirut: al-Maktab al-Islāmī, 1986).

Ibn Taymiyyah, *al-Radd* = Ibn Taymiyyah Aḥmad, *al-Radd ʿalā l-Manṭiqiyyīn*, ed. Muḥammad ʿAbd al-Sattār Naṣṣār and ʿImād Khafājī (Cairo: Maktabat al-Azhar, 1977).

Al-Juwaynī = Al-Juwaynī, Imām al-Ḥaramayn Abū l-Maʿālī, *al-Burhān fī Uṣūl al-Fiqh*, ed. ʿAbd al-ʿAẓīm al-Dīb (Qaṭar: 1399, A.H.).

Al-Maḥallī = Al-Maḥallī, Shams al-Dīn Muḥammad, *Sharḥ Matn Jamʿ al-Jawāmiʿ* (Beirut: Dār al-Fikr, 1982).

Al-Mawṣilī = Al-Mawṣilī, Muḥammad, *Mukhtaṣar al-Ṣawāʿiq al-Mursalah ʿalā l-Jahmiyyah wa-l-Muʿaṭṭilah li-Ibn Qayyim al-Jawziyyah* (Mecca: al-Maktabah al-Salafiyyah, 1349 A.H.).

Muḥibb Allāh = Muḥibb Allāh. b. ʿAbd al-Shakūr, *Sharḥ Musallam al-Thubūt*, 2nd edn. (Qum, Iran: Dār al-Dhakhāʾir, 1368).

Mullākhusrū = Mullākhusrū, *Ḥāshiyah ʿalā Ḥāshiyat al-Talwīḥ ʿalā Sharḥ al-Tawḍīḥ ʿalā l-Tanqīḥ* (Cairo: al-Maktabah al-Khayriyyah, 1306 A.H.).

PF = the principles of *fiqh* (i.e., *uṣūl al-fiqh*).

Al-Qarāfī, *Sharḥ Tanqīh* = Al-Qarāfī, Shihāb al-Dīn, *Sharḥ Tanqīḥ al-Fuṣūl fī Ikhtiṣār al-Maḥṣūl fī l-Uṣūl*, ed. Ṭaha ʿAbd al-Raʾūf Saʿd (Cairo: Maktabat al-Kulliyyāt al-Azhariyyah, 1973).

Al-Rāzī = Al-Rāzī, Fakhr al-Dīn, *al-Maḥṣūl fī ʿIlm Uṣūl al-Fiqh* (Beirut: Dār al-Kutub al-ʿIlmiyyah, 1988).

Al-Ruhāwī = Al-Ruhāwī, Yaḥyā, *Ḥāshiyah ʿalā Sharḥ al-Manār* (n.p. al-Maṭbaʿah al-ʿUthmāniyyah, 1319 A.H.).

Ṣadr al-Sharīʿah = Ṣadr al-Sharīʿah ʿUbayd Allāh b. Masʿūd, *Sharḥ al-Tawḍīḥ ʿalā l-Tanqīḥ* (Cairo: al-Maktabah al-Khayriyyah, 1306 A.H).

Al-Samarqandī = Al-Samarqandī, ʿAlāʾ al-Dīn Shams al-Naẓar Abū Bakr Muḥammad b. Aḥmad, *Mīzān al-Uṣūl fī Natāʾij al-ʿUqūl fī Uṣūl al-Fiqh*, ed. ʿAbd al-Malik ʿAbd al-Raḥmān al-Saʿdī (Baghdad: Maṭbaʿat al-Khulūd, 1987).

Al-Sarakhsī = Al-Sarakhsī, Abū Bakr Muḥammad b. ʾAhmad, *Uṣūl al- Sarakhsī*, ed. Abū l-Wafāʾ al-Afghānī (Beirut: Dār al-Kutub al-ʿIlmiyyah, 1993).

Al-Shāfiʿī, *Treatise* = Al-Shāfiʿī, Muḥammad b. Idrīs, *al-Risāla fī Uṣūl al-Fiqh: Treatise on the Foundations of Islamic Jurisprudence*, trans. Majid Khadduri, 2nd edn. (Cambridge: the Islamic Texts Society, 1987).

Al-Sharbīnī = Al-Sharbīnī, ʿAbd al-Raḥmān, *Taqrīrāt ʿalā Ḥāshiyat al-Bannānī ʿalā Sharḥ al-Jalāl al-Maḥlallī ʿalā Matn Jamʿ al-Jawāmiʿ* (Beirut: Dār al-Fikr, 1982).

Al-Sharīf al-Jurjānī, *Ḥāshiyah ʿalā Sharḥ al-ʿAḍud* = Al-Jurjānī, al-Sharīf, *Ḥāshiyah ʿalā Sharḥ ʿAḍud al-Millah wa-l-Dīn li-Mukhtaṣar al-Muntahā l-Uṣūlī*, 2nd edn. (Beirut: Dār al-Kutub al- ʿIlmiyyah, 1983).

Al-Sharīf al-Jurjānī, *al-Taʿrīfāt* = Al-Jurjānī, al-Sharīf, *al-Taʿrīfāt* (Tunis: al-Dār al-Tūnusiyyah li-l-Nashr, 1971).

Al-Shīrāzī, *Sharḥ al-Lumaʿ* = Al-Shīrāzī, Abū Isḥāq Ibrāhīm, *Sharḥ al-Lumaʿ*, ed. ʿAbd al Majīd Turkī (Beirut: Dār al-Gharb al-Islāmī, 1988).

Al-Shīrāzī, *al-Tabṣirah* = al-Shīrāzī, Abū Isḥāq Ibrāhīm, *al-Tabṣirah fī Uṣūl al-Fiqh*, ed. Muḥammad Ḥasan Haytū (Damascus: Dār al-Fikr, 1908).

Al-Subkīs, *al-Ibhāj* = Al-Subkī, ^{c}Alī b. ^{c}Abd al-Kāfi and al-Subkī, Tāj al-Dīn ^{c}Abd al-Wahhāb b. ^{c}Alī b. ^{c}Abd al-Kāfi, *al-Ibhāj fī Sharḥ al-Minhāj ^{c}alā Minhāj al-Wuṣūl ilā ^{c}Ilm al-Uṣūl*, ed. Sha^{c}bān Muḥammad Ismā^{c}īl (Cairo: Maktabat al-Kulliyāt al-Azhariyyah, 1981).

Al-Taftāzānī, *Ḥāshiyah ^{c}alā Sharḥ al-^{c}Aḍud* = Al-Taftāzānī, Sa^{c}d al-Dīn, Ḥāshiyah ^{c}alā Sharḥ ^{c}Aḍud al-Millah wa-l-Dīn li-Mukhtaṣar al-Muntahā l-Uṣūlī, 2nd edn. (Beirut: Dār al-Kutub al-^{c}Ilmiyyah, 1983).

Al-Taftāzānī, *Ḥāshiyat al-Talwīḥ ^{c}alā Sharḥ al-Tawḍīḥ ^{c}alā l-Tanqīḥ* (Cairo: al-Maktabah al-Khayriyyah, 1306 A.H).

Al-Tahānawī = Tahānawī, Muḥammad A^{c}lā b. ^{c}Ali, *Kashshāf Iṣṭilāḥāt al-Funūn*, ed. Muḥammad Wajīh and others. (Calcutta: The Asiatic Society of Bengal, 1862).

Weiss, *The Search* = Weiss, Bernard G., *The Search for God's Law: Islamic Jurisprudence in the Writings of Sayf al-Dīn al-Āmidī* (Salt Lake City: University of Utah Press, 1992).

Zādah = Zādah, ^{c}Azmī, *Ḥāshiyah ^{c}alā Sharḥ al-Manār* (n.p. al-Maṭba^{c}ah al-^{c}Uthmāniyyah, 1319 A.H.).

Chapter One
Introduction

1.1. GENERAL BACKGROUND

The term 'the principles (also the science of the principles, foundations or origins) of Islamic jurisprudence' has commonly been used as an English equivalent to the Arabic term *(uṣūl al-fiqh)*. Although the word 'jurisprudence' appears to be a good extensional translation[1] to the Arabic term *fiqh* in that both have to do with the study of law, the intensional imports (and the literal meanings) of the two words are noticeably different. For our purpose here, since we are dealing with the pragmatic thinking of the Muslim legal theorists, we would prefer to use the term *fiqh*, which literally means 'understanding', instead of 'jurisprudence', which does not have this meaning.

The legal theorists, however, frequently refer in their treatises to the fact that the pre-theoretical sense of the word *fiqh* is "the understanding of the speaker's intention"[2] or "the perception of concealed meanings" *(idrāku l-ashyāʾi l-khafiyyah)*.[3] This reference is probably made to indicate that the essential purpose of the principles of *fiqh* is "to grasp successfully the intentions of *Allāh* and His Prophet *via* the *Qur'ān* and *Sunnah*"[4] (the Traditions of the Prophet). Since merely receiving linguistic utterances does not fulfil that purpose, the legal theorists concerned themselves with additional devices, which we shall deal with later.

Ibn Taymiyyah (d. 728/1328) argues that since the signification of an utterance is intentional, and since utterances cannot communicate *per se*, but mean what speakers want them to mean, it follows that in order for communication to be successful, one must know the speaker's intention. Working through this chain of arguments, Ibn Taymiyyah reaches the conclusion that knowing[5] an utterance is not sufficient to understanding it successfully. Instead two things should be considered, namely knowing *(al- samᶜ)* and reasoning *(al-ᶜaql)* and that using both these capacities in understanding utterances is to use *fiqh*.[6]

As to the technical sense of 'the principles of *fiqh* (henceforth PF), the most straightforward definition of this term is the study of the rules by which legal judgements can be derived from their specific arguments directly.[7] The last restriction (directly) is stated partly to exclude grammar (in its broad sense) as it is considered to be one of the premises *(al-mabādiʾ)* upon which the research in this field is based (The other two are theology and *fiqh*). This exclusion underlies the fact that the legal theorists are interested exclusively in aspects that might be said to be of pragmatic character rather than the formal aspects of linguistic research on account of the fact that the latter are considered to be part of the premises whereas the former are part of the theorems *(al-masāʾil)* of the PF.

Thus, the linguistic concern of the legal theorists involves, as Imam al-Ḥaramayn al-Juwaynī (d. 478/1085) states, "the residue of the linguistic inquiry which has to do with the legal purposes and has been ignored by the scholars of the Arabic language".[8] Most, if not all, of such an inquiry can arguably be involved in the domain of pragmatics.

At this stage two points have to be mentioned:

Firstly, one should not expect the PF to have been the Islamic classical counterpart of pragmatics, although, as stated above, a considerable portion of its themes can fairly be assumed to fall within the domain of pragmatics.

Secondly, despite the fact that PF deals with some legal and theological theorems, which might be expected to be characterised by some metaphysical issues and doctrines accepted as a matter of faith, the pragmatic thinking of the Muslim legal theorists has the advantage of being noticeably based on an objective method. Of the many pieces of evidence that are available in this context, I would choose the following which shows that the legal theorists treat the texts of the *Qur'ān* and *Sunnah* in principle as typical Arabic utterances rather than extraordinary or unique divine messages:

> Whatever acceptable utterance produced by a native Arabic speaker is potential in the *Qur'ān* . . . [and *vice versa*] and what is unique to *Allāh* has nothing to do with languages.[9]

However, one might find some statements which appear to be incompatible with what has just been said. One such statement is: "the real question cannot be performed by *Allāh*"; another is "whatever *Allāh* says must be held to be true" and the like. These maxims should, in actual fact, be taken as important observations within the scope of a pragmatic account of how communication works, for pragmatists are interested, as far as the interpretation of utterances is concerned, in how beliefs, or, more precisely, the system of shared beliefs affects the pragmatic interpretation of utterances rather than evaluating the beliefs proper. Furthermore, if we take such maxims (the word 'maxim' here is employed in its pre-theoretical sense) in the context of Ibn Taymiyyah's version of *fiqh* and the communication principles formulated by the legal theorists, we will have to interpret, for instance, the interrogative sentences uttered by *Allāh* as indirect utterances. That is to say, they will be taken to have ulterior intentions. And this is indeed the common account of such utterances in the works of the legal theorists and the commentators of the *Qur'ān*.

So far the term 'pragmatic' has been used in a rather loose sense. Since the present study is not dealing with a modern pragmatic theory where the term 'pragmatic' is given a restricted technical sense, it seems to be appropriate to continue to do so. However, the general usage of this term in this study is not incompatible with its broad sense in the field of pragmatics where 'pragmatic' has to do with the study of language use and understanding or with meaning in relation to speech situations.

At this point, I shall state in non-technical language what can be regarded as the essential pragmatic insights in PF works. In the next chapters they will be discussed in detail either directly or indirectly. These insights include:

i The proper understanding of utterances cannot be achieved by merely understanding the meaning of sentences, but by grasping accurately the speakers' intentions. This view can be ascribed to the fact that the essential and ultimate goal of the PF is, as stated earlier, to reach a correct interpretation of the intentions of *Allāh* and His Prophet.
ii Communicative considerations and textual aspects are paramount in the understanding of utterances, without, however, ignoring the formal structure of language. This can be readily observed in the emphasis they place on the role of context (in its broad sense) in language use and understanding.
iii Utterances cannot be properly understood without using the intellectual capacities of the hearer. This view might be due to the

fact that languages are thought to be based upon what is shared between interlocutors such as innate linguistic and cognitive knowledge and convention.[10]

iv Two types of knowledge are generally distinguishable: knowledge of language as a set of *waḍ*ᶜ*s*, and that of language as use. This can be easily derived implicitly from the discussions of the distinction between what is called *waḍ*ᶜ *al-lughah* (the establishment of language) and *isti*ᶜ*māl* (use).

v A system consisting of a set of principles and a series of strategies which serves as a guide to solve the communicative problem is required. This system operates by virtue of two categories, namely 'the base' *(al-aṣl)* and 'the subsidiary' *(al-far*ᶜ*)*.

vi A distinction is made between what is understood explicitly and what is understood implicitly and also between what is understood directly from the utterance and what is inferred indirectly from it. This boils down to saying that there is a fairly subtle conception of the nature of meaning, which requires a fairly sophisticated proposal (might be regarded as more than one) of how the interpretation of utterances is reached.

vii Since the proper understanding of utterances is anchored in relation to communication in ideal set-ups, which implies the absence of what might be considered by the hearer to be contradictory to what is being said in actual situations, and the absence of such features as homonymy *(al-ishtirāk)*, figurative use *(al-majāz)*, polysemy *(al-naql)*, ellipsis *(al-iḍmār)* and so on, and since this is hardly ever the case in actual communication, it follows that what the hearer usually understands is regarded as *the most likely* intended messages which the speaker wishes to communicate rather than as the indubitable proper intentions of the speaker.[11] To put it Fakhr al-Dīn al-Rāzī's way (d. 606/1209), verbal signals are intended not to make the hearer absolutely certain but to make him think that he has successfully interpreted them.[12]

The frequent occurrence of the term *ḥaml* (interpretation) in the works of the legal theorists and their preference of it to the word *fahm* (understanding) would explain (as the name suggests) the fact that utterances are interpreted differently by different recipients. After all, it should be borne in mind that verbal signals can, according to the legal theorists, produce certainty if they are supported by sufficient contextual evidence that can efficiently make the hearer certain that his interpretation of the utterance is the sole possible one. The signification of the signals of this kind has commonly been called in the PF's terminology; 'deterministic signification' *(dalālah qaṭᶜiyyah)* whereas the signification of the former 'probabilistic signification' *(dalālah ẓanniyyah)*.

viii It is very often that, in particular utterances, addressees bypass the surface meaning of an utterance and appeal to an ulterior interpretation of that utterance in order to attain a proper understanding of the speaker's intention. An account of this can roughly be stated as follows:

The surface meaning of a given utterance must be taken in principle as the intended meaning of the utterance unless there is some contextual (context is being employed here in its broadest sense) evidence *(qarīnah)* to the contrary. If the literal meaning of the utterance is incompatible with the contextual evidence, the hearer will have to interpret *(yuʾawwil)* the utterance in such a manner that it will become in agreement with it.

Although this formation seems to oversimplify the Muslim legal theorists' account of how communication works and overlook its explanatory ramifications, it might hopefully be regarded as sufficient in presenting a general glance at their conception of indirect communication.

ix Legal texts must be handled as a whole and not isolated from their internal contexts. Thus, the *Qur'ān* must be treated as a complete text. The same is applicable to the traditions of the Prophet. Furthermore, they must not be separated from their external contexts, which involve the entire *Sunnah* in the case of the *Qur'ānic* verses and *vice versa*, as well as those things which are believed to be connected with the intentions of *Allāh* and His Prophet in the text in question. This includes the reasons of the revelation of the text *(asbāb al-nuzūl)*, the Arabs' way of thinking, their affairs, their customs and so on. This approach is advocated to avoid the pitfalls of the sentence and text based analyses, which disregard the context of the subject matter.

The sketch of the pragmatic thinking in the PF works outlined above can generally be incorporated into the domain of *general* pragmatics. However, not every thing in PF can be incorporated within this domain, owing to the fact that PF contains many features that are more peculiar either to the Arabic language or to the Islamic culture than to the universal structural features of language or to universal pragmatic issues, which are cross-culturally applicable. Thus, the inquiry made by the legal theorists into the pragmatic aspects of some particles (e.g. *wa, fa* and *thumma*), can be regarded as a good example of language-specific pragmatics while the inquiry into what has commonly been called 'performative expressions' *(ṣiyagh al-ᶜuqūd)*, e.g. 'I thereby divorce you' *(anti ṭaliq)*, which are generally based upon the judgements of the Islamic religion, can be deemed as good examples of culture specific pragmatics. However, in the next chapters I shall focus much more on the issues related to general pragmatics than those which are culture/language specific.

Having stated some of the Muslim legal theorists' insights into language and communication, the point that should be stressed here is that the linguistic and textual communicative studies are generally conceived of as an act of worship, for they are the key to a proper interpretation of the *Qur'ān* whose verses are the main basis upon which to formulate the law. Therefore, it is not strange that a lot of effort, time and money have been spent in searching for the best and the most proper way to understand the intentions of *Allāh* and His Prophet through the *Qur'ān* and *Sunnah*. It is true that Muslim scholars concern themselves with several branches of knowledge such as philosophy, logic, medicine, cosmology, metaphysics, etc., for their own sake, but they are much more interested in those topics which are related either directly or indirectly to the knowledge of the *Qur'ān* and *Sunnah*. It is for this reason that the Islamic civilisation is best described as text-oriented civilisation. There has always been controversy among Muslims about whether such topics as *falsafah* (i.e., Greek philosophy) merits the efforts spent in pursuing them, but such a criticism has never been raised against those who dedicated their life to the study of language and its related disciplines.

Among those who are interested in language and communication, the legal theorists are given a very special status. So, some scholars believe that introducing such extra-linguistic elements as addresser, addressee and context into the domain of interpretation makes the legal theorists more than just grammarians *"nuḥātun wa-ziyādah"*[13] or as ᶜAbd al-ᶜAlī al-Anṣārī (d. 1225/1810) puts it, "more skilful than *ahl al-ᶜarabiyyah* (Arabic linguists)".[14] The legal theorists are described in this manner because the interest of grammarians in terms of meaning is judged to be restricted solely to the literal meaning of utterances, which the legal theorists consider to be just one of a set of components that make interpretation possible. Thus, it can be stressed that the interests of the Muslim legal theorists in terms of meaning are similar to those of pragmatists, while the interests of the classical grammarians of Arabic are roughly similar to the interests of modern semanticists.

It is clear that relying on *waḍ*ᶜ *per se* can lead to failure in interpretation, should the speaker fail to produce an 'ideal discourse' (i.e., a maximally *waḍ*ᶜ-conforming discourse). Since actual communication involves some problematic features like ambiguity and metaphor, the interpreter has to be aware of some principles and strategies to deal with such features. And it was indeed the task of the legal theorists to provide a set of principles, strategies and rules of inference whose aim is to constitute an approach to tackling the problem of interpretation.

1.2. THE LEGAL THEORISTS' PRAGMATIC APPROACHES TO COMMUNICATION

In PF, there are at least two different pragmatic approaches to textual communication:

i The mainstream approach followed by the *Ash*ᶜ*arīs*, *Ḥanafīs* and *Mu*ᶜ*tazilīs*.[15]
ii The Salafite approach followed mainly by the *Ḥanbalīs*, traced back to the early generation and strongly advocated, defended and elaborated by Ibn Taymiyyah and his pupil Ibn Qayyim al-Jawziyyah (d. 751/1350).

It is part of this study to collect the scattered arguments of each of the above two schools, formulate their views into models and examine their positions over several communicative issues.

The mainstream legal theorists assume that any communication involves the following:

i *waḍ*ᶜ (assignment of meanings to expressions), which is carried out by the 'establisher' of the language;
ii *dalālah* (signification), which is a consequence of *waḍ*ᶜ and contextual information.
iii *isti*ᶜ*māl* (use) i.e., the production of an utterance by a speaker with the intention of a particular meaning.
iv *ḥaml* (interpretation), i.e., the hearer's own understanding of the intention of the speaker.

With the exception of non-*waḍ*ᶜ-based *dalālah*, the above constitutive factors are thought to take place in a linear order:[16] *waḍ*ᶜ first, *isti*ᶜ*māl* second, and *ḥaml* third (cf. 2.3). Each part is associated with an anchoring point in the chain: *waḍᶜ* is associated with the 'establisher', *dalālah* with *waḍᶜ* and context; *istiᶜmāl* with the addresser; and *ḥaml* with the addressee (cf. figure 1.1).

Communication is, therefore, more than a matter of encoding and decoding of utterances; it is, in fact, an integrated process in which both *naql* (the transmission of knowledge) and *ᶜaql* (an intellectual input) play a role.

What distinguishes the *Salafīs'* communication model from its mainstream rival is the neutralisation of the difference between *waḍᶜ* and use. The *Salafīs'* main contention is that conventions are not established in isolation from the communicative situations, but are, rather, set up, and modified by them. Hence, words have elastic rather than firmly fixed meanings so that they may change according to the verbal and non-verbal contexts in which they are uttered. Accordingly, if an expression is isolated from context, it will no longer be part of the language, simply because it cannot be used to communicate in a well defined manner.[17] Hence, much of the misconceptions in the mainstream account of *majāz* is due, according to Ibn al-Qayyim, to the confusion between a theoretical or abstract language *(al-kalām al-muqaddar)* and the language in use *(al-kalām al-mustaᶜmal)*.[18]

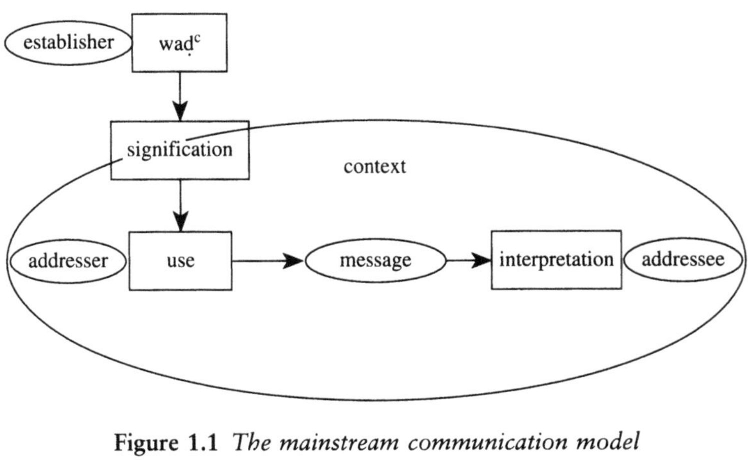

Figure 1.1 *The mainstream communication model*

The arrows indicate the chronological order. The rectangles represent the main constitutive processes of communication. With the exception of *waḍᶜ* and the *waḍᶜ*-based signification, all the constitutive processes of communication are contextualised.

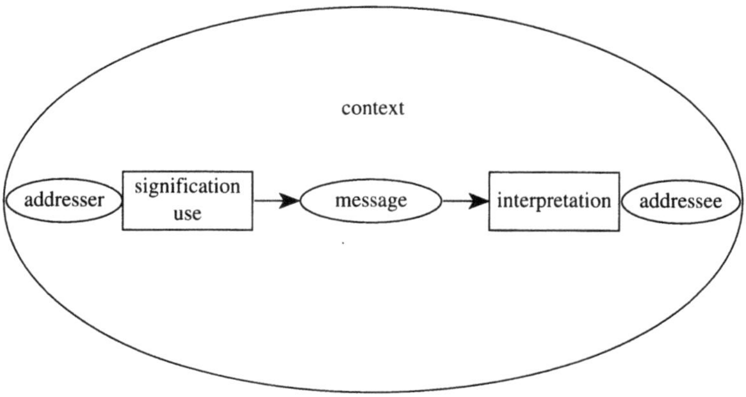

Figure 1.2 *The Salafite communication model*

Waḍ^c is omitted because the distinction between *waḍ*^{c} and use is neutralised. Signification is established and modified in the actual use of the utterance. The habitual use of the utterance, which is a contextual notion, is believed to play the role of the primordial *waḍ*^{c} in the mainstream model.

However, there is another distinct approach followed by the *Ẓāhirīs* which is based primarily on the non-pragmatic givens of the language and stresses the predetermined conventions of the language which are encoded in the linguistic structure of the texts as the essential, and perhaps the only requirements for communication. Extra-linguistic contexts are generally ignored and the inferential capacity of the hearer has almost no role to play in interpretation. This approach which has long been defunct will not be discussed in the present study since our concern is confined to the pragmatic thinking in the PF.

Finally, it should be pointed out that there are certain parallels between the distinction drawn in modern linguistics between semantics and pragmatics and the distinction drawn by the mainstream Muslim legal theorists between *waḍ*^{c} and use. Both *waḍ*^{c} and semantics are about the study of meaning in isolation of context: *waḍ*^{c} is generally about the assignment of expressions to meanings, semantics is about the study of meaning. Pragmatics, on the other hand, literally means the science of use and *isti*^{c}*māl* also means use. However, while semantics and pragmatics have come to be recognised as separate branches of linguistics, only *waḍ*^{c}, in the Islamic literature, was recognised as an independent branch of the Arabic linguistic sciences. ᶜAḍud al-Dīn al-Ījī (d. 756/1355) is said to be the first to have written on this subject outside the PF, but his treatise *(al-Risālah al-Waḍᶜiyyah)* "did not give rise immediately to a separate science".[19] According to Tāshkubrīzādah (d. 970/1561) who describes al-Ījī's treatise as "a drop in the ocean of the science of *waḍᶜ* and a sip from its river", the science of *waḍᶜ* had not yet become a written science *(lam yudawwan)*" in his time.[20] It was only in the eighteenth century, according to Weiss, that this body of knowledge gained "the status of a recognized written science".[21]

Hitherto we have generally been dealing with some pragmatic notions in the PF literature in an abstract way. In the next chapters I shall try to flesh out these notions in a way which expresses the specificity of PF, while at the same time displaying those features which demonstrate its general applicability.

1.3. AIMS AND SCOPE OF THE STUDY

As far as I can ascertain, this study is the first attempt to formulate the Muslim legal theorists' models of textual communication. There has been no study that examines the approaches followed by the *Salafīs* or the mainstream from a pragmatic viewpoint. In fact, there has been no attempt to explain the principles and the strategies utilised by the medieval Sunni Muslim legal theorists in their account of how communication works and how successful interpretation is achieved. Of course, a lot of traditional work has been done about different Islamic sects and their different positions over the interpretation of the *Qur'ān* and *Sunnah*. But these studies fall short of delving into the underlying communication principles that motivate their differences over interpretation.

However, I must acknowledge that Weiss's thesis about *'waḍᶜ al-lughah'* and its development was very beneficial and relevant to few points made in the second chapter, to which reference will be made in due course.

I must also acknowledge that my knowledge of the basic elements of modern linguistics and pragmatics was a great help to understanding the Islamic pragmatic theories. In particular, the Gricean framework contributes considerably to my formulation of the communication principles.

One of the primary aims of this study is to formulate and explore several PF's pragmatic theories, principles and views, construct them in the form of models and set them within a general uniform framework.

Another aim is to reveal a corpus of information and data, which, though highly relevant to modern pragmatics, is still unknown. I have endeavoured to make this corpus as accessible as possible to the reader who is acquainted with a basic knowledge of pragmatics.

The study is not restricted to outlining, systematising and clarifying. In fact, it goes beyond that so as to incorporate criticism, reconstruction and formulation of the Muslim legal theorists' own insights.

The issues discussed in the present work will not be diachronically approached, so the historical development of those issues will remain beyond the scope of this study.

Although my interpretation of the ideas of the legal theorists is very often an active ingredient in writing this work, I have tried my best to maintain their own technical apparatus and theoretical conceptualisations of the key ideas involved in this work and not to impose the essential elements of the current pragmatic theories on their formation of the subject. This can be made possible only by appealing to their own technical terms.

In order to provide a relatively true and precise picture of the Muslim legal theorists' insights into language and communication, I have consulted most of the essential works of the Sunni legal theorists which are available and relevant to my topic. This includes al-Shāfiᶜī's *al-Risālah* (d. 204/820), al-Baṣrī's *al-Muᶜtamad* (d. 436/1044), Ibn Ḥazm's *al-Iḥkām* (d. 456/1064), al-Shīrāzī's *Sharḥ al-Lumaᶜ* and *al-Tabṣirah* (d. 476/1083), al-Juwaynī's *al-Burhān* (d. 478/1085), al-Sarakhsī's *Uṣūl* (d. 490/1097), al-Ghazālī's *al-Mustaṣfā* (d. 505/1111), al-Rāzī's *al-Maḥṣūl* (d. 606/1209), al-Āmidī's *al-Iḥkām* (d. 631/1233), Ibn al-Ḥājib's *Mukhtaṣar al-Muntahā l-Uṣūlī* (d. 646/1248), al-Qarāfī's *Sharḥ Tanqīḥ al-Fuṣūl* (684/1285), al-Bayḍāwī's *Minhāj al-Uṣūl* (d. 685/1286), Ibn Taymiyyah's *Fatāwā* (d. 728/1328) and Ṣadr al-Sharīᶜah's *Sharḥ al-Tawḍīḥ* (d. 747/1346). The period covered in this study starts with al-Shāfiᶜī's *al-Risālah* (d. 204/820) and ends with Hārūn al-Marjānī's *Ḥāshiyah ᶜalā Sharḥ al-Tawḍīḥ* (d. 1306/1889).

In addition to the PF's works, the references also include:

i some medieval Arabic grammar sources like Ibn Yaᶜīsh's *Sharḥ al-Mufaṣṣal* (d. 643/1245–6), and al-Astarābādhī's *Sharḥ al-Raḍī ᶜalā l-Kāfiyah* (d. 688/1289);
ii some Arabic rhetorical sources like Abd al-Qāhir al-Jurjānī's *Asrār al-Balāghah* and *Dalā'il al-Iᶜjāz* (d. 471/1078–9);
iii Some Arabic logic sources like al-Ghazālī's *Miᶜyār al-ᶜIlm fī Fann al-Manṭiq;*

iv Arabic philology (al-Suyūṭī's *al-Muzhir fī ᶜUlūm al-Lughah wa-Anwāᶜihā* (d. 911/1505)).

Finally, this work is intended to be an extensive introduction to what might be called 'medieval Islamic pragmatics', since it introduces a number of the Muslim legal theorists' pragmatic insights and constructs from the data available several theories which lend themselves to a unified framework.

1.4. A NOTE ON TERMINOLOGY

The most important problem encountered in this work is finding exact English equivalents to Arabic terms. In dealing with this problem, I have followed a pragmatic rather than a predetermined approach in translating the technical terms. In many cases, one has to choose one of two methods: intensional or extensional translation. In the present study it is the former approach that is usually followed, although the latter is occasionally preferred.

One disadvantage of the intensional method is making the English counterpart of an Arabic term look like a literal equivalent to it. Another is that the connotations and the technical history of the term will be lost. In order to avoid this obstacle in the present study I have used the original term either alone or with its nearest English equivalent whenever necessary.

One of the main disadvantages of the extensional method, on the other hand, is that one has to apply, for the translation of a single Arabic term, as many different English words as the context requires whenever the Arabic term denotes different senses in different contexts.

1.5. THE STRUCTURE OF THE STUDY

This study deals with two models of communication: the mainstream model and the Salafite one. The mainstream model is based on four main pillars: (a) establishment *(waḍᶜ)*, (b) use *(istiᶜmāl)*, (c) interpretation *(ḥaml)* and (d) signification *(dalālah)*. This book aims to explore and formulate this model, and to show how it is different from the Salafite one. Since the two models overlap to a considerable extent, I will make the more complex one, which is the mainstream model the focus of attention. With the exception of the fourth chapter which deals with the Salafite model, all the other chapters deal primarily with the mainstream views on linguistic and communicative issues.

The present chapter provides the reader with a general background about the topics to be discussed in this study, including an informal outline of the legal theorists' pragmatic insights into textual communication.

The second chapter deals with the distinction drawn by the mainstream between *waḍ*ᶜ and use which constitutes the key to their model. Each utterance produced by a speaker or interpreted by a hearer is processed with reference to these two notions. So, it will be a concern of mine in this chapter to explain which aspects of an utterance pertain to *waḍ*ᶜ and which aspects belong to use. Under *waḍ*ᶜ, two distinctions will be examined: the distinction between universal and particular *waḍ*ᶜ, and the distinction between general and specific *waḍ*ᶜ. Under 'use', two related notions will be discussed: intention and context.

The third chapter investigates the notion *ḥaml* (interpretation) which makes up the third constitutive factor in the mainstream model. In this chapter, I will distinguish between *ḥaml*, understanding and *fiqh*, and discuss context from the addressee's point of view. An account of the mainstream model of interpretation is provided *via* examining five communication principles: the Principle of the Speaker's Disposition to Make his Intention Manifest, the Principle of the Speaker's Truthfulness, the Principle of *I*ᶜ*māl*, the Principle of Immediacy and the Principle of *Istiṣḥāb*.

The fourth chapter deals with the Salafite model of communication. This is taken up through a formulation of what I call 'Ibn Taymiyyah's contextual theory of interpretation'. The significance of my formulation of this theory is enhanced by highlighting its underlying philosophical principles. This involves relating it to his relevant ontological, epistemological and theological outlook. Besides, the inquiry includes his theory of cognitive relativism, his contextual theory of definition and his views on language, meaningfulness, the establishment-usè dichotomy, meaning-intention distinction and signification. More important is his critical view of the distinction between literal and non-literal meaning, and his model of interpretation.

The final chapter is concerned with two significational classifications: a semiotic classification and a text-based classification. The former involves natural, rational and *waḍ*ᶜ-based signification (which is divided into equivalence-signification *(dalālat muṭābaqah)*, incorporational signification *(dalālat taḍammun)* and implicational signification *(dalālat iltizām)*, the latter having two versions: the *Ḥanafī* version, which includes express meaning *(ʿibārat al-naṣṣ)*, alluded meaning *(ishārat al-naṣṣ)*, inferred meaning *(dalālat al-naṣṣ)* and required meaning *(iqtiḍāʾ al-naṣṣ)*, and the *Shāfiʿī* version, which includes required signification (*dalālat al-iqtiḍāʾ*), alluded signification *(dalālat al-ishārah)*, indicated signification (*dalālat al-tanbīh wa-l-īmāʾ*) and implicated signification (*dalālat al-mafhūm*). Implicated signification is divided into two types: congruent implicature *(mafhūm al-muwāfaqah)*, which is approved by the *Ḥanafīs* and counter implicature *(mafhūm al-mukhālafah)* whose validity is disputed by them.

NOTES

1 By extensional translation I mean that kind of translation in which the translator is concerned with the objects to which the term refers rather than with the attributes denoted by it. See Simpson and Weiner, *The Oxford English Dictionary*, V/597 (extension).
2 Al-Baṣrī, 1:4; al-Rāzī, 1/9.
3 Al-Qarāfī, *Sharḥ Tanqīḥ*, p. 16.
4 Ibn Taymiyyah, *Fatāwā*, 20/496.
5 Knowing is a rough translation of the term *al-samʿ*, which should be taken in this context to mean the previous knowledge of both the *waḍʿ* of that utterance (i.e., the linguistic meaning) and all that which has been received about it (i.e., the external context).
6 Ibn Taymiyyah, *Fatāwā*, 20/496.
7 Al-Ruhāwī, p. 19.
8 Al-Juwaynī, 1/169.
9 Al-Qarāfī, *Sharḥ Tanqīḥ*, pp. 259, 260.
10 See *ibid.*, p. 76.
11 See al-Rāzī, 1/493–494.
12 *Ibid.*, 1/493.
13 Al-Muṭīʿī, *Sullam . . .*, 2/350.
14 Al-Anṣārī, 1/315 and see 1/251.
15 It should be noted that most writers in PF are *Ashʿarīs*, *Ḥanafīs* (who usually hold Māturīdī doctrines) or Muʿtazilīs. There are only very few works written in this field by *Ẓāhirīs* and *Salafīs*. For this reason alone, I refer to the view shared by *Ashʿarīs*, *Ḥanafīs* and *Muʿtazilīs* or by most of them as the mainstream view.
16 See Mullākhusrū, 1/153.
17 Al-Mawṣilī, 2/41.
18 See *ibid.*, 2/41.
19 Weiss, "Language . . .", p. 92; al-Zahrāwī, "ʿIlm al-Waḍʿ", 3/454.
20 Ṭāshkubrīzādah, *Miftāḥ al-Saʿādah*, 1/130; see Weiss, "Language . . .", p. 92; al-Zahrāwī, "ʿIlm al-Waḍʿ", p. 454.
21 Weiss, "Language . . .", pp. 92–93.

Chapter Two
Waḍᶜ and Use

2.1. INTRODUCTION

The Muslim legal theorists did not concern themselves with differentiating between the formal and functional study of meaning, or with the distinction drawn in modern linguistics between semantic and pragmatic explanations. This was probably because their main motive for inquiry was chiefly to set up the general principles of an approach to comprehend the Holy *Qur'ān* and *Sunnah*. In other words, the scholars of the PF, as Muslim legal theorists, try, by virtue of their commitment to the commands of the Islamic religion, not only to understand the religious texts as accurately as they could, but also to derive from them the judgements concerning the life of the Muslims in this world and the hereafter.

The Western scholars of language, by contrast, began with investigations into the philosophy of language, focusing mainly upon the structures of languages, i.e., language as a system rather than as behaviour. When modern linguists, however, re-examined (particularly in the wake of the Saussurean distinction between *langue* and *parole* and more influentially after Morris's semiotic trichotomy of syntax, semantics and pragmatics) the ability of the traditional message-model of communication to account for how communication works, they came to the conclusion that this model was rather inefficient. Consequently, they adopted new approaches which presuppose that an accurate account of languages cannot be reached by studying them in isolation of the actual communicative situations.

Nonetheless, it might be argued that the legal theorists were more or less aware of the difference between the two levels of language and speech, but that they were much more interested in distinguishing between what they call the *waḍᶜ* (establishment)[1] and *istiᶜmāl* (use), which together with signification and interpretation are seen as the main constitutive factors of communication. The rough similarity between the two pairs (i.e., *langue* and *parole* on the one hand, and *waḍ*ᶜ and use on the other hand) is fairly striking and may not be overlooked in any serious study of this area of investigation. Correspondingly, the relation that holds between language and *waḍ*ᶜ, for example, was noticed by B.G.Weiss who states:

> Lughah [language] and waḍᶜ are here, as elsewhere, closely related terms; the knowledge of one is the same as the knowledge of the other.[2]

This relation can be clarified, as Weiss briefly did, by invoking the notion 'knowledge'. The knowledge of *waḍ*ᶜ, which involves both the *waḍ*ᶜ of vocabulary and grammatical elements, including morphological and syntactic patterns, implies the knowledge of language, in its capacity as a combination of lexicon and grammar, on the grounds that language is nothing, in fact, but the 'established' expressions *(al-lafṭ al-mawḍū*ᶜ*)*.[3] Similarly if we compare the Saussurean notion of *'parole'* with the notion of 'use' in Islamic legal thought, we will see on the whole a broad similarity between them for both pertain to the performance of language in actual situations.[4] However, there is an important difference between the legal theorists' and the Saussurean account of language which will be explained later (cf. 5.2).

2.2. WAḌᶜ

One discussion of the notion *waḍ*ᶜ in the PF literature will begin with a definition whose purpose is to show the way in which the notion is used in the Arabic intellectual tradition. According to Shihāb al-Dīn al-Qarāfī (d. 684/1285),[5] *waḍ*ᶜ is said to be

> employed to make an expression as a sign for a meaning [. . .] (this is what is called linguistic *waḍ*ᶜ), and to the most dominant use of an expression in a particular meaning so that this meaning becomes more well known than its other meaning(s) (and this applies to the legal *(al-shar*ᶜ*ī)* [. . .], general conventional *(*ᶜ*urfī* ᶜ*āmm)* [. . .] and special conventional, or technical, *(*ᶜ*urfī khāṣṣ) waḍ*ᶜ).[6]

Al-Qarāfī illustrates the latter class of *waḍ*ᶜ (i.e., the non-linguistic *waḍ*ᶜ) by three different examples, each of which represents one of the subclasses mentioned above:

The first example is *ṣalāh* (prayer), which in terms of the linguistic *waḍ*ᶜ means *du*ᶜ*ā'* (call) in its general sense. This term was later given a special meaning, i.e., that sort of religious ceremony practised by Muslims five times a day. This new meaning, which has become more common than the original linguistic meaning of the word *ṣalāh*, represents the legal *waḍᶜ*, for it had occurred by virtue of *sharīᶜah* (i.e., the revealed law of Islam).

The second example is *dābbah*, which literally means 'a moving creature'. This literal meaning is called 'linguistic meaning' *(al-maᶜnā l-lughawī)* since it is the meaning of an expression. Al-Qarāfī reports that the word *(dābbah)* came to mean (horse) as in Iraq or (donkey) as in Egypt in his time. This type of narrowing of meaning is commonly called 'general conventional *waḍᶜ (waḍᶜ ᶜurfī ᶜāmm)*.

The last example is *jawhar* (substance) *qua* a recognised theological term. Al-Qarāfī gives this example to show what is meant by the term 'special conventional *waḍᶜ*', which is applied to any operation of setting up a technical term in a given field of knowledge.[7]

Having defined the term *waḍᶜ* in the way mentioned above, al-Qarāfī adds that this term is also employed, in connection with the controversy over whether or not the figurative use of terms depends on *waḍᶜ*, to the extent that the single use of a given item by an Arab on a given occasion and only on that occasion is sufficient to underpin its *waḍᶜ*.[8] The word *waḍᶜ*, therefore, comes to be applied to any usage that has already been heard, on condition that it introduces into the language a new union between an expression and a meaning. The word 'use' *(istiᶜmāl)* in its technical sense is, however, reserved for producing an expression, and intending its designation (I shall return to the term later).

With reference to the distinction between language and speech, the question that needs to be answered here is why is it that the legal theorists and Muslim thinkers in general appeal to the term *waḍᶜ* instead of talking directly about language proper?

One possible answer to this question may partly be related to the well-known belief that has been so influential in Islamic thought, i.e., 'every action must have a maker and each created thing must have a creator'. Accordingly, language, as everything else, must have been created by someone. What is so special about Arabic, however, is that it has a unique status from the doctrinal point of view, which is reflected in its presumed eloquence. The inimitability of Arabic is said to make the way in which it is established and its creator (establisher, as it were) well worth investigating. This can be regarded as a major underlying motive for the utilisation of the notion *waḍᶜ* as a theoretical tool in any discussion of language and communication. However, it might be the case that the notion *waḍᶜ* is methodologically designed to refer to the given lexical units and the abstract grammatical patterns, which the speaker has to accept in order to make his communication successful.

In spite of the controversy concerning who was the creator of language, Muslim thinkers display a similarity of approach with regard to the extended treatment of the notion *waḍ*ᶜ. One of the influential matters agreed upon in this regard is that the creator of language, whether it is man or *Allāh*, is so wise that his creation is devoid of anything which might render it useless. Thus, every linguistic element must have been assigned to a given meaning. Therefore, for someone to understand a particular discourse, he must have the knowledge of the *waḍ*ᶜ of the language in terms of which the communication takes place.[9] If the utterance is unambiguous, the knowledge of *waḍ*ᶜ will be sufficient to enable the recipient to grasp it. If not, the intention of the speaker will not be correctly understood except when there is some contextual evidence associated with the utterance in question.[10]

2.2.1. Universal & particular waḍᶜ

The legal theorists make several classifications concerning the term *waḍ*ᶜ. Since our concern with the notion *waḍ*ᶜ is mainly restricted to what is related to the distinction between *waḍ*ᶜ and use, we will concentrate particularly on the difference between universal and particular *waḍ*ᶜ, as well as the difference between general and specific *waḍ*ᶜ, because of their strong connection with the *waḍ*ᶜ-use distinction.

In Islamic thought, the term 'particulars' *(al-juzʾiyyāt)* is applied to expressions referring to those things whose concepts are not in common to others. In Abū Ḥāmid al-Ghazālī's terms (d. 505/1111), "particular *(al-juzʾī)* is that thing whose conceptualisation in itself prevents other things from falling under its concept; such as 'Zayd' (as a proper name), 'this tree' and 'this horse'".[11] The conceptualisation of 'universal' *(al-kullī)*, in contrast, does not prevent others from falling within its concept like 'man', 'horse' and 'tree'. The phrase "in itself" is mentioned in the definition of 'particular' to exclude such expressions as 'sun' which, in spite of being singular in the external world, is not considered to be particular in terms of its concept, for the speaker can form a universal concept of it in his mind. In other words, it is the mental, not the external, existence that is regarded as the appropriate criterion by which an expression can be said to refer to either a universal or particular entity.

This view is closely related to the controversy over the manner in which expressions are assigned to their meanings. The controversy took the form of whether expressions were designations for the mental representations of their referents in the real world or for the extra-mental entities themselves.

Al-Rāzī, who holds the former view,[12] argues that expressions change according to the changes in the mental image rising in the speaker's mind. He provides two arguments to support his view.

The first, which concerns single items *(al-mufradāt)*, is that if you see a body from a distance and you think of it as a rock, you will call it a rock. If you come near to it and realise that it was an animal, but you thought of it as a bird, you will call it a bird. If you come closer to it and it turns out to be a man, you will call it a man. This shows that the same object may be named differently according to the mental representation, which it is thought to conjure up in the speaker's mind. On this basis it is possible that each mental representation conjures up a corresponding *waḍ^c*.[13]

The second, which concerns constructions *(al-murakkabāt)*, is that if you say 'Zayd has stood up', this utterance will not mean that Zayd has indeed stood up; rather, all it means is that you have stated that "Zayd has stood up" and reported it. Only if we recognise that the statement is empirically true, it will be taken as a sign for a state of affairs in the external world, which he calls *al-wujūd al-khārijī* (the external existence).[14]

However, Jalāl al-Dīn al-Suyūṭī (d. 911/1505) states that the view that expressions are designations for external entities, which is held by Abū Isḥāq al-Shīrāzī (d. 476/1083),[15] is the select one. He further mentions that al-Rāzī's argument concerning the single items was refuted by some scholars on account of the fact that the variation in the names at each stage in the process of thinking is not merely due to the change in the speaker's mental representation, but to an assumed corespondent variation in the external world.[16]

Nonetheless, al-Shīrāzī's view is open to many lines of criticism. Among them are the following:

i If expressions were designations for the external entities, the designations would be terminated the moment those objects ceased to exist.
ii If *waḍ^c* existed for the external entities proper, we would need a special expression for each particular entity to serve as a designation for it. This is obviously impossible.

In defending that position, the advocates of this view invoke the notion 'analogy' *(qiyās)*.[17] Thus, they say that although the Arabs have established a lexicon for those particular entities they had experienced; and that although those entities had vanished and then were replaced by other individuals, nonetheless Arabic speakers still use the 'old' lexical items for new objects by virtue of analogy.[18]

Since some Muslim thinkers view the pure Arabs as the makers (or the establishers) of the Arabic language, i.e., the sole authority entitled to assign expressions to meanings, all usages transmitted from the Arabs must be regarded not only as utterances performed to function as a means of communication, but also as acts manifesting their will of *waḍ^c*, hence the term a 'tested example' *(shāhid)*, which is applied to utterances transmitted from the pure Arabs and deemed as examples which must be followed by speakers who wish to speak correct Arabic.

To go back to the view that expressions are meant to be designations for concepts (or mental images), which was adopted by some Muslim philosophers, e.g., Abū Naṣr al-Fārābī (d. 339/950), Abū ^{c}Alī al-Ḥusayn Ibn Sīnā (d. 428/1037) and Abū-Ḥāmid al-Ghazālī and maintained by al-Rāzī, it seems that this view has dominated the literature concerning the notion *waḍ^c* in the PF.

According to this view, when the word *asad* (lion) was first uttered, the speaker did not intend to apply it merely to that particular 'lion', which was meant by his/her utterance, but also to any animal that has the same properties of that particular 'lion'. Consequently, any speaker of Arabic can use the word 'lion' whenever he wants as a sign for that animal. This can be applied to the various aspects of language, whether they are lexical or grammatical.

Al-Qarāfī who is one of the proponents of this majority view explained how the Arabs have assigned expressions to meanings:

> The Arabs have not 'established' [expressions] for what they saw with their own eyes, but, for what they pictured in their minds. What arose in the mind in the past is identical to that which arises in the mind now [. . .]. Nothing has been 'established' for the external entities except proper names.[19]

The point which has to be made here is that although the legal theorists (e.g., al-Qarāfī) apply the term *waḍ^c* to the process of introducing proper names, it should be noted that such names have not, as far as the notion of the *waḍ^c* of Arabic is concerned, been treated in the literature of Arabic as part of a language. The Arab grammarians, who are considered to be the authoritative arbiters on the formal characteristics of Arabic, state, as Ibn Yaᶜīsh (d. 643/1245) reports, that proper names can be substituted and changed without changing the character of the language. This is, however, not true of common names, for if you called a man a horse or a horse a camel, that would be tantamount to changing the language.[20] Al-Taftāzānī (d. 791/1389) puts it more clearly when he points out that "proper names, *qua* their *waḍᶜ* as proper names, cannot be attributed to a particular language rather than another".[21]

Given that proper names are not regarded as part of the language, it may, therefore, be said that what al-Qarāfī says above is applicable to universals. The establisher of language *(wāḍiᶜ al-lughah)*, according to this conceptual view, never concerns himself with particulars; rather he always 'establishes' universals. Not only lexical items are 'established' in such a way, but also grammatical patterns. To put it in the legal theorists' own terms:

> Just as the establisher of language has assigned each common name to a universal entity (*ḥaqīqah kulliyyah*) without going into the particulars subsumed under it, he has assigned each constructional pattern *(kull wāḥid min al-hayʾāt al-tarkībiyyah)* to its universal meaning without going into the particulars of that pattern.[22]

The well-known example of the latter kind of *waḍᶜ* is the *waḍᶜ* of 'the subject' *(al-fāᶜil)*. In this view the *waḍᶜ* of, say, *zaydun* in *qāma zaydun* (Zayd has stood up) as a subject is not meant to apply to this particular entity above, but to all entities that can perform its function in this particular slot. Thus, the function of 'Zaydun' as a subject in the above example is generalised or abstracted into a universal fact.[23]

Therefore, any item which functions as a 'subject' would be regarded as correct Arabic provided that the 'subject' is in the nominative case and that it meets all the other conditions that are applicable to subjects. The realisation of this view in individual instances is not considered to happen by analogy, and need not be so, since it is already subsumed under the so-called 'universal fact'. This is exactly what al-Sharīf al-Jurjānī (d. 816/1413) means when he points out that "When we put a given subject that has never been heard before in the nominative case, what is being done in effect is not an application of analogy, but the realisation of a universal rule".[24] However, the view that constructions were primordially established was subject to criticism. This criticism, which was put forward by some legal theorists, grammarians and other Muslim thinkers in general, could not, even though it led to the introduction of significant ideas about the nature of language, be taken to refute the fact that constructional patterns are established, mainly because it is directed at the view that constructions are individually established which is not an integral part of the thinking of the advocates of the conceptual view. The criticism is as follows:

> That which signifies by *waḍ^c*, as is the case with 'words' *(mufradāt)* and 'idioms' *(al-murakkabāt al-qā$^\circ$imah maqāmahā)*, must be listed and not added to. Consequently if utterances signified by virtue of *waḍ^c*, they would be treated in this manner, and also, just as we cannot use any word unless it has been used before, we would not speak utterances that had never been used before. Since this is not the case, this would be evidence for the fact that utterances do not signify by virtue of *waḍ^c*.[25]

It is worth mentioning here that Jamāl al-Dīn Ibn Mālik (d. 672/1273), who develops this argument, introduced a compelling notion which has long been of great importance in modern linguistics since it was introduced by Chomsky; namely, the idea that speakers, by virtue of their linguistic competence, can perform utterances that have never been heard before.

It is not the knowledge of *waḍ^c* but the intellectual capacity *(al-^{c}aql)* which, according to Ibn Mālik, can deal with the relationships that hold between words in sentences. This 'intellectual' view, was also criticised on the grounds that, just as languages have different lexicons, they vary in terms of their constructional patterns:

> The governing entity *(al-muḍāf)* precedes the governed entity of a genitive construction *(al-muḍāf ilayh)* in some languages whereas the contrary is true in other languages. If constructions had to do with the intellect, the meaning would equally be understood; thus, making no difference whether the governing entity precedes its partner or not.[26]

The answer to Ibn Mālik's criticism from those who advocated the view that constructions cannot be understood without the knowledge of *waḍ^c* is exemplified by Muḥammad al-Zarkashī (d. 794/1392):

> What the Arabs have 'established' is the types of constructions *(anwā^c al-murakkabāt)* rather than the particulars of those

> types. They have 'established' the category of 'the subject' *(bāb al-fāᶜil)* in order to predicate every action to its maker or doer, but they have not 'established' the particular subjects [. . .]. This is true of all types of constructions.[27]

Raḍī al-Dīn al-Astarābādhī (d. 688/1289) considers this issue in greater depth and explains the difference between the *waḍᶜ* of lexical items and that of constructional patterns:

> The establisher of language tends to establish either particular 'transmission-dependent expressions' *(alfāẓ muᶜayyanah samāᶜiyyah)*, the knowledge of which is dependent on lexicology *(ᶜilm al-lughah)*, or a canon *(qānūn)* by which we can know either the analogical items *(al-mufradāt al-qiyāsiyyah)* or [. . .] the analogical constructions *(al-murakkabāt al-qiyāsiyyah)*.[28]

By the canons by which one can know the analogical items he means what can roughly be called 'the derivational rules of word formation, which, according to al-Raḍī, are interpretable in relation to morphology. On the other hand, by the canons by which one can know the analogical constructions he refers to both the inflectional rules of word formation, "for the knowledge of which you need to consult morphology" and the grammatical rules of sentence formation, "for the knowledge of which syntax is needed".[29]

One of the significant distinctions made by al-Raḍī in the above quotation is the distinction between the linguistic elements that have lexical meanings, i.e., what he calls 'transmission-dependent expressions' and linguistic elements that have grammatical functions, i.e., what he calls 'analogical expressions'. This distinction is similar to Martinet's distinction between lexical and grammatical morphemes.[30] I will not concern myself with this correspondence here; rather I shall concentrate on the distinction between the two types of *waḍᶜ*, namely the *waḍᶜ* of individuals *(al-waḍᶜ al-shakhṣī)* and that of patterns *(al-waḍᶜ al-nawᶜī)* or, as Weiss renders them, "isolative and subsumptive *waḍᶜ*".[31]

The fundamental difference between the two types of *waḍᶜ* relates to the fact that the former is defined as singling out *(ifrād)* an expression for a particular meaning, whereas the latter is usually applied to setting up a general grammatical rule. This means that every speaker who wishes to learn Arabic is required to know each individual lexical item he needs in any communicative situation in order for him to be said to have a knowledge of the *individual waḍᶜ*.

Unlike the knowledge of the individual *waḍ*^{c}, the knowledge of universal *waḍ*^{c} enables the speaker to create a new lexically meaningless but grammatically meaningful 'utterance' that has never been introduced before, and which can rightly be attributed to a potential Arabic 'sentence'. Such an utterance can simply be transformed into an actual meaningful Arabic utterance by, say, lexicalizing it. Consider the following:

1) *ṣaghama l-ṣāghimu mutaṣaghghiman* [CaCaCa al-CāCiCu Muta-CaCCiCan].[32]
2) a *saraqa l-sāriqu mutakhaffiyan.*
   b *akala l-ṣā*^{c}*imu mutalahhifan.*
   c *dhahaba l-qātilu mutawa*^{cc}*idan.*

Although the abstract pattern being 'established' in a subsumptive way cannot be lexically processed, it is still possible for native Arabic speakers to regard a potential sentence as realisable in terms of the subsumptive *waḍ*^{c} of Arabic. Clearly the knowledge of subsumptive *waḍ*^{c} can enable the speaker to generate (the word is being used in its pretheoretical sense) an infinite number of utterances of the type exemplified in (2). According to the view that languages consist of a set of universal *waḍ*^{c}*s*, each utterance of the type we find in (2) would be regarded as an actual manifestation of the 'established' pattern represented in (1).

Ibn Khaldūn (d. 808/1406), who appears to hold this view, likens the producer of a spoken utterance to a builder or weaver, while the proper mental form *(al-ṣūrah al-dhihniyyah al-munṭabiqah)* is likened to the mould used in the building process, or the loom in weaving.[33] Thus, what the producer of an utterance does when he speaks is to build "his utterance in the 'moulds' used by 'the Arabs'". Such mental patterns (i.e., moulds or looms) "are known only to those who have expert knowledge of 'Arabic' speech, such that in their minds they have an absolute universal mould, which is the result of abstraction from specific individual moulds".[34]

To relate this view to the distinction between language (or more precisely *waḍ*^{c}) and use, we can say that the production of an utterance can be attributed partly to language and partly to use. What belongs to language is the set of the grammatical patterns and the lexical units being used in accord with *waḍ*^{c}. What pertains to use, on the other hand, is the selection of the very particular lexical units as well as the selection of the very particular grammatical patterns. Such a selection is intended to be typically controlled by the speaker's communicative intention. Accordingly, the judgement that a given sentence is not well-formed should be ascribed to its being incompatible with the common constructional patterns of the language in question whereas the judgement that an utterance is, for instance, true or false, conceivable or inconceivable, should be ascribed to the speakers' estimation. This is simply because:

> Language [according to ᶜAbd al-Qāhir al-Jurjānī (d. 471/1078)[35]] tends not to state nor to affirm or disaffirm[. . .]. That is to say, stating that 'beating' is Zayd's action or not, and that 'illness' is his condition or not, is something made by the speaker and is a claim he assumes. Consequently, whatever is levelled at this claim – whether it is belief, accusation of lying, acknowledgement, denial, approving or disapproving – is in fact a reaction directed to the speaker and has absolutely nothing to do with language.[36]

This statement shows that the distinction between language as an abstract system and the speaker's actual use of the language is a well-established one in Arabic literature.

2.2.2. General & specific waḍᶜ

We shall turn now to the distinction between general and specific *waḍᶜ*, which is related to the universal versus particular distinction discussed above. It seems that the simplest way of dealing with this classification is to approach it in terms of the 'generality' *(ᶜumūm)* and 'individuality' *(khuṣūṣ)* of both expressions and meanings.

According to al-Taftāzānī, the attention of the establisher during the assignment of an expression to a meaning can be directed to either of the following:

i The individuality of both the expression and the meaning, in which cases the establisher singles out a specific expression for a specific object, e.g., the particular expression 'Zayd' for the very particular person.
ii The individuality of the expression and the generality of the meaning, in which cases the establisher singles out a specific expression for a general meaning or generic signification, e.g., the very particular expression 'man' for every man.
iii The generality of the expression and the individuality of the meaning, in which cases the establisher does not consider a

particular expression, but a universal (or an abstract) pattern, e.g., the pattern *Fāᶜil* {CāCiC} (C stands for consonants), which is typically used for infinitive tri-consonantal lexemes in Arabic to indicate, in any given occasion, 'the active participle' *(ism al-fāᶜil)* of the corresponding lexeme.[37]

Al-Taftāzānī's classification does not constitute the common classification in the PF literature on *waḍᶜ* in terms of both the approach which underlies it and the terminology in which it is couched, nor is it the majority view in terms of its application to the connection between the expression and the meaning in linguistic *waḍᶜ*. Instead of talking about expression and meaning, the common custom of the legal theorists is to speak about *waḍᶜ* and 'object' *al-mawḍūᶜ lahu* (i.e., meaning). Regardless of the approach, terminology and application, it is most likely that the underlying reason behind this classification is the view among the legal theorists and others who were interested in the notion of *waḍᶜ* in general that there is something peculiar to the personal pronouns, demonstrative nouns, relative pronouns, definite noun phrase *(al-muᶜarraf bi-al)* and proper names with respect to the notion *waḍᶜ*.

One of the questions which occupied the legal theorists was how can the same pronoun or any of the other categories mentioned above be used to refer to different referents on different occasions? Another question was why these categories could not be meaningful when they lack their referents? The answers to these questions led to answers to two other important questions, namely which aspect of each one of these categories can be attributed to *waḍᶜ* and which to use?

One possible answer to the first two questions can be obtained from ᶜAḍud al-Millah wa-l-Dīn in his Commentary on Ibn al-Ḥājib (d. 646/1248). He points out that such expressions as demonstrative, personal and relative pronouns are assigned in a general manner to specific objects,[38] i.e., the establisher is not concerned with the individuality of such expressions; rather, his concern is exclusive to single out the expression *hādhā* (this), for example, for every particular relevant referent and *anā* (I) for every speaker and *alladhī* ('who/which' for masculine singular) for every referent identified by a relative clause.[39] This kind of *waḍᶜ* is different from the *waḍᶜ* of such expressions as 'man' in that 'the object' *(al-mawḍūᶜ lahu)* in the case of 'man' is general whereas the demonstrative pronouns and the other above categories are assigned, in consideration of the general meaning to the individuals subsumed under that general meaning.[40].ᶜAḍud al-Millah supported his view by arguing that if 'man' was used, exclusively for Zayd, it would be regarded as figurative in usage whereas if the generic meaning of 'man' (which is true of Zayd and others who are included under the concept of 'man') is considered, it would be regarded as displaying literal usage *(ḥaqīqah)*. By contrast, if *hādhā* ('this' for male), *anā* (I) or *alladhī* (who/which for masculine singular) is used to refer to individuals, it would be regarded as a literal usage. In fact, they are never used in the general sense, i.e., one never says 'this' nor 'I' with reference to an undefined referent.[41]

Al-Taftāzānī's view, which was outlined above, is no different from ᶜAḍud al-Millah's view on this matter in that even though the former scholar places expressions of this kind under class (ii), he nevertheless draws a distinction between them and expressions like 'man'.[42]

In this regard it would be interesting to consider al-Qarāfī's views on this subject and particularly his account of the personal pronoun *(al-muḍmar)*.

By the personal pronoun *(al-muḍmar)* al-Qarāfī means that expression which requires for its definition either another independent expression (in the case of the third personal pronoun) or some contextual evidence to show what the referent is (in the case of the first and second personal pronoun).[43] Al-Qarāfī's interest in this issue arises from his concern with whether the meanings of the pronouns can be regarded as universal or particular. He begins by pointing out that the majority view is that the pronouns are particular. The arguments adduced in this regard are as follows:

First, the Arab grammarians have unanimously agreed that the personal pronouns are definite nouns *(maᶜārif)*, which presupposes that they are particular, in contradistinction to entities that are indefinite *(nakirah)*, which are universal, because they apply to an infinite number of referents.

Second, if the personal pronouns were universal, they would necessarily be capable of applying to something else other than the corresponding particular individuals. Thus, according to the rational rule *(al-qāᶜidah al-ᶜaqliyyah)* that "what signifies the more general does not signify the more specific", the personal pronouns signify no particular individuals at all. But this is not the case with respect to the personal pronouns, because their referents can be identified, for example the 'I' must refer to the particular speaker.[44]

Al-Qarāfī points out that a minority of the legal theorists, including himself, hold the opposite view, which demands that the personal pronouns be regarded as universal. In putting forward this view, he develops the following argument:

> If the concept of personal pronoun was particular, it would not be true of another individual except by another *waḍᶜ* as is the case with the *waḍᶜ* of proper names, which, by virtue of being particular, are not applicable to any individual other than the one to which they are assigned except if sanctioned by another *waḍᶜ*.[45]

To bring the view that personal pronouns are universal within the orbit of the rational rule "What signifies the more general does not signify the more specific", al-Qarāfī ascribes the restriction of the reference of the definite noun to a particular individual to two factors:

a) The assignment of an expression to the individuality of an individual. This is the case with proper names like Zayd which is especially assigned to a certain person and consequently refers merely to that person.

   Here, it is not the case that Zayd signifies 'the more general' (i.e., more than one individual) and 'the more specific' (i.e., the very particular person) simultaneously, within the *proviso* that the proper name Zayd can refer to as many individuals as we wish but each time with a different *waḍᶜ*.

b) The expression is assigned to a general meaning and the situation *(al-wāqiᶜ)* proves that the designation of the expression has been restricted to a particular individual. That is to say, the reference of the expression to that particular individual is not due to its being assigned to it but to the restriction of its designation to it.[46] So if you say 'I', the pronoun 'I' will refer to you and you alone and the recipient will rely in identifying the referent of this pronoun on the fact that the situation is that nobody else say 'I' in this particular occasion. This account is applicable not only to personal names but also to the rest of the definite nouns. Therefore, if one says 'I have seen the judge *(al-qāḍī)* of Mecca', the utterance will refer to the judge *(al-qāḍī)* of Mecca at that time and it will refer to another judge of Mecca if it is uttered on another occasion and so forth.[47]

To sum up al-Qarāfī's account of the personal pronouns (and definite nouns in general) we may say that he believes that the definite nouns are 'established' in so general a manner that they are valid to refer to any relevant entity in the actual speech situation and that the participants in the process of communication are entitled to determine their references. Thus, the universal signification of these kinds of expressions is determined by virtue of *waḍ^c* but their particular reference is governed by use.

In connection with the fact that each one of the personal pronouns, demonstrative nouns, etc., can refer to different individuals on different occasions, one might raise the question why could not they be regarded as homonymous?

Al-Sharīf al-Jurjānī rules out this solution because, for example, the expression 'I' has not been assigned to its various referents by a multi-*waḍ^c* but by a single act of *waḍ^c* only.[48]

Thus, the ambiguity of expressions, as al-Qarāfī points out, is not caused exclusively by the facts of linguistic *waḍ^c* but may also be ascribed to what he calls 'rational possibility' *(al-tajwīz al-^caqlī)*. The distinction between the *waḍ^c*-based ambiguity and rationally-based ambiguity is very crucial to our subject matter, for it presupposes that ambiguity can be inherent in the language and can also result from its use.

2.3. USE

The term *isti^cmāl* (use) in the PF literature is commonly applied, but it is rarely defined. The most straightforward definition of this term in the works on the PF appears to be that given by al-Qarāfī. According to him:

> Use refers to the production of an expression by intending either its literal meaning (in the case of literal usage) or non-literal meaning on the strength of a 'relation' between the literal and non-literal meaning (in the case of figurative usage).[49]

The first point to comment on in this definition is that the term 'use' is not intended to involve the hearer. It is most likely that it is deliberately excluded in order to be covered by the term *ḥaml* (interpretation) which is employed to refer explicitly to the interpretation of the speaker's utterance by the hearer. Having introduced the threefold distinction between *waḍ^c*, use and interpretation, and defined each one of these terms, al-Qarāfī states that "*waḍ^c* is preceding *(sābiq)*, interpretation is subsequent *(lāḥiq)* and use is middle *(mutawassiṭ)*.[50] The importance of this statement relates to the fact that it portrays the process of communication as a product of at least three different elements, namely *waḍ*ᶜ, use and interpretation. Each element has its own maker and takes place at a different time. The maker of the intermediate element, i.e., the user, who concerns us here plays the most significant role in the communicative process, for he is the person whose communicative intention is the centre or axis around which the communicative process moves.

2.3.1. Intention

A further point to notice in al-Qarāfī's definition mentioned above concerns the notion of 'intention' (*al-qaṣd* or *al-irādah*) which was the subject of fierce controversy in the course of the long debate concerning the createdness of the Holy *Qur'ān*. The Muᶜtazilīs hold that communication takes place in the form of speech acts which involve making statements, asking questions, and issuing commands and prohibitions. This presupposes the existence of the addressee and the timing of the communicative situation. Applying this to the *Qur'ān*, they conclude that the *Qur'ān* must have been created at some point in time.[51] According to them, the assumption that the *Qur'ānic* speech acts are eternal would imply the eternality of the addressees and thus the multiplicity of the eternal. The *Ashᶜarīs* distinguish between two types of speech: *al-kalām al-nafsī* (mental speech) which can loosely be defined as the proposition which the speaker intends to convey and the physical manifestation of mental speech, which they call *al-ᶜibārah* (utterance).[52] The former is said to be eternal while the latter is not. The *Ḥanbalīs*, on the other hand, deny the creation of the *Qur'ān* and reject the *Ashᶜarīs'* distinction between mental and physical speech.[53] We shall not go into the details of this debate or its theological dimensions here. Instead, we will focus on the pragmatic aspects of this issue. The *Muᶜtazilīs* (an early Islamic sect who took part in this debate) uphold the belief that any action of issuing a command *(amr)* taking the form *ifᶜal* (Do!) involves three kinds of intentions or wills *(irādāt):*

i the intention of producing the form *ifᶜal;*
ii the intention of its signification as a command; and
iii the intention of getting the addressee to obey.[54]

The first intention is designed to exclude any command that might be issued by a sleeper in the course of his sleep. The second is designed to exclude such things as threat, e.g., *ifᶜal mā tashāʾ wa-sa-tarā* (lit, do what you want to do and you will see) and inviting somebody to enter your house, e.g., *udkhul* (come in) and so on. The last intention is designed to exclude situations involving indirect speech. Without the occurrence of the three intentions the form *ifᶜal* (do) cannot be a form of command. The *Muᶜtazilīs* argue that without the presence of intention we cannot distinguish whether a given form is a command or threat because intention is the sole signifying means.[55] By stressing the involvement of the above three types of intention, the *Muᶜtazilīs* aim at emphasising the role the participants play in the communicative process and the interaction between them, thus supporting their belief that the *Qur'ān* is not eternal.

The *Sunnī* scholars[56] concede the first kind of intention and deny the involvement of the other two in the operation of command. They argue that the intention of the speaker does not serve as a means of underlining the signification of command (or other meanings). In other words, this signification is understood, not through the speaker's intention but, by the context of situation *(qarāʾin al-aḥwāl)* according to Imām al-Ḥaramayn al-Juwaynī,[57] or by the facts of *waḍᶜ* in the case of literal usage *(al-ḥaqīqah)* and by context in the case of figurative usage as may be inferred from al-Qarāfī.[58]

The *Sunnī* view is based on the assumption that the intention of the speaker is "an internal object lacking a signifier" *(amr dākhilī yaḥtāj ilā muᶜarrif)*.[59] That is to say, "intention is not a signifier but a signified".[60]

In the light of what has just been said about the *Sunnī* view of 'intention', particularly the statement of al-Qarāfī, the above definition of use can be reformulated as follows: use is intending a meaning by producing either a *waḍᶜ*-based expression alone or with the consideration of some contextual evidence.

It should be stressed here that intention is very often used in contrast to meaning. In this case, meaning is intended to be more general than intention. That is to say, every expression has a meaning but does not necessarily involve an intention; for, as al-Qarāfī states, intention is required, not in the case of 'the signification of expressions' but, in the case of 'signifying by expressions', i.e., the use of expressions (cf. 2.3).[61] Another way of explaining the difference between meaning and intention is to say that meaning is the literal content of an utterance, whereas intention is the message communicated by the speaker and intended to be recognised by the hearer to yield a particular effect on him. Meaning is, thus, controlled by *waḍᶜ*; intention is, on the other hand, motivated by use. In other words, understanding meaning depends on well-formedness, but grasping intention is determined by context,[62] which leads to the fact that "a given meaning can be understood by reference to language-based knowledge without being intended".[63]

In pragmatics, the meaning vs. intention distinction usually takes the following forms: sense and force,[64] sentence meaning and utterance meaning;,[65] and utterance meaning and the speaker's meaning.[66]

In the PF literature, the distinction between these two meanings is of great significance particularly in the matter of figurative speech. The legal theorists occasionally employ 'the meaning established for' *(al-maᶜnā l-mawḍūᶜ lahu)* and 'the meaning used for' *(al-maᶜnā l-mustaᶜmal fīhi)* for literal and non-literal meaning respectively, and reserve the term 'intended meaning' *(al-maᶜnā l-maqṣūd)* for the latter only.[67] It is generally held that the speaker's intention should be grasped by the addressee in the actual communicative processes and that understanding the *waḍᶜ*-based meaning is not always sufficient in order to recover the speaker's intention. The question which should be considered then is how can the speaker's intention be perceived if understanding the conventional meaning of the speaker's words is not always sufficient for that purpose? The simplest answer to this question is that although use is controlled in principle by the constraints imposed on it by virtue of *waḍᶜ*, speakers do not restrict themselves to the idealised type of language, which fulfils the requirements of *waḍᶜ*. What is more, violating the literalism of language may well be considered to be a self-evident fact, which shows the speaker's efficiency of language[68] on condition that (i) he provides some contextual evidence for his departure from the idealised constraints of *waḍᶜ*, and (ii) there is a 'relation' *(ᶜalāqah)* or 'appropriateness' *(munāsabah)* between the *waḍᶜ*-based signification and the intended meaning.[69]

It should be borne in mind however that just as the amount of information intended to be conveyed by the utterance can be more than what the *waḍᶜ*-based elements can bear, the amount of information signified by the *waḍᶜ*-based elements can also be more than what the speaker intends to say. That is simply because "being included in the meaning does not imply being intended in it" *([inna] l-dukhūla taḥta l-murādi lā yastalzimu an yakūna murādan)*.[70]

It goes without saying that being intended by the speaker does not imply that it is meant by the *waḍᶜ*-based elements proper. These two fundamental canons are practically of great importance: when one says in Arabic *naḥnu ṭālibān* (we are two students) in reply to the question *mā mihnatukumā?* (lit, What is your profession?), the reply involves, in effect, some redundant elements, namely the dual mark *ān* in *ṭālibān*, which is imposed by the facts of *waḍᶜ* – i.e., required by conventions in order to meet the linguistic well-formedness – even though it is not intended, communicatively speaking, by the speaker. Consequently, if one says *naḥnu ṭalabatun* (we are students[71]) instead, one would be successful in conveying the message despite the violation of the grammar. On the other hand, when a native Arabic speaker says *zaydun kathīru l-ramād* (lit: Zayd has much ash) and means that 'Zayd is a noble generous man', he is not conveying the message exclusively by means of 'established' expressions but he is, in effect, relying to a considerable extent upon the inferential capacity of the hearer to grasp the inferred meaning of the utterance. In other words, the speaker presupposes that the hearer will infer from 'has much ash' that he very often burns firewood and sets fire for cooking → he cooks a great deal of food → he invites (or receives) a large number of guests → he is hospitable → he is a noble generous man. However, the inferential capacity of the hearer in itself is not sufficient in recognising the intention of the speaker. Therefore, this chain of inferences on the part of the hearer can lead to the recognition of the speaker's intention if and only if the speaker is speaking non-literally. Deciding whether the speaker is speaking literally or not depends upon the context.

So far we have mentioned three essential factors involved in communicative processes: the inferential capacity of the speaker, context and *waḍᶜ*. Maḥmūd al-Jawnafūrī (d. 1062/1652) distinguishes among these three factors and assigns each of these factors a function as follows:

> Rational inference suffices for implication, and context for intentionality, but well-formedness requires an additional dimension. This is the fact that there must be knowledge of *waḍᶜ (samāᶜ)* and allowance on the part of the Arabs for the usage, in order for an utterance to be compatible with their canons, and this is exactly the isolative *waḍᶜ*.[72]

The first point to make about al-Jawnafūrī's statement is that he does not mention the understanding of the literal meaning, which is generally held to be related to *waḍᶜ*.

A further point is that contexts serve for intentionality in roughly the same way as conventional expressions serve in conveying conventional meanings. In other words, expression and context function as signifiers whereas meaning and intention function as signified. However, although speakers can in principle 'intend' what their expressions do not 'mean', their freedom as to the use of expressions that are not assigned by virtue of *waḍ*ᶜ to their intended meanings is conditional on the ability of the expression (with the help of contextual information) to bear the intended meaning. Accordingly, "what the expression cannot bear is not considered [in the communicative process] even if it is intended",[73] as ᶜAbd al-Laṭīf Ibn al-Malik (d. 801/1399) puts it. Although it is not always possible to determine precisely the extent to which the intention of the speaker can depart from the *waḍ*ᶜ-based meaning, the accessibility of the expression is still the most important standard in the PF literature. In addition to *waḍ*ᶜ, context, as a means of rendering the intention of the speaker recognisable, should be taken into account when we talk about the understandability of expressions. Knowledge of context is very much needed when the expression is ambiguous, for it identifies the intended meaning among other meanings that the expression bears. So "what the expression bears is not considered relevant unless it is intended",[74] and of course identified by the context as the signifier of intentionality as al-Jawnafūrī pointed out in the quotation above.

2.3.2. Context

The term *qarīnah*,[75] which is the Arabic equivalent to 'context', literally means 'concomitant' *(muqārinah)*. In his technical dictionary '*al-Ta*ᶜ*rīfāt*', al-Sharīf al-Jurjānī defined the term as "a thing that refers to what is intended" *(amrun yushīru ilā l-maṭlūb)*.[76] In a more technical language, al-Tahānawī (d. after 1158/1745)[77] defines it as "what is set up to identify what is being intended".[78]

Although the above two definitions do not totally encompass the common use of the term, they focus upon a significant component of its technical import, namely its being evidence or indicative of the speaker's intention. We may therefore say that the senses of both 'concomitant' (or connection) and 'indication' constitute the central meaning of the term *qarīnah* in the PF literature. By considering these two components of the concept 'context', the term is intended to cover all the relevant features that contribute to the recognition of the speaker's intention.

Although the term 'context' *(qarīnah)* involves the linguistic and non-linguistic elements which are connected with the intended meaning, the legal theorists occasionally employ the term 'co-text' *(siyāq)* to refer to the uttered units that precede or follow the unit (whether it is a word or an utterance) in question.[79] However, when the term *siyāq* is used against the term *sibāq* (preceding), the former is restricted to the following units whereas the latter applies to the preceding ones.[80]

'Context' covers not only the immediate circumstances in which the utterance is uttered but also the mutual knowledge of the participants *(al-ᶜahd bayn al-mutakhāṭibīn)*[81] and the presuppositions of the hearer.[82]

It is common in the works of the legal theorists to distinguish between at least three types of context:

i Verbal context *(qarīnah lafẓiyyah, nuṭqiyyah* or *maqāliyyah)*, which includes any uttered element that is believed to contribute to clarifying the speaker's intention.[83]
ii Rational context *(qarīnah ᶜaqliyyah)*, which involves any cognitive facts that are believed to contribute to clarifying the speaker's intention.[84]
iii Situational context *(qarīnah ḥāliyyah)*, which involves the state of the speaker, his state of affairs, his previous history in terms of sincerity, any action or gesture carried out by him, and the situation in which the utterance is performed.[85]

As to the last one, al-Ghazālī states that "situational contexts [. . .] are unlimited and unpredictable".[86] This statement should be interpreted in the light of the belief that context is but a means of recognising the speaker's intention, as ᶜAzmī Zādah (d. 1040/1630) points out.[87] Accordingly, since the intentions of the speakers are inherently unlimited and unpredictable, so are the contexts which manifest them in communicative processes. This property of context is very important, for it sets out the role of context as a communicative element that can perform the function that 'established' expressions cannot, so much so that "whatever does not have an 'established' expression in language can be conveyed by context" *(kullu mā laysa lahu ᶜibāratun mawḍūᶜatun fī l-lughati fa-tataᶜayyanu fīhi l-qarīnah)*.[88]

With regard to the function of context, the legal theorists as well as rhetoricians differentiate between two kinds of context:

i Diverting context *(qarīnah ṣārifah)*, which indicates the impossibility of interpreting an expression literally.[89]

ii Guiding context *(qarīnah hādiyah)*, which directs the hearer to the intended meaning.[90]

Muḥammad al-Jurjānī (d. 729/1329) stresses that the diverting context by itself is not helpful in recognising the speaker's intention, "because not intending a particular thing does not necessitate intending another particular thing, so there must be a guiding context"[91] to achieve the intended meaning since the role of the diverting context is limited to indicate that the literal meaning is not the intended one.

However, it is customary in Arabic rhetoric and the PF to label the guiding context as 'relation' *(ᶜalāqah)* and to distinguish at least twenty-five types of relation[92] which are very often subsumed into four or five types: 'correspondence in form' *(al-ishtirāk fī l-shakl)*, 'correspondence in quality' *(al-ishtirāk fī l-ṣifah)*, 'considering the previous condition' *(iᶜtibār mā kān)*, 'considering the forthcoming condition' *(iᶜtibār mā sa-yakūn)* and 'proximity' *(al-mujāwarah)*. The last type is intended to be so vague that it covers any recognisable relation, including antonymy where utterances like 'you are a lion' is used ironically to mean 'you are a coward'. What is common to all these types of relation (the twenty-five relations) is that they are based on a survey of the potential associations that can take place between meanings either in the external world or in the speakers' minds. These types of relation were set up inductively through an investigation of the language.[93] It seems that the main goal of this survey is to recognise to which extent the ability of the speakers to reason can associate the literal meanings of utterances with the non-literal intentions of their speakers.

The conclusion arrived at by scholars in this field is that such relations should be distinct and well-known and that one should not be satisfied with any absolute connection no matter what.[94] This condition seems to have been adopted to stress the substantial contribution of the mutual knowledge *(al-ᶜahd)* acquired by the participants about the subject matter of speech to the success of communication. Thus, if one says 'Zayd is a lion' when one means 'he is brave', the utterance will properly be understood; but if one says the same utterance to mean 'his mouth has bad breath', or 'is suffering from halitosis', the utterance will not normally be understood, for the connection between the property of having bad breath and lion is neither distinct nor well-known.[95]

It is clear that 'the guiding context' (or relation) has very often much to do with cultural values, even though reasoning plays an essential part in its resolution. The difficulties facing non-Arabs in understanding such metonymy as 'Zayd has much ash' or 'Zayd's dog is a coward' (both mean 'Zayd is a hospitable host') would demonstrate the importance of the role that the environment plays in understanding linguistic utterances.

NOTES

1 I could not find a single word to stand for the Arabic term *waḍ*ᶜ, so I will use the following three different English words to get the import of this term, the preference of one of these terms over the other on a particular occasion depends on its relevance to the context:
   (i) 'to establish' (which represents the literal meaning of the Arabic word *waḍ*ᶜ);
   (ii) 'to assign' (in contexts like 'to assign a particular expression to a particular meaning');
   (iii) 'to designate' (in contexts like 'whether expressions are designed to be designations for mental images or external-entities').
   However, I will use the term *waḍ*ᶜ in its Arabic form whenever I find it more appropriate.
2 Weiss, "Language . . .", pp. 61–62.
3 Al-Ruhāwī, p. 51.
4 For comparison see al-Qarāfī, *Sharḥ Tanqīḥ*, pp. 20–22; Saussure, *Cours de Linguistique général*, pp. 30–38.
5 Shihāb al-Dīn Aḥmad b. Idrīs al-Qarāfī is an Ashᶜarī theologian and a distinguished *Mālikī* jurist and legal theorist. He was regarded by al-Suyūṭī as an independent *mujtahid* (not belonging to any of the four Sunnī legal schools). He wrote about twenty books among which are the following:
   – *Anwār al-Burūq fī Anwā*ᶜ *al-Furūq;*
   – *al-Dhakhīrah fī l-Fiqh al-Mālikī;*
   – *al-Iḥkām fī Tamyīz al-Fatāwā* ᶜ*an al-Aḥkām wa-Taṣarrufāt al-Qāḍī wa-l-Imām;*
   – *al-Istighnā*ᵓ *fī l-Istithnā*ᵓ*;*
   – *Nafā*ᵓ*is al-Uṣūl fī Sharḥ al-Maḥṣūl;*
   – *Sharḥ Tanqīḥ al-Fuṣūl fī Ikhtiṣār al-Maḥṣūl fī l-Uṣūl; and*
   – *Tanqīḥ al-Fuṣūl fī l-Uṣūl.*
   See Ibn al-Nadīm, *al-Fihrist;* al-Qarāfī, *al-Iḥkām . . .*, pp. 11–16.
6 Al-Qarāfī, *Sharḥ Tanqīḥ*, p. 20.
7 See *ibid.*, pp. 20–21.
8 *Ibid.*, p. 22.
9 See al-Ghazālī, *al-Mustaṣfā*, 1/339.
10 See *ibid.*
11 Al-Ghazālī, *Mi*ᶜ*yār . . .*, p. 43.
12 Al-Suyūṭī, *al-Muzhir . . .*, 1/42.
13 Al-Rāzī, 1/68; see *ibid.*, 1/42.
14 *Ibid.*, 1/68.

15 Al-Shīrāzī, *Sharḥ al-Lumaʿ*, 1/186.
16 See al-Suyūṭī, *al-Muzhir* . . ., 1/42.
17 Adrian Gully prefers to translate *qiyās* in this sense as "the sanctioning of linguistic data according to the rules governing the language". See Gully, *Grammar* . . ., p. 45.
18 See al-Qarāfī, *Sharḥ Tanqīḥ*, p.413; al-Shīrāzī, *Sharḥ al-Lumaʿ*, 1/186.
19 Al-Qarāfī, *Sharḥ Tanqīḥ*, p. 413.
20 Ibn Yaʿīsh, *Sharḥ al-Mufaṣṣal*, 1/27.
21 Al-Taftāzānī, *Ḥāshiyah ʿalā Sharḥ al-ʿAḍud*, 1/171. See, also, al-Baṣrī, 1/10–11.
22 Muḥammad al-Jurjānī, *al-Ishārāt* . . ., p. 23.
23 See al-Qarāfī, *Sharḥ Tanqīḥ*, p. 413.
24 Al-Sharīf al-Jurjānī, *Ḥāshiyah ʿalā Sharḥ al-ʿAḍud*, 1/183.
25 Al-Suyūṭī, *al-Muzhir* . . ., 1/43. *The Arabic text reads as follows: (inna l-dālla bi-l-waḍʿi lā budda min iḥṣāʾihi wa-manʿi l-istiʾnāfi fīh, kamā kāna fī l-mufradāti wa-l-murakkabāti l-qāʾimati maqāmahā, fa-law kāna l-kalāmu dāllan bi-l-waḍʿi wajaba dhālika fīhi, wa-lam yakun an natakallama bi-kalāmin lam nusbaq ilayhi, kamā lam nastaʿmil fī l-mufradāti illā mā sabaqa istiʿmāluhu, wa-fī dhālika burhānun ʿalā anna l-kalāma laysa dāllan bi-l-waḍʿi).*
26 *Ibid.*, 1/44.
27 *Ibid.*
28 Al-Astarābādhī, *Sharḥ al-Raḍī* . . ., 1/25.
29 *Ibid.*
30 See Martinet, *A Functional View of Language*, pp. 50–51; *idem*, *Elements of General Linguistics*, pp. 110–111.
31 Weiss, "Language . . .", p. 94.
32 C stands for consonants which are not part of the morphological patterns. The vowels, the definite article and *tanwīn* are represented as they are.
33 See Ibn Khaldūn, *al-Muqaddimah*, p. 474.
34 Ibn Khaldūn, *The Muqaddimah* . . ., 3/380.
35 ʿAbd al-Qāhir al-Jurjānī was an outstanding grammarian and rhetorician. It is widely held that he is the real founder of Arabic rhetoric. His two valuable books *Asrār al-Balāghah* and *Dalāʾil al-Iʿjāz* are highly influential in Arabic linguistics. Although he is not a legal theorist, the traditional interaction between Arabic rhetoric and PF, which is partly due to the fact that the vast majority of Muslim legal theorists are rhetoricians, makes his statement quite relevant here. (see al-Ziriklī, *al-Aʿlām* . . ., 1/95).
36 ʿAbd al-Qāhir al-Jurjānī, *Asrār al-Balāghah*, pp. 345–347.
37 See al-Taftāzānī, *Ḥāshiyah ʿalā Sharḥ al-ʿAḍud*, 1/187–188.
38 See ʿAḍud, 1/187.
39 See *ibid.*, 1/187–189.
40 See *ibid.*
41 See *ibid.*
42 See al-Taftāzānī, *Ḥāshiyah ʿalā Sharḥ al-ʿAḍud*, 1/188.
43 See al-Qarāfī, *Sharḥ Tanqīḥ*, p. 33.
44 See *ibid.*, pp. 34–35.
45 *Ibid.*, p. 35.

46 See *ibid.*, pp. 35–36.
47 See *ibid.*, p. 35.
48 Al-Sharīf al-Jurjānī, *Ḥāshiyah* [c]*alā Sharḥ al-*[c]*Aḍud*, 1/188.
49 Al-Qarāfī, *Sharḥ Tanqīḥ*, p. 20.
50 *Ibid.*, p. 22.
51 See Aḥmad, *Sharḥ al-Uṣūl al-Khamsah*, pp. 525–563.; Ibn Taymiyyah, *Kitāb al-Ṣafdiyyah*, 2/87.
52 Al-Juwaynī, 1/199–202; al-Sharīf al-Jurjānī, *Sharḥ al-Mawāqif* . . ., pp. 146–160.
53 Aḥmad Ibn Taymiyyah, *Kitāb al-Ṣafdiyyah*, 2/54–110.
54 See; al-Juwaynī, 1/204; [c]Aḍud, 2/78; al-Ghazālī, *al-Mustaṣfā*, 1/414.
55 Al-Rāzī, 1/198.
56 The term *Sunnī* in this particular context is being used in a narrower sense than elsewhere in the present study where it is used in opposition to *Shī*[c]*ī*.
57 Al-Juwaynī, 1/211.
58 Al-Qarāfī, *Sharḥ Tanqīḥ*, p. 138.
59 Al-Rāzī, 1/197.
60 Al-Qarāfī, *Sharḥ Tanqīḥ*, p. 218.
61 *Ibid.*, p. 136.
62 See Ṣadr al-Sharī[c]ah, 1/316.
63 Al-Anṣārī, 1/319.
64 See Leech, *Principles of Pragmatics*, p. 30; Marmor, *Interpretation and Legal Theory*, p. 15.
65 See Grice, "Meaning", pp. 53–59; *idem*, "Utterer's Meaning . . .", pp. 54–70; Levinson, *Pragmatics*, p. 19; Platts, *Ways of Meaning* . . ., p. 88–89.
66 Dascal, "On the Pragmatic Structure of Conversation", p. 41.
67 See, e.g., al-Harawī, 1/142.
68 See al-Taftāzānī, *Ḥāshiyah* [c]*alā Sharḥ al-*[c]*Aḍud*, 1/144; al-Anṣārī, 1/204.
69 See al-Harawī, 1/142.
70 Al-Taftāzānī, *Ḥāshiyah* [c]*alā Sharḥ al-*[c]*Aḍud*, 2/113.
71 This is the common answer in modern spoken Arabic and most languages.
72 Al-Anṣārī, 1/204. The Arabic text reads as follows: *(inna l-dalālata l-*[c]*aqliyyata takfī li-l-mafhūmiyyati wa-l-qarinata li-l-murādiyyati lākin lā budda li-ṣiḥḥati l-tarkībi min amrin zā*[ɔ]*idin, fa-lā budda mina l-samā*[c]*i wa-l-ijāzati minhum li-l-isti*[c]*māli ḥattā yakūna jāriyan* [c]*alā qawānīnihim wa-hādhā huwa l-waḍ*[c] *al-naw*[c]*ī).*
73 Ibn al-Malik, p. 140.
74 *Ibid.*
75 For a discussion of the term *qarīnah* in Islamic legal discourse, see Hallaq, "Brief Communications . . .", 475–480.
76 Al-Sharīf al-Jurjānī, *al-Ta*[c]*rīfāt*, p. 93.
77 Al-Ziriklī, *al-A*[c]*lām*, 6/290; Kaḥḥālah, *Mu*[c]*jam al-Mu*[ɔ]*allifīn* . . ., 11/47.
78 Al-Tahānawī, 2/969.(*al-isti*[c]*ārah*).
79 See Ibn al-Malik, p. 427; al-Ruhāwī, p. 427.
80 See Zādah, p. 427.
81 See al-Rāzī, 1/381.
82 See *ibid*, 1/140.
83 See *ibid;* al-Ghazālī, *al-Mustaṣfā*, 1/339.
84 See al-Ghazālī, *al-Mustaṣfā*, 1/340.

85 See al-Rāzī, 1/140; al-Ghazālī, *al-Mustaṣfā*, 1/340.
86 Al-Ghazālī, *al-Mustaṣfā*, 1/340.
87 See Zādah, p. 352.
88 Al-Ghazālī, *al-Mustaṣfā*, 1/340.
89 Muḥammad al-Jurjānī, *al-Ishārāt* . . ., p. 205.
90 See *ibid.*
91 *Ibid.*
92 See al-Taftāzānī, *Ḥāshiyah ᶜalā Sharḥ al-ᶜAḍud*, 1/143; al-Sharīf al-Jurjānī, *Ḥāshiyah ᶜalā Sharḥ al-ᶜAḍud*, 1/43–144; Muḥibb Allāh, 1/203.
93 Al-Taftāzānī, *Ḥāshiyah ᶜalā Sharḥ al-ᶜAḍud*, 1/145.
94 Al-Qarāfī, *Sharḥ Tanqīḥ*, p. 47. The Arabic text reads as follows: *(fa-innā nashtariṭu fī l-ᶜalāqati an yakūna lahā ikhtiṣāṣun wa-shuhrah, wa-lā yuktafā bi-mujarradi l-irtibāṭi kayfa kān).*
95 The second of Searle's principles of metaphor, which are designed to relate literal meaning to metaphorical meaning, involves a similar idea. See Searle, "Metaphor", p. 534.

Chapter Three
Interpretation

3.1. INTRODUCTION

In the Islamic legal literature, *al-ḥaml* (interpretation) has received intensive consideration. The most important underlying reason for this is that the whole life of a Muslim is associated with the evaluations derived from the divine text, which acts as the core part of a constellation of associated texts. Muslims believe that evaluations, values, and principles derived from the *Qur'ān* and *Sunnah* are suitable to all humankind, and applicable to any society, and that texts of this nature must be readable and interpretable forever. Thus, interpretation in this sense is viewed as a kind of searching for the intentions of *Allāh* and His Prophet, with the attendant requirement that any attempt to interpret such texts, or to establish an approach to tackle this task must take the above parameters into account.

Additionally, interpretation covers a large set of speech acts, which have social, legal and/or religious effects on Muslims in their everyday life. Examples of these speech acts are swearing, defaming and the so-called *ṣiyagh al-ᶜuqūd wa-l-fusūkh* (lit, forms of contracts and revocations), e.g., *Nakaḥtuki* (I hereby marry you), and *anti ṭāliq* (I hereby divorce you).

Jurists, who are conventionally entitled to decide whether a certain utterance has explicitly or implicitly such and such an effect, apply the same overall approach of the legal theorists in interpreting speech acts. It is generally accepted that the PF is the field that is concerned with constructing general principles and strategies that can be relied on in interpretation.

Al-ḥaml in PF is commonly understood as the hearer's own understanding of the intention of the speaker.[1] Any act of interpretation must consequently be preceded by an intended act of use, which leads to the view that an utterance performed by a sleep-talker, mad man or the like is judged not to merit interpretation, though the hearer may attempt to understand it. But there is a substantial difference between understanding an utterance and interpreting it. Thus, for an utterance to merit interpretation, it must meet at least three conditions:

i it must be uttered intentionally;
ii it must be intended to a particular hearer or hearers; and
iii the hearer must be rational and able to understand it.

These three conditions can readily be derived from the following definition suggested by some legal theorists for the term *al-khiṭāb* (discourse), which is considered to be the subject of interpretation: *al-khiṭāb* is "a conventional utterance intended to be communicated to whom is capable of understanding it".[2] "Conventional" *(al-mutawāḍa*[c] [c]*alayh)* in this context is taken to exclude what is called *al-alfāẓ al-muhmalah* (lit, disregarded expressions), i.e., "expressions that have no meaning by virtue of *waḍ*[c]" *(al-alfāẓu ghayru l-dāllati* [c]*alā ma*[c]*nan bi-l-waḍ*[c]*)*,[3] and, therefore, cannot be regarded as part of the lexicon of the language by which communication is taking place. Sayf al-Dīn al-Āmidī (d. 631/1233), who advocated this definition of discourse, insists on the intentionality of the speaker and the capability of the hearer to recover it, rendering the term discourse inappropriate to such utterances as those produced by sleep-talkers (condition (i) and (ii) above), and those addressed to hearers who are judged not to be rational (or not speaking the same language), and, therefore, unable to understand the full import of the discourse concerned (condition (iii) above). It can be assumed that the interpretative activity of the hearer is encouraged by the speaker's intent that his utterance is performed to be recognised insofar as the hearer feels that he is required to make some effort to grasp the intention of the speaker.

A further related notion that is given some emphasis is *al-ta*[c]*āwun* (co-operation), which is considered to be the motive behind communication in general. Co-operation, as far as communication is concerned, can occur by means other than language, for example, gestures and body language, but because of the properties of spoken discourse, language is believed to be the favoured and most significant means of communication. Some of the properties of spoken discourse are:

a) efficiency (i.e., it can refer both to existent and non-existent entities);

b) ease of use (i.e., the production of spoken utterances on the physiological side is viewed as an exploitation of the natural operation of exhalation without unnaturalness);
c) ephemerality (sounds vanish immediately after use); and
d) segmentability (by which an infinite number of utterances can be produced).[4]

Although 'co-operation' in PF is shown to contribute to communication, it is, however, not given the same prominence and methodological status attributed to it by Grice in his pragmatic account of how communication takes place.

In the PF account of communication, the hearer makes some presumptions about the degree to which the speaker is co-operative. These presumptions are based, whenever possible, on the hearer's knowledge of the speaker's habit of the use of language. This implies a connection between the hearer's knowledge of the speaker, and the success of communication. In other words, the more the hearer knows about the speaker's way of the use of language, the more likely it is that communication will be successful.[5]

Correspondingly, in order to achieve a proper interpretation for the intentions of *Allāh* and His Prophet, the legal theorists believe that at least the two following assumptions should be satisfied:

a) it is impossible that *Allāh* would say something without a prior intention; and
b) it is impossible that *Allāh* would set out to mean something contrary to what people understand[6] (i.e., He would not speak so ambiguously that people could understand the wrong message).

The importance of these assumptions here is that they serve as elements in a general principle that has to be considered in interpretation. Al-Qarāfī formulates this principle as follows:

> "'The base' is that expressions actualise their implicatures and designate their meanings".[7]

Thus, the hearer is required to act according to this principle, with the implication that the search for meaning is presumed until it is presumed to have been identified. Should the literal meaning be inconsistent with the context (in its broadest sense), the interpreter has to look for another meaning or meanings until the process is satisfactorily completed. There are particular strategies which guide this 'search' process (they shall be explored later).

Similarly, if the hearer believes that the speaker is sincere, he will consider his utterance meaningful even if its surface meaning seems unclear. The task of the hearer in such a case is to search for an ulterior meaning, which is guided by contextual features. So, if S tells H that he saw a smiling moon, he will presumably think that S is not speaking literally, provided that H believes that S is not telling a lie.

3.2. FIQH, UNDERSTANDING AND INTERPRETATION

The distinction drawn by the legal theorists between *fahm* (understanding) and *fiqh* shows a great insight into the problem of interpretation. Clearly, this distinction presupposes a further related distinction between meaning and intention.[8] It is customary in PF to define *fiqh* in its pre-theoretical sense as "understanding the intention of the speaker".[9] It is, as Ibn Qayyim al-Jawziyyah states, more specific than *fahm* (understanding), for it is more restricted than 'understanding' in its common sense.[10] Consequently, *fiqh* entails understanding, but not *vice versa*. Another way of explaining the difference between understanding and *fiqh* is to say that understanding is *waḍᶜ*-based construction, whereas *fiqh* is use-based one.

The term *fiqh* has a long history in the Islamic literature which can be traced back to the Holy Qur'ān, in which it is possible to find an implicit explanation of the meaning of this word and its derivatives, where they associate with commendable connotations, whereas the negation of the quality of *fiqh* suggests denial of praise and criticism of people who lack this quality.

Maclean points out that "those who read texts literally and not according to their [true] meaning are said to understand in a Jewish manner, as the Jews refuse to depart from the literal meaning".[11]In the Islamic literature, the *Ẓāhirīs* (lit, literalists: an Islamic sect), whose approach to texts is said to be based merely on the surface meaning of utterances, put themselves in a similar position. Since *fiqh* aims at the intention of the speaker, which presupposes extra-linguistic considerations, the legal theorists tend not to call this sect *fuqahāᵓ* (people who have the faculty of *fiqh*) on the grounds that they fail to go beyond the literal meanings of words.[12] In an attempt to explain why he thought that the *Ẓāhirīs* failed to understand the divine texts, Ibn Qayyim al-Jawziyyah raises the fact that they rely on literal meaning without considering other facts like the implications and references of expressions.[13] In setting out his position over this matter he calls the person who approaches a text in terms of what is said *lafẓī* (a verbal person), reserving the title *ᶜārif* (knowledgeable) to the person who asks about the intention of the speaker.[14] In modern pragmatics, the *Ẓāhirīs*'s approach would be called a code model, while the mainstream approach would be called an inferential model.[15]

Certainly, one of the crucial ideas of the Muslim legal theorists is the fact that they regard *ᶜaql* (reason) as one of the two operators in the process of *fiqh*.[16] The other operator is, of course, what they call *samᶜ* (information-knowledge), which includes the prior and immediate knowledge about the relevant elements that are believed to contribute to interpretation (e.g., *waḍᶜ*, common use, the speaker's habitual use of language, context, etc.). Hence, *fiqh* is a mixture of two integrative components: knowing and reasoning.

A further idea in PF is the intentions of the *Sharīᶜah*. The essence of this idea can be summarised by saying that the actual intentions manifested in the divine text are usually motivated, according to *Māturīdīs, Ḥanbalīs, Muᶜtazilīs,* and others, by wider, more abstract, and fundamental intentions. Contrary to the *Ashᶜarīs,* these theological schools hold the view that the interests of human beings are considered by *Allāh* in His actions and evaluations, and that the ultimate goals behind those actual intentions can potentially be identified.[17] Abū Isḥāq al-Shāṭibī (d. 790/1388), who places considerable emphasis upon the intentions of the *Sharīᶜah*, points out that the *Sharīᶜah* is established to maintain the five necessities: religion, life, posterity (*nasl*), wealth and intellect, insisting on the priority given to those five *ḍarūriyyāt* (necessities) over what they call *al-ḥājiyyāt* (the needs), and *al-ḥājiyyāt* over *al-taḥsīnāt* (amelioratives or luxuries).[18] The interpreter, in his attempt to derive evaluations from texts, should be aware of the relation between the intentions of the *Sharīᶜah* and their priorities, on the one hand, and the text in its literal form on the other. Any particular text that appears to be in disagreement, in some form or another, with a general principle must be reconciled with it, since the legislator has set that particular text with the intention of maintaining those principles.[19]

The idea of considering the intentions of the *Sharīᶜah* and generally any further intentions,[20] can be reasonably incorporated into the more abstract notion of the knowledge about the habit of the speaker in the use of language, which is believed to facilitate interpretation as an operation of searching for the actual intention represented in the text concerned.

Hitherto, we have three distinct, but connected, terms for the process of comprehending an utterance: *ḥaml* (interpretation), *fiqh* and *fahm* (understanding). In what follows, we will concentrate on *ḥaml* only, because, firstly, it is regarded as one of the four constitutive factors of communication, secondly, it is neutral (i.e., free of the favourable connotations that characterise the term *fiqh*), and, thirdly, it is so general that it can cover all speech acts whether they are of divine nature or not. The term *fiqh* will, however, be eliminated because it has juristic connotations owing to its being used as a label for the science of jurisprudence. With regard to *fahm,* its vagueness and the fact that it is regarded as a temporary process to achieve the interpretation of the speaker's intention make it unsuitable for discussion here (cf. Figure 3.1).

3.3 SIGNIFYING BY EXPRESSIONS AND THE SIGNIFICATION OF EXPRESSIONS

The distinction between *al-dalālah bi-l-lafẓ* and *dalālat al-lafẓ* (signifying by expressions and the signification of expressions), which seems to have been first introduced by al-Qarāfī, implies that what the speaker intends by his utterance and what the hearer interprets are two distinctively different things. Ibn Ḥalūl al-Qayrawānī (d. 895/ 1489) points out that al-Qarāfī's distinction in his work *Sharḥ Tanqīḥ al-Fuṣūl* seems to suggest that the two notions are completely different, but in his Commentary on al-Rāzī's *al-Maḥṣūl,* signifying by expressions appears to be more general than the signification of

The property	*ḥaml*	*fiqh*	*fahm*
waḍʿ based activity	–	–	+
use based activity	+	+	–
meaning oriented activity	–	–	+
intention oriented activity	+	+	–
suggests the possibility of indeterminacy	+	–	–
suggests the success of the hearer	–	+	+
has juristic connotations	–	+	–
has favourable connotations	–	+	+

Figure 3.1 *The differences between* **ḥaml, fiqh** *and* **fahm**

expressions, which is interpreted as understanding.[21] Al-Qarāfī managed to offer fifteen differences between the two processes.[22] Even if it is hard to assess how much importance can be given to each difference, many of them, it can be argued, seem not to have any clear significance since they have seemingly come to light only as a result of his determination to mention as many differences as he could rather than as being relevantly valuable dissimilarities.

Some of the considerations on which he relied in drawing his distinctions are

I The producer

Under this category three differences can be accommodated:

a) Signifying by expressions (henceforth SBE) is an activity of the speaker, whereas the signification of expressions (henceforth SE) is an activity of the hearer. To put it al-Qarāfī's way, SBE is a quality of the speaker, but SE is a quality of the hearer.[23]
b) SBE takes place in the articulatory system, whereas SE in the mind of the hearer.[24]
c) SE is preconditioned by life.[25]

Clearly, al-Qarāfī does not seem to be precise in his formulation of (b) above in that he concentrates upon the physical aspect for SBE and the intellectual aspect for SE. The reason for that may well be that he intends to render SBE so general to include any interpretable sound whether it is produced by man or an animate, or even inanimate object. This general sense of SBE is exactly what Ibn Ḥalūl understood from (c).[26]

The problem that arises from the extension of the term SBE in this way is that it leads to abandoning 'intentionality' as a condition for any act of communication. In another place in the same book, al-Qarāfī considers 'intentionality' to be a condition of SBE.[27] What is more, his definition of SBE as 'use' presupposes 'intentionality' as explained in the previous chapter. In order to reconcile the inclusion of 'intentionality' in SBE in some instances with his exclusion of it in his distinction between SBE and SE, we can say that intentionality is regarded in SBE in its narrow sense and disregarded in its broad sense. The noise of thunder can be a good example of SBE in its broad sense, for thunder does not intend to communicate any message, even if we can infer something when we hear it. Pragmatically and communicationally speaking, it is the narrow sense of SBE that concerns us in this work.

II Occurrence

SE is preconditioned by SBE, i.e., whenever SE occurs, SBE must have occurred, but SBE may occur without being followed by SE.[28]

III Causality

SBE is a cause, whereas SE is an effect.[29]

It is worth mentioning here, however, that the occurrence of the cause, as the legal theorists stress on various occasions, does not necessitate the occurrence of the effect as there might be an impediment. Accordingly, SBE may not be followed by SE owing to some communicational problems.

IV Types of signification

While SBE can be divided into two types: literally signifying and figuratively signifying, SE can be divided into three types: *dalālat muṭābaqah* (equivalence-signification), *dalālat taḍammun* (incorporational signification) and *dalālat iltizām* (implicational signification) (cf. 5.2.1.1).[30]

The three types of SE will be discussed in the fifth chapter, but at the moment let us consider the two types of SBE, which are involved in the following definition of SBE.

Al-Qarāfī defines SBE as "the use of an utterance either in its literal or figurative meaning".[31] The pragmatic significance of this definition (in fact, of the notion itself) relates to the fact that it implies a distinction between what words in themselves mean and what we mean by them, and, that it renders the speaker as the maker of the message insofar as the formation of the utterance would be determined by the extra-linguistic elements that he considers, specially his intention, context, rhetorical goals, the type of the hearer, and the expectations of the speaker about him.

With respect to the intention of the speaker, it is generally believed that it governs the speaker's selection of words and their order in a free-order language of the type to which Arabic belongs. In modern terms, it is the intention of the speaker that determines what Ferdinand de Saussure calls 'the paradigmatic and syntagmatic relationships" in a particular utterance. It seems reasonable to think, however, that the words selected from their paradigms and the very particular types of patterns chosen to be followed by the speaker constitute the speaker's message. Any linguistic element used by a rational speaker is largely held to be intentionally communicated, and its possible alternatives are, therefore, deliberately ignored. This can obviously be seen in the controversial notion *mafhūm al-mukhālafah* (counter implicature), which will be dealt with in the fifth chapter (cf. 5.3.3.1.2). Any kind of giving precedence to some parts of the utterance is also normally taken to be intended. In general, the common view in PF is that the signification of expressions is controlled by the intention of the speaker rather than self-controlled: *"dalālat al-alfāẓ laysat li dhawātihā, bal hiya tābiᶜatun li-qaṣdi l-mutakallim"*.[32]

It is widely held that context contributes to the forming of utterances. In a situation where the speaker is accompanying a hunter and suddenly tells him "gazelle", it is assumed that the speaker is pressurised to omit some parts of his utterance.

The speaker might also consider what is called in Arabic rhetoric and PF *al-aghrāḍ al-balāghiyyah* (rhetorical goals) to influence his hearer. *Al-taʾaddub* (politeness), *al-taᶜẓīm* (glorification) and *al-taḥqīr* (degradation) are examples of what is regarded as rhetorical goals, which are thought to have considerable effects on the utterance in terms of the quantity, quality and order of the linguistic elements used in the utterance.

Discourse is believed to be partially determined by the type of the hearer, and the expectations and assumptions the speaker makes about him.[33] Accordingly, the discourse addressed to a stupid person, for example, has to be explicit and detailed, and a hearer who is denying the proposition has to be addressed by emphatic words and so on.

A fundamental distinction can be drawn here between intended and interpreted meaning. This distinction is expanded to involve '*waḍᶜ*-based meaning' *(al-maᶜnā l-waḍᶜī)*. It is clear that intended meaning can be associated with SBE, and interpreted meaning with SE, while *waḍᶜ*-based meaning will be left without a counterpart in al-Qarāfī's distinction. The purpose of this tripartite distinction is to approach the question: When can communication be regarded as successful? And the first step would be to examine the possibilities of the occurrence of each meaning in relation to the other two meanings. Normally, the following five possibilities would be available:

I The *waḍᶜ*-based meaning is in agreement with the intended but not with the interpreted meaning. This is the case when the speaker is speaking in accordance with *waḍᶜ*, i.e., speaking literally, but the hearer fails to grasp the speaker's intention, perhaps because of some inherently problematic features attached to the language itself, for example ambiguity.

II The *waḍ*ᶜ-based meaning is in agreement with the interpreted but not with the intended meaning. This is the case when the speaker is speaking non-literally, and the hearer does not recognise that, thinking that the speaker is speaking literally, so he fails to grasp the intention of the speaker owing to some pragmatic reasons (e.g., misleading context).

III The intended meaning is in agreement with the interpreted but not with the *waḍ*ᶜ-based meaning. This is the case when the speaker is speaking non-literally and the hearer recognises it because of the presence of the sufficient contextual information and the success of the interlocutors in considering it.

IV The intended meaning is in disagreement with both the *waḍ*ᶜ-based and interpreted meanings. This is the case when the speaker is speaking non-literally and the hearer fails to recognise that owing to the same reasons mentioned in (II).

V The interpreted meaning is in agreement with both the *waḍ*ᶜ-based and intended meanings. This is the case when the speaker is speaking literally and the hearer recognises this fact because there is no 'diverting context' to the contrary. Obviously, this is the ideal form of communication in which all the communicative elements are acting in conformity with what tends to be called in PF *al-uṣūl* (the bases) (cf. 3.5.1).

As we have seen, the success of communication rests upon the agreement between the intended and interpreted meaning (notice No III & V) rather than between the *waḍ*ᶜ-based meaning and only one of

	waḍᶜ-based m	intended m	interpreted m	success of communication
I	+	+	–	**un**successful
II	+	–	+	**un**successful
III	–	+	+	**successful**
IV	–	+	–	**un**successful
V	+	+	+	**successful**

Figure 3.2 *When is communication regarded as successful?*

the other two meanings (notice No I & II). This leads to the conclusion that *waḍ*^{c} (establishment) is similar to any contextual feature whose value is dependent on how much it is needed in actual communication, which means that it can be abandoned. However, this conclusion is inaccurate for the mainstream legal theorists, for even if the *waḍ*^{c}-based meaning is not the ultimate goal of the interlocutors in many communicative situations, it still functions as a means to achieve the intention of the speaker as it is believed to have some relation with it. This thesis is reflected in PF in the emphasis on what is called *^{c}alāqah* (relation) or sometimes *munāsabah* (relevance). According to the legal theorists, any non-literal use must involve a relation between the literal and non-literal meaning (cf. 3.5.1.4); otherwise any expression can be employed to convey any meaning, which is false.[34] However, not any *munāsabah* would be sufficient, but only that one which is being considered by the interlocutors can be relied upon in non-literal communication.[35] Since there is no correlation between the speaker's and the hearer's consideration[36] (i.e., the kind or aspect of relation considered by the speaker might differ from the one considered by the hearer), it follows that the communicative act is subject to failure as a result. It should be stressed, however, that failure in communication does not imply failure in interpretation. This is because the hearer can rightly be said to have managed to interpret a particular utterance if he manages to understand the linguistic meaning of the utterance, considers the relevant contextual features, and follows the appropriate pragmatic principles and strategies; regardless of whether he succeeds in grasping the intention of the speaker (i.e., in communication) or not. This obviously demonstrates the significance of the differentiation between *fiqh*, which, as mentioned above, suggests the success of communication, and interpretation, which is neutral in this respect. In the light of what has just been said about the difference between success in communication, and success in interpretation,[37] it seems appropriate to think of al-Qarāfī's distinction between SBE and SE in terms of types of signification, which presupposes that the SBE is clue-giving, as it were, whereas SE is intention-searching, and that the speaker has his own way of giving the clue (he may speak literally or non-literally, directly or indirectly, explicitly or implicitly and so on), and the hearer has his own way of searching (he may give priority to the linguistic givens over the extra-linguistic settings or to the explicatures over the implicatures and so on). Strangely enough, the speaker might succeed in his SBE, and so might the hearer in his SE in a particular communicative situation, but the communication fails. That is exactly what happens when both of the interlocutors follow the proper principles and strategies in using and comprehending utterances, but they diverge in their consideration of the relation between the literal and non-literal meaning, probably as a result of considering different contextual features.

3.4. CONTEXT FROM THE VIEWPOINT OF THE ADDRESSEE

3.4.1. Comprehensive sight of text

One of the most important characteristic features of the pragmatic thinking in the PF is the fact that the *Qur'ān* and *Sunnah* are treated as one utterance *"ka l-lafẓati l-wāḥidah"* and that each part of this utterance has to be dealt with in relation to the other relevant parts.[38] No text, accordingly, can be taken separately.[39] The interpreter, therefore, has to be aware of all other relevant texts in dealing with a particular one. Failure to do so, as al-Shāṭibī points out, results in failure to achieve the intention of the legislator unless the goal of the hearer is only to reach an understanding of the surface meaning, which rests merely upon the linguistic givens, without seeking the intention of the speaker.[40] The idea behind this comprehensive sight is that the whole contains more than the sum of its parts.[41] A very much-quoted example to explain this idea is the following verses from which one can, by joining two connected texts together, infer a proposition that cannot be inferred from either of the two texts alone.[42]

> (1)- "We have enjoined on man
> Kindness to his parents:
> In pain did his mother
> Bear him, and in pain
> Did she give him birth.
> The carrying of the (child)
> To his weaning is
> (A period of) thirty months".[43]
>
> (2)- "The mothers shall give suck
> To their offspring
> For two whole years".[44]

By considering the two texts together, jurists infer that the minimum period of pregnancy is six months. Consequently, should any wife give birth to a fine healthy baby before six lunar months from her marriage, her husband has the right to deny it.[45]

The legal theorists regard the texts that have to be considered when a particular text is being interpreted as a verbal context on the grounds that it has some influence on its interpretation. This is generally in conformity with their definition of context as "what is set up to identify what is being intended"[46] (cf. 2.3.2). The question that arises here is how can the same linguistic element be regarded as a context and text at the same time? And the simple answer to this question is that the legal theorists see each text in the Holy *Qur'ān* and *Sunnah* as a part of a whole in a sense that the parts interact in a way which makes the proper interpretation of a given text dependent on all the other relevant texts.

3.4.2. Context as a signifying element

In PF context is treated as a signifying element and is given a position similar to that of linguistic forms (versus meanings), in that both the relevant contextual features and the linguistic forms are meant to be used as a means of communication. There are of course some differences especially in terms of dependency, where context, unlike linguistic forms, cannot function independently. This is, however, what the word 'context' both in Arabic and English seems to suggest. A significant difference in this regard is that the linguistic forms are conventional signifiers, whereas the contextual features are instantaneous signifiers. This difference is notably related to the distinction between *waḍ*^{c} and use (cf. 2.1), where the linguistic forms are held to be *waḍ*^{c}-givens, whereas contexts are generally viewed as use-related features.

Al-Zarkashī declares that the function of *al-siyāq* (co-text) consists of

- i clarifying the obscure;
- ii determining the intention of the speaker;
- iii particularising the general;
- iv qualifying the unqualified; and
- v varying signification.[47]

Thus, context can be described, as far as its function is concerned, as confining or modifying rather than informing, as it were. This might partially, at least, explain why it is that context is viewed as a sign of the intention of the speaker whereas the speaker's words are taken as signs of their literal meanings. The addressee is, therefore, required to realise which one of the available contextual elements is considered by the addresser in order to secure successful communication. At this point, a distinction should be drawn between available and actually considered contexts. Correspondingly, the task of the addressee is not the awareness of the available contexts but the knowledge of what the addresser has chosen, among them, to be the sign of his intention. Hence, the expression *"naṣb al-mutakallim qarīnah"* (setting up a context by the speaker), which occurs frequently in both PF and Arabic rhetoric, implies a favourable quality because it suggests that context is meant to function as a means to reveal the speaker's intention.[48]

Having said that, a large portion of misunderstanding in communication can be assigned to the multiplicity of possible contexts, where the interlocutors consider different contexts, and, therefore, form different interpretations. Consider the two following examples:

1) On his way to Medina accompanied by the Prophet (in their secret *Hijrah* (emigration) from Mecca to Medina in 622 A.D.) Abū Bakr would be asked by some of the unbelievers about his companion. His answer would be:

   "Hādhā l-rajulu -lladhī yahdīnī l-sabīl" (lit. this is the man who is guiding me to the way).[49]

2) On his way to *Badr* (the first battle in Islam), the Prophet was asked by one of his enemies: "Where do you come from?" He replied:

   "We come from *māʾ*.[50]

In both (1) and (2) the addressee misunderstood the intention of the speaker. In (1) the addressee understood the word "way" as the path in its surface meaning, whereas Abū Bakr intended it to be the way leading him to his interest in this life, and Paradise in the hereafter. In (2) the addressee interpreted " *māʾ* " (lit, water) as a name of a particular tribe while the Prophet intended it to be 'water' as water is the origin of human beings.[51]

Examples of this type show:

i choosing one interpretation over another is due to giving priority to a particular context over another. Accordingly, the legal theorists are justified in considering context to be the signifying element of the speaker's intention in actual communication.

ii giving priority to a particular context over another is in turn due to the fact that the addressee tends to localise his interpretation by considering the most immediate context, which is the fact that the meeting took place in the desert in (1), and that the addressee was a tribesman in (2). This factor, which determines interpretation in this way is referred to in PF as *al-tabādur* (immediacy) (cf. 3.5.1.4).

3.4.3. Types of context

Although three types of context are sometimes distinguished, namely verbal, rational and situational context (cf. 2.3.2), the twofold distinction, in which the last two types are integrated under what is called *al-qarīnah al-maᶜnawiyyah* (non-verbal or situational context), appears to be more frequent and less ambiguous.[52] There is not much to say about verbal context (or co-text) other than what has already been briefly said (cf. 2.3.2 and 3.4.1). My concern will, therefore, be the non-verbal context in which the legal theorists incorporate the following:

i The speaker's habit.
ii *Al-ᶜahd* (mutual knowledge).
iii Cultural practices.
iv *Al-bisāṭ* (the carpet).

(i) The speaker's habit:

By this term is meant the speaker's usual way of deploying expressions to convey meanings so that the addressee, if he is familiar with the speaker's habit, can immediately recover his intention through his utterance regardless of what the utterance seems to mean. Ibn Taymiyyah, who attaches great importance to the speaker's habit, argues that since the signification of expressions is intentional *(qaṣdiyyah)* and wilful *(irādiyyah)*, i.e., expressions signify what the speaker intends them to signify and do not signify by themselves, it follows that hearing expressions without the knowledge of the speaker and his custom would signify nothing.[53] Although Ibn Taymiyyah seems to exaggerate to a certain degree the role that the knowledge of the speaker's habit is assumed to play in everyday communication, clearly it plays a significant role in the domain of text-based analysis, especially religious texts, which probably form the scope of his statement.

The concept of the speaker's habit is usually linked with what is known in PF as *al-waḍᶜ al-ᶜurfī,*[54] but the justification for handling it within the notion context is the fact that this concept is sometimes widened to cover not only the verbal habit of the use of language, but also some of what can be accommodated under the speaker's history such as the speaker's sincerity.

The legal theorists believe that the assumptions the addressee makes about the addresser's reliability have a direct effect on his interpretation of the utterance in that they determine, in many cases, whether the utterance should be taken non-literally or as a false statement.[55] The general basis is that if the surface meaning of the utterance is not in correspondence with reality, the utterance should be taken as untrue unless the hearer has a reason to hold the following assumptions:

a) The assumption of the speaker's sincerity: (The hearer assumes that the speaker is sincere).
b) The assumption of the speaker's rationality: (The hearer assumes that the speaker is rational).
c) The assumption of the legal plausibility of the utterance;: (The hearer assumes that the utterance is in agreement with the general principles of religion) (cf. 5.3.1.4).

Once an utterance that has an untrue surface meaning is, by virtue of the above assumptions, accepted to be true, the hearer has to search for an ulterior acceptable meaning. There are various reasons, according to al-Rāzī, to take a particular seemingly untrue utterance as a figurative utterance: one of them is to know or to think that the speaker does not tell a lie.[56] With respect to the texts of the *Qur'ān* and *Sunnah*, any text seemingly conflicting with the speaker's sincerity, his rationality or the utterance's legal plausibility is said to have been intended to be taken non-literally since the utterer of the text is believed to be sincere.

It is generally accepted that the knowledge of the speaker's habit of the use of language including his reliability facilitates the communication process and that, as Ibn al-Qayyim points out, the more knowledge the hearer has about the speaker, his intentions, his language and his habit, the more complete and more perfect his knowledge of the speaker's intention will be.[57] Furthermore, the assumptions which the addressee forms about the addresser contribute to the interpretation of utterances.

(ii) *Al-ᶜahd* (mutual knowledge):

The legal theorists usually apply this concept to *al-maᶜārif* (definite nouns) with the definite article in particular, where the subject of the conversation is mutually assumed to be shared by the interlocutors. Any contribution by the speaker in such cases would be related by the hearer to what both assume to be mutually known to them.[58] The general principle that can be formulated in this context is that the addresser refers to the nearest referent. The application of this principle can be found in Arabic grammar in the discussion of the definite article.

(iii) Cultural practices:

There are different contextual features pertaining to cultural practices which are believed to contribute to interpretation, but without being given a special name in the sources. In his discussion of the requirements of understanding the *Qur'ān*, al-Shāṭibī states that knowledge of the Arab customs, their ways of using language, their ways of behaviour and their current affairs at the time of the revelation is necessary for this purpose.[59] One of his examples is the following *Qur'ānic* verse:

> (3) "*Wa atimmū l-Ḥajja wa-l-ᶜUmrata li-Allāh*"
> "And complete
> The *Hajj* or *'umra*
> In the service of God".[60]

The reason why the *Qur'ān* uses the verb *atimmū* (complete) instead of *addū* (perform) is the fact that the Arabs used to perform the *Ḥajj* and *ᶜUmrah*[61] before Islam even if not in a complete manner.[62]

The term *ᶜurf* (custom) is commonly used as a synonym for *ᶜādah* (habit). Some scholars, however, discriminate between the two terms, employing *ᶜādah* for actions and *ᶜurf* for expressions.[63] The *ᶜurf* is held to be a vital factor in determining the reference of expressions. Al-Rāzī argues that the angels and thieves are not intended when someone says (4), and that restricting the utterance in this way is due to *ᶜurf*.

> (4) Whoever enters my house will be treated hospitably.

(iv) *Al-bisāṭ* (the carpet):

Al-bisāṭ, which is regarded as a form of context, received relatively careful consideration by the *Mālikī* school of law particularly in the subject of *al-yamīn* (oath). By this term, which literally means 'the carpet', is understood the underlying reason behind someone's oath. According to the *Mālikīs*, the interpretation of oaths is highly determined by the motives behind them. They assume that the effects of *al-bisāṭ* on the interpretation of oath-taking are manifest in one of two forms:

First, *al-takhṣīṣ* (restriction), where an expression is modified by *al-bisāṭ* to refer to less than what it literally does. Consider the following example:

(5) I swear that I will never go to that market again.

Given that there is believed to be a particular reason that made the interlocutor take this decision (e.g., the market is overcrowded or not safe), his oath should be taken to be restricted solely to the cases where the relevant condition exists. Thus, the full utterance of the speaker should be interpreted as: I swear that I will never go to that market again <u>as long as such and such a thing exists</u>. The underlined part of this utterance is assumed to be recoverable from *al-bisāṭ*.

Second, *al-taᶜmīm* (generalisation), where the expression is construed to refer to more than what it literally does. So, if one angrily says (6) to somebody who reminded him of a favour he owes, his words in such an example should not be taken literally. Consequently, if he receives any benefit from the speaker in some form or another, his oath will be taken to be broken even if he is not given water to drink.[64]

(6) I will never drink water from you.

3.5. THE MAINSTREAM INTERPRETATION MODEL

The legal theorists construct a set of *uṣūl* (singular, *aṣl* (bases or principles)) and a series of strategies to describe how interpretation can be achieved. In this section, a formula of their fundamental principles and postulates will be offered as a model of their representation of interpretation. This model presumes that interlocutors follow certain norms in communication processes, and handle linguistic utterances in accordance with the *uṣūl* to be examined later.

Before proceeding further, it should be noted that the Arabic term *aṣl* (base or principle) is misleading. Although the word literally refers to the origin of something[65] or the part on which something is based,[66] the following explanations are provided to identify its technical senses:

i *al-dalīl* (evidence) e.g., the *aṣl* of this evaluation is *al-Qur'ān* and *Sunnah;*
ii *al-qā^cidah al-kulliyyah* (general rule);
iii *al-ghālib* (preponderant);
iv *al-rājiḥ* (outweighing); and
v *al-mustaṣḥab* (roughly, presumption).[67]

With the exception of (i), all these senses are relevant to the notion 'base or principle' in this subject. The notion 'base or principle' is usually formulated in one of the following forms:

- the *aṣl* is such and such, e.g., *al-aṣl al-ḥaqīqah* ('the base' is the literal use);
- such and such is an *aṣl,* e.g., *al-ḥaqīqah aṣl* (the literal use is a base); and
- such and such is in violation of the *aṣl,* e.g., *al-majāzu khilāfu l-aṣl* (the non-literal use is in violation of 'the base').

Although it is not easy to assess exactly how significant a base is in interpretation, it can generally be said that the import of each base is sensitive to how much it is required in actual situations. There are, however, some *uṣūl* which operate in the majority, if not all, speech situations. One may be tempted to call these particular *uṣūl* principles, reserving the term 'bases' for the *uṣūl* which are applicable only to particular discourses. However, the Arabic word *(aṣl)* allows one to do so; and, moreover, the way in which what I would call 'bases' are handled in PF is noticeably different from those which I would call 'principles'.

One of the main differences between 'bases' and 'principles' is that the former are designed to depict *discourse* in its ideal form (which is in conformity with *waḍ^c*), whereas the latter are intended to describe the *behaviour* of the interlocutors in the course of the communicative process.

More importantly, the violation of the bases; can generate *ba^cḍ al-aghrāḍ al-balāghiyyah* (some rhetorical intentions) or what Grice calls implicatures. The violation of the principles, on the other hand, would lead to problems in communication. For example, if the speaker flouts the 'literalness' base (i.e., 'the base' is the literal use (cf. 3.5.1.5)), his utterance will be taken as figurative in nature, but if he infringes the principle of truthfulness, his utterance will be taken to be false, leading to the breakdown of communication. The reason is that in violating *'the base'*, the speaker sets up a context which indicates this violation, thus making his intention manifest. In the case of violating *the principle*, the speaker, by contrast, intends to mislead the addressee.

Thus, the above difference is manifested in the fact that speakers in the case of violating the bases depart from what is presumed to be dominant or base in the language veering towards the less common or subsidiary *(al-far^{c})* for a particular purpose by invoking some extra-linguistic elements (i.e., *al-qarā^{ɔ}in al-^{c}aqliyyah* (rational contexts)), which cannot be made manifest except by moving from *waḍ^{c}* to use. In the case of violating the principles, speakers, however, depart from what is presumed to be the common behaviour of the users of language (e.g., truthfulness) to the exception (e.g., telling a lie) without purposefully making this departure clear to the addressee.

Briefly, although both kinds of violation pertain to the manifestation of language in actual situations, the violation of bases; relates to use (versus language), whereas the violation of principles concerns the users themselves (e.g., their credibility).

As far as I can ascertain, pragmatists do not draw the difference between principles and maxims within the Gricean framework (which might be thought of as parallel to the principles-bases dichotomy) in this manner. However, they would face serious difficulties if they did so, since the Gricean distinction between principles and maxims is not formulated with reference to the same underlying premise. A quick look at Grice's maxims will show that they are nothing but instructions intended to show what speakers should do in actual communicative situations in order to be co-operative. This, however, is not true of bases in their capacity as depicters of the ideal, or *waḍ^{c}*-conforming, discourse. More crucially, unlike the violation of bases, the violation of some of the Gricean maxims does not necessarily generate what Grice calls 'implicatures', but rather it leads to failure in communication. Thus, if one flouts the Gricean maxim of quality (Try to make contribution one that is true[68]) by telling a lie, he will probably cause a communication problem. In contrast, if 'the base' of literalness is violated by speaking figuratively, this would lead to an implicature.

However, one might claim that there is no difference between speaking figuratively and telling a lie which would justify placing them in different categories since both arise from the speaker's linguistic performance. This, however, is an implausible claim since the telling of a lie, even if it is a product of the use of a language, is not a property of the language *per se*,[69] for, as ᶜAbd al-Qāhir al-Jurjānī subtly expounds:

> Language tends not to state nor to affirm or disaffirm [. . .]. That is to say, stating that 'beating' is Zayd's action or not, and that 'illness' is his condition or not, is something made by the speaker and is a claim he assumes. Consequently, whatever is levelled at this claim – whether it is belief, accusation of lying, acknowledgement, denial, approving or disapproving – is in fact a reaction directed to the speaker and has absolutely nothing to do with language.[70]

Thus, the ethical basis of utterances in actual situations, though it does have fundamental influence on communication in terms of success or failure, is not attributable to the facts of language structure. Therefore, it would not be appropriate to say that lying is a feature of language in the same way it would be appropriate to say that figurative use is. For that reason, it is by no means accurate to place some kind of lies (e.g., the well-known lies) in the dictionary as a part of a certain language in the same way lexicographers do with some metaphors (i.e., dead or frozen metaphors).

The PF interpretation model is intended mainly to show how a plausible interpretation of the religious and related texts can be achieved. It is generally assumed that language as a product of *waḍᶜ* (i.e., as an abstract system) is not a sufficient basis in interpreting texts, since performing utterances presupposes extra-linguistic elements in the communicative process. Any process of *fiqh* or interpretation (cf. 3.2) in general would involve some kind of cognitive facts. Hence, it is false, as Ibn Taymiyyah argues, to claim that expressions signify without the involvement of cognitive contexts.[71]

As drawn by the legal theorists, the *waḍᶜ*-based (or the highly idealised) discourse must at least be:

i determinate (i.e., has one meaning);
ii intended to be taken literally;
iii taken in its generality;
iv independent (i.e., free from ellipsis);
v devoid of tautology; and
vi following standard syntactic order.[72]

However, this idealised form of communication does not always manifest itself in actual communication. Accordingly, knowledge of *waḍ*ᶜ on its own, even if it can be relied on in identifying linguistic meaning, as al-Ghazālī points out,[73] would not be sufficient for recognising the intention of the speaker in non-ideal communication.

According to the legal theorists and Arab rhetoricians, the native speaker, who is presumed to have knowledge of *waḍ*ᶜ, has the ability not only to form this ideal discourse, but also to discover how much a given discourse on a particular occasion is in agreement or in disagreement with ideal communication, and also to recognise the relationship holding between ideal and actual discourse.

This idealised form of discourse is sometimes called *ᶜibārat al-mutaᶜāraf*[74] (conventionalised discourse) as it does not require to be supported by contextual evidence in actual communication. Any departure from this common discourse, by contrast, needs to be joined by a relevant context in order for successful communication to be guaranteed. The task of the addressee in such a case is to eliminate the *waḍ*ᶜ-based discourse and search for an ulterior one. To make the task of the addressee possible, the speaker has to set up two kinds of context:

i Diverting context *(qarīnah ṣārifah)*[75] to proclaim that the literal meaning is not intended. By reference to this context the addressee recognises that the literal interpretation is nonsense, unlikely or impossible.[76]

ii Guiding context *(qarīnah hādiyah)*[77] to make the intention of the speaker manifest to the hearer.[78] In Arabic rhetoric, this kind of context is called *ᶜalāqah* (relation).[79] It should, however, be pointed out that the employment of the term *ᶜalāqah* for guiding context is not precise since the relation between literal meaning and intended meaning is only part of this kind of context, "which is designed to rule out the competition of other interpretations".[80]

As elucidated in the second chapter, expressions are controlled by isolative *waḍ*ᶜ (cf. 2.2.1.), while grammatical rules and pragmatic precepts are guided by subsumptive *waḍ*ᶜ. Part of subsumptive *waḍ*ᶜ is the following precept: "every expression assigned [by virtue of *waḍ*ᶜ] to a certain meaning should, given the preventing context *(al-qarīnah al-mānīᶜah)*, be assigned to another specifically related meaning".[81] Consider this traditional example:

(1) I saw a lion delivering an address from the pulpit (*Raʾaytu ʾasadan yakhṭubu ᶜalā l-minbar*).

In this example, the hearer receiving this message is assumed:

i to know that lions (in the literal sense) cannot deliver a speech (diverting context), thus eliminating the literal interpretation.
ii to believe that there must be another meaning (the principle of *iᶜmāl* (to make sense of the expressions) (cf. 3.5.1.3).
iii to search for the most possible related meaning (the principle of *tabādur* (immediacy) (cf. 3.5.1.4). The relation ought to be distinct and well-known for both of the interlocutors (cf. 2.3.2.).

Since both of the addresser and the addressee belong to the same linguistic community, and they mutually know that 'courage' is the most well-known and distinct property of lions, and that the hearer expects the speaker to intend the most immediate interpretation (the principle of *tabādur)*; it follows that the hearer would conclude that the speaker intended to say that 'he saw a courageous man'.

However, there must be some reason, according to the legal theorists, for flouting 'the base' (or abandoning the use of *ᶜibārat al-mutaᶜāraf* (conventionalised discourse)), by alternatively appealing to something that is in violation of 'the base'[82] (the subsidiary). Several reasons or motives, which are mainly related to the effective use of communication, are promulgated in this connection. Some of them are held to be *lafẓiyyah* (stylistic); others, which are labelled as *maᶜnawiyyah* (related to meaning) have more to do with rhetorical or communicative intentions, for example *al-taᶜẓīm* (glorification), *al-taḥqīr* (degradation), *targhīb* (arousal of acceptance) and *tarhīb* (intimidation).[83]

3.5.1. The uṣūl *(principles and bases)*

The legal theorists widely believe that *al-taᶜāwun* (co-operation) is the underlying motive behind the establishment of language. To this effect they argue that:

> man cannot live independently of others, for, unlike animals, he cannot content himself with the natural goods [. . .]. For his survival, he has to manufacture his synthetic needs such as food, shelter and wear. The acquisition of such things can be accomplished only by co-operating, participating and dealing with others [. . .], which, undoubtedly, require people to inform each other of the needs related to their livelihood.[84]

The fact that people have a mutual interest in expressing their needs is subtly linked with the question of how communication works. It is generally assumed that the purpose of the establishment of language is to reach a successful communication *(al-tafāhum)*[85] and that the goal of utterances is to guide the hearer and to make the intention of the speaker manifest to him.[86] To achieve this goal, two things, according to Ibn al-Qayyim, are required, namely *bayān al-mutakallim* (speaker's making of his intention manifest) and *tamakkun al-sāmi*^{c} *min al-fahm* (hearer's success in understanding).

In what follows I shall try to answer the two following fundamental questions:

i How is it that the speaker makes his intention manifest to the hearer?
ii How can the hearer recover the intention of the speaker?

The answer to these two questions is largely obtainable by appealing to the five following principles, each of which is treated in PF as a necessary guarantee for the success of communication:

i *Bayān al-mutakallim* (the speaker's disposition to make his intention manifest).
ii *Ṣidq al-mutakallim* (the speaker's truthfulness).
iii *Al-i*^{c}*māl* (lit, operation).
iv *Al-tabādur* (immediacy).
v *Al-istiṣḥāb* (the presumption of the continuity).

It should be noted, however, that the assumption that co-operation is both the motive behind the *waḍ*^{c} of language and the goal of communication is the axis around which these principles operate.

3.5.1.1. The Principle of the Speaker's Disposition to Make his Intention Manifest

By *bayān al-mutakallim* (the speaker's disposition to make his intention manifest;) the legal theorists mean "the speaker's revelation of his intention to the hearer".[87] Abū al-Ḥusayn al-Baṣrī (d. 436/1044) offers four arguments to prove that the speaker intends his audience to recognise his intention:

> [Firstly] Should the speaker not intend his intention to be recognised, that would contradict his position as addresser (*mukhāṭib lanā*) since what is understood from being an addresser is to address, and that would mean nothing except to intend the addressees to understand.

> [Secondly] Should he not intend the addressees to recognise his intention immediately – despite the fact that his utterance seems as an address to them, and the fact that if one addresses his audience in their language, it would mean that he intends them to believe that he has meant what they mean by the same discourse – that would mean he intends the addressees not to know.
>
> [Thirdly] Since the goal of communication is to make the addressee understand [something], it would be futile if the addresser did not intend the addressee to recognise his intention.
>
> [Finally] If it was thinkable that he does not intend us to understand, it would be thinkable to speak in Sudanese *(zinjiyyah)* to an Arab who cannot speak it; rather this is more conceivable as in Sudanese the Arab cannot find an ostensive interpretation that he might hold.[88]

In order for the speaker to be said to have applied this principle, he ought to intend his discourse to be taken in its ostensive interpretation, otherwise the speaker would be intending something which his discourse does not signify.[89] Thus, the speaker has either to use his utterance in accordance with *waḍᶜ* or to indicate his departure from it by contextual evidence. In other words, he ought to conform to the bases or to introduce a valid context to show the addressee that he has violated one or more bases. Failure to do so results in what is called *al-taᶜqīd* (complication),[90] which leads to failure in communication.

Ibn al-Qayyim insists on the hearer's knowledge of this principle, regarding it as one of two requirements the hearer must fulfil in order to be able to grasp the intention of the speaker. The other requirement is, according to him, the knowledge of the speaker's language and his habit in the use of the language[91] (cf. 3.4.3).

However, there is no contradiction between the principle of the speaker's disposition to make his intention manifest; and the fact that speakers frequently use vague expressions since their aims can be the identification of their intentions either in general or in detail.[92] Zayd, for example, may know that ᶜAmr is in the house, but his aim could be to make Khālid know that (a) ᶜAmr is in the house, or alternatively to make him know that (b) a man is in the house.[93] In both cases he can be said to have observed the principle as long as he fulfils the condition mentioned in the previous paragraph no matter whether he is very specific as in (a) or otherwise as in (b).

In brief, the importance of this principle with reference to interpretation is manifested in the fact that the hearer is committed by virtue of this principle to take *al-ẓāhir* (the apparent interpretation) as the intended one. Thus, any interpretation which is in disagreement with the apparent interpretation has to be, at least temporarily, eliminated. However, the senses in which the term *al-ẓāhir* (the apparent interpretation) are employed vary from one context to another, yet in this context it is usually used as equivalent to *al-maᶜnā l-mutabādir* (immediate interpretation), i.e., the first interpretation that occurs to the mind of the hearer (cf. 3.5.1.4).

3.5.1.2. The Principle of the Speaker's Truthfulness

The principle of *ṣidq al-mutakallim* (the speaker's truthfulness) does not receive adequate exposition by the legal theorists, probably because they believe that the truthfulness of the utterances of *Allāh* and the Prophet, which are their main concern, is by no means questionable. However, there are some statements that offer some laconic, but not shallow, answers to questions such as: what is the importance of presuming that the speaker is sincere? Why is it that hearers presume so? What is the relationship between this principle and the presumption of co-operation?

With respect to the first question, al-Rāzī points out that if it is known or presumed that the speaker is not telling a lie, it will be known that the utterance is intended to be taken non-literally.[94] Conversely, it can be argued that if the hearer presumes that the speaker is lying, he will halt the process of 'making sense of' (or searching for the purpose in) the speaker's utterances, which is required, by virtue of the principle of *iᶜmāl* (cf. 3.5.1.3) in order for communication to be successful.

Thus, in order for language to function properly, we have to take the speaker's statement to be true unless there is evidence to the contrary; thus if one says *zaydun qāma* (Zayd has stood up) we will, according to al-Qarāfī, understand that the addresser asserted this proposition, and take it to be true, because of the presumed truthfulness of the addresser, thus believing what the proposition asserts is indeed the case in reality.[95]

The principle of the speaker's truthfulness can be explained in terms of al-Qarāfī's statement: "language is truthfulness not falsehood" (*al-lughatu hiya l-ṣidqu dūna l-kadhib*)[96] by which he seems to render truthfulness as an inherent feature in language to the effect that language cannot function properly without it. In fact, he goes much further to claim that "the Arabs 'established' *al-khabar* (the declarative sentence) for truthfulness but not for falsehood".[97] To furnish the proof for this claim, he reports "the consensus of the grammarians and linguists that the meaning of *zaydun qāma* (Zayd stood up) is the occurrence of the standing in the past" and adds "nobody said that its meaning is the possibility of standing and not standing".[98] It is worth mentioning here that al-Qarāfī has no objection to the definition of the declarative sentence as the sentence that can be true or false, but his account is that the possibility of falsehood "comes not in terms of *waḍ*ᶜ but in terms of the speaker".[99]

However, the claim that truthfulness is an inherent feature in language does not appear to be in harmony with the common view which presupposes, as al-Zarkashī explains, that "the Arabs established the patterns of constructions, but not the particulars of these patterns [. . .] and referred meaning [i.e., the pragmatic meaning] to the speaker's choice".[100] According to this view, truthfulness or its denial has absolutely nothing to do with language;[101] rather they are generated by the performance of the speaker. That is to say, sentences are neutral in terms of truthfulness and other qualities, which, in fact, only emerge when sentences are rendered as utterances in actual situations.

Nevertheless, there are at least two possible interpretations of al-Qarāfī's statement that "language is truthfulness not falsehood": the literal one, which has just been explained; and the non-literal according to which he might be taken to mean that any violation of this principle would lead to the disablement of language as a means of communication.

The difference between the two views (i,e., al-Qarāfī's view and the common view) is, however, not applicable to falsehood in that both views treat this quality as a non-linguistic behaviour of the speaker. Consequently, both views do not contradict the distinction between *majāz* (non-literal use) and falsehood owing to the fact that the former, unlike the latter, has to be joined by contextual evidence which qualifies it as an efficient alternative to literal use in communication.

So far, only one indirect answer to the question 'why is it that hearers presume that the speaker is sincere?' has been provided, namely al-Qarāfī's presumption that truthfulness is an inherent feature in language. There is a further answer derived from the general presumption in PF that people tend to be truthful in communication because they feel that it is in their interest to do so. The legal theorists agree that the tendency towards truthfulness is generally governed by *al-ilf* (familiarity), *al-ᶜādah* (habit), *madhhab* (belief) and *iᶜtiqād* (ideology), and that *al-ᶜaql al-mujarrad* (mere reason) prefers truthfulness to falsehood.[102] However, they acknowledge that speakers may flout the principle of truthfulness for specific purposes, but this cannot demolish the principle altogether, for although *al-muqtaḍī* (the cause) might fail to produce its *ḥukm* (issue) for a certain impediment, 'the base' is that the occurrence of *al-ḥukm* is an inevitable consequence of the occurrence of *al-ᶜillah* (the cause).[103] But, as al-Rāzī's argument implies, if this principle was abandoned, and the reliability of the speaker became dependent on the non-existence of an ulterior interest, which is impossible to prove, it would be impossible to understand the discourse in its ostensive form[104] and, consequently, communication would break down. Obviously, the correlation presumed by al-Rāzī between the violation of this principle and the failure of communication implies that co-operation, which is held to be the motive behind the establishment and use of language, could not be achieved without the maintenance of this principle.

3.5.1.3. The Principle of Iᶜmāl

The principle of *iᶜmāl* (lit, to make something operate) is designed to describe what the addressee has to do when he receives the speaker's utterance. The essence of this principle is that the hearer tends to make the received discourse and the relevant contexts operate by exploiting them to their maximum capability as they are, roughly speaking, the clue to the intention of the speaker. The hearer, according to this principle, searches for any clue that can lead to the intention of the speaker, presuming that interlocutors have mutual interest in communicating with each other. This principle also means that just as the speaker makes his remark manifest as clearly as possible to render his intention recognisable, the hearer has to make the speaker's utterance operate by assuming that it is meaningful in a way which allows for the recovery of his intention. To explain this principle in a simple and pretheoretical English, the *iᶜmāl* of an utterance or an expression is to make sense of, or to search for the purpose in it.

In PF, the principle of *iʿmāl* (operation) is formulated in different ways, but the most common and precise formulation is the following:

i *"iʿmālu l-Kalāmi awlā min ihmālih"* (Making sense of the utterance is given priority to disregarding it).[105]

ii *"inna ḥamla l-kalāmi ʿalā fāʾidatin awlā min ilghāʾih"* (Making sense of the utterance is given priority to cancelling it).[106]

Thus, the first step for the hearer in dealing with a certain discourse is to take all the speaker's utterances as operative signifiers for their meanings, for "the failure of a signifier to stand for its signified is in violation of 'the base'".[107] However, if there is evidence that expressions are not being used in their literal meanings "they must be interpreted figuratively in order to avoid the cancellation of the utterance and leaving the expression without intention".[108] So, if a parent declares that he leaves his possessions to *awlādih* (his children), the word *awlād* (children) must, given that his immediate children are dead, be interpreted to mean 'his descendants' since the literal interpretation is *mutaʿadhdhir* (impossible), thus upholding the general signification of *awlād* in order to avoid the disregard of the expression.[109]

Moreover, if the hearer has to choose between an informative interpretation and a more informative one (richer in meaning), he would, as maintained by this principle, choose the more informative one, since its selection leads to what is called *"takthīr al-fāʾidah* (increasing the value) and enables him to obtain maximum information from the expression. Similarly, should a conflict occur between taking the utterance as a fresh contribution or as *taʾkīd* (diaphora), the former would be more appropriate as a course of action[110] since 'the base' stipulates "that the expression fulfils its requirement, and signifies its meaning".[111] Besides, if the hearer receives two utterances, one of which is more specific, he is required to give prominence to the more specific on the grounds that this would guarantee the *iʿmāl* of the two utterances, which is regarded by the legal theorists as more appropriate *"liʾanna iʿmāla l-dalīlayni aḥrā ay awlā"*.[112]

3.5.1.4. The Principle of Immediacy

The principle of *tabādur* (immediacy) is used to identify the most likely proper interpretation. By *tabādur* the legal theorists presume that *al-mubādir* or *al-sābiq* (the immediate, i.e., the first interpretation that occurs to the hearer) is the one which is most likely to be the intention of the speaker. Any other possible interpretation that occurs later is called *mubādar* (literally means *masbūq* (preceded)). However, not any interpretation that comes to the mind is acceptable, but only that which the addressee believes to be intended by the speaker.[113] The intention behind this constraint is to rule out the infinite inferences that can be derived from utterances if taken independently from the intention of the speaker.[114]

Al-tabādur is regarded as the primary criterion on which the addressee bases himself in his selection of the proper interpretation. This is reflected in the way in which this principle is formulated: "*al-mubādarah awlā*" (priority is given to immediacy).[115]

At this stage, two separate, but connected, questions arise:

i Why is it that the immediate interpretation is the most likely to be the proper interpretation?
ii What kind of interpretation is qualified to fulfil the requirements of immediacy?

The simple answer to the first question is that the speaker and hearer are both presumed to have a mutual interest in communicating with each other, so they are eager to facilitate the communicative process. On the speaker's part, this would, as previously mentioned, involve following the bases, or, alternatively, indicating his departure from them by means of a relevant context. Bearing in mind that the speaker should behave in this manner, the hearer presumes that unless there is evidence to the contrary, the intention of the speaker would be what is understood from the ostensive interpretation.

With respect to the second question, the following answers can be offered:

i The first interpretation which occurs to the speaker is the one in accordance with bases.
ii The first interpretation which occurs to the speaker is the one in accordance with *waḍ*[c].
iii The first interpretation which occurs to the speaker is the most expected one.
iv The first interpretation which occurs to the speaker is the most 'related' interpretation to the literal meaning.

(i) The first interpretation which occurs to the speaker is the one in accordance with bases.

> [According to al-Qarāfī], *al-ḥaqīqah* (literal interpretation) is given priority because its occurrence to the mind of the

> speaker is more immediate than *al-majāz* (the figurative interpretation); and this immediate occurrence *(al-sabq)* is what is meant by "the base [. . .] in speech is literal use".[116]

However, if the literal interpretation is eliminated by contextual evidence, the alternative would be the figurative interpretation,[117] or more precisely "the figurative interpretation nearest to the literal one".[118]

Since bases are formulated in accordance with the requirements of *waḍ*^{c}, the answer to the second question can be stated as in (II):

(ii) The first interpretation which occurs to the speaker is the one in accordance with *waḍ*^{c}.[119]

(iii) The first interpretation which occurs to the speaker is the most expected one.

The hearer's expectations about the speaker's utterance are heavily dependent on his knowledge of the speaker's history including his habit of the use of the language in the sense that "the more knowledge the hearer has about the speaker, his intentions, his language and his habit, the more complete and perfect his knowledge of the speaker's intention will be".[120] This may be illustrated by the Prophet's example cited above (cf. 3.4.2), where the addressee interprets " *mā*$^{\supset}$ " as a name of a particular tribe while the Prophet intends it, in fact, to be "water" in the sense that water is the origin of human beings. The success of Abū Bakr (and presumably anybody who has the same relevant knowledge) in grasping the intention of the speaker could be explained by invoking their presumed knowledge of this matter. Consequently, it can be assumed that grasping the ulterior intention of the Prophet would partially depend on his prior knowledge that the Prophet (i) would not provide the unbeliever with an explicit answer to his question as this would lead to the destruction and, therefore, the suppression of his mission, and (ii) would not tell a lie. It would also partially depend on knowing that human beings are created, according to Islam, from water. Since these expectations (or presumptions) were not held by the addressee (the tribesman), he failed to grasp the ulterior intention of the Prophet, though he understood the apparent meaning of his utterance.

However, temporal and spatial circumstances are believed to contribute to the expectations about the intention of the speaker, and this appears to be the justification for recording what is called *asbāb al-nuzūl* (the reasons for revelation) of the *Qur'ānic* verses, and for specifying the places in which they were revealed. The reference to Abū Bakr's example (cf. 3.4.2) might be helpful to explain this idea, where the addressee understood the word "way" in Abū Bakr's answer "this is the man who is guiding me to the way" as 'road', whereas Abū Bakr intended it to be 'the way' leading to the furtherance of his well-being in life, and Paradise in the hereafter. In this example, it seems reasonable to ascribe the addressee's failure to recover Abū Bakr's intention to the fact that the meeting took place in the desert, which makes the addressee inclined to equate the speaker's intention with the most ostensive meaning of the utterance. However, the failure of the addressees to recover the addressers' intentions in these two examples does not undermine the view that the first interpretation that occurs to the hearer is the one most likely to be the intention of the speaker since these two examples do not illustrate what is held to be the common way of the use of language. On the contrary, these two examples may be judged to demonstrate the correlation between the violation of the principle of the speaker's disposition to make his intention manifest;; (the principle which is held to be a presupposition for this view) and the failure of communication.

Furthermore, the more accessible a phenomenon or an object, the greater the possibility that the hearer would expect it to be part of the speaker's intention. As al-Qarāfī points out, if a given currency becomes the dominant one in a particular place, currency-related expressions will be taken to refer to it.[121] Consider:

A) How much is a cup of tea?
B) Eighty.

It is obvious that if this exchange takes place in Britain, the "eighty" will probably be interpreted as eighty pence, but it would be interpreted differently in different places.

(iv) The first interpretation which occurs to the speaker is the most related one.

This presumption is not necessarily in contrast with (III) above, since in most cases, they actually express the same idea but from two different angles. However, the term *ᶜalāqah* (relation) is usually associated with the notion *majāz*, which seems to be more general than what the English term 'figurative' refers to, since a great deal of what is labelled as 'implicatures' in the Gricean sense is covered by this term.

Relation in PF is designed to account for the connections between sentence meaning and utterance meaning; or to use PF's terminology, between *maᶜnā* (meaning) and *murād* (intention), which are, according to Dascal, "the business of pragmatic interpretation".[122] Moreover, "the task of pragmatic theory is to account for the means whereby this is achieved".[123] As Dascal points out, some "of these means are certainly the Gricean maxims, notably the maxim of relevance".[124] If this is conceded, it can be assumed that the legal theorists offer a workable theory to account for interpretation in terms of relevance. According to this theory, every act of *majāz* involves a relation and context. By context, they mean, in fact, a set of contexts, some of which function as diverting contexts while the others serve as guiding contexts. The former are intended to eliminate the irrelevant interpretations, whereas the latter indicate the relevant ones (cf. 3.5). The literal interpretation is discarded if it conflicts with *qarīnah ṣārifah* (diverting context) in any way. Some of the instances in which the conflict occurs are:

- i If the literal interpretation contradicts logical or customary facts *(li-taᶜadhdhurihā ᶜaqlan aw ᶜādatan)*.[125]
- ii If the literal interpretation contradicts the hearer's assumptions about the world.[126]
- iii If the literal interpretation contradicts another verbal context.[127]
- iv If the proposition is already known by the hearer and the speaker knows that.

However, the legal theorists investigate further cases concerning specific kinds of sentences, such as conditional and imperative sentences, where the literal interpretation is eliminated if

- i the speaker knows that the condition he makes already exists;
- ii the speaker knows that the condition he makes is impossible to meet; or
- iii the speaker knows that the demand he makes is impossible to perform.[128]

With regard to 'guiding context', the term context is sometimes employed in so broad a manner that it incorporates some, if not all, of the principles of communication, distinctly the principle of truthfulness (cf. 3.5.1.2). In his exemplification of *al-qarīnah al-ḥāliyyah* (situational context) al-Rāzī regards the hearer's knowledge or assumption that the speaker is not lying as a way of recognising that the speaker is speaking figuratively. According to him, *al-qarīnah al-ḥāliyyah* includes any indication made by the speaker or inferred from the situation, that the speaker is speaking non-literally.[129]

However, some scholars, particularly Arab rhetoricians, see the guiding context as equivalent to what is meant by *ᶜalāqah* (relation).[130] As it has been pointed out earlier (cf. 3.5), this view is highly suspect since the relation is not the sole guide to the speaker's intention. Thus, it can be said that, with the exception of those falling under the scope of diverting context, all the relevant assumptions involved in non-literal communication can be covered by the term guiding context. Nevertheless, I shall concentrate below on 'relation' as it forms the other part of what can be labelled as the theory of relevance in PF.

In PF, relation is viewed as a matter of degree which allows speakers some freedom as to the clarity between the linguistic meaning of an utterance and the speaker's intention. Given that, according to the communication principles, speakers are bound to communicate clearly and, therefore, successfully, there must, the legal theorists say, be limitations on relation. Consequently, the figurative use of an utterance is acceptable only if the relation is close *idhā qarubat ᶜalāqatuhu.* Any figurative use lacking this condition is characterised as *majāz al-taᶜqīd* (complex figurative use).[131] This kind of *majāz,* which needs too many relations to be interpreted, is *mumtaniᶜ* (inaccessible) in communication.[132] Plainly, this view is based on the assumption that language is established and systematically used in a co-operative manner in communication, and that this in turn means that the more an utterance conforms to this principle the more successful the communicative act will be and *vice versa*. This applies to all kinds of implicational significations.[133]

This condition of *qurb al-ᶜalāqah* (the closeness of relation), which is sometimes alternatively expressed as the immediate occurrence to mind of the intended object of communication *sabqu l-dhihni mina l-musammā ilayh,* is taken as a criterion to decide whether or not a particular act of non-literal use is accessible and, also, to evaluate which one of the two or more possible interpretations should be given priority over the other. Al-Rāzī, who reports the consensus of the legal theorists in giving priority to *ḥaqīqah* (literal use) over *majāz* (non-literal use), formulates the following workable criterion to justify this matter:

"Dependence on one factor is more appropriate than dependence on many".[134]

In his implementation of this criterion on *majāz*, al-Rāzī states that unlike *ḥaqīqah*, *majāz* requires the following:

i the existence of *ḥaqīqah*;
ii the existence of what is qualified to be *majāz*;
iii the relation whereby *majāz* would be justifiable; and
iv the impracticality of *ḥaqīqah*.[135]

Al-Rāzī also points out that diverting the expression from *ḥaqīqah* to *majāz* needs "*nawᶜ taʾammul wa-istidlāl* (some kind of mediation and reasoning)".[136] In modern pragmatics, this has been shown to be true.[137] However, the issue is not as simple as it seems to be, owing to the difficulty of providing a water-tight distinction between literal and non-literal use. In PF, criteria are provided for making the distinction clear between the two types of use, but, some of the legal theorists doubt these criteria.[138] What is more, some scholars, the *Salafīs* in particular, deny the plausibility of the distinction altogether, claiming that this distinction is a technical construct, and that it has no empirical basis (cf. 4.8). Nonetheless, there seem to be different degrees of literalness in linguistic utterances that are sufficient enough to justify the assumption that some utterances take more time and effort to process than others.

However, there are further criteria for identifying which one of the possible non-literal interpretations would have priority over the other(s). Ibn Ḥājib mentions the following:

i the prominence of the relation *(shuhrat al-ᶜalāqah)*;
ii the strength of the relation *(quwwat al-ᶜalāqah)*;
iii the closeness of the *majāz*'s sense to the literal meaning *(qurb jihatih)*;
iv the predominance of its contextual evidence (*rujḥān dalīlih*); and
v the prominence of its use (*shuhrat istiᶜmālih*).[139]

Al-Taftāzānī condenses all these criteria[140] in these words: "briefly, the more prominent *(ashhar)*, stronger *(aqwā)* or more apparent *(aẓhar)* the relation of one of the non-literal interpretations is to the literal meaning, the more appropriate that interpretation will be".[141]

Relation is classified into different types, each of which is held to be subsumptively established (*wuḍiᶜat waḍᶜan nawᶜiyyan)* and, therefore, mutually known by interlocutors. The particular actualisations of these types of relations are dependent on the speaker's choice. In other words, speakers can create as many new *majāz* as they wish provided that the relation between the literal meaning and the intention is in accordance with the subsumptive *waḍ*ᶜ in its general meaning. Thus, by virtue of these types of relation one might (given the relevant context and the absence of any impediment) for example,

i utter the cause *(al-sabab)* and intend the effect *(al-musabbab)*;
ii utter the effect and intend the cause;
iii utter something and intend its approximation *(mushābihih)*;
iv utter a part of something *(al-juz*ᵓ*)* and intend the whole *(al-kull)*;
v utter the whole and intend the part;
vi utter the general *(al-*ᶜ*āmm)* and intend the particular *(al-khāṣṣ)*;
vii utter the particular and intend the general;
viii utter the place *(al-maḥall)* and intend its content *(al-ḥāll)*;
ix utter the content and intend its place;
x utter what is implying *(al-lāzim)* and intend the implicatum *(al-malzūm)*;
xi utter the implicatum and intend the implying;
xii utter the unqualified *(al-muṭlaq)* and intend the qualified *(al-muqayyad)*;
xiii utter the qualified and intend the unqualified;
xiv utter something and intend its function; and
xv utter something and intend its opposite *(ḍiddah)*.[142]

The idea behind these types of relation is better explained in terms of the view that "meaning attracts another meaning but not the expression".[143] The essence of this view is that expressing meaning can be carried out by one of two ways: (a) by producing an expression to signify its conventional meaning or (b) by producing an expression to indicate the implicational signification of its conventional meaning. In order for speakers to understand each other, there must be a kind of relationship between expression and meaning on the one hand, and between meaning and intention on the other. The relation between the expression and its conventional meaning is held to be arbitrary (*i*ᶜ*tibāṭiyyah*)[144] whereas the relation between the conventional meaning and its implicational signification (*dalālatuh al-iltizāmiyyah*) – or what ᶜAbd al-Qāhir al-Jurjānī calls *ma*ᶜ*nā l-ma*ᶜ*nā* (the meaning of meaning)[145] is implicational.[146] Implication is meant to be so general that it covers the inference of meaning from meaning, which is presumed to be based on one of the types of relations stated above. It should be noted, however, that this implication is, as al-Rāzī puts it, not a *mūjib* (cause) but only a condition.[147] That is to say, it is, as al-Asnawī explains, not the implication in itself which is the cause that leads to the implicational signification, but that the cause is, in fact, the production of the utterance[148] with the consideration of the context.[149] In other words, these types of relations alone are not sufficient to enable speakers to infer one meaning from another, but there must exist contextual evidence to determine which one of the possible implicata is intended in any given actual situation. On the other hand, speakers are not free to use any expression (or more precisely any meaning) to generate an implicature, but there must exist a relevant relation between the conventional meaning and the intention of the speaker so that the speaker can render his intention manifest to the hearer by virtue of the fact that relations of this type are mutually known by both of them. Thus, it can be said that the above types of relations roughly function as a set of bridges between the meaning of an expression and the implications derivable from it, while the guiding contexts function as 'road signs' to guide the hearer to the appropriate bridge that should be followed in order to reach the intention of the speaker.

3.5.1.5. The Principle of Istiṣḥāb

This principle, which is usually presented in this form: "*al-aṣlu baqāʾu mā kāna ʿalā mā kān*"[150] (lit, 'the base' is the maintenance of the status quo[151]), is frequently combined with the notion of *al-aṣl* and *al-farʿ*, so it would be useful to examine these notions in relation to each other. *Al-aṣl* (the base) is usually understood in relation to what is considered to be its opposite, namely *al-farʿ* (the subsidiary). The notion of *al-aṣl* and *al-farʿ* is given great importance not only in PF, but also in different domains of the Arabic sciences. It is recognised by the grammarians, the rhetoricians and the jurists in their respective disciplines. It is clear from this that *aṣl* and *farʿ* are important notions in the Arabic intellectual tradition.

The idea behind the notion of *al-aṣl* and *al-farʿ* seems to be the fact that humans tend, in the absence of any instantaneous evidence, to form an initial intuition-based presumption about the situation they encounter. By virtue of the principle of *istiṣḥāb,* this presumption is maintained unless it conflicts with some contextual evidence. However, although the two notions (the base-subsidiary notion and the notion *istiṣḥāb)* appear to operate jointly, they should be kept distinct. However, it should be noted that assuming the continuity of something logically necessitates the assumption of its prior existence, and that is why the two notions are occasionally investigated together in PF and the other branches of the Arabic sciences in general.

There are fundamental general assumptions concerning the base and subsidiary which can be found in PF either explicitly or implicitly. The following are examples of these assumptions:

i 'The base' cannot be renounced for 'the subsidiary' without justification,[152] which may be a reason, condition, contextual evidence, motive or goal, depending on the viewpoint being considered.
ii 'The subsidiary' must have some connection with 'the base',[153] these connections, however, vary in terms of degree and type.
iii It is typically possible to attribute a certain subsidiary to its base by way of abstraction (or decontextualisation).
iv 'The subsidiary' can be explained by reference to its base.
v 'The subsidiary' is potentially exposed to some environmental variations which are not attached to 'the base'.
vi Bases and subsidiaries are relative concepts; that is, some bases may be regarded as subsidiaries in relation to other bases, and some subsidiaries may be regarded as bases in relation to other subsidiaries.
vii Some bases can be arranged in hierarchical order, and the lower bases, in this case, might be governed by the higher.
viii Bases may sometimes conflict with each other, which might be resolved by what is called *qawā^cid al-tarjīḥ* (rules of preference).

However, there are certain characteristics that can be attached to bases and others to subsidiaries. These characteristics are not necessarily applicable to each base or subsidiary, but at the same time no element can be regarded as a base or subsidiary without displaying some of the relevant characteristics given below, see figure 3.3.

The legal theorists formulate a set of bases, which they assume obtainable in any act of communication if there is no evidence to the contrary. It should, however, be noted that some bases are formulated in a variety of ways in the literature:

i *Al-aṣlu isti^cmālu l-ṣīghati fī musammāhā*"[154] (lit. 'the base' is to use the form in its meaning) (i.e., the original state is to use the form to signify its predetermined meaning).
"*Al-aṣlu ^cadamu l-naqli wa-l-taghyīr*"[155] (lit, 'the base' is the non-existence of transfer or change) (i.e., the original state is to exclude any transfer or change of established features).
"*Al-naqlu khilāfu l-aṣl*"[156] (lit, transference is in violation of 'the base').(i.e., transference deviates from the original state).

Figure 3.3

The base	The subsidiary
dominant	less dominant
intuitive	calculated
hypothetical	factual
abstract	concrete
potential	actual
independent	dependent
arbitrary	explainable
conventional	contextual
simple	complex

ii "*Al-aṣlu l-ḥaqīqah*"[157] (lit, 'the base' is literalness).
"*Al-majāzu khilāfu l-aṣl*"[158] (lit, non-literalness is in violation of 'the base') (i.e., the original state is to rule out the opposite of the prior state of literalness).

iii "*Al-iḍmāru khilāfu l-aṣl*"[159] (lit, ellipsis is in violation of 'the base').
"*Al-aṣlu ᶜadamu l-iḍmār*"[160] (lit, 'the base' is the non-existence of ellipsis) (i.e., the original state is to rule out the opposite of the prior state of complete manifestation).

iv "*Al-aṣlu ᶜadamu l-ishtirāk*"[161] (lit, 'the base' is the non-existence of indeterminacy) (i.e., the original state rules out indeterminacy).
"*Al-ishtirāku khilāfu l-aṣl*"[162] (li, indeterminacy is in violation of 'the base') (i.e., the original state is to rule out the opposite of the single expression of function).

v "*Al-aṣlu ᶜadamu l-ijmāl*"[163] (lit, 'the base' is the non-existence of obscurity) (i.e., the original state is the exclusion of obscurity).
"*Al-ijmālu khilāfu l-aṣl*"[164] (lit, obscurity is in violation of 'the base').

vi "*Al-mutarādifu ᶜalā khilāfi l-aṣl*"[165] (lit, synonymy is in violation of 'the base') (i.e., synonymy is a deviation from the original state, which is the one-for-one meaning relation).

vii "*Al-aṣlu ᶜadamu l-taqyīd*"[166] (lit, 'the base' is unqualification) (i.e., the original state is to exclude qualification).

viii "*Al-aṣlu ᶜadamu l-taqdīm wa-l-taʾkhīr*"[167] (lit, 'the base' is the non-existence of 'preposing and postposing') (i.e., the original state is to exclude 'preposing and postposing').

Thus, priority ought to be given to

> literal use over non-literal use *(al-ḥaqīqah dūna l-majāz)*, the general over the particular *(al-ᶜumūm dūna l-khuṣūṣ)*, determinacy over indeterminacy *(al-ifrād dūna l-ishtirāk)*, unqualification over qualification *(al-iṭlāq dūna l-taqyīd)*, originality over tautology *(al-taᵓṣīl dūna l-ziyādah)*, order over 'preposing and postposing' *(al-tartīb dūna l-taqdīm wa-l-taᵓkhīr)*, initiation over emphasis *(al-taᵓsīs dūna l-taᵓkīd)*, continuation over abrogation *(al-baqāᵓ dūna l-naskh)*, legal; over rational [interpretation] *(al-sharᶜī dūna l-naqlī)*, technical over linguistic [interpretation] *(al-ᶜurfī dūna l-lughawī)*; unless there is evidence to the contrary.[168]

Al-Qarāfī insists that a base does not always have priority in interpretation since the principle of immediacy demands that the hearer chooses the dominant interpretation whether it is a base or not. In other words, bases are given priority only by default. He says:

> Turning into the dominant [interpretation] is obligatory, even if it is in violation of 'the base'. Do not you see that non-literal use is in violation of 'the base', yet if it appears most likely by evidence, it will become inevitable. This applies also to particularity, ellipsis and the rest of the things that are in violation of 'the base'.[169]

Let us now turn to the principle of *istiṣḥāb* (lit, "seeking a companion or link").[170] As mentioned above, by virtue of this principle the initial presumption is to maintain the *aṣl* until evidence to the contrary is made manifest. The notion of *istiṣḥāb* or the presumption of continuity is based on the assumption that the status *quo* is presumed to obtain as long as there is no evidence to the contrary. This assumption is believed to play an essential role not only in the scientific thinking of the Arabs but also in everyday life. As ᶜAḍud al-Millah wa-l-Dīn puts it,

> were it not for this presumption, no sane person would justify corresponding wirh people who live far away from him [since sending a letter to somebody presumes that he/she is still alive and living in the same place], the engagement in works that take time [to yield] such as ploughing (*ḥirāthah*) and commerce, the dispatching of consignments and gifts from country to a remote country, loan or debt; and if it were not for this assumption, all that would be impudence.

NOTES

1 See al-Qarāfī, *Sharḥ Tanqīḥ*, p. 20; al-Subkīs, *al-Ibhāj*, 1/263; al-Muṭīʿī, *Sullam* . . ., 2/142.
2 Al-Āmidī (1986), 1/136; see al-Tahānāwī, 1/372.
3 Al-Sharīf al-Jurjānī, *al-Taʿrīfāt*, p. 124 *(al-muhmalāt)*.
4 See al-Rāzī, 1/65; al-Bayḍāwī, 1/193; al-Subkīs, *al-Ibhāj*, 1/193; ʿAḍud, 1/115–116; al-Sharīf al-Jurjānī, *Ḥāshiyah ʿalā Sharḥ al-ʿAḍud*, 1/115–116.
5 See al-Mawṣilī, 1/121.
6 See al-Bayḍāwī, 2/191–192; al-Asnawī, 2/192.
7 Al-Qarāfī, *Sharḥ Tanqīḥ*, p. 123.
8 This distinction is sometimes presented as a distinction between *dalālat al-lafẓ* (the signification of expression) and *irādat al-mutakallim* (the intention of the speaker). See al-Taftāzānī, *Ḥāshiyat al-Talwīḥ*, 1/322.
9 Al-Baṣrī, 1/4; al-Rāzī, 1/9; Ibn Qayyim, *Iʿlām al-Muwaqqiʿīn* . . . 1/241; al-Subkīs, *al-Ibhāj*, 1/28.
10 Ibn Qayyim, *Iʿlām al-Muwaqqiʿīn* . . ., 1/241; al-Subkīs, *al-Ibhāj*, 1/28.
11 Maclean, *Interpretation and Meaning* . . ., p. 142.
12 See al-Subkīs, *al-Ibhāj*, 1/28.
13 See Ibn Qayyim, *Iʿlām al-Muwaqqiʿīn* . . ., 1/377.
14 See *ibid.*, 1/241.
15 See Sperber and Wilson, *Relevance* . . ., p. 2.
16 See, e.g., Ibn Taymiyyah, *Fatāwā*, 20/496.
17 See Turkī, *Munāẓarāt* . . ., p. 479.
18 See *ibid.*, p. 486–487.
19 Al-Shāṭibī, *al-Muwāfaqāt* . . ., 3/8–10; see *ibid.*, p. 490.
20 On the notion of further intentions see Marmor, *Interpretation and Legal Theory*, p. 166.
21 See Ibn Ḥalūl, *Ḥāshiyah* . . ., p. 23.
22 See al-Qarāfī, *Sharḥ Tanqīḥ*, p. 26.
23 See *ibid*; al-Subkīs, *al-Ibhāj*, 1/207; al-Asnawī, 2/38.
24 See al-Qarāfī, *Sharḥ Tanqīḥ*, p. 26; al-Subkīs, *al-Ibhāj*, 1/206; al-Asnawī, 2/38.
25 Ibn Ḥalūl, *op. cit.*, p. 23.
26 See *ibid.*
27 See al-Qarāfī, *Sharḥ Tanqīḥ*, p. 136.
28 See al-Subkīs, *al-Ibhāj*, 1/206; al-Asnawī, 2/38.
29 Al-Subkīs, *al-Ibhāj*, 1/207; al-Asnawī, 2/38.
30 See al-Qarāfī, *Sharḥ Tanqīḥ*, pp. 24–26; al-Subkīs, *al-Ibhāj*, 1/206; al-Asnawī, 2/38.
31 Al-Qarāfī, *Sharḥ Tanqīḥ*, p. 26; al-Subkīs, *al-Ibhāj*, 1/206; al-Asnawī, 2/38.
32 Al-Āmidī (1986), 1/35; see Ibn al-Shāṭ, *Idrār al-Shurūq* . . ., 2/15, Ibn Taymiyyah, *Fatāwā*, 20/496; al-Subkīs, *al-Ibhāj*, 1/192.
33 See al-Shāṭibī, *op. cit.*, 3/347; al-Muṭīʿī, *op. cit.*, 2/54.
34 Al-Asnawī, 2/164; ʿAḍud, 1/142; al-Taftāzānī, *Ḥāshiyah ʿalā Sharḥ al-ʿAḍud*, 1/142; al-Sharīf al-Jurjānī, *Ḥāshiyah ʿalā Sharḥ al-ʿAḍud*, 1/142; al-Harawī, 1/142.

35 Al-Harawī, 1/142.
36 *Ibid.*, 1/142.
37 On this notion see Marmor, Interpretation and Legal Theory, pp. 29–30.
38 See Ibn Ḥazm, *al-Iḥkām . . .*, 3/371.
39 See *ibid.*
40 Al-Shāṭibī, *op. cit.*, 3/413–414.
41 Al-Sharīf al-Jurjānī, *Ḥāshiyah ᶜalā Sharḥ al-ᶜAḍud*, 1/67.
42 See al-Rāzī, 1/179.
43 Ali's Translation of THE HOLY QURᵓĀN, 46/15.
44 *Ibid.*, 2/233.
45 Al-Subkīs, *al-Ibhāj*, 1/385.
46 Al-Tahānawī, 2/969 (al-istiᶜārah).
47 Al-Zarkashī, *al-Burhān . . .*, 2/200.
48 See al-Ṭarūdī, *Kitāb Jāmiᶜ al-ᶜIbārāt . . .*, pp. 245–247.
49 Al-Bukhārī, *Ṣaḥīḥ al-Bukhārī*, bāb al-Hijrah: 5/79; see al-Rāzī, 1/99.
50 Al-Suyūṭī, *al-Rawḍ . . .*, 3/34.
51 See Ali, *Waṣf . . .*, pp. 141–142.
52 See Ṣadr al-Sharīᶜah, 1/343; al-Tahānawī, 2/1228 *(al-qarīnah)*.
53 Ibn Taymiyyah, *Fatāwā*, 20/496. Ibn Sīnā seems to hold the same view. See al-Marjānī, *Ḥāshiyah . . .*, 1/317.
54 See al-Tahānawī, 2/957 *(al-ᶜādah)*.
55 See al-Rāzī, 1/140.
56 *Ibid.*
57 Al-Mawṣilī, 1/121.
58 See; al-Rāzī, 1/381; ᶜAḍud, 2/131.
59 See al-Shāṭibī, *op. cit.*, 3/351.
60 *THE HOLY QURᵓĀN*, 2/196.
61 The *Ḥajj* is visiting "the Sacred Mosque, the Kaᶜba. The Season of regular Hajj culminates in the visit to ᵓArafāt on the ninth day of the month of Zul-ḥajj, followed by the circumambulation of the Kaᶜba. A visit to the Sacred Mosque and the performance of the rites of pilgrimage at any other time is called an ᵓUmra" (Aliᵓs Translation of THE HOLY QURᵓĀN, p. 62. Note 62).
62 See al-Shāṭibī, *op. cit.*, 3/351.
63 See al-Taftāzānī, *Ḥāshiyat al-Talwīḥ*, 1/335; al-Tahānawī, 2/957–958 *(al-ᶜāda)*.
64 See al-Qarāfī, *al-Iḥkām . . .*, pp. 238–240. note no (1).
65 Al-Qarāfī, *Sharḥ Tanqīḥ*, p. 15.
66 Al-Ruhāwī, p. 18; al-Anṣārī, 1/8; al-Sharīf al-Jurjānī, *al-Taᶜrīfāt*, p. 16; al-Tahānawī, p. 85 *(al-aṣl)*.
67 Al-Ruhāwī, pp. 18–19; al-Qarāfī, *Sharḥ Tanqīḥ*, p. 15; al-Anṣārī, 1/8; al-Asnawī, 2/170.
68 Grice (1975), p. 46.
69 A similar point can be found in Leech, *Principles of Pragmatics*, p. 8.
70 Al-Jurjānī, ᶜAbd al-Qāhir, *Asrār al-Balāghah*, ed. H., Ritter, pp. 345–347.
71 Ibn Taymiyyah, *Fatāwā*, 20/459.
72 See al-Rāzī, 1/151–152; al-Qarāfī, *Sharḥ Tanqīḥ*, p. 112.
73 Al-Ghazālī, *al-Mustaṣfā*, 1/339.

74 See al-Tahānawī, 1/901–902 *(al-iṭnāb).*
75 It is also called *qarīnat al-ilghāʾ* (the context of cancellation). See al-Anṣārī, 1/203.
76 See *ibid.,* 1/221.
77 It is also called *qarīnat al-iʿmāl* (the context of operating). See *ibid.,* 1/203.
78 See al-Fanārī, *Ḥāshiyah . . .,* 1/200.
79 Muḥammad al-Jurjānī, *al-Ishārāt . . .,* p. 206.
80 Al-Fanarā, *op. cit.,* 2/64.
81 Al-Muṭīʿī, *Sullam . . .,* 2/147.
82 Ṣadr al-Sharīʿah, 1/1343.
83 See Ṣadr al-Sharīʿah, 1/343–344; al-Asnawī, 2/176; al-Bayḍāwī, 2/176; Mullākhusrū, 1/154.
84 Al-Sharīf al-Jurjānī, *Ḥāshiyah ʿalā Sharḥ al-ʿAḍud,* 1/115; see al-Rāzī, 1/64; ʿAḍud, 115; al-Asnawī, 2/13–14; al-Bayḍāwī, 2/11.
85 See Ibn Ḥazm, *op. cit.,* 3/371; see al-Āmidī (1983), 2/322.
86 Al-Mawṣilī, 1/50; al-Rāzī, 1/82.
87 Al-Sharīf al-Jurjānī, *al-Taʿrīfāt,* p. 26.
88 Al-Baṣrī, 1/316; see al-Rāzī, 1/488–489. However, in modern pragmatics, similar remarks are made by D Sperber and D Wilson: "It is generally true that ostensive communicators try to be optimally relevant. When addressees are disappointed in their expectations of relevance, they rarely consider as a possible explanation that the communicator is not really trying to be optimally relevant. It would be tantamount to assuming that the apparent communicator is not really addressing them, and perhaps not communicating at all" (Sperber and Wilson, *Relevance . . .,* p. 159).
89 Al-Baṣrī, 1/223.
90 Al-Sharīf al-Jurjānī, *al-Taʿrīfāt,* p. 33 *(al-taʿqīd);* see al-Tahānawī, 2/955 *(al-taʿqīd).*
91 See al-Mawṣilī, 1/120.
92 *Ibid.,* 1/320.
93 Al-Baṣrī, 1/320.
94 Al-Rāzī, 1/140.
95 See al-Qarāfī, *al-Istighnāʾ fī l-Istithnāʾ,* p. 458; see also al-Qarāfī, *Sharḥ Tanqīḥ,* p. 248.
96 Al-Qarāfī, *Anwār . . .,* 1/24.
97 *Ibid.*
98 *Ibid.*
99 *Ibid.*
100 Al-Suyūṭī, *al-Muzhir . . .,* 1/45; see Ali, *Waṣf . . .,* p. 278.
101 ʿAbd al-Qāhir al-Jurjānī, *Asrār al-Balāghah,* pp. 345–347; see Ali, *Waṣf . . .,* p. 278.
102 They are, nevertheless, in dispute about whether *al-ʿaql al-mujarrad* (the mere reason) would be able to judge that truthfulness is worthy of religious reward and falsehood is worthy of religious blame and punishment. Contrary to the *Salafīs* and *Muʿtazilīs*, *al-Ashʿarīs* hold the view that only *al-sharʿ* (the Revelation) is entitled to do that. See al-Rāzī, 1/29–40.

103 *Ibid.*, 1/38.
104 *Ibid.*
105 Al-Suyūṭī, *al-Ashbāh wa-l-Naẓāʾir* . . ., p. 142.
106 *Ibid., p.* 143.
107 Al-Qarāfī, *Sharḥ Tanqīḥ*, p. 248; al-Āmidī (1983), 2/279.
108 Al-Taftāzānī, *Ḥāshiyat al-Talwīḥ*, 1/322.
109 See al-Suyūṭī, *al-Ashbāh wa-l-Naẓāʾir* . . ., p. 143.
110 Al-Rāzī, 1/271; al-Āmidī (1983), 2/274; al-Sharīf al-Jurjānī, *al-Taᶜrīfāt*, p. 28 *(al-taʾsīs)*; see al-Tahānawī, 1/28 (al-taʾsīs); al-Ruhāwī, p. 351.
111 Al-Qarāfī, *Sharḥ Tanqīḥ*, p. 132.
112 Al-Asnawī, 2/466; al-Āmidī (1983), 2/48; al-Muṭīᶜī, *op. cit.*, 2/475.
113 See al-Taftāzānī, *Ḥāshiyah ᶜalā Sharḥ al-ᶜAḍud*, 1/148, 2/76; *idem*, *Ḥāshiyat al-Talwīḥ ᶜalā l-Tawḍīḥ*, 1/322.
114 On a similar view, see Blakemore, *Understanding Utterances* . . ., p. 30.
115 Al-Qarāfī, *Sharḥ Tanqīḥ*, p. 247.
116 *Ibid.*, p. 120.
117 See al-Qarāfī, *al-Iḥkām* . . ., p. 62.
118 Mullākhusrū, 1/330.
119 Al-Anṣārī, 1/265.
120 Al-Mawṣilī, 1/121.
121 See al-Qarāfī, *Sharḥ Tanqīḥ*, p. 120.
122 Dascal, "On the Pragmatic Structure of Conversation", p. 41.
123 *Ibid.*
124 *Ibid.*
125 See al-Anṣārī, 1/221.
126 Ibn al-Malik, p. 428.
127 *Ibid., p.* 427.
128 See al-Samarqandī, pp. 323–324; al-Qarāfī, *Sharḥ Tanqīḥ*, p. 146.
129 See al-Rāzī, 1/140.
130 Muḥammad al-Jurjānī, *al-Ishārāt* . . ., p. 206.
131 See al-Qarāfī, *Sharḥ Tanqīḥ*, p. 114.
132 *Ibid.*
133 Al-Subkīs, *al-Ibhāj*, 1/375.
134 Al-Rāzī, 1/154, see al-Asnawī, 2/160.
135 Al-Rāzī, 1/154.
136 *Ibid.*, 1/158.
137 Akmajian and others formulate the presumption of literalness as follows, "Literal utterances seem to have communicative priority in that we presume a person to be speaking literally unless there is some reason to suppose the contrary" (pp. 404–405). There also seems to be some psychological evidence to prove this presumption (p. 455). See Akmajian, Demers and Harnish, Linguistics . . . .
138 See, e.g., al-Baṣrī, 1/25–27; al-Rāzī, 1/148–151; Ibn al-Ḥājib, 1/145; ᶜAḍud, 1/145–153; al-Taftāzānī, *Ḥāshiyah ᶜalā Sharḥ al-ᶜAḍud*, 1/146–153; al-Sharīf al-Jurjānī, *Ḥāshiyah ᶜalā Sharḥ al-ᶜAḍud*, 1/146–153; al-Harawī, 1/146–152; al-Samarqandī, 1/197–198 and see the editor's note (38).
139 Ibn al-Ḥājib, 2/312; ᶜAḍud, 2/313; al-Taftāzānī, *Ḥāshiyah ᶜalā Sharḥ al-ᶜAḍud*, 2/313.

140 Wilson and Sperber offer two similar criteria to account for relevance:
(1) "other things being equal, the greater the contextual effects, the greater the relevance" (Sperber and Wilson, *Relevance . . .*, p. 119).
(2) "other things being equal, the greater the processing efforts, the lower the relevance" (Sperber and Wilson, *Relevance . . .*, p. 124).
See Sperber and Wilson, *Relevance . . .*, pp. 119–125; see also Barton, *Nonsentential Constituents . . .*, pp. 200–201.

141 Al-Taftāzānī, *Ḥāshiyah ᶜalā Sharḥ al-ᶜAḍud*, 2/313.

142 Al-Rāzī, 1/134–137; Ibn al-Ḥājib, 1/141; ᶜAḍud, 1/142–143; al-Taftāzānī, *Ḥāshiyah ᶜalā Sharḥ al-ᶜAḍud*, 1/142–145, al-Sharīf al-Jurjānī, *Ḥāshiyah ᶜalā Sharḥ al-ᶜAḍud*, 1/142–145; al-Harawī, 1/142–145; al-Samarqandī, pp. 532–533; al-Bayḍāwī, 2/164; al-Asnawī, 2/164–169; Muḥammad al-Jurjānī, *al-Ishārāt . . .*, pp. 206–237.

143 Muḥibb Allāh, 1/186; al-Anṣārī, 1/186.

144 Since introduced by De Saussure the notion of the arbitrariness of the linguistic signs has become not only an unquestionable postulate, but also "one of the cornerstones of modern linguistics". (See Leech, *Principles of Pragmatics*, p. 25. In PF, although some *Muᶜtazilīs*, notably ᶜAbbād al-Saymarī, claim that the relationship between expression and meaning is *munāsabah dhātiyyah* (intrinsic relation), most scholars argue against this view. Some of their counter-arguments are as follows:
(i) If the signification of expression was intrinsic, it would not vary across regions and nations. Besides, everybody would be able to have access to any language (Al-Rāzī, 1/58; see Ali, *Waṣf . . .*, pp. 31–32.
(ii) This view is contradicted by the phenomenon of *al-aḍdād*, where one linguistic form has two opposite meanings, e.g., *jawn* for black and white, and *qurʾ* for menstruation and non-menstruation (See Ibn al-Ḥājib, 1/192; ᶜAḍud, 1/192–193; al-Taftāzānī, *Ḥāshiyah ᶜalā Sharḥ al-ᶜAḍud*, 1/192–193; al-Sharīf al-Jurjānī, *Ḥāshiyah ᶜalā Sharḥ al-ᶜAḍud*, 1/192–193).

145 According to ᶜAbd al-Qāhir al-Jurjānī, if you say *balaghanī annaka tuqaddimu rijlan wa-tuʾakhkhiru ukhrā* (lit, I hear that you put one foot forward and the other backward), "you cannot convey your intention by the expression alone, but rather the expression will signify its ostensive meaning and then the hearer infers from this meaning another meaning [which he calls the meaning of meaning] which is your intention". ᶜAbd al-Qāhir al-Jurjānī, *Dalāʾil al-Iᶜjāz*, p. 184; see Ali, *Waṣf . . .*, pp. 179–180.

146 See Muḥammad al-Jurjānī, *al-Ishārāt . . .*, pp. 206.

147 Al-Rāzī, 1/76.

148 Al-Asnawī, 2/35.

149 See Mullākhusrū, 1/303; al-Muṭīᶜī, *Sullam al-Wuṣūl li-Sharḥ Nihāyat al-Sūl*, 2/35 note no (1).

150 Al-Asnawī, 2/160; al-Rāzī, 1/231; see al-Āmidī (1983), 2/342; al-Tahānawī, 1/809 *(al-istiṣḥāb)*.

151 See Netton, *A Popular Dictionary of Islam*, p. 130 *(al-istiṣḥāb)*. On a similar notion in modern pragmatics, see Brown and Yule, Discourse Analysis, p. 65.

152 See Ṣadr al-Sharīᶜah, 1/343.
153 See *ibid.*, 1/343.
154 Al-Qarāfī, *Sharḥ Tanqīḥ*, p. 139.
155 *Ibid.*, pp. 137, 235, 247; al-Qarāfī, *al-Istighnāʾ fī l-Istithnāʾ*, p. 457; al-Asnawī, 2/218.
156 Al-Rāzī, 1/129; al-Bayḍāwī, 2/159; al-Asnawī, 2/160.
157 Al-Rāzī, 1/146, 381; al-Āmidī (1983), 2/291, 322; al-Qarāfī, *Sharḥ Tanqīḥ*, PP. 123, 130, 193, 235; al-Bayḍāwī, 2/226; al-Asnawī, 2/186, 239; al-Taftāzānī, *Ḥāshiyat al-Talwīḥ*, 1/314; al-Suyūṭī, *al-Ashbāh wa-l-Naẓāʾir*. . ., p. 69.
158 Al-Rāzī, 1/144; al-Qarāfī, *Sharḥ Tanqīḥ*, p. 130; al-Bayḍāwī, 2/170; al-Asnawī, 2/172, 269; al-Suyūṭī, Jalāl al-Dīn, *al-Muzhir fī ᶜulūm al-lughah wa-anwāᶜihā*, 1/361.
159 Al-Āmidī (1983), 2/364, 366, 377; al-Asnawī, 2/254.
160 Al-Qarāfī, *Sharḥ Tanqīḥ*, p. 112.
161 Al-Āmidī (1983), 1/105, 2/191; al-Qarāfī, *Sharḥ Tanqīḥ*, pp. 130–131, 192.
162 Al-Āmidī (1983), 2/190, 192, 342; al-Anṣārī, 1/311.
163 Aḍud, 2/258.
164 Al-Āmidī (1983), 2/343, 378.
165 Al-Rāzī, 1/130.
166 Al-Qarāfī, *Sharḥ Tanqīḥ*, p. 113.
167 Al-Rāzī, 1/176.
168 Al-Qarāfī, *Sharḥ Tanqīḥ*, p. 112.
169 Al-Qarāfī, *al-Iḥkām* . . ., p. 62.
170 Netton, *A Popular Dictionary of Islam*, p. 130 *(al-istiṣḥāb)*.

Chapter Four

Ibn Taymiyyah's contextual theory of interpretation

4.1. INTRODUCTION

Taqī l-Dīn Aḥmad Ibn Taymiyyah, jurist, theologian and religious reformer (661/1262–728/1328), is one of the most influential and controversial figures in Islamic history. He was imprisoned several times for his political opinions and polemic arguments against the dominant religious and political powers in his time. His emphasis on the literal interpretation of the *Qurānic* verses concerning the attributes of *Allāh* angered many scholars and "aroused public opinion against him". Moreover, his anti-*taqlīd* (the uncritical adherence to a particular *madhhab)* attitude and some other common jurisprudential issues brought him into conflict with other orthodox and non-orthodox jurists. Although Ibn Taymiyyah is considered to be a *Ḥanbalī* scholar for his acceptance of the essential principles on which the *Ḥanbalī madhhab* is founded, he rejects a considerable number of Ibn Ḥanbal's opinions. He was well-known for his intolerant criticism of non-*Salafī* sects including the Muʿtazilīs and Ashʿarīs.[1] Similarly, he was very critical of Muslim philosophers, like al-Fārābī and Ibn Sīnā, for what he calls 'their blind adherence to Greek philosophy'.[2]

> He was particularly critical of the concept of universals, since for him universals are nothing more than the human mind's intellectualization of the external realities which may or may not conform to those realities. For him realities are always specific and particular.[3]

Logicians distinguish between two types of knowledge: *taṣawwur* (forming concepts) and *taṣdīq* (making judgements) and hold that there are two methods to achieve them: *ḥadd* (definition) by which *taṣawwur* is tested and *qiyās* (syllogism) through which *taṣdīq* is reached. In his *al-Radd ʿalā l-Manṭiqiyyīn* and other treatises Ibn

Taymiyyah endeavoured to refute these two methods on which Aristotelian logic is based.[4] Demonstrating a deep understanding of Greek philosophy and logic, he developed persuasive arguments against the basic principles of these two branches of knowledge. His pragmatic approach allowed him to identify several weak points in the structure of the formal construction of Greek logic. Following the same approach he managed to formulate a number of compelling views on language and communication, many of which are very much in line with the latest trend in modern pragmatics.

In the course of his extended discussion of the two controversial topics of *majāz* (figurative use) and *taʾwīl* (diverting to non-apparent meaning), Ibn Taymiyyah advances scattered, but powerful, arguments in favour of a contextual approach to interpretation. These arguments can be interpreted as a polemic criticism against what can be called atomism (i.e., the view that certain meanings are ultimately simple and unqualified)[5] and foundationalism (i.e., the doctrine that meanings are predetermined and a priori 'established') as developed by the adherents of the notion of *waḍᶜ*, in favour of a well-developed version of compositionalism and contextualism. My task in this chapter will be to integrate these scattered arguments into a coherent form so that they appear as a highly evolved theory of interpretation. Moreover, my formulation will involve relating it to Ibn Taymiyyah's relevant ontological and epistemological concepts but with less emphasis on his theological outlook. Besides, the inquiry will include an outline of what can be assumed to be the two other related pragmatic theories which they form, together with the theory at issue, a consistent pragmatic paradigm. The other two are his theory of definition and his theory of cognitive relativism. What these theories have in common is that all of them lay great emphasis on context and make the participants (i.e., the actual agents) the principal element in forming the subject, whether it is a definition, interpretation or cognition. Thus, it will be demonstrated that context-dependency is a firmly established notion in Ibn Taymiyyah's thinking and that his contextual theory of interpretation constitutes only one of at least three theories in which the notion of context-dependency is manifested.

In spite of its originality, Ibn Taymiyyah's pragmatic position does not seem to have been considered before in a serious study if at all. In fact, his call for a contextual approach to interpretation is almost always understood by his opponents either as a dogmatic denial of the existence of *majāz* in the language or as a naive call directed at the adherents of *ta'wīl* (cf. 4.9.1) for the abandonment of the attention they give to non-apparent meanings of the *Qur'ānic* and *Sunnī* texts. Unfortunately, even his followers – with the exception of his eminent disciple Ibn al-Qayyim who shows in his elaboration of Ibn Taymiyyah's ideas a deep understanding of his remarkable insights – do not seem, as far as I am aware, to give to his ideas the consideration they merit. Hence, this chapter is tantamount to an attempt to reveal some of Ibn Taymiyyah's pragmatic thought and re-evaluate a significant aspect of his unknown insights.

4.2. CALL FOR A CONTEXTUAL APPROACH

Ibn Taymiyyah's main thesis is that "there is no entity that is free from any qualification in the external world" *(lā yūjadu fī l-khāriji shay'un mawjūdun khārijun ʿan kulli qayd)*.[6] Consequently, there is no such a thing as unqualified expression or unqualified meaning; other than the mental representations of real expressions and meanings, which are in effect nothing but abstract constructs having no reality in the external world. The essence of his argument is that the formal approaches attempted by Greek and Muslim philosophers[7] to discover the truth failed owing to their appeal to abstract structures instead of dealing with reality, and that a plausible inquiry can be achieved only by an empirical approach which takes the overall situation of a particular phenomenon into account. The philosophers' misconception is, says Ibn Taymiyyah, due to a confusion between the world *per se* and their assumptions about the world. They incorrectly think that what they construct in their minds represents the external reality, although their mental representations are decontextualised and divested of the individual variations of the external entities which are generated by their individuation and which, he believes, is the sign of their real existence in the physical world.

It may be helpful to point out that this approach is patently consistent with his theological doctrines. Chief among them is the belief that *Allāh* has real external existence with actual unique attributes on the grounds that nothing can be said to have real external existence unless it is entitled to be assigned particular attributes. He strongly rejects Ibn Sīnā's and al-Rāzī's notion of *al-muṭlaq al-maḥḍ* (the pure absolute), "which cannot be characterised by oneness or plurality, or existence or non-existence, or otherwise" *(alladhī lā yattaṣifu bi-waḥdatin wa-lā kathratin, wa-lā wujūdin wa-lā ʿadmin, wa-lā ghayri dhālik)*.[8] The pure absolute, like any universal, is a mental construct which has no real existence in the external world.

4.3. PHILOSOPHICAL BACKGROUND

The basic idea Ibn Taymiyyah is attempting to convey in the course of his discussion of *majāz* is that meaning is context-dependent. This view of meaning can readily be related to his philosophical framework, particularly his ontological and epistemological ideas, as well as to his theory of cognitive relativism and his theory of definition. The next three sections are devoted to these issues, together with a sketch as to how his ontological and epistemological ideas can be related to his contextual theory. Before proceeding further, it is essential to point out that the preoccupation with the universals versus particulars dichotomy is one of the main concerns of any epistemological and, especially, ontological discussion, and that the ontological positions of a philosopher are usually explained in terms of his view over the existence and nature of universals and particulars and the relationship between them.

As pointed out earlier (cf. 2.2.1), there is some connection between the distinction between *waḍ*^{c} and use and the distinction between universals and particulars[9] in a way which permits us to say that sentences, which are based on *waḍ*^{c}, are *universals*, while utterances, which are motivated by use, are *particulars*. Thus, whatever Ibn Taymiyyah assigns to universals can be assigned to sentences; and whatever he assigns to particulars can be assigned to utterances. Hence, the distinction drawn in modern linguistics between sentences and utterances is very useful here to identify what is universal and what is particular in relation to language structure and, consequently to show how Ibn Taymiyyah's ontological and epistemological conceptions can be related to his contextual theory.

Although Ibn Taymiyyah does not distinguish explicitly between sentences and utterances, neither does he constantly use technical terms to refer to this dichotomy, this distinction is, nevertheless, central to the explanation of his contextual theory. However, Ibn Taymiyyah seems to be very aware of the difference between the actually-produced signals (utterances) and the abstract structures which underlie them (sentences), but he insists on the invalidity of any operation involving a kind of abstraction which leads ultimately to the disregard of the very distinctive peculiarities of the individuals (e.g., the relevant contextual features of the actual utterances in the case of abstracting sentences from utterances). This amounts to the neutralisation of the distinction between sentences and utterances and of the other two pertinent distinctions, namely the traditional distinction between *waḍ^c* and use (cf. 2.1) on the one hand, and between *waḍ^c*-based meaning and intention (cf. 2.3.1) on the other.

One way of relating these two distinctions to that between sentences and utterances is to say that sentence-meanings (and sentence-structures) are based on *waḍ^c* whereas utterance-intentions (and the production of utterances) are motivated by use.

4.3.1. Ibn Taymiyyah's ontological position

Within Ibn Taymiyyah's ontological framework, the following philosophical attitudes seem to be relevant to his contextual theory:

(i) Contrary to the realists, Ibn Taymiyyah holds that *al-kullī l-ṭabī^{c}ī* (the natural universal), that is, *al-muṭlaq lā bi-sharṭ* (the unconditionally absolute universal)[10] exists only in the mind and has no actual existence in the physical world.[11] Nonetheless, one may say that "a universal does have a reality in the external world, but only as a particular and individual; thus, there can be nothing in the external world other than a particular human with a particular animality and a particular 'ability to speak' (*nāṭiqiyyah mu^{c}ayyanah*)".[12]

Applying this view to the sentences-utterances dichotomy leads to the conclusion that sentences as abstract entities have no objective reality in the extra-mental world independent of the corresponding utterances. This is based on Ibn Taymiyyah's conception that universals are the result of an abstraction from the particulars, which means that they can be conceptualised only by the conceptualisation of the relevant particulars; or as he puts it, "if one cannot conceptualise the particular existing thing, how can he be able to conceptualise its kind and type" (*jinsah wa-naw^{c}ah*)?.[13] Thus, utterances are the true manifestations of a language, while sentences are mental constructions.

This position contrasts with the Platonic realist's doctrine according to which universals exist prior to particulars. According to Katz, who has swung from Chomsky's conceptualism[14] to realism,; sentences exist prior to utterances and "grammars are theories of abstract objects (sentences)".[15] Katz as a Platonist philosopher and linguist "conceives of sentences in much the same way that Platonist philosophers of mathematics (and many working mathematicians) conceive of numbers and mathematical spaces"[16] assuming that mathematical and logical facts exist "prior to our mathematical and logical Adams and Eves".[17]

Ibn Taymiyyah strongly rejects both the Pythagorean view that numbers and measures (*al-aᶜdād wa-l-maqādīr*) exist in the external world independently of the corresponding entities counted or measured (*al-maᶜdūdāt wa-l-muqaddarāt*), and its platonic version that the universal essences (*al-ḥaqāʾiq al-nawᶜiyyah*), which are thought to be immutable realities, exist in the physical world externally to their relevant individuals.[18]

(ii) Properties of individuals are not independent of them and their existence is not prior to the existence of the individuals in the external world.[19] Ibn Taymiyyah emphasises that the cognition of an object and its properties depends on *al-ḥiss al-ẓāhir* ('exterior sense' or perception) or *al-ḥiss al-bāṭin* (lit, inner sense, or 'introspection') whereas the cognition of a relation (e.g., generality, particularity, sameness, resemblance, contrast) between a property of a given object and a property of another is constructed by the mind.[20] For instance, there is no objective similarity in the physical world between the external entities that are said to be similar; but it is the mind that constructs and identifies this kind of relation. It is for this reason that the construction of a relationship may vary from one person to another, and that it is, consequently, plausible to criticise 'the analogists' (*al-qiyāsiyyūn*) when they concentrate on the point of resemblance and disregard the distinctive feature.[21] Thus, Ibn Taymiyyah denies that these types of relation have reality in the physical world assuming that they are nothing but mental constructions. For him, the cognition of particulars takes place by means of either exterior or interior sense, whereas the cognition of universals is an immanent act of the mind.[22]

While Ibn Taymiyyah assigns the knowledge of mathematics, logic and meanings to innate faculties (or mental abilities), he insists that knowledge of expressions can be acquired only on the basis of knowledge of *waḍᶜ*.

Ibn Taymiyyah sharply criticises the assumption that there is knowledge of the presumed, abstracted and priori existing structure of language, which is represented by the PF mainstream in the intuition-based notion knowledge of the first *waḍᶜ* (*maᶜrifat al-waḍᶜ al-awwal*).

(iii) Ibn Taymiyyah strongly rejects al-Fārābī's and Ibn Sīnā's distinction between *al-māhiyyah* (essence) and *al-wujūd* (existence)[23] in that both have objective realities.[24] In addition, he objects to the distinction between what they call *dhātī* (contingent) and *lāzim li-l-*

māhiyyah fī l-wūjūd wa-l-khārij (essential for the essence both mentally and extra-mentally) arguing that there is no real difference in the external world between them. What appears to be differences is essentially conceptual (*iᶜtibāriyyah*) and motivated by *waḍᶜ*, the selection of the establisher and his own conceptualisation.[25]

This misconception, according to Ibn Taymiyyah, is again due to a confusion between mental worlds (or mental existence) and real worlds (or objective existence). To put it his way:

> The reason behind their delusion [the philosophers'] is that they see that an object can be known and intended *(yuᶜlam wa-yurād)* before its existence and that it is possible to distinguish between what is possible and what is impossible. Consequently, they say if this object were not existent, it would not be the case. They are also confused by the fact that we are able to speak about the substances of objects (i.e., their essences) irrespective of their existence in the external world, which leads them to think that these substances and essences are existent in the external world. But the truth is that all these are mental facts; and that mental constructions are larger in number than the real entities in the physical world "*al-muqaddar fī l-adhhān awsaᶜ mina l-mawjūd fī l-aᶜyān*" [. . .]. Thus, the proper difference is that essence is the mental representation of an object, whereas existence is its actuality in the extra-mental world.[26]

In his attempt to show that the distinction between *dhātī* and *lāzim* is based on a construction rather than an actual knowledge, Ibn Taymiyyah maintains that "the external facts which are independent from us are not dependent upon our conceptualisations; thus, it is not the case that if we assume that such-and-such is prior and such-and-such is posterior, they would be so in the external world".[27]

Although the above ontological attitudes in general appear to be related to his view that actual utterances have a chronologically prior existence to the unobservable and abstracted structure of utterances (i.e., sentences), it is not clear whether the above three ontological attitudes are based on this view or *vice versa*. Nonetheless, the following reasons make the former possibility more likely:

a) The alternative possibility (i.e., that his *general* ontological philosophy is the rationale behind his *particular* conception that utterances are prior to sentences) might be seen as self-contradictory, since, as this doctrine implies, a *universal* is a product of generalisation from the corresponding *particulars*, but not *vice versa*.

b) The motive behind his inquiry into the distinction between *ḥaqīqah* and *majāz*, on which his contextual theory is presumably founded, is, as pointed out by Ibn al-Qayyim,[28] to find rational arguments to refute the strongly-held doctrines of *ahl al-taʾwīl* (the advocates of the non-apparent interpretation of the *Qur'ānic* verses) especially those pertaining to the attributes of *Allāh*. Thus, it is the textual, rather than the philosophical, inquiry that appears to have been his starting point.

c) The hallowed status of the actual utterances of the *Qur'ān* for him as a Muslim generally and as a *Salafī Ḥanbalī* in particular[29] may have contributed not only to his giving precedence to utterances over sentences but also to assuming that utterances are prior to them and concluding, consequently, that particulars are prestigiously superior, and chronologically prior, to universals.

At this stage, three points have to be made:

Firstly, despite of what has just been said about the probability of the priority of his linguistic (or pragmatic) inquiry over his philosophical investigation, the opposite possibility should not be ruled out.

Secondly, no matter how insignificant the above investigation about whether Ibn Taymiyyah's linguistic or philosophical inquiry is prior, the fact that this investigation shed light on the probable justification of his pragmatic approach into language is almost undeniable.

Finally, (b) and (c) above should not be construed as to undermine Ibn Taymiyyah's ontological arguments on the grounds that they are motivated by doctrinal beliefs rather than philosophical convictions. They are, in actual fact, approached in a highly critical and scholarly way.

4.3.2. Ibn Taymiyyah's theory of cognitive relativism

According to Ibn Taymiyyah's theory of cognitive relativism, the acquisition of knowledge has no objective standard since determining whether a given proposition is discursive or self-evident depends on the individual's mental ability rather than the nature of the proposition itself. To put it his way, the difference between a discursive and self-evident proposition "is relative and comparative (*innamā huwa bi-l-nisbati wa-l-iḍāfah)*, what is discursive for a given person can, thus, be self-evident for another".[30] His argument is based on the fact that mental abilities are different from one individual to another. Consequently, contrary to the traditional logic, the middle term (*al-ḥadd al-awsaṭ*) is, according to Ibn Taymiyyah, dispensable for people who are exceptionally quick at conceptualising propositions. Hence, the propositions that are *ḥissiyyah* (perceptible), *mujarrabah* (empirical), *burhāniyyah* (evidential) or *mutawātirah* (i.e., one that has a large "number of reliable transmitters"[31]) for many people cannot be attainable for others except by meditation and demonstration.[32]

4.3.3. Ibn Taymiyyah's contextual theory of definition

According to Ibn Taymiyyah, the process of conceptualisation is quite different from the process of signification and reference in that the former is a natural process, whereas the latter two processes are *waḍ*ᶜ-based and contextual ones. "The name [i.e., the expression] *per se* cannot induce the conceptualisation of *al-musammā* (nominatum) for a person who is not able to conceptualise it, but can only produce its signification and its reference (*al-dalālah* ᶜ*alayh wa-l-ishārah ilayh*)".[33] This seems to be based on the view that signification is a relationship between an expression and meaning, and reference is a relationship between an expression and extra-mental referent. On the other hand, conceptualisation is a relationship between a meaning and referent (cf. figure 4.1).

However, the common sense between names and logical definitions is that they are both not qualified to make the hearer conceptualise the entities that he has never conceptualised before. This idea seems to be based upon his philosophical view that names and logical definitions[34] do not add any new proposition to the set of assumptions the hearer already possesses, since both the nominatum and definiendum (the concept defined); are not only conceptualisable without them but their conceptualisation is a necessary pre-condition for names and definitions to signify their meanings.[35] Hence, languages are not designed to signify the meanings of single expressions (*al-lafẓ al-mufrad*), because signifying the meaning of a single expression depends on the knowledge that the expression is assigned, by virtue of *waḍ*ᶜ, to it; and the only way to know that the expression is assigned to a particular meaning is to conceptualise both the expression and meaning. Thus, if the aim of *waḍ*ᶜ was to produce the meanings of single expressions, the argument would be circular.[36] For this reason,

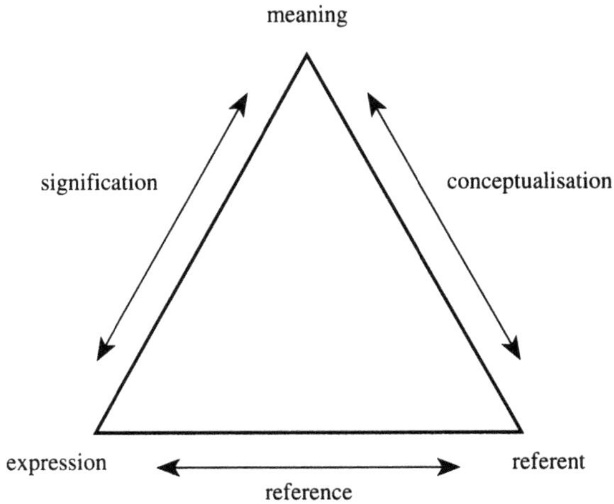

Figure 4.1

"all people [i.e., scholars] agree that a meaningful utterance (*al-kalām al-mufīd*) can be nothing but a full sentence".[37]

What Ibn Taymiyyah seems to be trying to say is that since the relationship between expression and meaning is conventional, saying a single word to somebody who is not aware of the convention would not convey any sense. If he is, however, aware of the convention, the word would only refer to the subject, but since references cannot properly be made in isolation from a defining context, it follows that saying single words would be nothing more than gibberish.

Definitions, in Ibn Taymiyyah's view, should be used to identify the intention of the speaker.[38] To put it another way, "the use of definitions is to identify the nominatum of the name. It is, therefore, the intention and the language of the user of the name that should be consulted for this matter".[39] Thus, the intention of the speaker is not only the goal of communication but also the goal of definitions. This boils down to saying that a successful definition is, therefore, that one which apprises the speaker's intention. According to Ibn Taymiyyah, it is only the nominal definitions that are capable of doing this.

Nominal definition can involve:

i *ism murādif* (synonym);
ii *ism mukāfī* (equivalent, but not synonymous, name), two expressions are not synonymous unless they denote the same

ṣifah (quality), and refer to the same *dhāt* (referent); if they refer to the same referent but denote different qualities, they are 'equivalent names', e.g., *al-ṣārim* (distinctively sharp sword), and *al-muhannad* (sword made of Indian steel); or

iii *mithāl* (example). Ibn Taymiyyah includes in this class any kind of exemplification aiming at the identification of the nomintatum in order to be recalled, e.g., pointing at a loaf of bread for somebody who asks: 'What is bread?; "since the knowledge of the individual [e.g., the particular loaf of bread] leads to the recognition of the kind [bread in general]."[40]

What he means by nominal definitions is, therefore, definitions which identify the meaning, the referent or the translation of a term.[41] Thus, the wording of nominal definitions is not a firmly fixed and predetermined scheme, but rather a temporary and procedural process as it varies according to the actual communicative situations. The same thing can, therefore, be described differently depending on the way the speaker selects and sees as sufficient to identify his intention in the very particular situation. So, in a certain situation one may refer to a glass of water by 'the large one', and in another situation he can refer to the same glass by 'the one in the middle', or 'the dirty one' etc. according to the condition, position or any other contextually distinctive peculiarities of the glass in the communicative situation. Ibn Taymiyyah's view of definition may well be understood as a call for the abandonment of the Aristotelian way of forming definitions and treating them instead as context-based descriptions. If the argument that Aristotelian definitions are not qualified to make the hearer conceptualise the entities that he cannot conceptualise without them is accepted, it would be reasonable to say that unless they are seen as context-based descriptions, definitions would be useless. This view can best be appreciated if definitions are investigated from a communicative point of view; and this is what Ibn Taymiyyah seems to have done since he associates them with language use to render the intened meaning as a unique individual in the corresponding situation by both the expression and the relevant contexts. If definitions are, however, examined from a scientific viewpoint, as is the case when water, for example, is defined chemically as the sum of one part oxygen and two parts hydrogen, his view would be questionable. However, scientific definitions may well be contextual since the definition of water for example may vary from field to field according to the purposes of the definers.

Nonetheless, Ibn Taymiyyah does not deny that definitions can produce a new proposition provided that the hearer already knows the constituents of the concept to be defined, but this applies only to complex concepts. In this case, "definition signifies the definiendum but does not identify its particular intended referent" (*fa-l-ḥaddu yufīdu l-dalālata ᶜalayhi lā taᶜrīfa ᶜaynih).*[42]

It should be noted, however, that Ibn Taymiyyah does not claim that *al-taᶜyīn* (referring) is the only way to make definitions.[43] In fact, he holds that definitions can also be made by *al-waṣf* (description). At first glance, the claim that definitions can be made by *waṣf* does not seem to be in harmony with his strict pragmatic approach to definitions, since it seemingly undermines his insistence on context as an indispensable element in forming definitions. This implication is, nevertheless, not necessarily applicable, since the claim that the use of definitions is to make the intention of the speaker manifest does not necessarily imply that referring is the only way to make definitions. In fact, one can form a descriptive definition, which can still be regarded as a proper pragmatic definition provided that he takes into account the contextual considerations such as the need and purpose of the hearer.[44] This conception of definition is applicable also to Ibn Taymiyyah's account of meaning, where he takes 'intention' in so broad a sense that it encompasses both intended referent and intended meaning. His sole condition for both meaning and referent to meet the requirements of what he calls *murād al-mutakallim* (the intention of the speaker) is that they should not be taken out of their contextual realisations.

Thus, the gist of Ibn Taymiyyah's thesis is that the aim of the use of names and definitions is to distinguish the respective nominatum and the respective definiendum from others.[45]

4.4. IBN TAYMIYYAH'S CONTEXTUAL VIEW OF LANGUAGE AND MEANINGFULNESS

Ibn Taymiyyah maintains that language is nothing but a means to make predications, so one can never be considered to be speaking language by uttering merely a single word in isolation from any defining context. Although he does not dispute the claim that names and definitions do have references, he nevertheless reserves the terms *lughah* (language) and *kalām* (speech or utterance) for making predications since references, in his view, cannot be made without predications. He mentions, however, some instances where speakers may use single names for purposes such as *tanbīh* (e.g., warning, awakening and calling) and *ishārah* (pointing)[46] but even in such cases, words are not being used for the same meanings being intended by *al-kalām* (linguistic utterances).[47] He distinguishes quite clearly between mentioning a word without the intention of communicating a certain proposition and the process in which the user intends to convey a particular message to the hearer. It is only the latter case that can, in his view, be said to pertain to the use of language. This distinction is very useful for understanding his conception of meaningfulness and his rejection of the distinction between *ḥaqīqah* and *majāz*, where he claims that words such as 'lion' taken in isolation from every context would never be meaningful, let alone characterised as *ḥaqīqah*. This is meant to be a counter-argument against the claim of the advocates of the distinction between *ḥaqīqah* and *majāz* that an expression is *ḥaqīqah* if it signifies independently of context[48] (*in dalla bi-lā qarīnah*) and *majāz* if it does not signify without context (cf. 4.8.1.1).

Ibn Taymiyyah maintains the claim that an expression is never used in an unqualified way. An expression cannot be meaningful prior to its being 'knotted' and 'combined' with other expressions; but even knotting and combining *(al-ᶜaqd wa-l-tarkīb)* alone are not sufficient for an expression to be meaningful. It is, therefore, necessary for the hearer to know not only the speaker, but also his communicative habits *(ᶜādātih bi-khiṭābih)*. Information of this type would be needed to render the speaker's intention manifest.[49] Thus, language in his view is a medium for speakers to express their communicative intentions, which are inexpressible by merely decontextualised words.

Ibn Taymiyyah lays great emphasis on the significance of the syntagmatic relationship holding between the items of language in the determination of the speaker's intention. For example, *al-iḍāfah* (annexation), among others, plays a significant role in determining the meanings of words.

There is a consistent correlation between qualification and meaningfulness, i.e., the more restricted the expression the more meaningful it is, and *vice versa*. Hence, absolute and abstracted expressions (*al-lafẓ al-muṭlaq al-mujarrad*) have no meanings at all.[50] It should be noted, however, that the terms 'absolute expression' and 'abstracted expression' are usually used by Ibn Taymiyyah and Ibn al-Qayyim in a specific technical sense, where they refer to the completely decontextualised expression, which, in their view, can never be part of language. Ibn al-Qayyim argues that the goal of communication is the maintenance of the interests of human beings by means of understanding and making others understand, which can be available only by the appeal to qualified meanings and qualified expressions. The absolute is, however, nothing but a mental image that has no existence in the external world.[51] Thus, the highly decontextualised concept *ẓahr* (surface or back), for example, is viewed as an eminently abstracted image which is derived from the individuals in the external world but has no counterpart in it. For this reason, "it cannot be used in the language unless it is combined with a revealing adjunct" (e.g., *ẓahr al-ṭarīq, ẓahr al-insān, ẓahr al-faras, ẓahr al-jabal).*[52]

This view implies that what the linguists and philosophers do when they decontextualise some concepts for their own special purposes is not necessarily applicable to what the speakers of language do in actual communication. So, as Ibn al-Qayyim explains, "the expression that is abstracted from all its contexts is not used by the sane whether they are Arabs or not, and can never be used without qualifications since use would certainly restrict it".[53] Thus, all the names of the entities which can be expressed by the language are in reality contextualised, and no expression would be meaningful if it has not been contextualised.

4.5. IBN TAYMIYYAH'S CONTEXTUAL VIEW OF THE *WAḌ*ᶜ-USE DISTINCTION

The distinction between *waḍᶜ* and use adopted by the PF mainstream was subject to sharp criticisms by the *Salafīs.*[54] Expressions, according to Ibn al-Qayyim, cannot be abstracted in isolation from use: just as movement is anchored to the mover *(al-mutaḥarrik)*, so also expressions are anchored to use. Ibn al-Qayyim agrees that expressions may be abstracted from use in the mind; however, he does not call them in such cases expressions, but assumed expressions *(alfāẓ muqaddarah).*[55]

Ibn al-Qayyim's main concern about the notion *waḍᶜ* is with the claim that expressions are 'established' in isolation from context *(anna l-lafẓa wuḍiᶜa waḍᶜan muṭlaqan lā muqayyadan).*[56] He points out that the position of the proponents of this claim is similar to the position of the logicians who abstracted the meanings and took them in isolation from all qualifications; and when they realised that their conclusions are contradicted by the fact that these meanings are not disengagable from their qualifications in their external existence, they found themselves in a dilemma as to whether to deny external existence or to renounce those entities which they assumed to be abstract and unqualified. They consider the entities without their external qualifications in such a manner that

> they profess a human that is neither tall nor short; neither white nor black; neither in time nor in place; neither motionless nor moving; neither in the world nor out of it; with no flesh, no bone, no nerve, no nail; has no stature or shadow; and cannot be characterised or restricted. And when they noticed that the external human is different from all that, they said that these are irrelevant characteristics to its sense, rendering the imaginary image as its sense (*ḥaqīqatahu*).[57]

Thus, in order to avoid the traditional philosophers' misconception of entities, we have to consider the entities as they are in reality, that is, to take them as a whole without ignoring any of their features whether they are contingent (*dhātī*) or essential (*lāzim*). To apply this procedure to meaning requires taking the overall actual context of the utterance into account.

4.6. IBN TAYMIYYAH'S CONTEXTUAL VIEW OF THE MEANING-INTENTION DISTINCTION

Although the term 'meaning' was frequently used by the PF mainstream in a rather vague sense, it was, nonetheless, given a distinct definition. Generally speaking, the term was employed to refer to the mental image which the expression denotes, but since the so-called mental image was given different names, it may be helpful to introduce these names in order to know what exactly is meant by meaning, and to show the differences between these various terms. Before proceeding, it would be essential to remember that all the terms to be introduced are referentially synonymous as they refer to the same thing, namely the mental image. If this image is seen as being intended by the expression, it is called *maᶜnā* (meaning); if it is seen as being conjured up by the expression in the mind, it is called *mafhūm* (concept); if it is viewed as an answer to the question *mā huwa ?* (What is it ?), it is called *māhiyyah* (quiddity); if it is viewed as an existing entity in the external world, it is called *ḥaqīqah* (fact); if it is perceived as being distinguished from the others, it is called *huwiyyah* (identity);[58] if it is seen as being an object for an 'established' name, it is called *musammā* (nominatum);[59] and finally if it is seen as derived from the expression, it is called *madlūl* (signified).[60]

With the exception of the contexts in which the *Salafīs* employ it merely for the sake of the argument, the term 'meaning' in the above sense has no room in their framework. They do not seem to accept that word-meaning can be accounted for independently of use. According to Ibn al-Qayyim, signification, which he defines as "understanding a meaning from an expression at the time of its production" *(fa-inna l-dalālat hiya fahmu l-maᶜnā mina l-lafẓi ᶜinda iṭlāqih)*, can never take place without use.[61] Since intention is defined as 'meaning in use', taking Ibn al-Qayyim's definition of signification (which has just been mentioned) for granted would lead to the equation of meaning with intention. Obviously, the neutralisation of the differentiation between meaning and intention (cf. 2.3.1) is founded upon the rejection of the notion *waḍᶜ* in its folk sense. However, it should be noted that it is essential to be aware of the consequences of conflating the two ideas, i.e., meaning and intention. One consequence is that this conflation (or neutralisation) would entail that conventional meaning is trivialised to the advantage of contextual meaning. To put it Searle's way, the adherents of this procedure do not "make a clear distinction between what is conventionally expressed by means of language and what someone actually intends by his utterance".[62] This was intended to be an objection directed against Grice who followed this practice. Defending Grice's position, Wunderlich points out that "Grice's neutralisation of this distinction is fully intentional. The conventions of a language do not exist independently of the numerous situations in which one could communicate in the language; conventions are established, stabilized and modified in them".[63]

In order to prove that conventions are set up in actual communicative situations rather than being established independently of contexts in a one-to-one relationship between expressions and meanings, Ibn Taymiyyah and Ibn al-Qayyim refer to the natural way of language acquisition where the child gradually masters his mother-tongue *via* the actual communicative processes until he manages to have a full command of it without need for others to agree with him on a prior convention (*waḍᶜ mutaqaddim*).[64] However, it may be the case that speakers in a child's environment explain to him some words he may occasionally inquire about in the same way texts are translated to somebody who does not know the language, but this is not meant to be a kind of establishing conventions. Ibn Taymiyyah and Ibn al-Qayyim do not deny, however, the fact that new conventions for new ideas are established from time to time[65] "particularly for specialists who have to establish their own technical terms which are required to fulfil their communicative needs".[66] But this, according to Ibn al-Qayyim, is a special case "in which a *wad*ᶜ prior to use is known", and does not fall within his enquiry.[67]

It may be worth mentioning that, in contemporary pragmatics and cognitive studies, there are others who share this view: Peter Bosch, for example, proposes that "we should give up the notion of the meaning of, or the interpretation of, a sentence or utterance as an identifiable unit or thing" propounding that 'meaning' in his model "is not only procedural but also 'holistic'. It is holistic, as it were, to the extent of self-sacrifice: 'meaning' as such disappears entirely and, as it would seem, without loss".[68] On the other hand, there are other linguists who believe that meaning can be accounted for independently of context. The firm version of this view is held by Katz who assumes that the error of those who identify a natural language "with the concrete realization of the linguistic rules in the heads of its speakers" lies in "conflating a language with its empirical exemplifications. [. . .] A language is not itself subject to the fate of the mortals who speak it. It is some sort of abstract entity, whatever it is that this means".[69] He argues that there is "some given, natural level of context-independent meaning, and that sentence-meaning can be described independently and prior to utterance meaning".[70]

Katz's position seems similar to the position of the advocates of the assumption that the establisher has 'established' the types of constructions, but not the particulars of those types (cf. 2.2.1). There is, however, a significant difference between his explanation of meaning and the view of those who see meaning as a mental image whose views he criticises.[71]

4.7. IBN TAYMIYYAH'S CONTEXTUAL VIEW OF SIGNIFICATION

Within the *Salafī* framework, the term *dalālah* (signification) is employed in a special sense. Showing a discernible consistency in his pragmatic approach, Ibn al-Qayyim points out that the term *dalālah* is intended to refer either to *fi*ᶜ*l al-dāll* (the action of the signifying agent),[72] that is to say, the use of the utterance by the speaker as a signifier to the hearer *(wa-huwa [i.e., the action] dalālatuhu li-l-sāmi*ᶜ*i bi-lafẓih)* or the speaker's understanding of the meaning of that utterance.[73] The rationale behind adopting this definition is not only his insistence on the inclusion of the agents as indispensable elements in the production and understanding of the linguistic utterances, but also his wider belief that sentences cannot be properly handled in isolation from the situations in which they occur.

Maintaining that the signification of an utterance is intentional and wilful, Ibn Taymiyyah distinguishes between two types of signification: *dalālah wujūdiyyah and dalālah ᶜadamiyyah* (existential and non-existential signification). By existential signification, he intended to cover any process in which the speaker utilises an actual signifying element, whether it is a mark (*ᶜalāmah*), word or the like to convey a meaning. If the speaker, on the other hand, relies for this purpose on an abstract (zero) element, he will be said to apply a non-existential signification. The notion of non-existential signification could be seen as an attempt to maintain consistency in his claim that expressions cannot be used without contextual qualifications; especially if we take into account the fact that he regards non-existential significations as intentional qualifications made by the speaker. To make this idea clear, it may be beneficial to quote his statement that "uttering an expression without qualifications is a qualification" (*fa-nafsu l-takallumi bi-l-lafẓi mujarradan qayd)*, and that "abstinence from specific qualifications is a qualification" (*fa-l-imsāku ᶜani l-quyūdi l-khāṣṣati qayd)*.[74] In other words, "[non-existential] signification is not [made by] the expression itself, but rather [by] the expression, the speaker's confinement to it, and his abstaining to add something to it" (*fa-laysati l-dalālatu hiya nafsa l-lafẓi, bali l-lafẓu maᶜa l-iqtiṣāri ᶜalayhi wa-ᶜadami l-ziyādati ᶜalayh)*.[75] Accordingly, the relevant silence of the speaker during the conversation is treated as an informative process and, consequently, given a certain communicative function. It should be noted, however, that not any just silence (or more precisely abstinence) is said to be communicatively meaningful, but only abstinence from what he calls 'specific qualifications' by which he seems to mean the qualifications that the speaker knows that they are expected by the hearer in a given situation.

> Hence, the speaker of an utterance proceeds in one of two ways: he sometimes stops talking while intending a particular meaning, and sometimes combines an expression with another to indicate a meaning that is different from the meaning designated by the first expression alone. The first expression has, therefore, two forms: it is either followed by silence, abstinence and the omission of the qualifier (*tark al-ṣilah*), or combined with another expression. Thus, it is

common for the speaker to intend a particular meaning if he abstains, and to intend another if he combines; in both cases his intention would be manifest, since he couples his utterance with what makes his intention clear.[76]

4.8. IBN TAYMIYYAH'S CRITICAL REVIEW OF *ḤAQĪQAH* AND *MAJĀZ* DICHOTOMY

From the time of Aristotle and up until recently, linguists and philosophers in general have taken the classical distinction between literal and figurative meaning for granted. However, in recent years there has been a growing tendency among some contemporary pragmatists, language philosophers and researchers in artificial intelligence to question this distinction either entirely or partially. To take one example, Sperber and Wilson state that it "is possible that the whole idea of tropes and their classification is destined to go the same way as the notion of humors in medicine[. . .]. Quite independently of the existence of irony, there are already strong grounds for rejecting the notion of figurative meaning".[77]

One of the points that have recently been added to the inquiry into metaphor is the question whether metaphor is a matter of meaning or a matter of use. To put it another way: Is metaphor a subject of semantics or pragmatics? Arguing against traditional views and in favour of an adequate theory of metaphor, Searle insists on the need to distinguish between what he calls speaker's utterance meaning and word or sentence meaning. Searle ascribes the "endemic vice" of traditional theories of metaphor to their failure to appreciate this distinction and their attempt "to locate metaphorical meaning in the sentence or some set of associations with the sentence".[78] Similarly, Davidson holds that metaphor, unlike literal meaning which "can be assigned to words and sentences apart from particular contexts of use"[79] "concerns not the meaning of words but their use".[80]

As will appear, despite their revolutionary contributions, these recent approaches are still closer to the Islamic traditional than to Ibn Taymiyyah's radical approach, since their fundamental assumptions such as the assumption that metaphor is a matter of use rather than a matter of linguistic meaning are already held by the traditional Muslim theory of *majāz*. However, what distinguishes Ibn Taymiyyah's radical theory is its emphasis on the neutralisation of the distinction between *ḥaqīqah* and *majāz* within a contextual framework.

In the next three sections three issues will be discussed:

i the view of the adherents of *ḥaqīqah* and *majāz* dichotomy and their arguments in favour of this distinction;
ii the *Salafīs'* arguments against this distinction; and
iii Ibn Taymiyyah's account of *majāz*.

4.8.1. The view of the adherents of ḥaqīqah and majāz dichotomy

The first point that has to be made here is that the distinction between *ḥaqīqah* and *majāz*[81] is commonly explained by reference to the notion of *waḍ*ᶜ. Abū l-Ḥusayn al-Baṣrī l-Muᶜtazilī defines *ḥaqīqah* as "that which is used to convey the meaning for which it is 'established' in the code [language] of communication" (*mā ufīda bihā mā wuḍiᶜat lahu fī aṣli l-iṣṭilāḥi -lladhī waqaᶜa l-takhāṭubu bih).*[82] According to the view of the adherents of *ḥaqīqah* and *majāz* dichotomy (which is the mainstream view in the works of the Muslim legal theorists), if an expression is used to convey more than one meaning, this expression is characterised either as a homonym (*mushtarak*), polysem (*manqūl*) or metaphor (*mustaᶜār*). The difference between the first category, on the one hand, and the other two categories, on the other, may be explained in terms of the relatedness of meaning.[83] If there is a recognisable connection between the different meanings of a given multi-meaning expression, the expression is classified either as a *manqūl* (polysem) or as a *mustaᶜār* (metaphor); if this connection is not made, the expression is then classified as a *mushtarak* (homonym). For the legal theorists, the difference is commonly defined in terms of the way in which the expression is held to have been assigned its meaning in the primordial *waḍ*ᶜ: if the expression is judged to have been assigned two or more meanings by virtue of different acts of *waḍ*ᶜ – whether the assignments are made by the same establisher or by different establishers – the expression is classified as a homonym;[84] if the expression is, however, judged to have been primordially assigned only one meaning, and the other meaning or meanings are thought to have been obtained by a fresh convention (ᶜ*urf*), or alternatively as a result of the progressive use of the language, the expression is categorised either as a polysem (*manqūl*) or as a (*mustaᶜār*) respectively. Another way of explaining the difference between a homonym and the other two categories is to say that, unlike polysems and metaphors, homonyms signify, as al-Suyūṭī points out, their different meanings *equally.*[85] To put it al-Ghazālī's way, none of the meanings of a homonym can be regarded as more suitable to be rendered as *aṣl* (original or base) than its partner(s).[86] As has already been explained in the previous chapter, treating a kind of meaning as *aṣl* means giving it a number of privileges, chief among which is that it is held to be the first to occur to the mind of the hearer in the communicative process. And this is what is assumed to form the fundamental parameter by which one can judge whether a given multi-meaning expression should be seen as a homonym or not. Thus, the important point to notice is that in PF, the meanings of a homonym are presumed in the absence of any contextual evidence to occur simultaneously to the mind, whereas only the literal meaning of a polysem and metaphor is believed to occur to the hearer's mind if there is no evidence to the contrary.

With respect to the difference between polysem and metaphor, it may be briefly said that although the two categories are generally covered by the term *majāz* and sometimes studied as a single class, some legal theorists attempt to draw a distinction between them. To clarify the difference between a polysem and metaphor, al-Ghazālī takes recourse to a special test which may be called 'the constancy test'. Al-Ghazālī applies the term *manqūl* (polysem) to refer to the expression that is transferred from its original meaning to another *(yunqalu ᶜan mawḍūᶜihi ilā maᶜnā)*, treated invariably as a constant name for it, and used to convey both the original and new meaning.[87] For example, the expression *ṣalāh* is held to have been originally assigned to, or technically speaking, 'established' for *duᶜāᵓ* (call) in its wide sense and then used narrowly to refer to the Islamic prayer. To take more examples, *ḥajj*, which is said to have been originally assigned to *qaṣd* (intention); and *kufr*, which is primordially assigned to *taghṭiyah* (covering) are given in the *Qur'ān* and *Sunnah* new Islamic meanings, namely 'the Islamic pilgrimage to Mecca' and 'unbelief' respectively. The process of assigning a new meaning to an old expression in this way is, thus, interpreted as a process of transferring an expression from its original meaning to a new one. The pretheoretical meaning of *naql* (transferring) and *istiᶜārah* (borrowing) may well be useful here to pinpoint the terminological contrast between *manqūl* and *mustaᶜār*, which have only technically been translated as polysemy and metaphor.[88] Just as borrowing implies that borrowed objects are customarily returnable, so also *mustaᶜār* (metaphor) entails that the non-literal message conveyed by a metaphoric expression is only contextually implied, rather than conventionally signified, by the expression.

It is essential, however, to point out that while homonymy (*ishtirāk*) is assumed to be a *waḍ*ᶜ-based phenomenon and treated as *ḥaqīqah*,[89] metaphor is widely judged to be a partially use-motivated one. The qualification made here by the adverb 'partially' is meant to indicate that metaphor is also based on a kind of *waḍ*ᶜ, namely the so-called subsumptive *waḍ*ᶜ *(al-waḍ*ᶜ *al-naw*ᶜ*ī)* (cf. 2.2.1), which, unlike individual *waḍ*ᶜ (*al-waḍ*ᶜ *al-shakhṣī*), gives the speakers a great deal of freedom to use innovative utterances. As to polysemy (*naql*), it is held to be brought about either by the *Sharī*ᶜ*ah*-based *waḍ*ᶜ (*al-waḍ*ᶜ *al-shar*ᶜ*ī*) by virtue of which the *Sharī*ᶜ*ah*-based terms are coined, or by the conventional *waḍ*ᶜ (*al-waḍ*ᶜ *al-*ᶜ*urfī*). The latter involves both the general conventional *waḍ*ᶜ (*al-waḍ*ᶜ *al-*ᶜ*urfī l-*ᶜ*āmm*) and the special conventional *waḍ*ᶜ (*al-waḍ*ᶜ *al-*ᶜ*urfī l-khāṣṣ*). The difference between the general and special conventional *waḍ*ᶜ is that the latter is made by the specialists in a particular field, whereas the former is made by ordinary speakers of the language (cf. 2.2). It should be noted that the fresh expressions entering the language by *Sharī*ᶜ*ah*-based *waḍ*ᶜ, or by the conventional *waḍ*ᶜ, can be counted as *ḥaqīqah*-expressions since they satisfy the definition of *ḥaqīqah* mentioned above. What this definition suggests is that determining whether a given expression is *ḥaqīqah* or *majāz* is relative to the code [language] in which the communication takes place. Accordingly, the expression *ṣalāh* (the Islamic prayer) is counted as *ḥaqīqah*-expression in relation to the *Sharī*ᶜ*ah*-based *waḍ*ᶜ and *majāz*-expression in relation to the original (or the linguistic) *waḍ*ᶜ.[90]

4.8.1.1. *Arguments in favour of the distinction between ḥaqīqah and majāz*

Since the issue of the existence of *majāz* in languages has long been taken for granted, there is no need to introduce all the arguments that are developed by the proponents of *majāz* to support their claim that there is a distinctive type of speech called *majāz*. Instead, it might be wise to select the ones that seem most powerful. These arguments can be outlined as follows,

1) Unlike the recovery of a *ḥaqīqah*-expression, the recovery of a *majāz*-expression depends on contextual evidence. Hence, the word 'lion' can stand alone to mean "the ravenous animal", but needs to be supported by an appropriate context to refer to a brave man.[91]

2) Some meanings of a multi-meaning expression tend to occur to the mind prior to others, which means that they are the proper nominatums of the expression. Therefore, it is reasonable to distinguish those meanings as *maᶜānī ḥaqīqiyyah* (proper meanings) and the others as *maᶜānī majāziyyah* (figurative meanings).[92]

These two arguments can be combined and reformulated in the following manner:

3) If a native speaker is asked about the meaning of an expression such as 'lion' in isolation from any context, his reply can typically be said to be satisfactory if and only if he states what is known as the literal meaning of the word, which in this example is something like 'the king of Beasts' or 'the ravenous animal'. This demonstrates that some of the meanings of such expressions, that is, the literal meanings, are more entitled to be their proper meanings than others.

4.8.2. Arguments against the distinction between *ḥaqīqah* and *majāz*

Prior to embarking on the discussion of Ibn Taymiyyah's arguments against the distinction between *ḥaqīqah* and *majāz*, it would be necessary to point out that we will confine ourselves to the arguments and remarks that are of universal nature, that is, those which are not distinctively and exclusively related to Islamic history and culture. It is also necessary to stress that in order to do full justice to Ibn Taymiyyah and his disciple Ibn al-Qayyim, their position on the notion *majāz* will be taken as one element of a complex pragmatic theory.

Challenging the advocates of the distinction between *ḥaqīqah* and *majāz* to introduce any reliable distinction between *ḥaqīqah* and *majāz*, Ibn Taymiyyah and Ibn al-Qayyim advance several arguments against this distinction; the following are some of these:

I The distinction between *ḥaqīqah* and *majāz* is based upon a false claim that there is *waḍᶜ* prior to use. Ibn Taymiyyah and Ibn al-Qayyim assume that the distinction between *ḥaqīqah* and *majāz* is acceptable only if it can be proven that
   [a] a group of sane people held a meeting, and agreed to assign names to designate entities in the extra-linguistic world;
   [b] and then used those expressions for those meanings; and

[c] after holding another meeting they agreed to use the same expressions for different meanings by virtue of the relatedness between the original meanings and the accidental ones; and referred to the expressions signifying the original meanings as literal, and to the expressions signifying the accidental meanings as non-literal.[93]

The essence of this argument is that the etymological and diachronic account of *majāz* is invalid since it is founded upon non-demonstrable assumptions. In other words, the claim that a given meaning of a multi-meaning expression is a literal meaning on the grounds that it is the first meaning to have been assigned to the expression is a non-verifiable claim. It should be noted, however, that Ibn Taymiyyah does not deny the existence of relationships holding between literal and figurative meanings or the possibility that one meaning is chronologically prior to the other(s), but what he disputes is the possibility of finding reliable tests by which one can judge that a particular meaning is *ḥaqīqah* or *majāz*. Thus, according to Ibn Taymiyyah, it is untenable to assume that *dhawq* (taste) in one of the following phrases is more suitable to be classified as *ḥaqīqah* than the others: *dhawq al-ᶜadhāb* (the taste of punishment), *dhawq al-mawt* (the taste of death) or *dhawq al-ṭaᶜām aw al-sharāb* (the taste of food or drink). It will be made clear that Ibn Taymiyyah develops an alternative synchronic account of *majāz*, which will be dealt with later (cf. 4.8.3).

II Responding to the claim that an expression is *ḥaqīqah* if it signifies independently of context *(in dalla bi-lā qarīnah)* and *majāz* if it does not signify without context,[94] Ibn Taymiyyah argues that there is no meaningful expression that may signify in isolation from all contexts.

Similarly, he refuses the claim that an expression is *ḥaqīqah* if it is satisfied with a verbal context – which, unlike situational context, is assumed to be a *waḍᶜ*-based or conventionalised one – and *majāz* if it requires a situational context.[95] Defending this position, Ibn Taymiyyah states that

> An expression is never used without *waḍᶜ*-based verbal qualifications. Furthermore, situation (i.e., the speaker's and hearer's situation (*ḥāl al-mutakallim wa-l-mustamiᶜ*)) must be taken into account in all kinds of utterances. For knowledge

> of the speaker would reveal a great deal of the speaker's meaning, which cannot be understood otherwise. This is because knowledge of the speaker's habit of the use of the language depends on knowledge of the speaker himself, and because an expression cannot be meaningful unless the 'language' of the speaker, that is, his habit and custom which he usually observes in his speech, is known. What is more, the signification of an expression for its meaning is intentional *(qaṣdiyyah)*, wilful *(irādiyyah)* and freely chosen *(ikhtiyār-iyyah)*.[96]

It seems that Ibn Taymiyyah's statement that "an expression is never used without *waḍ*ᶜ-based verbal qualifications" appears to be irreconcilable with Ibn al-Qayyim's notion 'unqualified meaning', more of which later (cf. 4.8.3). However, there is in fact a way of reconciling the two positions since what Ibn Taymiyyah means by qualifications is so general that it embraces not only what the speaker utters, but also his relevant silence during the conversation.

III In his attempt to refute the second argument of the adherents of *majāz*, Ibn Taymiyyah argues that although a particular meaning of a multi-meaning expression tends to occur to the mind prior to the others, this does not justify the distinction between *ḥaqīqah* and *majāz*. For the meanings of some *ḥaqīqah*-expressions may also tend to occur to the mind prior to others. For example, lexicographers agree unanimously that the word *ẓahr* (back) is literally used to refer to all animal backs, but the back of a human may, nevertheless, be the one which occurs immediately to many people's mind *(wa-ma*ᶜ*a hādhā fa-kathīrun mina l-nāsi qad lā yasbiqu ilā dhihnihim illā ẓahru l-insān)*. They do not think of the back of a dog, fox, wolf, weasel, ant or louse. Similarly, if someone takes an oath that he will never eat *ru*ᵓ*ūs* (heads) or eggs, his utterance would be taken to mean, according to the jurists, the heads and eggs that are usually eatable but not the heads of ants and fleas or the eggs of fish.[97] Thus, *tabādur* (immediacy), within Ibn Taymiyyah's framework, is not a fixed, predetermined or predictable, but rather context-dependent, process such that what occurs first to the mind in a given situation could not be the same in all other situations. That is to say, there is no constant immediate meaning attached to each word in the language, but the context in which the word is processed determines which

> interpretation is most likely to be the first to occur to the hearer's mind.[98] To put it another way, the occurrence of a particular meaning rather than another in the mind is not due to variation in the nature of the speech itself, but to other extra-linguistic factors such as the frequency of the words in the speech, the relevance of the meaning and a host of psychological factors related to the way in which memory operates. Hence, the reason why a back of a human rather than a back of an ant is most likely to occur to the mind when the word *al-ẓahr* (the back) is mentioned relates to the fact that the back of a human is the most frequent meaning expressed by the word *al-ẓahr* (the back) in the everyday use of the language.[99]

Thus, according to Ibn Taymiyyah, there is no distinctive feature in the expression itself by which one can distinguish *ḥaqīqah* from *majāz* in the same way that one can distinguish a declarative sentence from an interrogative one. However, if it is the case that no distinctive feature inheres in the expression itself which can help in identifying *ḥaqīqah*-expression from *majāz*-expression, then why cannot *tabādur* (immediacy) be regarded as a well defined parameter by which *ḥaqīqah* can be distinguished from *majāz*, especially if we take into account that the native speakers of the same linguistic community are usually capable of recognising the immediate meanings of most, if not all, the words in the language? Putting it in a modern context, Ibn Taymiyyah's position on this issue would be tantamount to saying that just as there is no need to render the Canadian dollar, for example, as the literal meaning and the American dollar as the figurative meaning of the word 'dollar' if it is used in Canada, so also there is no need to regard 'the ravenous animal' as the literal meaning and 'the fearless man' as the figurative meaning of the word 'lion', since the intended meaning of these words is identified by the situations in which they are employed.[100]

Thus, instead of saying that since 'a ravenous animal' is more likely to occur to the mind as a meaning for 'lion' than 'a fearless man', which qualifies the former to be regarded as the literal meaning and the latter as the figurative meaning for 'lion', the opponents of *majāz* would prefer to say that what occurs to the mind first in the actual respective situation is the intended and, consequently, the proper meaning.[101]

IV On the basis of the postulate that the conventions of the language are set up in the actual communicative situations rather than being established independently of contexts in a one-to-one relationship between expressions and meanings, Ibn al-Qayyim develops two arguments:

a) The claim that *waḍ*ᶜ is independent from, and prior to, use theoretically implies that it is possible to assign another meaning to an expression without being previously used in its first meaning, which leads to the inadmissible consequence that there can be *majāz* without being preceded by *ḥaqīqah*.[102]
b) Since signification, which he defines as "understanding the meaning of an expression when it is produced", never takes place without a preceding use, and since use is either equivalent to *ḥaqīqah* or *majāz* according to those who define *ḥaqīqah* as the use of an expression to convey its *waḍ*ᶜ-based meaning, or one of the constituents of *ḥaqīqah*[103] for those who define *ḥaqīqah* as the expression that is used to convey its *waḍ*ᶜ-based meaning, it follows that the claim that *waḍ*ᶜ (i.e., the assignment of a meaning to an expression) is independent from, and prior to, use leads to saying that an expression, before being used, is free from both *ḥaqīqah* and *majāz* while at the same time signifying one of them, which is a paradox.[104]

V The distinction between *ḥaqīqah* and *majāz* is unfounded, whether it is taken in terms of signifier *(al-dalīl)*, signified *(al-madlūl)* or signification *(al-dalālah)*.

> As far as the signifier is concerned, the invalidity of the distinction between *ḥaqīqah* and *majāz* is indisputable inasmuch as no sane person would say that an expression, regardless of its meaning can be divided into *ḥaqīqah* and *majāz*. Looking at the same issue from the angle of the signified, the distinction between *ḥaqīqah* and *majāz* is invalid because the signified on its own cannot be conceived of as being *ḥaqīqah* or *majāz*, but can only be asserted or negated [. . .]. The distinction between *ḥaqīqah* and *majāz* is similarly false when considered from the angle of signification. This is because signification is intended to refer to two things: first, the action of the signifying agent [i.e., the speaker], that is, his signifying something to the hearer by means of the expression *(dalālatuhu li-l-sāmi*ᶜ*i bi-lafẓih)*; [. . .] and, second, the hearer's understanding of that expression [. . .]. In these two senses of signification, the intended meaning of an expression

> is its proper or literal meaning (*ḥaqīqatuh*) regardless of how clear or unclear the expression is, or the ability or inability of the speaker to make his intention manifest, or, finally, whether the hearer knows the language of the speaker, including his speech habit (*ʿādat khiṭābih*).[105]

Hence, much of the misconception in the mainstream account of *majāz* is due, according to Ibn al-Qayyim, to the confusion between a theoretical or abstract language (*al-kalām al-muqaddar*) and the language in use (*al-kalām al-mustaʿmal*).[106] By the former he seems to mean the set of the assignments of the single words to their meanings which the mainstream assume to have been made by the establisher and by virtue of which they claim that these meanings are the proper or literal meanings.

The major mistake in the analysis of the adherents of *majāz* is that

> They abstract single expressions from the qualifications which apply to them, examine them in isolation from their contexts, and apply the same conclusions to the expression when it is combined with other expressions. Thus, they say that 'lion' taken in isolation from context is the specific animal and that 'sea', in isolation is a large quantity of water. But this is fallacious, because 'lion', 'sea' and the like, when used in isolation, are not utterances or parts of utterances, nor do they mean anything; they are nothing in fact but sounds used for cawing (*wa-huwa ṣawtun yunʿaqu bih*).[107]

4.8.3. Ibn Taymiyyah's account of *majāz*

Ibn Taymiyyah argues that since language is used as a means to express the contents of the external world, there must be a correspondence between the structure of reality and the use of language in such a way that the structure of reality is reflected in the language. Consequently, since there is no abstract thing in the external world but all entities are conceived to be qualified in some way, it follows that there would be no unqualified expressions in the language to signify it.[108]

> Thus, in a language there is no such a thing as blackness, whiteness, tallness and shortness independently of black, white, tall or short objects, or in isolation from any

> qualification. However, expressions in isolation can indeed be found in the works of lexicographers, but this is because these abstract expressions are understood by lexicographers to represent the common range of what native speakers mean in different utterances.[109]

This is intended to be a counter-argument against the advocates of the distinction between *ḥaqīqah* and *majāz* who hold that single expressions such as 'lion' are *ḥaqīqah* if it is considered in isolation from any context and *majāz* if there exists a contextual indicator that the speaker means 'a brave man'.

Since Ibn Taymiyyah strongly believes that simple expressions (e.g., *dhawq* in its abstract sense) are not meaningful and, accordingly, cannot unequivocally signify objects in the extra-linguistic world, it follows that his empirical conception of the relationship between language and reality differs fundamentally from the view of logical atomists. According to this view, "Every simple expression of the language would have a single meaning and this could be described, either directly or by reduction, in terms of the relationship holding between the expression and the object or class of objects which the expression stood for, or named, in the external world".[110] The fact that languages vary in their structures and that word-for-word translation is not usually a good procedure for a proper translation of texts raises major difficulties for this view, which may lend credit to Ibn Taymiyyah's thesis that meaningfulness is a context-dependent notion.

The remainder of my discussion of Ibn Taymiyyah's account of *majāz* will be introduced in three points. The first is his emphasis on the following principles without which no expression can be seen as an actual part of the language:

Firstly, no expression can be meaningful unless it is combined with others to form, at least, a sentence.[111]

Secondly, expressions never signify without the following conditions being satisfied:

- i the speaker is rational and uses the language in a conventionally accessible manner, this being his habit of speech.
- ii the hearer has a knowledge of the speaker's habit of the use of his utterance.
- iii the speaker speaks in agreement with this habit.
- iv the hearer assumes this is the case.[112]

However, one could argue that Ibn Taymiyyah is wrong in insisting that meanings are so contextualised to the extent that it would be impossible to recover the meaning of 'back' when it occurs in isolation. In response, Ibn Taymiyyah would argue that although an expression like 'back' may conjure up a mental picture of 'human back', it is still an expression that does not refer to one object in particular in a one-to-one relationship nor can it be used for predication. Also since expressing intentions is the ultimate goal for communication, and because it is not possible to assign any intention to an expression in isolation, it follows that the expression in question cannot be regarded as part of language.

The second important point in Ibn Taymiyyah's account of *majāz* is that he equates metaphors with what is called in PF *al-mushakkikāt*, derived from *shakkaka* (to make somebody doubt something). Al-Qarāfī points out that the reason why a *mushakkik*-expression is given this name has to do with the fact that the investigator doubts as to whether to classify it as a *mushtarak* (homonym) or as *mutawāṭi*ᵓ (lit, concurrent or accordant). By *mutawāṭī*ᵓ is meant "an expression assigned for a universal meaning which applies *equally* to its referents". For example, the expression 'man' applies equally to all objects that have the following features (+ human + adult + male). *Mushakkik*, by contrast, is defined as "an expression assigned for a universal meaning which applies *differently* to its referents".[113] 'Light', for example, is employed to refer to 'sun light' and 'lamp light', although they are different from each other. Similarly, there are different kinds of existence, such as the eternal and everlasting existence of *Allāh*, the existence of His mortal creatures, physical and metaphysical existence, and mental and external existence; these different kinds of existence are, nevertheless, covered, at least in some languages, by one term. Therefore, there is no essential difference, according to Ibn Taymiyyah, between metaphors and *mushakkikāt* which would allow us to place them under different categories and, therefore, treat them differently. In the mainstream analysis, metaphors are distinguished from *mushakkikāt* by reference to *waḍ*ᶜ. If the assignment of two or more meanings to an expression is assumed to be carried out by a single act of *waḍ*ᶜ, the expression is classified as *mushakkik*, and the meanings are consequently treated as one meaning. Thus, the different kinds of existence, which have just been mentioned, are treated as one meaning, rather than multi-meanings. If the assignment of meanings to an expression is, however, assumed to be made by more than one act of *waḍ*^c at different points in time and, also, the creator of the new meaning is thought to have relied on the relatedness between the old and new meaning, the expression is classified as a *majāz*-expression, thus allowing for the existence of figurative meaning. For Ibn Taymiyyah, this criterion is unsatisfactory, because in the first instance there is no means by which one can identify which meaning is prior to the other, and, second, the only way to know that the assignment of the meanings to an expression is made by more than one act of *waḍ*^c at different points in time is to assume that the expression is *majāz*, which is circular.

However, there is one element that both the mainstream and Ibn Taymiyyah have in common in their different accounts of *majāz*, namely the relationship between the so-called literal and figurative meaning. According to Ibn Taymiyyah, this relationship is existent in *mushakkik* as well. Thus, just as it is not reasonable to say that 'existence' in its abstract meaning is the literal meaning and the actual qualified meanings (like the eternal and everlasting existence of *Allāh*, the existence of his mortal creatures, physical and metaphysical existence) are the figurative meanings, so it is not reasonable to say that 'lion' in its abstract meaning is the literal meaning and the actual qualified meaning 'a brave man' is the figurative meaning of the expression 'lion'. It should be pointed out here that what is meant by abstract meaning is essentially different from unqualified meaning. 'Abstract meaning' refers to the mental construction of the meaning of an expression resulting from considering it in isolation from all its actual contexts. With respect to unqualified meaning, it would be better to explain it in line with Ibn Taymiyyah's distinction between *dalālah wujūdiyyah and dalālah ^cadamiyyah* (existential and non-existential signification) (cf. 4.7). As mentioned earlier, if the speaker intentionally abstains from qualifying his expression in a conventionally recognisable manner, his abstention will be interpreted as an attempt on his part to use the expression in its unqualified meaning, that is, the meaning understood from the expression together with the speaker's abstention. Accordingly, the word 'lion' in 'I saw a lion yesterday' is used to convey an unqualified meaning, while in 'I saw a lion delivering an address from the pulpit' is used to convey a qualified meaning. Unlike abstract meanings, unqualified meanings can be described as linguistically relevant and consequently regarded as meaningful. Hence, it can be said that although the *Salafīs* acknowledge the existence of 'single meaning', they, nevertheless, employ it in a special sense which is compatible with their thesis that expressions are meaningful only if they are used in particular communicative situations.

The question that has to be raised here is why the *Salafīs* refuse to regard unqualified meanings as *ḥaqīqah* (literal meanings) and qualified meanings as *majāz* (figurative meanings). According to Ibn al-Qayyim, the reason pertains to the elasticity, inconsistency, and open-endedness of this distinction in empirical terms *(ghayru munḍabiṭin wa-lā muṭṭaridin wa-lā munᶜakis)*. Furthermore, this distinction involves an unnecessary differentiation between totally similar notions, since the adherents of *majāz* do not apply *majāz* to all those expressions whose meanings vary according to unqualification and qualification, which form the majority of, if not all, expressions in a language. However, Ibn al-Qayyim's point is this: if each expression whose unqualified meaning is different from its qualified meaning is regarded as *majāz*, the whole language would be regarded as *majāz*, since this is the case with every expression in the language. But this (i.e., that the whole language is *majāz*) is, according to Ibn al-Qayyim, self-evidently false because it is obvious that most expressions are used to convey their literal meanings. Besides, the majority of the adherents of *majāz* acknowledge that each *majāz* must have a *ḥaqīqah*. Consequently, *ḥaqīqah* in their view is prior to, and more commonly used than, *majāz*. Moreover, they acknowledge that *ḥaqīqah* is the base *(al-aṣl)* and *majāz* is the derivative *(al-farᶜ)*. However, if the whole or the majority of the language was *majāz*, would not *majāz* have to be considered the base, and, therefore, would inevitably have to be given priority in interpretation, which would inevitably lead to confusion in language and communication.[114]

Thus, Ibn al-Qayyim's basic point is that a single meaning is either unqualified (*muṭlaq*) or qualified (*muqayyad*). Unqualified meanings are designated by unqualified expressions, and qualified meanings are designated by qualified expressions. Both unqualified and qualified meanings belong to *ḥaqīqah* type (the term '*ḥaqīqah*' is being employed here in a special sense where it refers to the proper use of language). Accordingly, 'lion' is a *ḥaqīqah*-expression whether it is used to refer to the ravenous animal or to a fearless man since the intended meaning in both cases is determined by the situational context and since it does not matter whether context is *wujūdī* (existential) or *ᶜadamī* (non-existential). Although the distinction between existential and non-existential contexts does not seem to have been explicitly drawn by Ibn Taymiyyah or Ibn al-Qayyim, it is, nonetheless, quite vital in their framework, especially in connection with the existential/non-existential signification dichotomy and the unqualified/qualified meaning dichotomy; for it is doubtful that these two dichotomies can be explained without reference to this distinction.

If one is to compare Ibn Taymiyyah's account with the mainstream account of *majāz*, one may say that Ibn Taymiyyah's account is committed to a wide sense of meaning which can accommodate both what the mainstream call *ma^cnā ḥaqīqī* (literal meaning); and *ma^cnā majāzī* (figurative meaning). Therefore, instead of saying that *baḥr* (sea) literally means a huge quantity of water and could be used metaphorically to refer to a person who possesses wide knowledge, Ibn Taymiyyah would say that *baḥr* unqualifiedly means 'very wide' and thus can be used, given the relevant context, to refer to the sea or to a person who possesses wide knowledge.[115] Thus, there is no difference, according to the *Salafīs'* approach, between the relationship holding between 'the blackness of ink' and the 'blackness of tar' and the relationship holding between 'sea' and 'an extremely knowledgeable person'. Just as the *mushakkik*-expression 'black' covers both 'the blackness of ink' and 'the blackness of tar' and can be employed to refer to either of them, so the word *baḥr* can be used to refer to 'a huge quantity of water' or to 'an extremely knowledgeable person'.[116]

Thus, the Arabic word '*dhawq*' (taste) is treated by the mainstream as having only one literal meaning (to experience the sensation of food or drink in the mouth). The other meanings of this word are viewed as figurative. This conception, in Ibn Taymiyyah's view, is inaccurate, because the meaning of *dhawq* is in actual fact "to experience the sensation of something", as al-Khalīl Ibn Aḥmad al-Farāhīdī (one of the classical Arab lexicographers (d. 175/791)) says, whether it is food or not. Ibn Taymiyyah quotes several Arabic texts to support his claim; the following Qur^ʾānic verses constitute some of these examples:[117]

> (1) *Wa-la-nudhīqannahum mina l-^cadhābi l-adnā dūna l-^cadhābi l-akbari la^callahum yarji^cūn.*
>
> And indeed We will make
Them taste of the Penalty
Of this (life) prior to
The supreme Penalty, in order
That they may (repent and) return.[118]

(2) *fa-dhāqat wabāla amrihā*

Then did they taste
The evil result of
Their conduct.[119]

(3) *lā yadhūqūna fīhā l-mawta illā l-mawtata l-ūlā*

Nor will they there
Taste Death, except the first
Death.[120]

(4) *lā yadhūqūna fīhā bardan wa-lā sharāban illā ḥamīman wa-ghassāqā*

Nothing cool shall they taste
Therein, nor any drink,
Save a boiling fluid
And a fluid, dark, murky,
Intensely cold.[121]

Thus, instead of saying that *dhawq* literally means 'to experience the sensation of food or drink' and can be used metaphorically to refer to other kinds of sensation, Ibn Taymiyyah says that *dhawq* can be used to refer to any experience of sensation of any kind and the context provides real means by which the speaker's intended meaning can be recovered.

Although this account of *majāz* may appear to be rather strange, some lexicographers such as Ismāᶜīl Ibn Ḥammād al-Jawharī seem to find it practical to the extent that they prefer to treat words like *baḥr* as having a broad scope of application rather than having different meanings, so *baḥr* applies to sea because of its deepness and vastness, to the horse that has wide steps (used for fast horses) and to every great river.[122]

The third point we need to highlight in Ibn Taymiyyah's account of *majāz* concerns the relationship between an abstract expression like *janāḥ* (wing) and its actual variants, which are divided by the mainstream into *ḥaqīqah*-expressions like *janāḥ al-ṭāʾir* (bird's wing) and *majāz*-expressions like *janāḥ al-dhull* (the wing of humility) as one involving the general (*al-ᶜāmm*) and the specific *(al-khāṣṣ)* or between the unqualified *(al-muṭlaq)* and the qualified *(al-muqayyad)* respectively. The difference between the general *(al-ᶜāmm)* and the unqualified (*al-muṭlaq*) is that the former is used to refer to a class of entities (to which it conventionally applies) regardless of their individual variety whereas the latter is used to refer to them regardless of their qualitative variety. Thus, 'man' can be seen as a general expression since it is applicable to Zayd and 'Umar despite of their difference; and can also be seen as an unqualified expression since it is applicable to a bad and good man regardless of their qualitative variety.[123] However, this difference between general and unqualified expression is not essential here, since the intended referent or the meaning of the expression in both cases is relative to the situation in which the expression is uttered. In other words, the point of resemblance between a *majāz*-expression like 'lion' in 'I saw a lion delivering an address from the pulpit', on the one hand, and a specific and qualified expression like 'Zayd' and 'the good man', on the other, is that all of them are indexical expressions.

In addition to specific, qualified and *majāz* expressions, there are others that are treated as context-dependent categories in Ibn Taymiyyah's framework. These are *asmāʾ al-maʿārif* (definite nouns), which involve

i personal pronouns (*al-muḍmarāt*), e.g., 'I', 'you' and 'he';
ii demonstrative nouns (*asmāʾ al-ishārah*), e.g., 'this' and 'that';
iii relative pronouns (*al-asmāʾ al-mawṣūlah*), e.g.,

(4) *alladhīna yuqīmūna l-ṣalāta wa-yuʾtūna l-zakāta*

"those who
Establish regular prayers
And regular charity".[124]

iv definite nouns (*al-asmāʾ al-muʿarrafah bi-al*), e.g., *al-rasūl* (the messenger);
v proper names (*al-asmāʾ al-aʿlām*), e.g., *Ibrāhīm, Ismāʿīl* and *Ramaḍān*;
vi what is annexed to any of these categories to form a genitive construction (*al-muḍāf ilā l-maʿrifah*), e.g., *baytī* (my house), *baytu hādhā l-rajul* (this gentleman's house), *baytu -alladhī dhahaba -alʾān* (the house of that who has just left), *baytu l-rasūl* (the House of the Messenger) or (the Messenger's House), *baytu Ibrāhīm* (*Ibrāhīmʾs* House) or (the House of *Ibrāhīm*,); and
vii *al-munādā l-muʿayyan* (the definite noun in the vocative), e.g., the prophet Yūsuf's statement,

(5) "*yā abati innī raʾaytu aḥada ʿashara kawkaban*",[125]

"O [. . .] father
I did see eleven stars".[126]

Ibn Taymiyyah points out that such expressions as *rasūl* (messenger) and *bayt* (house) can be intended to denote the general meaning or refer to a more specific meaning (i.e., a particular house). To illustrate this, he considers these examples:

> (6) "*innā arsalnā ilaykum rasūlan shāhidan ᶜalaykum ka-mā arsalnā ilā firᶜawna rasūlan; fa-ᶜaṣā firᶜawnu l-rasūla*"
>
> "We have sent to you,
> (O men!) an apostle,
> To be a witness concerning you,
> Even as We sent
> An apostle to Pharaoh.
> But Pharaoh disobeyed
> The apostle . . .".[127]
>
> (7) "*lā tajᶜalū duᶜāʾa l-rasūli baynakum ka-duᶜāʾi baᶜḍikum baᶜḍan*",
>
> "Deem not the summons
> Of the apostle among yourselves
> Like the summons of one
> Of you to another".[128]

The expression *al-rasūl* (the apostle) in these two different texts is the same expression, but it refers to different people: the messenger Moses in (6) and the messenger Muḥammad in (7).[129] Similarly, 'I' and 'you', 'this' and 'that' can be used to refer to different referents in different situations.

Ibn Taymiyyah's basic point here is that although this type of expression is never used without a context for identifying the entity to which it refers, and although the signification of this type of expression consists of the expression and a context serving to identify the referent, it is, nevertheless, treated as *ḥaqīqah* and no sane person could claim that it was *majāz*.[130]

According to Ibn Taymiyyah, the pronoun (I) has never been uttered unqualifiedly (*muṭlaqan*) owing to the fact that the average universal abstract speaker does not exist in the external world, since each speaker is particular and distinctive. So, in order to know its referent and its meaning, one has to know the speaker.[131] In the *Salafīs'* view, just as there is no abstract speaker, so there is no such a thing as an abstract *janāḥ* (wing), *dhawq* (taste), *dhahr* (back), or *bayt* (house). What exists in the external world, and what speakers do refer to in their communications, is the qualified *janāḥ* (wing), *dhawq* (taste), *dhahr* (back), and *bayt* (house). Consider these examples:

> (8) Thy Lord hath decreed
> That ye worship none but Him,
> And that ye be kind
> To parents. Whether one
> Or both of them attain
> Old age in thy life,
> Say not to them a word
> Of contempt, nor repel them,
> But address them
> In terms of honour.
> And, out of kindness,
> Lower to them the wing
> Of humility, and say:
> "My Lord! bestow on them
> Thy Mercy even as they
> Cherished me in childhood.[132]

> (9) But lower thy wing
> in gentleness
> To the Believers.[133]

> (10) There is not an animal
> (That lives) on the earth,
> Nor a being that flies
> On its wings, but (forms
> Part of) communities like you.[134]

The word 'wing' in all these examples is being used in a qualified way to refer to a specific entity in the extra-linguistic world. It is not typical of speakers to use 'wing' or any other expression in an unqualified way; so, there is no difference between *anā* (I) and *janāḥ* (wing) that can justify subsuming them under different categories. Furthermore, the connection between *janāḥ* (wing) in its abstract sense and *dhull* (humility) in "Lower to them the wing of humility" is similar to the connection between *janāḥ* (wing) and *ṭāʾir* (bird) in 'the bird's wing', so why is it, Ibn al-Qayyim asks, that the expression *janāḥ* (wing) is rendered as *ḥaqīqah* in the latter and *majāz* in the former although the speakers of the language use each of them in its respective qualified manner. If someone says, Ibn al-Qayyim adds, but 'humility' has no wing, we would say to him it is indeed the case that 'humility' has no wing covered by feathers but has an immaterial wing that suits it.[135] I shall not go any further into the question why the *Salafīs* do not conceive of 'the bird's wing' as *ḥaqīqah* and 'the wing of humility' as *majāz* as it has already been dealt with in this section.

Let us sum up this point by saying that context is the essential element in identifying the intended meaning in each linguistic utterance, especially in utterances involving *mushakkik*, *mutawāṭiʾ* and *mushtarak* expressions; and that each pair of the so-called *ḥaqīqah*-expression and *majāz*-expression represents two variants of a wider unqualified expression. Thus, instead of saying that 'the bird's wing' is a *ḥaqīqah*-expression, and 'the wing of humility' is a *majāz*-expression, *Salafīs* would say that both 'the bird's wing' and 'the wing of humility' are two different variants of 'wing', which only has mental, not actual, existence. In other words, just as the *mushakkik*-expression 'white', given the appropriate context, is capable of referring to the whiteness of ice and the whiteness of milk, the *mutawāṭīʾ*-expression 'man' refers equally to Zayd and 'Umar, and the *mushtarak*-expression '*al-mushtarī*' is applicable to a 'buyer' and 'Jupiter', in the same way that the personal pronoun 'I' can refer to different speakers in different situations; thus the expression 'wing' can be applied equally to 'a bird's wing' and 'the wing of humility', subject to the condition that identifying which one of them is the intended meaning will depend on context.

Ibn Taymiyyah's account of *majāz* is assumed to have at least one advantage over the account of the adherents of *majāz*, namely the advantage of being relatively objective. There are at least three reasons which make Ibn Taymiyyah's account more objective than its rivals:

i It does not presuppose a chronological priority for one meaning over another.
ii It does not claim that one meaning is more deserving to be the primary meaning of an expression than its other meaning(s).
iii It does not give priority in interpretation to one meaning over another, but assumes that an interpretation that is supported by contextual evidence is the only possible and intended one.

Furthermore, Ibn Taymiyyah does not accept the idea that the use of the so-called *majāz* involves a departure from what the mainstream assume to be *al-aṣl* (the original state or the norm).[136] *Majāz* in Ibn Taymiyyah's view is not a decorative alternative of expressing *ḥaqīqah*, for what is expressed by *majāz* is inexpressible by *ḥaqīqah*. Determining whether to use an unqualified expression or qualified one rests on the communicative situation rather than the speaker's choice; and the relationship between the use of unqualified expressions and the use of qualified ones is integrative rather than substitutive. Also, although he accepts that speech varies in terms of eloquence and ambiguity, he, nevertheless, does not believe that this justifies dividing speech into *majāz* and *ḥaqīqah*.[137]

4.9. IBN TAYMIYYAH'S MODEL OF INTERPRETATION

Compared with the mainstream model examined in the previous chapter, Ibn Taymiyyah's model of interpretation appears to be more straightforward. In what follows I shall sketch out the principles of the mainstream model, and then highlight the differences between the mainstream model and Ibn Taymiyyah's one.

As has already been elucidated, the mainstream model consists of the following principles *(uṣūl)*:

- i The Principle of the Speaker's Disposition to Make his Intention Manifest *(bayān al-mutakallim)*: the speaker tends to make his intention as clear as possible.
- ii The Principle of Truthfulness *(ṣidq al-mutakallim)*: the hearer takes the speaker's utterance as being true.
- iii The Principle of *Iᶜmāl* ('making sense of' expressions): the hearer treats the text as meaningful as possible.
- iv The Principle of Immediacy *(tabādur)*: the hearer takes the interpretation that occurs to the mind first as the intended interpretation.
- v The Principle of *Istiṣḥāb:* the hearer takes the interpretation that is compatible with the base as the intended interpretation.

It is clear that there is a striking similarity between the Principle of Immediacy and the Principle of *Istiṣḥāb*, but there is also, it should be noted, an important difference, which makes the mainstream model and Ibn Taymiyyah's model diverge. Whereas the Principle of Immediacy operates in relation to the whole communicative situation, the Principle of *Istiṣḥāb* operates only by default, that is, in isolation from the actual contexts in the communicative situation.

It is because of this difference that the *Salafīs* appeal to the Principle of Immediacy rather than that of *Istiṣḥāb*, owing to the fact that it harmonises well with their belief that valid interpretations are not obtainable in isolation from communicative situations. Furthermore, the *Salafīs* believe that the Principle of *Istiṣḥāb* is incompatible with the Principle of the Speaker's Disposition to Make his Intention Manifest, which forms with the Principle of Immediacy the cardinal postulates in their model of interpretation. They defend this position in this regard by pointing out that in recovering the signification of an utterance the hearer does not have to move from a literal-base meaning to a non-literal subsidiary or derivative one. In fact, the *Salafīs* believe that the intended meaning strikes the hearer directly by virtue of the Principle of the Speaker's Disposition to Make his Intention Manifest; and the Principle of Immediacy. In other words, the hearer's mind goes directly to the intention of the speaker without the need for mediating meanings, simply because it is the appropriate context, not the context-independent meaning, of the expression which provides the effective guide to the speaker's intention.

Let us now consider the difference between Ibn Taymiyyah's model of interpretation and that of the mainstream in dealing with the example 'I saw a lion delivering an address from the pulpit'.

Let us begin with the mainstream model of interpretation:

- i The hearer takes the word 'lion' in its literal sense (the Principle of *Istiṣḥāb* + literalness base).
- ii The hearer recognises that this meaning is irrelevant (by virtue of a diverting context).
- iii The hearer assumes that the speaker is not telling a lie (the Principle of Truthfulness).
- iv The speaker must, therefore, be intending another meaning since the utterance cannot be without meaning (the Principle of *I*^{c}*māl*).
- v The hearer concludes that the speaker intends 'lion' to be 'a brave man' (guiding context: 'delivering an address from the pulpit'.

Let us now deal with Ibn Taymiyyah's model of interpretation:

- i The hearer assumes that the speaker is interested in making his intention manifest; consequently, he provides him with a sufficient relevant context to display his communicative intention (the Principle of the Speaker's Disposition to Make his Intention Manifest).
- ii Both the speaker and the hearer belong to the same linguistic community and the hearer knows the speaker's habit in the use of language (the presumption of knowing the speaker's habit).
- iii The hearer presumes that the speaker will speak in accordance with his habit (the Principle of the Speaker's Disposition to Make his Intention Manifest).

iv Provided that all the previous conditions are fulfilled, the hearer concludes that the speaker intends 'lion' to be 'a brave man' since this is the first interpretation to strike the hearer's mind (guiding context plus the Principle of Immediacy).

The main difference between the mainstream model and Ibn Taymiyyah's model of interpretation is that the mainstream model presupposes that the hearer tends to form one interpretation as the most likely to represent the speaker's intention and assumes that other interpretations are possible. If the first interpretation, which is usually formed in accordance with *uṣūl*, is ruled out by a diverting context, the hearer will look for other interpretations until a proper one is found. Ibn Taymiyyah's model, on the other hand, presupposes that the hearer goes directly to the contextually relevant interpretation. As a result, the mainstream model can be characterised as indeterminate since it leaves the way open for other possible interpretations whereas Ibn Taymiyyah's model is determinate.

4.9.1. *Taʾwīl* (diverting to non-apparent meaning)

The Arabic word *taʾwīl* literally means *taṣyīr, 'to* make something be something else'[138] and *tarjīᶜ* 'to bring something back'[139] but in Islamic literature, it is used as a technical term to refer to one of the following:

i According to a majority of late traditional Muslim Jurists and legal theorists, *taʾwīl* is the diversion of an expression from *al-iḥtimāl al-rājiḥ* (the preponderant, probable interpretation) to *al-iḥtimāl al-marjūḥ* (the outweighed, improbable interpretation) on the strength of contextual evidence accompanying it.[140]
ii In the common terminology of the commentators of *Qur'ān*, as well as that of the *Salafī* jurists and scholars of *Ḥadīth*, *taʾwīl* is equated with *tafsīr* (exegesis).
iii In the *Qur'ān*ic usage, *taʾwīl* is employed to designate the entity or the referent in the external world to which the expression is referring.[141]

Among these three different senses of *taʾwīl*, it is only the first that concerns us here. *Taʾwīl* in this sense is a kind of interpretation that typically involves a diversion from the apparent *(al-ẓāhir)* meaning of an expression to an ulterior meaning of that expression by virtue of contextual evidence. In PF, the term *al-ẓāhir* belongs to a cluster of terms designed to describe the supposedly different levels of clarity of texts. Muslim legal theorists offer two main different versions of the possible levels of clarity in which the message of the speaker appears to the hearer: the mainstream version and the *Ḥanafī's* version.

According to the mainstream version, the speaker's message can either be determinate or indeterminate. In the latter case, it is typically sensitive to more than one reading. In those instances where there is no room for other interpretations, the meaning (or sometimes the expression itself) is called *naṣṣ* (prominent),[142] which is literally derived from the verb *naṣṣa* meaning 'to raise something and make it manifest' (*rafaᶜa wa-aẓhara*), though 'unequivocal' would be a better translation for this technical term in this context. If the speaker's message, by contrast, is indeterminate, the hearer has to take the first meaning that comes to mind as the most probable intended meaning; and this meaning is usually referred to as *al-ẓāhir* (the apparent). However, it may be the case that none of the possible interpretations is qualified to outweigh the other set of interpretations. This typically happens when the speaker's utterance contains a homonym without there being a guiding context by which one can select one of the meanings over the others. *Taʾwīl* in this case is not applicable because it is only *al-ẓāhir*, according to the mainstream, that can be made liable to *taʾwīl*. For *taʾwīl*, as understood by the mainstream, is a process of switching from discerning an ostensible meaning to the postulation of a less probable meaning on the basis of supporting evidence, but since there is no ostensible meaning in the case of homonyms, by virtue of the fact that all the meanings of a homonym are literal, it follows that none of the meanings can be the apparent meaning. However, since 'apparent meaning' is generally regarded as equivalent to 'literal meaning', we are inclined to accept al-Ghazālī's view that "each process of *taʾwīl* involves a diversion from *ḥaqīqah*-mode to *majāz*-mode".[143]

The *Ḥanafī's* version, on the other hand, compromises four levels of clarity: *ẓāhir*, *naṣṣ*, *mufassar* and *muḥkam*; although it is only the first three that are relevant here. The difference between *ẓāhir* and *naṣṣ* is explained by reference to the distinction between meaning and intention: the term *ẓāhir* is employed to describe the level of clarity of the linguistic meaning while *naṣṣ* is used to describe the level of clarity of the speaker's intention. Viewed from these different perspectives, the same utterance can be regarded as *ẓāhir* and *naṣṣ* at the same time. Consider the following example:

(11) That is because they say:
"Trade is like usury",
But *Allāh* hath permitted trade
And forbidden usury.[144]

The utterance *"wa-aḥalla Allāhu l-bayʿa wa-ḥarrama l-ribā"* (But *Allāh* hath permitted trade and forbidden usury) is considered to be *ẓāhir* because any native speaker of Arabic would understand the linguistic meaning (*al-maʿnā l-lughawī*) of this utterance without calculation (*min ghayri taʾammul*).[145] The same utterance is regarded as *naṣṣ* in view of the fact that the context (i.e., "they say: "Trade is like usury"") indicates that the utterance is intended to state that trade is distinct from usury. Thus, the accessibility of the grammatical structure and the clarity of the lexical meaning of the utterance qualify it to be classified as *ẓāhir;* while the context, which is assumed to make the speaker's intention manifest renders it as *naṣṣ*. It is important to notice that in the *Ḥanafīs'* framework both *ẓāhir* and *naṣṣ* are liable to *taʾwīl*. Therefore, what is understood from the *ẓāhir* in the above *Qur'ānic* verse, that is, the unqualified permission of trade and the unqualified forbidding of usury can in fact be qualified, and, consequently, subjected to *taʾwīl* depending on other contextual indicators that show that some forms of trade were forbidden and some forms of usury were permitted. Equally, what is indicated by the context, that is, the unqualified denial of the similarity between trade and usury, can be laid open to *taʾwīl*.

What distinguishes *mufassar* (lit, uncovered) from *ẓāhir* and *naṣṣ*, however, is its being completely clear and definite, and, consequently, its being unavailable for *taʾwīl*. A very much-quoted example in this context is the word "eighty" in the following verse:

(12) And those who launch
A charge against chaste women,
and produce not four witnesses
(to support their allegations), _
Flog them with eighty stripes;
And reject their evidence
Ever after: for such men
Are wicked transgressors.[146]

There is no way here to go beyond the literal meaning of "eighty" since any attempt to cancel, increase or decrease the number would provoke a contradiction between what the expression conventionally denotes and what the hearer construes, which is considered by the legal theorists to be a violation of one of the conditions of the proper *taʾwīl*, more of which later.

Ḥanafī scholars distinguish between two types of *mufassar*: one whose clarity is due to structure, which has already been illustrated; the other is one whose clarity is due to contextual evidence. In order to illustrate the latter type, let us consider the following example:

(13) *fa-sajada l-malāʾikatu kulluhum ajmaʿūn*
So the angels prostrated themselves,
All of them together.[147]

The word *al-malāʾikatu* (the angels) *per se* can be taken to refer to some, rather than all, of the angels, but since it was followed by the phrase 'all of them', this possibility is ruled out. Yet, without the addition of the word "together" the possibility of *taʾwīl* is still open, for it is not clear yet whether the angels prostrated separately or together; it is only by the existence of the word "together" that the utterance has become determinate.[148]

To sum up what has already been said about the degrees of the clarity of texts, it can be said that while the *Ḥanafīs* hold that both *ẓāhir* and *naṣṣ* are liable to *taʾwīl*, the mainstream believe that *taʾwīl* is applicable to *ẓāhir* only. However, the term *ẓāhir* in the mainstream framework covers both *ẓāhir* and *naṣṣ* in the *Ḥanafī* use of these terms, while the *Ḥanafī* term *mufassar* is an equivalent to *naṣṣ* in the mainstream sense.

4.9.1.1. *The limitations of taʾwīl*

Taʾwīl is one of the most controversial topics in PF as well as in most, if not all, of the domains of the Muslim intellectual pursuit. The legal theorists' controversies over *taʾwīl* can be attributed to differences over the possible range in which *taʾwīl* operates, methodological and terminological canons and, not infrequently, the actual applications of *taʾwīl*.

Before proceeding further, it is worth pointing out that the legal theorists seem to agree that any process of *taʾwīl* should be regarded as a deviation from the norm *(aṣl)*, but they entertain different views concerning the range to which the interpreter can go beyond the apparent meaning. There are at least three different views on this issue. On the assumption that the *Salafī* view is the moderate one,[149] there would be two extreme views – the *Ẓāhirī* view, which is generally known as having an anti-*taʾwīl* attitude, and the mainstream view,[150] which is criticised by the *Salafīs* for making *taʾwīl* on some *Qur'ānic* and *Ḥadīth* texts that should be taken in their apparent meanings. Among the mainstream proper, there are often different positions on various issues, which provokes some arguments and mutual criticisms specially between *Shāfiʿīs* and *Ḥanafīs* where the former criticise the latter for going too far beyond the apparent meaning in their interpretations of a number of texts.[151]

With respect to the *Ẓāhirī* approach, Abū Muḥammad Alī Ibn Ḥazm (the most distinguished advocate of the *Ẓāhirī* school (d. 456/1064)) considers any diversion from the linguistic meaning of an expression *(mafhūmihi fī l-lughah)* as distortion *(taḥrīf)*.[152] In his discussion of *taʾwīl*, Ibn Ḥazm maintains that language is established for *al-tafāhum* (communication) and for making the speaker's intention manifest to the hearer. This can happen only if each expression has a specific meaning; otherwise *bayān* (i. e. the speaker's making of his intention manifest to the hearer[153] (cf. 3.5.1.1)) would never take place. The main contention of the *Ẓāhirī* school is that the intention of the speaker is obtainable in the apparent meaning *(al-maʿnā l-ẓāhir)* of his utterance (and hence the name *ẓāhirī*),[154] and, therefore, the hearer need not make much calculation to recover it. In other words, all the hearer has to do in order to grasp his addresser's intention is to follow the conventions of the language. Thus, extra-linguistic context, according to *Ẓāhirīs*, has almost no role to play in communication. Furthermore, the general intentions (including those of *Sharīʿah* in the case of interpreting the *Qur'ānic* and *Sunnāic* texts) are generally ignored by *Ẓāhirīs* in the process of interpreting a particular text.

As to the mainstream view, *taʾwīl* is assumed to be applicable to any utterance containing an equivocal expression (i.e., *ẓāhir*-expression, according to the non-*Ḥanafīs*, and *ẓāhir*-expression and *naṣṣ*-expression in the *Ḥanafī* sense of these terms) provided that there is a contextual indicator to support the process of *taʾwīl*. It is widely accepted that an act of *taʾwīl* involves a departure from the most immediate interpretation to the hearer's mind, which presupposes the assumption that the speaker is not co-operating sufficiently in communication. This assumption attracts strong criticism from the *Salafī*s on the grounds that it is not consistent with the Principle of the Speaker's Disposition to Make his Intention Manifest,[155] which is regarded by all parties as the primary principle behind any process of successful communication.

Thus, within the mainstream, the *Shāfiᶜīs* distinguish between three types of *taʾwīl*: accessible (*qarīb*), far-fetched (*baᶜīd*) and impossible (*mutaᶜadhdhir*).[156] Although both accessible and far-fetched *taʾwīl* can be acceptable *(sāʾighah)* if they are supported by appropriate contexts, accessible *taʾwīl* is, nevertheless, less in need of contextual evidence to become more preponderant than a far-fetched one. However, there are at least three conditions that have to be met in order for *taʾwīl* to be acceptable; if any of these conditions fail to be fulfilled, *taʾwīl* will be classified as *mutaᶜadhdhir* (impossible). These conditions are

i the expression must be capable of accepting *taʾwīl*, that is, it must be *ẓāhir*-expression or even *naṣṣ*-expression in the *Ḥanafī* sense of the term;
ii the expression must be capable of bearing *taʾwīl;* that is to say, the non-apparent meaning which the interpreter assumes to be the intended meaning must be one of the possible meanings of the expression; and
iii *taʾwīl* should be based on sufficient contextual evidence to make the non-apparent, rather than the apparent, meaning the intended one.[157]

Salafīs accept these three conditions, but differ from the PF mainstream in postulating the possibility that the speaker who conforms to make his intention manifest may prefer to be less forthcoming in co-operating with the hearer putting the onus on him in recovering the intention behind the utterance. The *Salafīs* believe that it is not wise for the speaker to do so,[158] whereas the PF mainstream think that it is possible. Applying this to *Allāh* as a speaker, the *Ashᶜarīs* hold that *Allāh* does what He wishes while the *Muᶜtazilīs* say that it is possible that there is a concealed purpose behind making His speech indeterminate.[159] In a special chapter devoted to elucidating how that the speaker's supposed intention to make the addressee take his utterance in its non-apparent meaning contradicts the intention of exposition and guidance, Ibn al-Qayyim argues that

> Since the goal of *al-khiṭāb* (communication) is to guide the hearer and introduce the speaker's intention into his mind through the utterance [. . .] in the most accessible ways, communication then hinges upon two things: the speaker's making of his intention manifest and the hearer's success in understanding. If the speaker's making of his intention manifest does not take place or it does take place but the

> hearer does not manage to understand, the speaker will not achieve his purpose [. . .]. Therefore, if *Allāh* or His Prophet had not intended his discourse to be taken in its proper and apparent meaning (*ḥaqīqatihi wa-ẓāhirihi*), which the speaker can understand, they would have commanded the addressee to understand his intention through a non-indicative means, or even through what signifies the contrary of his intention.[160]

Moreover, the *Salafīs* and the PF mainstream disagree on the nature of the expression which is liable to *taʾwīl*. As explained earlier, the PF mainstream hold that *taʾwīl* is applicable to *any ẓāhir*-expression, provided that there is a contextual indicator that the apparent meaning is not the meaning intended by the speaker. For the *Salafīs*, this is not necessarily true. They confine *taʾwīl* to those *ẓāhir*-expressions whose signification in a particular context appears, as Ibn al-Qayyim puts it, to be different from its equivalents *(khārijan ʿan naẓāʾirihi). Taʾwīl* is, thus, viewed as an attempt "to return the anomaly to its [normal] equivalents".[161] This 'returning' can be carried out by making use of the knowledge of the speaker's habit, by which one can know what the speaker consistently means by the respective utterance in such an occasion. To put it another way, if the hearer notices that the apparent meaning of the utterance is not in conformity with what the speaker habitually means by such an utterance in such a situation, then he has to interpret it in line with the speaker's own lexicon *(ʿurf al-mukhāṭib)* and 'his consistent habit' *(ʿādatihi al-muṭṭaridah)*.[162] This is the only circumstance, according to the *Salafīs*, in which *taʾwīl* accurately operates. Of the other examples designed to show how the adherents of *taʾwīl* apply it improperly, Ibn al-Qayyim points out that interpreting 'the seeing of *Allāh*' as the seeing of his reward[163] in such texts as "*tarawna rabbakum*" (you will see your Lord), "*tanẓurūna ilā rabbikum*" (you will look at your Lord) and "*ilā rabbihā nāẓirah*" (Looking at their Lord) is invalid because 'the seeing of his reward' does not obtain in any *Qur'ānic* and *Ḥadīth* text in a way which sanctions the use of 'reward' instead of '*Allāh*'.[164]

Ibn Taymiyyah ascribes the misapplication of *taʾwīl* to the emphasis placed on the possible linguistic meanings of the expression instead of the speaker's intention (cf. 4.9). He goes further to say that any *taʾwīl* not intended to disclose the speaker's intention through the proper means and ways by which the speaker's intention is recoverable, means that the interpreter is distorting the speaker's utterance.[165] However, what Ibn Taymiyyah has in mind when he talks about 'the means and ways by which the speaker's intention is recoverable' is not very clear, but we may find some clues as to what he means in Ibn al-Qayyim's explanation of a similar issue. Following the contextual approach to meaning and interpretation, Ibn al-Qayyim stresses that "the speaker expresses his intention through his utterance, and his utterance signifies via its system (or structure)" *(fa-l-mutakallimu dāllun bi-kalāmihi, wa-kalāmuhu dāllun bi-niẓāmihi).* And in order to know whether the speaker intends to make his intention manifest through the apparent meaning of his utterance, the hearer refers to the speaker's habitual use of utterances *(wa-dhālika yu^crafu min ^cādati l-mutakallimi fī alfāẓih).*[166]

But the question that arises here is how can the hearer be certain that the speaker speaks in accordance with his habit? Ibn al-Qayyim develops the following two points to establish this knowledge:

> First, the signification of the expression is founded upon the speaker's habit, which is observed in his words and upon the rationale behind his language in which he habitually speaks. If the hearer knows the meaning of the expression and knows that it is the speaker's habit to use that expression in its meaning, he will then know for certain that that meaning is the speaker's intention. Otherwise no speaker's intention can ever be known, which is impossible.
>
> Second, if the goal of the speaker is to make his utterance understood by the hearer, and the addressee [. . .] knows via the speaker's character and the way he speaks that the speaker wants to make his intention manifest and not to deceive him, the addressee will, given he obtains the knowledge of both the above matters [i.e., he knows the meaning of the expression and knows that it is the speaker's habit to make his intention manifest], be fully certain of the speaker's intention and never to doubt it. If, by contrast, he fails to recover the speaker's intention, it would mean that there is something wrong either with his knowledge of the meaning of the expression or with his knowledge of the speaker's way of speaking, his character and his goal.[167]

Thus, the *Salafīs*' main contention is that if the hearer knows that the speaker is able and willing to make his intention manifest, it would be wise to think that he intends his utterance to be taken in its apparent meaning.

It is essential here to note that by virtue of their neutralisation of the distinction between *waḍ*[c] and use, 'apparent' within the *Salafīs*' framework is usually equated with immediate. This practice, however, is not in agreement with the mainstream framework where being apparent does not necessarily entail being immediate to the mind, for the quality of being apparent is given to the expression by virtue of *waḍ*[c] and the bases, while the quality of being immediate is applicable only in the actual communicative situation. Therefore, one may, according to the mainstream view, veer away from the apparent meaning (i.e., literal meaning) without violating the Principle of Immediacy (cf. 3.5.1.4), which typically happens when a diverting context and a guiding one signal that.

This methodological difference between the *Salafīs* and the mainstream thinkers may well explain why they may agree as to the interpretation of an utterance, but still differ with regard to the methodologies by which this is achieved. Thus, what the former regard as *ta*ʾ*wīl*, the latter consider as literal interpretation.

NOTES

1 See Lewis, Pellat and Schacht, *Encyclopaedia of Islam*, 951–955; al-Ziriklī, *al-A*[c]*lām . . ., 1/144.*
2 See Serajul Haque, *Imām Ibn Taimīya . . .*, p. 164.
3 Majid, "Ibn Taymiyya . . .", p. 224.
4 Serajul Haque, *Imām Ibn Taimīya . . .*, pp. 164–165.
5 According to Ibn Taymiyyah, what is called *basā*ʾ*iṭ* (atoms) which are assumed to be unqualified components of *al-anwā*[c] (the species) has no reality (Ibn Taymiyyah, *al-Imān*, p. 102). They are in fact merely postulated abstract objects. This leads him to question the validity of the distinction between what is known in the traditional logic as *taṣawwur* (conceptualisation) which he explains as "the conceptualisation of a simple object which is free from any qualification" (*Ibid.*, pp. 101–102) and *taṣdīq* (propositional apprehension) which can roughly be explained as the cognition of a proposition, arguing that *taṣawwur* in this sense does not take place. (*Ibid.*, p. 102).
6 *Ibid.*, p. 101.
7 Ibn Taymiyyah's arguments aim at refuting Greek philosophy and its Islamic versions particularly those of al-Fārābī and Ibn Sīnā (Avicenna).
8 *Ibid.*, p. 102.
9 To remind the reader of the difference between universals and particulars, it might be loosely said that the term 'universal' is used to refer to a class of people, entities or qualities. The individuals subsumed under that class are referred to as its 'particulars'.
10 According to Muslim philosophers, the natural universal "is distinguished from two other types of universals, the mental universal *(al-kullī al-*[c]*aqlī)*,

which is nature insofar as it is a universal, that is, nature conditioned by universality *(bi-sharṭ lā-shayʾ)*, and the logical universal (*al-kullī al-manṭiqī)*, which is the concept of universality itself. Heer, "al-Jāmī's Treatise on Existence", p. 227; see Ibn Taymiyyah, *Kitāb al-Ṣafdiyyah*, 1/298.

11 Ibn Taymiyyah, *al-Radd*, 1/159; see also, Ibn Taymiyyah, *Darʾ*. . ., 1/286–295; Ibn Taymiyyah, *Bayān Talbīs al-Jahmiyyah* . . ., 1/15–16.

12 Ibn Taymiyyah, *al-Radd*, 1/191.

13 *Ibid.*, 1/147.

14 For Katz's conceptual position see Katz, Linguistic Philosophy . . . .

15 Katz, *Language* . . ., p. 3.

16 *Ibid.*, p. 22.

17 *Ibid.*, p. 181

18 Ibn Taymiyyah, *al-Radd*, 1/164. For a discussion of this idea in the Philosophy of Ikhwān al-Ṣafāʾ, see Netton, *Muslim Neoplatonists* . . ., p. 12.

19 Ibn Taymiyyah, *al-Radd*, 1/174–175.

20 Ibn Taymiyyah, *Fatāwā*, 9/49, 58, 60.77.

21 *Ibid.*, 9/62.

22 *Ibid.*, 9/78.

23 "Latin translations attributed to Avicenna [Ibn Sīnā] the notion that existence is an accident to essence". Runes, *Dictionary of Philosophy*, p. 31 (Avicenna).

24 Ibn Taymiyyah, *al-Radd*, 1/160. For more discussion of this distinction, see Netton, *Allāh Transcendent* . . ., pp. 109–114.

25 Ibn Taymiyyah, *Fatāwā*, 9/97–101; Ibn Taymiyyah, *al-Radd*, 1/98.

26 Ibn Taymiyyah, *Fatāwā*, 9/97–98.

27 *Ibid.*, 9/99.

28 See al-Mawṣilī, 2/29.

29 It should be noted that the term *Ḥanbalī* is not employed here in its strict sense, since Ibn Taymiyyah is widely considered to be *mujtahid muṭlaq* (roughly independent jurist) rather than *Ḥanbalī*. However, this term is remarkably suggestive in this context for readers who are aware of

(i) the *Ḥanbalīs*' denial of *al-Ashʿarīs*' notion of *al-Kalām al-nafsī* (mental speech);

(ii) Ibn Ḥanbal's *miḥnah* (inquisition) during al-Maʾmūn's rule because of his strong objection to the *Muʿtazilite* doctrine of the createdness of the *Qur'ān;*

(iii) the *Ḥanbalī* position on *Allāh*'s attribute of speech; and

(iv) Ibn Taymiyyah' strong adherence to all these *Ḥanbalī* positions.

30 Ibn Taymiyyah, *Fatāwā*, 9/103.

31 Netton, A Popular Dictionary of Islam, p. 185 (mutwātir).

32 Ibn Taymiyyah, *Fatāwā*, 9/103.

33 Ibn Taymiyyah, *al-Radd*, 1/113, 184–185.

34 He treats definitions in the same way he treats names, for " a definition is nothing but a name, two, or three names". *Ibid.*, 1/66.

35 *Ibid.*, 1/110–114.

36 Ibn Taymiyyah, *al-Radd*, 1/113–114. The same argument had been used by al-Rāzī. See al-Rāzī, 1/67.

37 Ibn Taymiyyah, *al-Radd*, 1/114.
38 *Ibid.*, 1/133.
39 Ibn Taymiyyah, *Fatāwā*, 9/51, 58–67.
40 Ibn Taymiyyah, *al-Radd*, 1/137.
41 See *ibid.*, 1/133.
42 Ibn Taymiyyah, *al-Radd*, 1/144.
43 *Ibid.*, 1/142–150.
44 See *ibid.*, 1/150.
45 *Ibid.*, 1/73. He traces this view back to *al-nuẓẓār* (Muslim speculative theologians) from different schools, attacking the Aristotelian view that the purpose of definition is "to have the definiendum conceptualised, and to identify its sense" *(taṣawwur al-maḥdūd wa-ta^crīf ḥaqīqatih). Ibid.*, 1/73–77.
46 See *ibid.*, 1/114.
47 See *ibid.*
48 Unlike *Salafīs* who confine meaningfulness to the full utterances, the adherents of *majāz* claim that both single expressions and full utterances can be characterised as meaningful. For single expressions, 'meaningful' is explained by Abū l-Ḥusayn al-Baṣrī al-Mu^ctazilī (one of the distinguished figures of the adherents of *majāz* died 436/1044) as being 'established for' (or assigned to) a particular meaning and, consequently, potentially used to convey this meaning. With respect to utterances, Abū l-Ḥusayn employs the term 'meaningful' to refer exclusively to an utterance involving a predicative relation.
49 Ibn Taymiyyah, *Fatāwā*, 20/412.
50 Al-Mawṣilī, 2/57.
51 *Ibid.*, 2/58.
52 Ibn Taymiyyah, *Fatāwā*, 20/431.
53 Al-Mawṣilī, 2/63.
54 The term *salafiyyah* in this context is employed in a very restricted sense where it refers solely to Ibn Taymiyyah, Ibn al-Qayyim and their followers in this contextual theory.
55 *Ibid.*, 2/7.
56 *Ibid.*, 2/52.
57 *Ibid.*, 2/59
58 See al-Sharīf al-Jurjānī, *al-Ta^crīfāt*, 116; al-Kafawī, *al-Kulliyāt*, 4/251.
59 Al-Taftāzānī, *Ḥāshiyat al-Talwīḥ*, 1/298.
60 Al-Sharīf al-Jurjānī, *al-Ta^crīfāt*, p. 104.
61 Al-Mawṣilī, 2/8.
62 Wunderlich, *Foundations of Linguistics*, p. 271; Searle, *Speech Acts . . .*, p. 43f.
63 Wunderlich, *op. cit.*, p. 272.
64 Ibn Taymiyyah, *al-Imān*, p. 87; al-Mawṣilī, 2/70.
65 Ibn Taymiyyah, *al-Imān*, pp. 87–88; al-Mawṣilī, 2/70.
66 Al-Mawṣilī, 2/70.
67 *Ibid.*
68 Bosch, "Context Dependence and Metaphor", p. 165.
69 Katz, *Semantic Theory*, p. 16.
70 Levinson, *Pragmatics*, p. 20.

71 Katz, *Semantic Theory*, pp. 7–8.
72 This definition is found in Ibn Ḥazm, *al-Iḥkām* . . . , 1/41.
73 Al-Mawṣilī, 2/68. Ibn al-Qayyim remarks that it is common to devote *dilālah (bi-kasri l-dāl)* to the former sense and *dalālah (bi-fatḥi l-dāl)* to the latter (2/68).
74 Ibn Taymiyyah, *Fatāwā*, 20/413.
75 *Ibid.*, 20/414–415.
76 *Ibid.*, 20/413.
77 Sperber and Wilson, "Irony and the Use-Mention Distinction", pp. 550–564, pp. 551–552.
78 Searle, "Metaphor", pp. 520–524.
79 Davidson, "What Metaphors Mean", p. 496.
80 *Ibid.*, p. 502.
81 For a discussion of the history of the terms *ḥaqīqah* and *majāz* in Islamic and Arabic literature, see the following:
- Jonn Wansbrough, *Quranic* Studies (Oxford University Press, 1977).
- Ella Almagor, "The Early Meaning of *Majāz* and the Nature of Abū ᶜUbayda's Exegesis", Studia Orientalia Memoriae D.H.Baneth Dedicata (Jerusalem: Magnes, 1979), pp. 307–326.
- Heinrichs, "On the Genesis of the *Ḥaqīqa* and *Majāz* Dichotomy", pp. 111–140.
- Gully, *Grammar* . . . .

82 Al-Baṣrī, 1/11. The same definition is adopted by some of his successors, such as al-Rāzī who adopts the definition without any alteration; al-Qarāfī who substitutes "that which is used" with "the expression used" and uses the word *ᶜurf* (convention) instead of *iṣṭilāḥ* (code) which can also be translated in this context by language or terminology, and al-Sharīf al-Jurjānī with the replacement of "that which is used" with "the word used". See: al-Rāzī, 1/112; al-Qarāfī, *Sharḥ Tanqīḥ*, pp. 42–43; al-Sharīf al-Jurjānī, *al-Taᶜrīfāt*, p. 48 *(al-ḥaqīqah)*.
83 See Lyons, *Semantics*, 2/551–552; Lyons, *Language and Linguistics* . . . , p. 147.
84 See al-Āmidī (1983), 1/24–25.
85 Al-Suyūṭī, *al-Muzhir* . . . , 1/369; see also, al-Samarqandī, 1/208.
86 Al-Ghazālī, *Kitāb Miḥakk al-Naẓar* . . . , p. 21.
87 See al-Ghazālī, *Miᶜyār* . . . , p. 56.
88 Both polysemy and metaphor are Greek terms, polysemy is composed of two parts: poly (of many) and semy (meaning). See Ali, *Waṣf* . . . , p. 346. Metaphor is, however, "a derivative of the Greek metapherein, to 'transfer'". Weiss, *The Search*, p. 141. Consequently, polysemy and metaphor are only the technical, but not the literal, equivalents of *naql* and *istiᶜārah* respectively. In fact, the literal meaning of metaphor qualifies it to be a good literal, but not technical, counterpart for *naql* (transferring).
89 Emphasising that homonyms are *ḥaqīqah*-expressions, al-Baṣrī employs the term *al-ḥaqīqah al-mushtarakah* (homonymous *ḥaqīqah*-expression) for homonyms versus *al-ḥaqīqah al-mufradah* (univocal *ḥaqīqah*-expression). See al-Baṣrī, 1/16–17.
90 See *ibid.*, 1/11–12.

91 Al-Mawṣilī, 2/21.
92 See al-Baṣrī, 1/23–24; al-Rāzī, 1/148–149; Ibn Taymiyyah, *Fatāwā*, 20/405–406; al-Mawṣilī, 2/18.
93 Al-Mawṣilī, 2/6.
94 See the first of the arguments developed in favour of the distinction between *ḥaqīqah* and *majāz* (the previous section).
95 Ibn Taymiyyah, *al-Imān*, pp. 109–110.
96 *Ibid., p.* 110.
97 Ibn Taymiyyah, *Fatāwā*, 20/436–437, 449.
98 *Ibid.*, 20/449–450.
99 *Ibid.*, 20/436.
100 See *ibid.*, 20/437. Note that Ibn Taymiyyah's example has been altered to make his idea clear.
101 See al-Mawṣilī, 2/68.
102 See *ibid.*, 2/7.
103 The other constituent seems to be *waḍ*ᶜ.
104 See *ibid.*, 2/8.
105 See *ibid.*, 2/68.
106 See *Ibid.*, 2/41.
107 *Ibid.*
108 See Ibn Taymiyyah, *al-Imān*, pp. 103–104.
109 *Ibid.*, p. 104.
110 Lyons, Semantics, 1/140.
111 Ibn Taymiyyah, *Fatāwā*, 20/450.
112 *Ibid.*, 20/446, 450, 459.
113 Al-Qarāfī, *Sharḥ Tanqīḥ*, pp. 30–31.
114 Al-Mawṣilī, 2/22–23.
115 See Ibn Taymiyyah's quotation of the debate between an opponent and a proponent of *majāz*. Ibn Taymiyyah, *Fatāwā*, 20/490–491.
116 *Ibid.*
117 See Ibn Taymiyyah, *al-Imān*, pp. 104–105.
118 Ali's Translation of THE HOLY QURᵓĀN, 32/21.
119 *Ibid.*, 65/9.
120 *Ibid.*, 44/56.
121 *Ibid.*, 78/24–25.
122 Al-Jawharī, *al-Ṣiḥāḥ . . . , (baḥr).*
123 See al-Qarāfī, *Sharḥ Tanqīḥ*, pp. 38–40.
124 Ali's Translation of THE HOLY QURᵓĀN, 5/55, 27/3, 31/4.
125 Ibn Taymiyyah, *Fatāwā*, 20/429.
126 Ali's Translation of THE HOLY QURᵓĀN, 12/4.
127 *Ibid.*, 73/15–16.
128 *Ibid.*, 24/63.
129 Ibn Taymiyyah, *Fatāwā*, 20/427–428.
130 *Ibid.*, 20/430–431.
131 *Ibid.*, 20/430.
132 Ali's Translation of THE HOLY QURᵓĀN, 17/23–24.
133 *Ibid.*, 15/88.
134 *Ibid.*, 6/38.
135 Al-Mawṣilī, 2/20–21, 28–29.

136 See Ibn Taymiyyah, *Fatāwā*, 20/462.
137 See *ibid.*, 20/462–463.
138 Al-Mawṣilī, 1/10.
139 Al-Sharīf al-Jurjānī, *al-Ta^{c}rīfāt*, p. 28 (*al-taʾwīl*).
140 For more definitions of *taʾwīl* in this sense, see al-Ghazālī, *al-Mustaṣfā*, 1/387.
141 See Ibn Taymiyyah, *Fatāwā*, 3/55–57, 5/35–36, *idem, Darʾ*. . . , 1/14; al-Mawṣilī, 1/11–14.
142 In addition to this sense, the term *naṣṣ* is very often used to refer to what is usually translated as text (e.g., *naṣṣ qurʾānī* (Qur'ānic text)).
143 Al-Ghazālī, *al-Mustaṣfā*, 1/387.
144 Ali's Translation of THE HOLY QURʾĀN, 2/275.
145 Al-Samarqandī, 1/505.
146 Ali's Translation of THE HOLY QURʾĀN, 24/4.
147 *Ibid.*, 15/30.
148 See al-Sarakhsī, *Uṣūl al- Sarakhsī*, 1/163–165; Ibn al-Malik, p. 353.
149 This assumption is based on purely linguistic and communicative considerations.
150 See note (1) p. 9.
151 For the *Shāfi^{c}īs'* arguments, see al-Ghazālī, *al-Mustaṣfā*, 1/389–401. For the *Ḥanafīs'* arguments, see al-Anṣārī, 2/22–32.
152 Ibn Ḥazm, *al-Iḥkām* . . . , 3/304.
153 Al-Sharīf al-Jurjānī, *al-Ta^{c}rīfāt*, p. 26 (*bayān*).
154 It is important here to notice that the derivational relationship between *ẓāhir* (apparent) and *Ẓāhiriyyah* (the name of the school) is suggestive.
155 See Ibn Taymiyyah, *Fatāwā*, 6/361–362.
156 Ibn al-Ḥājib, 2/69; al-Anṣārī, 2/22.
157 See Zaydān, *al-Wajīz* . . ., p. 341; al-Darīnī, *al-Manāhij* . . ., 1/204–220; Weiss, *The Search*, p. 477.
158 See al-Mawṣilī, 1/55–57.
159 See; al-Rāzī, 1/465–466.
160 Al-Mawṣilī, 1/50.
161 *Ibid.*, 1/68.
162 *Ibid.*
163 In Islamic theology, some Muslim sects, noticeably the Mu^{c}tazilah and Ibāḍiyyah, strongly deny the seeing of *Allāh* in the hereafter, thus appealing to the *taʾwīl* of the *Qur'ānic* and *Ḥadīthic* texts whose apparent meanings refer to that possibility.
164 See *ibid.*, 1/68–69.
165 Ibn Taymiyyah, *Darʾ* . . ., 1/12.
166 Al-Mawṣilī, 1/120.
167 *Ibid.*, 1/120.

Chapter Five

Ways of signification

5.1. INTRODUCTION

'Signification' is meant to be a rough translation of the Arabic term *dalālah*, which is inherently ambiguous. The wide-ranging application of this term in different domains of the Arabic intellectual tradition contributes considerably to its looseness. There are at least three distinct meanings assigned to *dalālah:* signification, implication and demonstration. It is only the first two meanings that concern us here, since they are the meanings that *dalālah* is intended to cover when we deal with what is known as *ṭuruq al-dalālah* (ways of signification). It is important to highlight that the sense of the English word 'signification' has been so widened here to incorporate the sense of 'implication', which is not usually recognised as a standard meaning for 'signification' in the current use of the word, as well as one of its standard meanings, namely 'the act of signifying (meaning)'.

Muslim legal theorists discuss two different models of significational classification: the first is a text-based categorisation; the other represents a semiotic viewpoint adopted from the traditional Arab philosophers. Since we are interested in the pragmatic thinking and the textual analysis in the works of the legal theorists, the former model will be given most of the space allocated to this chapter; the latter will only briefly be discussed.

Signification is commonly defined as "the fact of something being in a state where the cognition of it necessarily implies the cognition of something else" *(kawnu l-shayʾi bi-ḥālatin yalzamu mina l-ʿilmi bi-hi l-ʿilmu bi-shayʾin ākhar).*[1] The word *ʿilm* in this definition is frequently regarded as synonymous with *idrāk* (cognition), which covers both *taṣawwur* (conceptualisation or non-propositional apprehension) and *taṣdīq* (judgement or propositional apprehension). Al-Tahānawī mentions four possibilities in which the cognition of a signifier necessarily implies the cognition of the signified associated with it:

I the conceptualisation of a signifier necessarily implies the conceptualisation of a signified *(an yalzama min taṣawwuri l-dālli taṣawwuru l-madlūl)*, e.g., the signifier 'apple' necessarily implies the signified 'apple', i.e., the particular fruit;

II the propositional apprehension of a signifier necessarily implies the propositional apprehension of a signified *(an yalzama mina l-taṣdīqi bi-l-dālli l-taṣdīqu bi-l-madlūl)*, e.g., the signifier 'the apples are red' necessarily implies the signified 'the apples are red', i.e., the proposition of this statement;

III the conceptualisation of a signifier necessarily implies the propositional apprehension of a signified *(an yalzama min taṣawwuri l-dālli l-taṣdīqu bi-l-madlūl)*, e.g., the signifier *aḥ aḥ* (i.e., coughing) in some circumstances necessarily implies that the utterer has a chest problem; and

IV the converse of (III).[2] That is to say, the propositional apprehension of a signifier necessarily implies the conceptualisation of a signified. Examples of this possibility are hard to find, specially if al-Tahānawī means by *taṣdīq* the apprehension of a statement consisting of subject and predicate. However, he may mean the apprehension of idioms where a single concept is derived from a construction, e.g., *jabān al-kalb* (having a coward dog) means *karīm* (generous).

Since conceptualisation is thought to be a precondition for propositional apprehension, (I) would be the most frequent process of signification as it operates in all the above possibilities.

5.2. THE SEMIOTIC CLASSIFICATION OF SIGNIFICATION

It may be helpful to begin this section with highlighting the fact that in traditional Arabic literature, there is a general tendency among philosophers, the legal theorists and linguists to talk about the process of signification instead of talking about the 'sign' itself, as is the case in modern semiotics and linguistics. This tendency would be appreciated if it is seen as part of a more general and consistent approach to the study of communication from the standpoint of communicative processes rather than from the standpoint of the objects and participants proper. To take an example, while the legal theorists devote a large space of their work to such topics as *waḍᶜ*, use, interpretation and signification, which are held to be the components of the communicative process, they pay comparatively little attention to the establisher, user, interpreter and sign. The reason behind this procedure seems to relate to the fact that the legal theorists see language as a system of significations rather than a system of signs, as it is seen by Ferdinand de Saussure and his followers in modern linguistics. The difference between these two positions has to do with the fact that Ferdinand de Saussure views language as an abstract system of signs, and assigns the realisations of these signs to a different domain, which he calls *parole*,[3] whereas the legal theorists see language as a complex system pertaining partially to the primordial *waḍ*^{c} (including general and special conventional *waḍ*^{c}) and partially to the actual processes of use. Muslim thinkers seem to have found 'signification' more suitable than 'sign' to incorporate such elements as intention, non-existence and rationality, thus preferring to say intentional, non-existential, or rational signification than to 'say intentional, non-existential, or rational sign.

Muslim scholars distinguish two types of signification: verbal *(dalālah lafẓiyyah)* and non-verbal signification *(dalālah ghayr lafẓiyyah)*. Each type is subdivided into further types: verbal signification is classified into *waḍ*^{c}-based *(waḍ*^{c}*iyyah)*, rational *(*^{c}*aqliyyah)* and natural *(ṭabī*^{c}*iyyah)* types. Non-verbal signification, on the other hand, is classified into *waḍ*^{c}-based and rational types. For the linguists and legal theorists *waḍ*^{c}-based verbal signification (or linguistic signification) is the most important type of signification. As mentioned earlier, a distinction is commonly made between three different types of this kind of signification: 'equivalence-signification' *(dalālat muṭābaqah)*, 'incorporational signification' *(dalālat taḍammun)* and 'implicational signification' *(dalālat iltizām)* (cf. figure 5.1).[4]

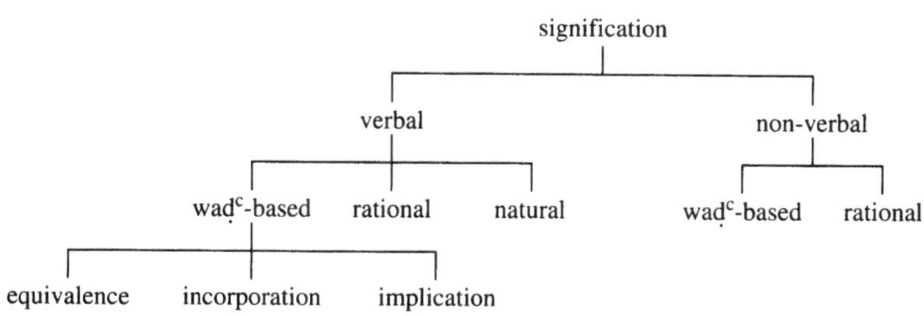

Figure 5.1 *The majority classification of signification*

Although this is the common classification of signification, it is, nevertheless, not the only one. Al-Āmidī and Ibn al-Ḥājib, for example, distinguish between verbal and non-verbal signification and divide the former into 'equivalence' and 'incorporational', while treating 'implicational' signification as a non-verbal category (cf. figure (5.2).[5]

Let us now sketch out what is meant by these types of signification:

I Verbal signification is any type of signification derived from a sound whether it is linguistic or not. Therefore, it applies to the production of any non-linguistic sound indicating a particular state of affair (e.g., screaming) as well as the utterance of any linguistically meaningful element.

II Rational signification is a kind of signification involving an intrinsic relationship *(ᶜalāqah dhātiyyah)* between a signifier and a signified. 'Intrinsic relationship' refers to that kind of relationship by virtue of which the existence of a signifier necessarily implies the existence of a signified, without the need to invoke external coding. As is clear from figure (5.1), rational signification can be verbal, or non-verbal. An example of the former is the relationship between the speaker's production of a particular sound and his existence or his being alive; an example of the latter is the causal relationship between smoke and fire.

III Natural signification is a kind of signification involving a natural relationship by virtue of which the mind switches from a signifier to a signified. The term 'natural' in Arabic is imprecise and misleading. One consequence of this is that there is a clear overlap between the 'extension' of this kind of signification and rational signification. One way of drawing the line between these two kinds of signification is to confine natural signification to that resulting from the sounds created by animals, or instinctively produced by human beings, indicating a particular psychological

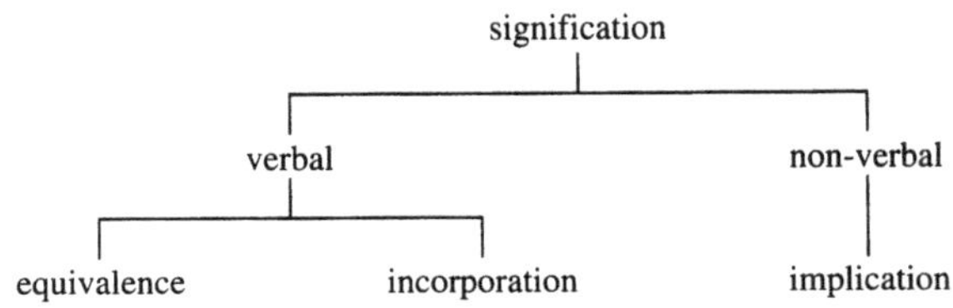

Figure 5.2 *al-Āmidī and Ibn al-Ḥājib's classification of signification*

> state or temper. Interpreting natural signification in this narrow sense would justify and explain why it is restricted to verbal signification and not subsumed under the non-verbal type in the above majority model (cf. figure 5.1). Those who adopt this narrow interpretation of natural signification say that natural signifiers (which are called 'symptoms' *(^{c}awāriḍ))* are part of the psychological state of the utterer. Thus, the cry of pain, for example, is believed to form one operator in a complex psychological process. The reason why it is called 'natural' relates to the fact that it occurs instinctively.[6]

There are others, however, who extend natural signification to cover cases such as redness as an indication of being shy, and yellowness as an indication of being in fear. The direct outcome of this procedure is to render natural signification able to accommodate both verbal and non-verbal signification, thus adding a third subdivision to the two already subsumed under the non-verbal type, namely *waḍ*^{c}-based and rational signification. And this is exactly what Ḥasan al-Harawī does in his commentary on al-Jurjānī.[7] Another outcome is to undermine to some extent the distinction between verbal and non-verbal signification, since all kinds of signification, whether *waḍ*^{c}-based, rational or natural, can be verbal or non-verbal (cf. figure 5.3).

Thus, the distinction between rational and natural signification does not seem to be very well-founded, since it is very hard to see any real difference between redness as a sign of being shy, which is seen as a natural signifier and smoke as a sign of fire, which is viewed as a rational signifier. Al-Tahānawī's explanation of this is that a particular signification could be seen as natural, rational or even *waḍ*^{c}-based depending on the viewpoint under consideration.[8]

IV *Waḍ*^{c}-based signification: '*waḍ*^{c}-based' can 'extensionally' be taken to mean conventional, for all that which is *waḍ*^{c}-based is

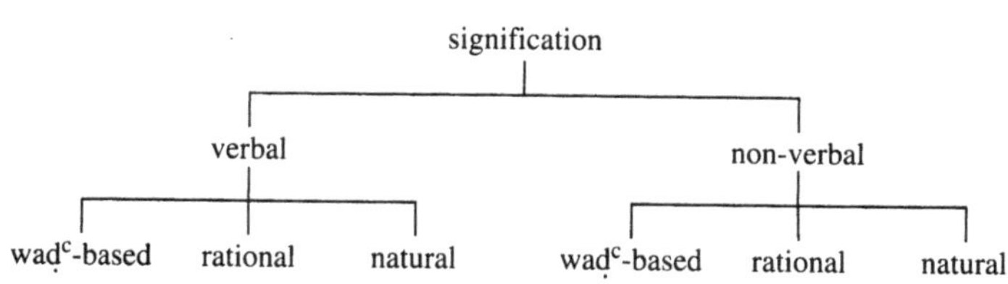

Figure 5.3 *al-Harawī's classification of signification*

> in fact conventional. However, there is a respected tradition in medieval Arabic literature which sanctions the use of the neutral term '*waḍ*ᶜ-based' *(waḍᶜiyyah)*, rather than conventional *(iṣṭilāḥiyyah* or *muwāḍaᶜiyyah)*, to avoid the controversy concerning whether language is invented by *Allāh* or set up by people, as well as the controversy concerning the way in which it is set up for those who say that language is conventionally established.

As is clear from figures (5.1) and (5.3), *waḍ*ᶜ-based signification can be verbal or non-verbal. In PF, there is nothing to say about the latter type, apart from emphasising the fact that it is based on a *waḍ*ᶜ-based, rather than intrinsic or natural, relationship, and offering some examples: hand gestures to tell numbers,[9] sunset as a sign for the time for *al-maghrib* prayer, and the use of *dhirā*ᶜ (lit, arm)[10] for a given measurement.[11] As for the former type, it will be taken up in the next section.

5.2.1. *Waḍ*ᶜ-based verbal signification

'*Waḍ*ᶜ-based verbal signification' is the most important type of signification from both the communicative and linguistic points of view. It is the type which is usually meant when the word 'signification' is unqualifiedly used.[12] Muslim thinkers offer at least two common definitions of this kind of signification. According to the first, "signification is the ability of an expression to be meaningful when it is produced" *(kawnu l-lafẓi bi-ḥaythu idhā uṭliqa dall)*. According to the second, "signification is the hearer's understanding of the exact meaning, or the entailment or the implication of the exact meaning, of an expression from the speaker's utterance" *(fahmu l-sāmiᶜi min kalāmi l-mutakallimi kamāla l-musammā aw juzʾahu aw lāzimah)*.[13]

If we are to make comparison between these two definitions, which are traced back to Ibn Sīnā, and are widely quoted in PF, we will notice that the former emphasises the potential ability of a sign to be meaningful and interpretable without invoking any interpersonal, social or contextual element, whereas the latter equates signification with interpretation, rendering signification as process made by the hearer instead of seeing it as a quality of the expression itself. The advocates of the latter definition argue that judging whether an expression signifies something depends on whether something is understood from it: i.e., an expression can be said to signify something if and only if speakers understand something from it. This demonstrates, the argument continues, that the connection between the signification of an expression and the understanding of it is similar to the connection between names and their nominata, thus, signification can be rendered as a name for understanding. The advocates of the former definition reject this argument on the grounds that signification and understanding are two different things, since the former is a quality of the expression while the latter is an attribute of the hearer.[14]

> Moreover, signification is an established relationship *(ᶜalāqah makhṣūṣah)* between expression and meaning. It is in effect a quality which makes an expression meaningful. This being so, it is possible to see the signification of an expression as a cause for the understanding of it. And, since the same thing cannot be the cause and the effect at the same time, it follows that signification is something different from the understanding of a meaning from an expression and consequently cannot be used as a label for it".[15]

The first part of the above criticism applies also to Ibn Ḥazm who defines signification as "the action of the signifying agent" (*fiᶜl al-dāll*),[16] thus assigning signification to the speaker instead of the expression. It is worth mentioning, however, that although Ibn al-Qayyim applies 'signification' to both the speaker's action (the use of the utterance) and the hearer's action (the hearer's understanding of the meaning of the utterance),[17] he, nevertheless, is not liable to the above criticism. The reason is due to the fact that Ibn al-Qayyim's position is consistent with his *Salafite* contextual framework within which signification is anchored to the actual use of the language in communicative situations, which requires the existence of a speaker and hearer. As was explained in the previous chapter, the *Salafīs* always insist on the participants and context as indispensable elements in any communicative process. The PF mainstream, on the other hand, distinguish between 'signification' and other processes which operate in communication: while the participants and context are essential elements for use and interpretation, signification may operate in isolation, since [*waḍᶜ*-based] signification, as they say, is "chronologically prior to use" *(mutaqaddimatun ᶜalā l-istiᶜmāl)*.[18] Accordingly, *waḍᶜ*-based verbal signification in the mainstream sense is the result of the interaction between three elements only:

i expression;
ii meaning; and
iii *waḍ*ᶜ (the assignment of a meaning to an expression).[19]

The legal theorists often employ *dalīl* (sign) to refer to a meaningful expression which, in reality, is the product of the assignment of a meaning to an expression. And in order to maintain consistency and derivational symmetry in their terminology, they tend to use *dāll* (signifier) and *madlūl* (signified), which share with *dalīl* (sign) and *dalālah* (signification) the same derivational root, in preference to *lafẓ* (expression) and *ma*ᶜ*nā* (meaning).

Since the language comprises elements pertaining to use as well as *waḍ*ᶜ-based material, *waḍ*ᶜ-based signification constitutes only part of linguistic meanings; the other part being the inferences drawn from communicative situations. Therefore, sentences which represent the *waḍ*ᶜ-based aspect of the language on the syntactic level do not have to preserve their predetermined established meanings when they are actualised in real communicative situations. Thus, as ᶜAlī al-Subkī (d. 756/1355) and Tāj al-Dīn b.ᶜAlī b. al-Subkī (d. 771/1369) put it, although establishing a particular sign means making it potentially capable of signalling its meaning when it is actually used by the speaker in the primordially determined way, what is actually informative in reality *(al-mufīdu fī l-ḥaqīqah)* is the speaker. The expression is nothing but the means by which the speaker can inform.[20] Accordingly, in order for the utterance *qāma l-nās* (the people stood up) to be meaningful, three conditions have to be met:

i the utterance is not contradicted by a preceding one *(an lā yabtadi*ᵓ*ahu bi-mā yukhālifuh)*;
ii the utterance is not contradicted by a following one *(an lā yakhtimahu bi-mā yukhālifuh)*; and
iii the utterance is intentionally produced *(an yakūna ṣādiran* ᶜ*an qaṣd)*.[21]

One can, therefore, say that the meaning of an utterance is not determined by the *waḍ*ᶜ-based signification of that utterance alone, since non-*waḍ*ᶜ-based components such as the context, are ultimately the determining factor for recovering the intention of the speaker. However, there is disagreement among Muslim thinkers as to whether or not signification can operate without intention. Generally speaking, linguists tend to make intention as a necessary condition for signification, since "signification, in their view, is the understanding of intention, not meaning in its unqualified sense",[22] (cf. the distinction between meaning and intention 1.3.1). Logicians, on the other hand, believe that signification is "the understanding of meaning whether it is intended by the speaker or not".[23] As for the legal theorists, although it is very difficult to make generalisations,[24] one may be tempted to say that the *Salafīs* strongly deny that signification is obtainable in isolation of a particular communicative situation, while most scholars hold that there are some meanings which can be abstracted from actual utterances and identified as *waḍ*ᶜ-based. There is no clear-cut view about what kind of meaning can be characterised as *waḍ*ᶜ-based. Some believe that it is the meaning of single words,[25] but this would involve what is called 'individual *waḍ*ᶜ' only and would fall short of accommodating 'subsumptive *waḍ*ᶜ' on the syntactic level (cf. 2.2.1). Furthermore, Muslim legal theorists entertain different views as to whether *majāz*-meaning is based on *waḍ*ᶜ or use or is partially related to *waḍ*ᶜ and partially to use. Those who adopt the latter view say that *majāz* is an outcome of the interaction between 'subsumptive *waḍ*ᶜ' and use, thus emphasising that an expression taken before use and after *waḍ*ᶜ cannot be characterised as *ḥaqīqah* or *majāz (al-lafẓu qabla l-istiᶜmāl baᶜda l-waḍᶜ lā yusammā bi-wāḥidin minhumā)*.[26] As indicated in the previous chapter, this view is criticised by the *Salafīs* (cf. 4.8.2).

5.2.1.1. Types of waḍᶜ*-based verbal signification*

Following Muslim logicians, legal theorists distinguish between three types of signification: 'equivalence-signification' *(dalālat muṭābaqah)*, 'incorporational signification' *(dalālat taḍammun)* and 'implicational signification' *(dalālat iltizām)*.[27] If the expression *rajul* (man), for example, is used to refer to an 'adult human male', the expression is said to be used to signify its equivalent meaning, since this is the meaning to which the expression is assigned. In addition to this meaning, the legal theorists say that the word *rajul* entails each one of the following features: 'adult' 'male' and 'human'. Drawing inferences this way is commonly referred to as 'incorporational signification', which is widely seen as a relationship between the specific and the general, where the specific word incorporates *(tataḍamman)* the general one. In PF, one can find some logical rules relating to this type of signification. The following are some of these:

a) the assertion of the specific necessarily entails the assertion of the general,[28] so, (1) entails (2), (3) and (4):

   (1) there is a man in the house.
   (2) there is an adult in the house.
   (3) there is a male in the house.
   (4) there is a human in the house.

b) the negation of the general necessarily entails the negation of the specific,[29] so each one of (5), (6) and (7) entails (8).

   (5) there is no adult in the house
   (6) there is no male in the house.
   (7) there is no human in the house.
   (8) there is no man in the house.

As will be explained later, this particular rule (and may be the following one too) does not seem to lend itself to the definition of incorporational signification. It is one of what I will call inclusional signification (cf. 5.2.1.2).

c) the assertion of the general does not necessarily entail the assertion of the specific,[30] so (2), (3) or (4) does not entail (1).
d) the negation of the specific does not necessarily entail the negation of the general,[31] so (8) does not entail any of (5), (6) or (7), since (8) does not deny that there could be a child, female or animal in the house.

Incorporational signification is widely defined as "the process in which an expression signifies one of the components of its nominatum" *(dalālatu l-lafẓi ᶜalā juzʾi musammāhu)*.[32] This definition does not seem to be precise, because it would imply that incorporational signification covers both entailment and presupposition as they are commonly defined in modern semantics and pragmatics, while it is designed to introduce the former notion only. Let us introduce a brief explanation of the differences between the two notions. Entailment is a relation between two sentences *(p)* and *(q)* such that *p* entails *q* if the truth of *q* arises from the truth of *p*.[33] Consider these two sentences where (9) *(p)* entails (10) *(q)* such that whenever (9) is true, (10) must be true.

   (9) I can see a dog.
   (10) I can see an animal.[34]

The difference between entailment and presupposition can be briefly explained by saying that if *p* is false, entailment requires that *q* may be true or false, while presupposition requires that *q* must be true. Thus, the relationship between (9) and (10) is of entailment, since it is the case that if (9) is false, (10) can be true (if one can see any other kind of animal) or false (if one cannot). The relationship between (11) and (12), by contrast, is of presupposition, since it is the case that even if (11) is false, (12) must be true.

(11) He has stopped beating his wife.
(12) He has beaten his wife.[35]

It is clear that (12) is part of the meaning of (11), which means that the above definition of incorporational signification is applicable to presupposition.

In PF, there is a notion similar to the notion of presupposition in the above sense commonly called *iqtiḍāʾ* (requirement). The notion of *iqtiḍāʾ*, which is placed under the third type of *waḍᶜ*-based signification, is very often illustrated by the following pair of sentences where (13) presupposes (or more precisely 'requires' (*taqtaḍī*)) (14).

(13) I manumit this slave.
(14) I own this slave.[36]

According to the Islamic *Sharīᶜah*, if somebody says *aᶜtaqtu hādhā l-ᶜabd* (I manumit this slave), it would mean that he already owns or commits himself to own the slave, and he, by virtue of the law, sets the slave free.[37] There are three kinds of *iqtiḍāʾ*, which will be dealt with later, however let us now deal with 'implicational signification' as the third kind of *waḍᶜ*-based signification.

Implicational signification is loosely defined as "the process in which an expression signifies its implication" *(dalālatu l-lafẓi ᶜalā lāzimihi)*.[38] The notion of implication *(iltizām)* is intended to cover all that which is excluded from equivalence and incorporational signification. Broadly speaking, the implications of a given word are the connotations associated with it: 'courage', for example, is an implication *(lāzim)* of 'lion',[39] and 'capable of learning' is an implication of 'human'.[40] As we have already seen, the signified in incorporational signification is one of the essential and defining components of the concept (e.g., 'man' signifies 'adult', 'human' or 'male') while it is the sum of the entire components of the concept in equivalence-signification (e.g., 'man' signifies an 'adult human male').

The signified in implicational signification, by contrast, is not an essential or defining feature of the concept.

Implicational associations *(al-lawāzim)* are of two different kinds: mental *(dhihnī)* like the association between sight and blindness, and external *(khārijī)* like the association between blackness and crow. However, implicational associations can be both mental and external at the same time as is the case between 'lion' and 'courage', and between 'bed' and 'height' where it is customarily impossible, say the legal theorists, to imagine or to find in the actual world a lion without courage or a bed without height. Although both Muslim logicians and legal theorists agree that *mental* implicational associations serve as the bases for several kinds of implicational signification, they are, nevertheless, in disagreement over *external* implicational associations; thus, while the legal theorists see them as valid bases for implicational signification, logicians say they are not. The legal theorists argue that disregarding external implicational associations would narrow the scope of implicational signification, since several kinds of *majāz* are based on them. Logicians reject this argument saying that non-literal meanings are not, in fact, purely external, but also mental, implicational associations, although context is essential for an external implicational association to become *majāz*.

In his explanation of the relationship between implicational association *(al-luzūm)* and implicational signification, al-Rāzī points out that the former is not a cause *(mūjib)* for the latter but only a condition for it.[41] To put it another way, although implicational signification cannot be possible without there being implicational association, the speaker's production of the utterance[42] and the contextual evidence[43] are the actual causes behind the engendering of implicational signification (cf. 3.5.1.4).

It is worth noting, however, that saying that implicational signification is not obtainable without the production of an utterance and setting up a context implies that intention is a basic element in the generation of implicational signification, which is another bone of contention between Muslim logicians and legal theorists. This contention is usually ascribed, as has already been discussed, to disagreement over the definition of signification in general. However, there is a dispute among the legal theorists themselves concerning whether all the three types of signification, or only equivalence-signification, are/is taken to be intentional: while the majority of them hold that all types of signification are intentional,[44] the *Ḥanafīs* believe that only equivalence-signification is intentional. In his clarification of the Ḥanafīte view, Hārūn al-Marjānī (d. 1306/1889) states that

> The expression is used for equivalent meaning *(al-maᶜnā l-muṭābiqī)* only which it primarily conveys and to which it calls attention. It is only equivalence-signification that can be regarded as independent and relevant to intention and use. Incorporational and implicational meanings, in contrast, are never meant to be conveyed as the primary import of the expression; they are only indirectly and secondarily intended and can be only subordinately and implicitly understood from the equivalent meaning.[45]

What al-Marjānī seems to be trying to say is that if somebody says (15), his statement will 'incorporationally signify' (16) and 'implicationally signify' (17), no matter whether he intends that or not; but if he says (18), the utterance can 'equivalently signify' (19) or (20) depending on the intention of the speaker which is recoverable by means of contextual information.

(15) there is a man in the house.
(16) there is an adult in the house.
(17) there is a potential smoker in the house.
(18) there is a lion in the house.
(19) there is a 'large yellow flesh-eating cat' in the house.
(20) there is a 'brave man' in the house.

Thus, the difference between figurative signification, which is considered to belong to the equivalence-signification type, on the one hand, and incorporational and implicational signification on the other, is that the latter may function in isolation of context while the former is a context-dependent notion. So, (15), 'incorporationally signifies' (16) and 'implicationally signifies' (17) in any possible situation in which it is uttered, while (18) 'equivalently signifies' (20) only if the speaker intends to convey this figurative meaning.'

Al-Marjānī's view is similar to that of al-Qarāfī, which is based on his distinction between SBE and SE (signifying by expressions and the signification of expressions). According to al-Qarāfī, the classification of signification into figurative and non-figurative has nothing to do with its classification into implicational, incorporational or equivalence type: while the former is related to SBE, the latter is related to SE. And since intention is required, not in the case of SE but, in the case of SBE, (cf. 3.3), it follows that intention is irrelevant to the classification of signification into implicational, incorporational and equivalence type. Thus, if someone says *zaydun jabānu l-kalb* (Zayd has a coward dog), the implicational signification (i.e., Zayd is generous) may be derivable, whether the utterance is meant to be taken literally or not. Recovering the speaker's intention, however, is always dependent on determining whether the speaker is speaking figuratively or not.

It is important to notice that the sense in which the term 'equivalence-signification' is being employed here is so general as to cover figurative as well as non-figurative use. However, equivalent meaning will vary according to whether the discourse is figurative or not. In non-figurative discourse, equivalent meaning is the literal meaning, while in figurative discourse equivalent meaning is the non-literal force.

Finally, we may conclude by saying that the equivalent meaning of an utterance is its truth-value (or its propositional content). Thus, (21) and (22) are synonymous in terms of their equivalent meanings because they have the same truth-values, since (21) can be true if and only if (22) is true and *vice versa*. This means that just as the assertion of one of this pair of sentences necessarily implies the assertion of the other, the negation of one also implies the negation of the other.

(21) there is a man in the house.
(22) there is an 'adult human male' in the house.

In contradistinction, the relationship between (23) and (24) is different from that between (21) and (22), for, although the assertion of (23) necessarily implies the assertion of (24), the reverse is not true. Furthermore, the negation of (23) does not necessarily imply the negation of (24), though the reverse is true.

(23) there is a man in the house.
(24) there is an adult in the house.

5.2.1.2. Criticisms of the classification

The following criticisms may be levelled against the above triadic classification of signification:

First, the classification is by no means exhaustive. To furnish the proof for this claim, al-Qarāfī points out that this classification does not embrace the kind of signification in which the general *(ṣīghat al-ᶜumūm)* signifies one of its individuals. The way in which *al-*

mushrikīn (the polytheists), for example, signifies 'the polytheist Zayd' in particular as one of the individuals to which this word may refer is not subsumable, according to al-Qarāfī, under any category of this classification.[46] In other words, the above classification scheme has nothing to offer to explain how (1) entails (2)

(1) there is no polytheist in the house.
(2) Zayd is not in the house.

Although al-Qarāfī is perhaps right in his remark that the classification is not exhaustive, his explanation, nonetheless, does not appear to be correct, simply because the kind of signification he mentions is irrelevant here. The reason for this has to do with the fact that the above threefold classification of signification deals with meaning independently of non-linguistic factors, while the inclusion of a given individual (e.g., Zayd) in a corresponding general term (e.g., the polytheists) is something pertaining to knowledge about the world. That is to say, the assumption that Zayd is a polytheist or not is not a logical or linguistic fact, but an assumption derived from the background knowledge. Therefore, it is an instance of reference rather than of signification.

In fact, the signification which is not captured by the above classification is not the process in which the general refers to an individual or particular included in its extension (i.e., the one to which al-Qarāfī refers), but that kind of signification in which the general intensionally embraces the specific. Consider the following two utterances, where (3) necessarily entails (4).

(3) there is no adult in the house.
(4) there is no man in the house.

As this kind of signification, which I shall call 'inclusional signification', does not fall within the scope of any of the three types of signification recognised by the Muslim logicians and legal theorist as verbal *waḍ*[c]-based signification, there will be four kinds of signification:

i equivalence-signification (e.g., man » 'adult + human + male');
ii incorporational signification (e.g., man » 'adult', 'human', or 'male');
iii implicational signification (e.g., man » 'potential smoker' or 'potential laugher'); and
iv inclusional signification (e.g., no adult » 'no man and no woman').

An alternative way of covering the kind of signification in which the general intensionally embraces the specific is to extend the definition of incorporational signification to accommodate both incorporational and inclusional signification. If we do so, we will have what modern semanticists call 'entailment' as defined earlier (cf. 5.2.1.1), which is not restricted to the cases in which the speaker incorporates the general.

Second, the above classification is based on a false assumption that implicational signification is verbal. This criticism comes from al-Āmidī and Ibn al-Ḥājib who argue that the import of implicational signification is drawn not from the signifier itself but from the signified.[47] To put it in ᶜAbd al-Qāhir al-Jurjānī's terms, an implicational import is in fact a meaning for a meaning rather than a meaning for an expression (cf. 3.5.1.4). This amounts to saying that the relationship between the signifier and the signified in implicational signification is rational rather than conventional (or '*waḍᶜ*-based' to use the Muslim thinkers' terminology). Consequently, implicational signification is not subsumable under verbal *waḍᶜ*-based signification (cf. figure 5.2).

Al-Rāzī and his followers, however, go much further to claim that it is only equivalence-signification that can be characterised as *waḍᶜ*-based, arguing that both incorporational and implicational types of signification are rational.[48] There is no justification, according to them, to classify incorporational signification as verbal, and implicational signification as rational, since both are based on the same principle. Al-Rāzī and his followers argue that the claim that incorporational signification is verbal is based on one of the following assumptions:

A) the signified is understood from the expression,
B) the expression is primordially assigned to it;
C) the expression can be employed to refer figuratively to it; or
D) the signified (which is one of the sense-components of the expression) is included in the nominatum.

Therefore, the claim that incorporational signification is verbal is unwarranted because (A) and (C) are applicable to implicational signification as well, (B) is false, and (D) is a purely dogmatic contention.[49]

This disagreement is, however, taken by some scholars to be terminological,[50] because it is argued that if we take the three different types of signification as being engendered by virtue of the intermediation of the *waḍᶜ* of a meaning to an expression, all types of signification would be characterised as *waḍᶜ*-based. If we, however, consider the fact that the understanding of an implication – whether it is a defining feature (*dākhil* (a component included in the definition)) or a non-defining feature (*khārij* (an excluded component)) – is based on a mental switch from the meaning of the expression to the implication, which is a rational process, then equivalence-signification would be characterised as *waḍ*ᶜ-based, while incorporational and implicational signification as rational.

Finally, since determining the type of signification rests on judging whether the signified represents

a) the components of the corresponding concept (in which case, signification is said to be of equivalence type); or
b) one of its defining components (in which case, signification is referred to as incorporational signification); or
c) one of its non-defining components (in which case, signification is called implicational signification),

the point which needs answering concerns the basis for regarding a given component as a defining or non-defining feature. In dealing with this issue, which perplexes so many Muslim scholars, al-Qarāfī points out that there is no way that the distinction can be drawn by mere reason.[51] There are only two ways by which one can include a particular feature in, or exclude it from, a definition:

> First, to learn from the establisher of the expression that the expression is assigned to the [sum of] two components, thus concluding that each is included in the nominatum [. . .]. It is understood, for example, that the Arabs have assigned *insān* (human being) to 'the potentially speaking animal' *(al-ḥayawān al-nāṭiq)*, the feature 'potentially speaking' is thus included and 'potentially laughing' is excluded. Accordingly, if it was the case that it was understood that the Arabs have assigned *insān* for the 'potentially laughing' instead of the 'potentially speaking animal', [the reverse would be true].
>
> Second, the mind invents a concept consisting of two [or more] components and assumes that any feature except these components are excluded.[52]

It seems to me that what al-Qarāfī has in mind is consistent with the distinction drawn by modern linguists between universal sense-components and sense-components specific to a particular language. This distinction, which is based on the assumption that linguistic meanings are to a notable extent culturally dependent, implies that a universal sense-component, which is typographically marked by small capitals (e.g., HUMAN) is not necessarily equal to, or, equivalent with, a language-specific one (e.g., human).[53] To take al-Qarāfī's example, the sense-components of oxymel (*sakanjabin,* i.e., a home-made medical syrup used by Medieval Arabs as a cure for yellow fever) vary according to the ingredients that go into it. Should the ingredients of which this mixture is made differ across cultures, the sense-components would vary accordingly. A comparison between al-Qarāfī's own definition of oxymel (a mixture of sugar and vinegar) and that provided by the Oxford English Dictionary "syrup compounded of vinegar and honey, sometimes with other ingredients"[54] shows how the sense-components of the same concept are culturally dependent, thus backing up al-Qarāfī's claim. There seems to be no semantic field which may be said to be safe from being conceptualised differently across cultures. Not only social customs and activities, such as marriage and divorce, but also apparently universal concepts such as 'boy' and 'girl' may have different definitions in different linguistic communities.[55]

Following his rigorously contextual approach, Ibn Taymiyyah argues that there is no reliable criterion by which one can judge whether a given component is a defining or non-defining feature. As has already been pointed out, definitions in Ibn Taymiyyah's view are context-dependent: the defining features of a concept are determined by the speaker's intention, which is recoverable by contextual information as well as the knowledge of the speaker's habitual use of the language. So, instead of saying that determining the type of signification rests on judging whether the sense-components are defining or non-defining features, Ibn Taymiyyah says determining whether the sense-components are defining or non-defining features rests on whether the speaker intends the sense-component to be signified incorporationally or implicationally.[56] But the problem with this contention is that Ibn Taymiyyah does not explain how one can know whether the speaker intends the sense-component to be signified incorporationally or implicationally.

5.3. THE TEXT-BASED CLASSIFICATION OF SIGNIFICATION

In the previous section we discussed the predominantly semantic classification of signification as introduced by Muslim logicians, and adopted and developed by the legal theorists. In this section, we shall be concerned with the rigorously pragmatic classification of signification, which is put forward by the legal theorists on their own initiative. The difference between 'semantic' and 'pragmatic' is interpreted here as elsewhere as a distinction between what pertains to the study of sentences in isolation of context and what pertains to the study of sentences in context. This being so, it would be important to mention that describing the classification of signification dealt with in the preceding section as 'predominantly' rather than 'purely' semantic is due to the fact that some, if not most, of the legal theorists do not exclude context in their explanation of that classification despite the fact that the original formulation of the classification as made by the logicians is of strictly formal and semantic nature. It would also be important to point out that the ongoing classification is deliberately described as 'rigorously pragmatic' in order to emphasise the fact that it is based on the meanings and inferences drawn in what the legal theorists call *al-maqāmāt al-khiṭābiyyah* (communicative situations).[57] This fact manifests itself in many ways: the legal theorists' (specially the *Ḥanafīs'*) emphasis on the employment of the term *naṣṣ* (text) with each type of signification, their acknowledgement of the speaker's intention, their distinction between 'what is said' *(al-manṭūq)* and 'what is implicated' *(al-mafhūm)* and so on.

In PF, there are two common proposals for what I have called 'text-based classification of signification': the majority proposal known as the *Shāfiᶜī* method of dividing signification; (which is sometimes called the speculative theologians' way *(ṭarīqat al-mutakallimīn)* of dividing signification) and the *Ḥanafī* one. I shall begin with a relatively brief discussion of the *Ḥanafī* classification.

5.3.1. The *Ḥanafī* method of dividing text-signification

The *Ḥanafī* scholars distinguish four types of meaning at the textual level:

i the express meaning *(ᶜibārat al-naṣṣ);*
ii the alluded meaning *(ishārat al-naṣṣ);*
iii the inferred meaning *(dalālat al-naṣṣ);* and
iv the required meaning *(iqtiḍāʾ al-naṣṣ).*[58]

5.3.1.1. The express meaning of text

Broadly speaking, this is the meaning which is taken to be the main import the speaker intends to convey by his utterance. To put it more literally, the meaning "at which the utterance is driven" *(al-masūqu lahu l-kalām)*.[59] It should be noted, however, that it is very frequent in PF's terminology to speak of 'expression', 'utterance' or 'text' as being driven *at* some meaning, but driven *to* somebody. The meaning of 'driven' *(masūq)* in the former phrase is said to be somewhat similar to the meaning of 'intended' *(murād or maqṣūd)*. The difference between the two words relates to their being used in different contexts: while the former is employed for expressions, the latter is used for meanings.[60] On the surface, what the text is 'driven at' is thus tantamount to what the speaker intends to convey, but the reality is that they are two quite different matters. In order to be aware of the difference, we need to distinguish three different levels of 'intentionality' in which 'meaning' may be seen. According to al-Tahānawī, the meaning signified by an expression can either be

a) primarily intended;
b) subordinately intended; or
c) presupposed

(a) and (b) are illustrated by the following Qurʾānic text:

> (1) That is because they say:
> "Trade is like usury",
> But *Allāh* hath permitted trade
> And forbidden usury.[61]

Among the meanings inferred from this Qurʾānic verse is the permission of trade and the forbidding of usury, and the distinctness of trade from usury, the former belonging to (b) while the latter belonging to (a). (c), on the other hand, is illustrated by the Prophet's saying:

> (2) "The price of a dog is ill-gotten property" *(inna min al-suḥti thamana l-kalb)*, where one may infer the legal validity of this sale.

According to al-Tahānawī, while the meaning of type (a) is always 'driven at' *(masūq ilayh)*, the meaning of type (c) can, on no account, be said to be 'driven at'. As for (b), it can be looked upon as being 'driven at' on the grounds that the speaker designs it to be an integral part of his communicative intention and it can, by contrast, be regarded as 'non-driven at' since it is necessarily embodied to impart the speaker's primary intention rather than being specifically intended.[62]

Although the *Ḥanafīs* agree that the above verse conveys at least two meanings:

i an apparent meaning: the permission of trade and the forbidding of usury; and
ii an unequivocal one: the distinctness of trade from usury

they are, nonetheless, in disagreement as to whether only (ii) is, or both (i) and (ii) are, to be regarded as being 'driven at'. ᶜUbayd Allāh Ṣadr al-Sharīᶜah (d. 747–1346), who holds the former view, says that (i) is derivable from the express meaning and (ii) from the alluded meaning of the text (more of which later), whereas the majority believe that both (i) and (ii) are conveyed by the express meaning of the text.[63] This amounts to saying in more technical language that, by virtue of the majority definition, both *naṣṣ* (unequivocal meaning) and *ẓāhir* (apparent meaning) fall within the scope of 'express meaning' while only *naṣṣ* is captured by Ṣadr al-Sharīᶜah's definition (cf. 3.9.1).

It may be important here to mention that the notion of 'driving' *(al-sawq)* always involves a context-dependent import. In order for the audience to get this import in a particular situation, he has to take into account the overall drift of the speaker's utterance and the relevant contextual information. And the cardinal issue the addressee has to consider in this direction concerns the relevance of the speaker's utterance. Applying this to the above verse would show that it seems more plausible to share Ṣadr al-Sharīᶜah's view that the above verse is 'driven at' (ii) than to concur with the majority that both (i) and (ii) are 'driven at' since the passage is clearly designed to be an answer to those who say "Trade is like usury".

Finally, it may also be worth mentioning that the difference between 'what is driven at' and 'what is not driven at' corresponds in some way or another to the distinction drawn by some modern linguists between what is presupposed and what is in focus.[64]

5.3.1.2. The alluded meaning of text

This term is used by the *Ḥanafī* scholars to refer to the meaning which, according to Ḥāfiẓ al-Dīn al-Nasafī (d. 710/1310), is "conveyed by the linguistic construction of the utterance, but does not represent the intention of the speaker at which the text is driven" *(mā thabata bi-naẓmi l-kalāmi lughatan, lākinnahu ghayru maqṣūdin wa-lā sīqa lahu l-naṣṣ)*.[65] This definition, which is adopted by al-Sharīf al-Jurjānī in his encyclopaedic dictionary,[66] compromises two defining specifications: 'conveyed by the linguistic construction of the utterance' and 'being unintended'. We have already dealt with the latter specification in the preceding subsection, so we shall be concentrating here exclusively on the former. As we shall see later, according to the *Ḥanafī* classification of signification, express and alluded meanings are derivable from the linguistic construction of the utterance, inferred meaning is derivable by deduction, and required meaning is at least partly deducible by inference together with the knowledge of the relevant aspects of *Sharīᶜah* (the revealed Islamic law). Hence, if the phrase 'conveyed by the linguistic construction of the utterance' is proven to be inaccurate, then the validity of this version of the classification will be questionable. However, it should be pointed out that there are two possible interpretations for the above phrase: an apparent one, by virtue of which 'what is conveyed by the linguistic construction' *(mā thabata bi-naẓmi l-kalāmi lughatan)* is taken in a relatively narrow sense, and a more probable one in which the phrase is taken to include the implicated aspects of the utterance meaning. In what follows we will examine some examples given to this kind of signification to see whether or not it is based purely on the linguistic construction of the utterance in its narrow sense, then we shall turn to the more probable interpretation.

> (1) "*Wa-l-wālidātu yurḍiᶜna awlādahunna ḥawlayni kāmilayni li-man arāda an yutimma l-raḍāᶜāta wa-ᶜalā l-mawlūdi lahu rizquhunna wa-kiswatuhunna bi-l-maᶜrūf*"
>
> (The mothers shall give suck to their offspring for two years if they wish to complete the term, but it is the duty of the person to whom they are born to bear the cost of their food and clothing on equitable terms).[67]

This *Qur'ānic* verse is a well-studied example of alluded meaning, in which the phrase 'to whom they are born' is said to allude to the implication that the child's descent *(nasabuhu)* is attributed not to the mother but to the father. This inference is derived from the use of the above underlined phrase instead of 'father' which is seen by Muslim scholars as a deliberate departure from a common wording to a less common, but more indicative, one to indicate this implication.[68] However, it is doubtful that this type of meaning is conveyed by purely formal expression, since this meaning cannot be ascribed to any grammatical or lexical form in that phrase as its conventional meaning. Moreover, there are allegedly other alluded meanings drawn from the above phrase, among which is the inference that the father is permitted to take what he necessarily needs from his child's possessions without having to take his or her permission.[69] So, if this meaning was also conveyed by the linguistic construction of the utterance in its narrow sense, what would be its corresponding form? And how would it be related directly or indirectly to this form and to the form of the first alluded meaning on a mere linguistic basis? It is very unlikely to find any, let alone convincing, answers to such questions. However, one may raise the same questions for those *express* meanings which are derivable by way of incorporation and those derivable by implication, since they are similarly irrecoverable by the linguistic construction alone. Consequently, both express and alluded meanings should be seen as capable of being non-linguistically conveyed, a conclusion which would be unacceptable to the *Ḥanafīs* who hold that both these types of meaning are linguistic meanings *(thābitun bi-ṣīghati l-kalām)*. It is true that the *Ḥanafīs* distinguish between express and alluded meaning in that the former, unlike the latter, is immediate and incalculable, but this is only because the former is 'driven at' and the latter is not. As we will make clear, 'non-calculation' *(ᶜadam al-taʾammul)* and 'immediacy' *(al-tabādur)* (cf. 3.5.1.4), are very important tests to prove that a particular meaning is intended to be indeterminate, but not sufficient to prove that it is inferential rather than being linguistically constructed (cf. 5.3.3.1.2.2).

In any case, in order to understand the linguistically constructed meaning of an utterance, one needs to know its lexical and grammatical meaning. Thus, to understand the phrase *l-mawlūdi lahu* (to whom they are born), we need to know, for example, the meaning of the lexeme *walada* (bear), that *l* (to) means 'for the sake of' and that *mawlūd* (were born) is passive participle, and so forth. However, if we widen the sense of 'linguistic' a little so as to include reference assignment and disambiguation, we may also need to identify the reference of *hu* (whom) and know that the whole phrase means 'father'. But, if one wishes to account for how the alluded meaning(s) in this phrase is/are generated, one has to go beyond all that, that is, the lexical and grammatical meaning, the assignment of the reference and the linguistic disambiguation. Particularly, one has to reason out the purpose of the use of this phrase in preference to *wālid* (father) which is more common and more relevant in this context (specially if we take into account the use of *wālidāt* for 'the mothers' in the same verse). Hence, the non-linguistic contexts, specially the co-operation maxims and the background knowledge, will play the essential role in recovering the allusions imported by the phrase.

However, so far we have been employing 'linguistic construction' in its narrow sense, but we should point out here that by virtue of the broad interpretation of the phrase 'conveyed by the linguistic construction', which is more likely to represent what the *Ḥanafīs* have in mind, all the above constituents of the alluded meaning are taken to be part of the linguistic construction. To fortify this interpretation, we need to consider what is exactly meant by 'construction' *(naẓm)*. According to al-Sharīf al-Jurjānī, *naẓm* in its technical sense is the composition of words and sentences such that their meanings are semantically systemised and their significations are arranged in accordance with the requirements of reason".[70] That is to say, to put words and sentences in a coherent and cohesive way. Thus, in order for the hearer to 'deconstruct' the speaker's message, he has not only to decode the conventional meaning, but also to reason about the rational way in which the utterance is constructed. This may involve a consideration of the shared background knowledge and the communication principles governing the linguistic construction of the text.

Another example of alluded meaning is the following *Qur'ānic* verse:

> (2) *"li-l-fuqarāʾ i l-muhājirīna -alladhīna ukhrijū min diyār-ihim wa-amwālihim".*
>
> (Some part is due)
> To the indigent, the Muhājirs,
> Those who were expelled
> From their homes and their property.[71]

The express meaning of this *Qur'ānic* passage is that a portion of the booty is due to those who were expelled from their homes and their property. The alluded meaning, on the other hand, is that their properties and wealth left in *Makkah* (their fatherland) are no longer counted as being held by them. I would assume that the pattern of reasoning by which this allusion is generated runs as follows:

A) these people are referred to as 'the indigent';
B) since there is no 'diverting evidence' to the contrary, this description is meant to be taken literally (the Literalness base);
C) since this describing reference is fresh rather than mutually known reference, it follows that the expression 'the indigent' is being used

attributively rather than referentially (the Principle of Unknown Reference plus the Principle of *I^{c}māl);*

D) as those people were expelled from their homes and their property (shared background knowledge), the relevant allusion engendered from their being described as 'indigent' will be that their properties and wealth left in *Makkah* are no longer counted as being under their control (conclusion).

With the exception of what I call 'the Principle of Unknown Reference', all the above communication principles have already been dealt with. I will shortly explain what I mean by 'the Principle of Unknown Reference', but before that I need to point out that referring to those people as the *Muhājirs* would have been enough to identify them since this is the most common and well-known defining feature for their identification; this raises the point as to the communicative aim behind the use of the expression 'the indigent'. According to 'the Principle of Unknown Reference', for a describing reference to be interpreted by the hearer as being used purely referentially, the hearer must be in a position which enables him to believe that the speaker assumes that the hearer knows that the describing reference is sufficient to make him identify who, or what, is being talked about. In our present example, the describing reference does not satisfy the above condition, because the people referred to are unknown to be poor. In fact, what the audience know about them is that they left homes and possessions in *Makkah*. So, the reference is innovative rather than mutually known and the audience would, accordingly, take this use of describing reference as an act of attribution rather than an act of reference. That is to say, the expression would be interpreted as being used to attribute the quality of indigence to the *Muhājirs*. To put it another way, the expression alludes to the fact that the properties and wealth of the *Muhājirs* left in *Makkah* are no longer counted as being under their control and, consequently, they should no longer be regarded as being comfortably off.

One condition appears to be necessary for this kind of structure (i.e., 'the x' structure) to be regarded as being used attributively, that is, it must be followed by a defining clause. Consider the following examples;

(3) The teacher who saved the drowned yesterday was very brave.

(4) On my way to the university this morning, I saw the teacher who saved the drowned yesterday.

Provided that the speaker believes that the hearer knows 'who saved the drowned yesterday' but does not know the fact that he is a teacher, 'the x' structure in (3) and (4) will be taken as being used attributively. As in the above *Qur'ānic* example, the alluded meaning is engendered by wondering on the part of the hearer about the purpose of the use of 'the teacher', instead of a more general term such as 'man' or 'person'.

To sum up, there are at least four necessary, though not sufficient, characteristics which should hold for a communicative import to be regarded as alluded meaning:

I it must be presupposed rather than 'driven at';[72]
II it must be derivable from the linguistic construction of the utterance;[73]
III it must be calculable;[74] and
IV it must not be immediate.[75]

There will be more elaboration on (II) when we discuss the *Shāfiᶜī* method of dividing text-signification, where the distinction between 'what is said' and 'what is implicated' will be more technically relevant.

5.3.1.3. The inferred meaning of text

Several definitions are offered to pinpoint the notion of inferred meaning, each emphasising some features of the notion, but without any of them being sufficiently exhaustive. So, I will selectively consider two of these definitions in order to give some indication of the properties the *Ḥanafīs* have in mind when they are discussing inferred meaning.

According to ᶜAlāᵓ al-Dīn al-Bukhārī's definition (d. 730/1330), inferred meaning is "the understanding of an unstated meaning from the stated meaning on the basis of the consideration of the context and the illocutionary import of the utterance" *(fahmu ghayri l-manṭūqi mina l-manṭūqi bi-siyāqi l-kalāmi wa-maqṣūdih).*[76] It is obvious that this definition, which appears to be a modified form of al-Ghazālī's definition,[77] is based on equating signification with understanding, a view which is rejected by some Muslim thinkers on the grounds that signification and understanding are two different constructs (cf. 5.2.1). However, I will be concentrating on three different notions involved in al-Bukhārī's definition, each of which represents a distinct form of meaning in the broad sense of the term. These notions are

i the stated meaning *(al-manṭūq)*;
ii the unstated meaning *(ghayr al-manṭūq)*,
iii the illocutionary import of the utterance *(maqṣūd al-kalām)*.

In order to illustrate these different forms of meaning we need to consider the passage "Say not *ʾuff* to them" in the following *Qur'ānic* verse:

> (1) Thy Lord hath decreed
> That ye worship none but him,
> And that ye be kind
> To parents. Whether one
> Or both of them attain
> Old age in thy life,
> **Say not *uff* to them**, nor repel them,
> But address them
> In terms of honour.[78]

The stated meaning of this passage is the prohibition of saying *uff* (Fie) to parents, a meaning which is encoded in the conventional wording of the utterance. But this clearly stated meaning amounts to something else, that is, the prohibition of striking them, insulting them, and so forth. The prohibition of each one of such despicable acts is considered by the legal theorists as an unstated meaning of the utterance. Such meanings are said to be generated by a consideration of the context, which leads in turn to the realisation of the illocutionary import of the utterance. In the above *Qur'ānic* verse, it is clear that the whole context is driving at urging people to respect their parents. This being so, the illocutionary import of the passage will be the prevention of harm to parents. Once one grasps this illocutionary import of the passage, it will be clear for him that any act or behaviour causing harm to parents will fall within the scope of the prohibition intended in the above *Qur'ānic* verse.

In a similar definition, Muḥibb Allāh. b. ʿAbd al-Shakūr (d. 1119/1707) interprets inferred meaning as "the result of attributing the rule of the stated meaning to the unstated meaning on the strength of the consideration of the effective cause on a linguistic basis" *(thubūtu ḥukmi l-manṭūqi li-l-maskūti li-fahmi l-manāṭi lughatan)*.[79] What is striking about this definition is that it renders the consideration of 'the effective cause' *(al-manāṭ)* as the basis for generating an inferred meaning. It should be pointed out here that there is a long-standing controversy in the PF concerning whether *Sharīʿah*-related analogical reasoning *(al-qiyās al-sharʿī)* or only linguistic considerations are the key to inferred meaning. At first sight, ʿAbd al-Shakūr appears to opt for the former view, but a moment of reflection would show that this is not the case. In fact, the qualification "on a linguistic basis" *(lughatan)* seems to be deliberately made to display his rejection of this view. Before we spell out the positions of each part of the controversy, it is worth mentioning that not only the *Ḥanafīs*, but also the *Shāfiʿīs*, are divided over this issue. So in order to avoid repeating the same thing during the discussion of 'congruent implicature' *(mafhūm al-muwāfaqah)*, i.e., the *Shāfiʿī* counterpart of 'inferred meaning', all the arguments concerning this controversy whether they are advanced by the *Shāfiʿīs or Ḥanafīs* will be dealt with here. Those who hold that inferred meaning is derived through purely linguistic considerations base their view on the argument that, unlike *Sharīʿah*-related analogical deduction *(al-qiyās al-sharʿī)*, inferred meaning has the following properties:

i It needs no knowledge about *Sharīʿah*, thus, any speaker of the language, whether he is a jurist or not, is capable of deriving this type of meaning.[80]
ii The process of deriving this type of meaning does not involve a great deal of calculation.[81]
iii It is a necessary condition for this kind of inference that the point of resemblance *(al-maʿnā l-munāsib li-l-ḥukm)* (i.e., "the governing consideration" or "the concern to promote rationality"[82]) is more relevant to the derivative than it is to the antecedent.[83] To go back to our example, the prohibition of striking parents is more relevant to the prevention of harm to them than saying *uff* to them.
iv The antecedent, in the case of this kind of inference, can be subsumed under, or made part of, the derivative.[84] According to al-Āmidī, if a master says to his slave "do not give someone a grain", it is understood that the slave is disallowed to give any larger amount including a single grain.[85]

The advocates of the rival view, on the other hand, equate this kind of inference with deduction by analogy because

a) it involves some sort of calculation; and

b) it necessitates the same pillars involved in analogical reasoning, namely 'the antecedent' *(al-aṣl)* (e.g., saying *uff*), 'the derivative'*(al-far^c)* (e.g., striking) and common effective cause *(^{c}illah jāmi^{c}ah mu$^{\prime}$aththirah)* (e.g., the prevention of harm to parents).[86] But, since this kind of inference is so plain, it is called 'manifest analogy' *(qiyās jalī)*.

In response to the arguments (i) and (ii), Abū Isḥāq al-Shīrāzī ascribes the accessibility of inferred meaning to ordinary speakers to its being plain and apparent, a quality which should not, according to him, prevent it from being subsumed under analogical reasoning.[87] As for (iii) and (iv), they are, I would say, invalid arguments because the properties assigned to inferred meaning in those two arguments do not contradict the very nature of analogical reasoning. It is true that the notion of inferred meaning (or 'congruent implicature', according to the *Shāfi^{c}īs*) is remarkably embodied in the above properties, but this does not disqualify it from being a special kind of analogy.

Some scholars, however, treat this type of inference as a kind of *majāz*, subsuming it under what they call 'the use of the specific to indicate the general'. To return to our example, the specific is 'do not say *uff* and the general is the prohibition of causing harm to one's parents.[88] This account is invalidated on the grounds that it is a necessary condition for an expression to be a *majāz* that the literal meaning is truth conditionally disregarded on the strength of a diverting context, but what we have here is a case in which both the literal and figurative meanings are included in the speaker's intention of the utterance.[89]

However, one may be tempted to say that the prohibition of saying *uff* to one's parents is not necessarily derived from the literal meaning, but could be tacitly understood from the more general meaning, that is, the prohibition of causing any kind of harm to one's parents, since the verse is primarily driven at the prohibition of causing any kind of harm to one's parents rather than to the prohibition of saying *uff* in its strictly literal form. This assumption can be accurate if and only if al-Gazālī's claim that the unstated meaning is more immediate than the stated meaning is accurate.[90] But this is very unlikely, because it is very hard to imagine that the unstated meaning (the prohibition of striking one's parents), which represents just one of the possible manifestations of the illocutionary import (the prohibition of causing any kind of harm to one's parents), strikes the mind before the literal meaning (the prohibition of saying *uff*), by means of which the illocutionary import itself is recovered. This being the case, both the literal and non-literal meanings are integral to what the speaker is intending, which means that the above criticism (i.e., that this kind of expressions cannot be counted as *majāz* for their literal meanings are integral to what the speaker is intending) still holds.

Furthermore, classifying such inferences under the heading of *majāz* would be open to another criticism: the distinction between *ḥaqīqah* and *majāz* is something different from the distinction between stated and unstated meaning, the former is drawn from the classification of use, while the latter is drawn from the classification of signification. To put it al-Qarāfī's way, the former is related to SBE, while the latter is related to SE (cf. 3.3).

To sum up, inferred meaning is a special case of analogical reasoning in which an unstated meaning is derived on 'all-the-more-reason basis' from a stated meaning by virtue of the consideration of the context and the speaker's illocutionary import. This definition represents the outcome of modifying and integrating the two separate definitions developed by al-Bukhārī and ᶜAbd al-Shakūr in the light of the above discussion.

5.3.1.4. The required meaning of text

The term *iqtiḍāᵓ al-naṣṣ* (the required meaning of text) is commonly used to refer to the semantic content of ellipted parts of an utterance which is believed to be essential to the meaningfulness of the whole utterance. As explained earlier (cf. 3.5.1.3), Muslim legal theorists lay great importance on the addressee and his role in the communicative process. Chief among the tasks expected from him is the function of "making sense of the expressions". This function which is formulated in the 'Principle of *Iᶜmāl* (cf. 3.5.1.3) is particularly important in interpreting those utterances whose apparent meanings do not appear to be compatible with the rationality or the legal validity of the text, or the principle of the speaker's truthfulness. Relying on the immediate context and his background knowledge, and motivated by the principles of communication, the addressee is assumed not only to divert the expression from its face-value meaning, but also to enlarge the discourse such that it becomes most relevant to the communicative situation. In the case of 'required meaning', the hearer is believed to assume that the speaker omits some parts of the utterance on the strength that the speaker is capable of recovering them from the context. The hearer's assumption that some parts of the utterance are omitted and intended to be part of the force of the speaker's utterance is envisaged by the legal theorists as an extension *(ziyādah)* to the actual discourse. The motive behind – or the requiring for *(al-muqtaḍī)*, to use the legal theorists' terminology – this 'extension' is "the maintenance of communication" *(ṣiyānat al-kalām)* and "its prevention from balderdash" *(ṣiyānatuhu ᶜan al-laghw)*.[91] In other words, it is the participants' need for proper communication which constrains the existence of this type of meaning.

Having outlined the notion of 'required meaning, we need to examine some of the definitions offered by the *Ḥanafīs* to explore the idea further. According to Abū Bakr al-Sarakhsī (d. 490/1097), the required meaning *(al-muqtaḍā)* is "a presupposed extension to the stated proposition, whose being presumed is a necessary condition for the utterance to be meaningful (or for its illocutionary force to occur), and without which the utterance does not make sense".[92] For example, the *Qur'ānic* verse (1) must be taken to mean that 'unlawful to you is the marriage of your mothers, daughters . . .'.

> (1) "Prohibited to you are your mothers, daughters, sisters . . .",[93]

The recovery of the unmentioned word 'marriage' is dependent on a set of assumptions and communication principles:

i that the apparent meaning is inaccessible (diverting context);
ii that the speaker is truthful (the Principle of Truthfulness) and has a particular communicative intention to convey (the Principle of the Speaker's Disposition to Make his Intention Manifest).
iii that there must be an ulterior meaning for the utterance (the Principle of *Iᶜmāl*); and
vi that the verse must be taken to mean that 'unlawful to you is the marriage of your mothers, daughters . . .' (guiding context).

Among the points to notice in al-Sarakhsī's definition is his distinction between the value of the utterance *(fāˀidat al-kalām)* and its legal illocutionary force *(ḥukmuhā l-sharᶜī)* where the former refers to the intended meaning of the utterance whereas the latter refers to its legal effect (which is here the prohibition of marrying the mother). Contrary to the case of the above *Qur'ānic* verse where the value of the utterance and its illocutionary force are almost the same, it is very frequent in Islamic jurisprudence that jurists, while agreeing about the value of the text, differ in determining its legal illocutionary force. I will not go into the details of this issue, but it suffices here to point out that both the value of the utterance (which represents the speaker's intention) and its illocutionary force are different from its meaning in that the latter does not require a great deal of reflection and calculation to grasp.

Another point in al-Sarakhsī's definition is his use of the term *iᶜmāl* where he makes the assumption that some parts of the utterance's structure are omitted as the only way to make sense of the utterance. The term *iᶜmāl* (making sense of the expression) refers here (as elsewhere) to the process in which the addressee assesses all the possible interpretations on the strength of the context in which the utterance is uttered (cf. 3.5.1.3).

The second definition to be introduced here is the one quoted by al-Bukhārī without mentioning who suggested it. According to this definition, the required meaning *(al-muqtaḍā)* is "that which is assumed to have been omitted for some purposes such as the preservation of the speaker's truthfulness" *(mā uḍmira fī l-kalām ḍarūrata ṣidqi l-mutakallimi wa-naḥwih)*.[94] The significance of this definition lies in highlighting the addressee's tendency to take the speaker's utterance as an informative message even in a situation in which the speaker's utterance appears inaccessible, which tacitly implies the importance of the Principle of *Iᶜmāl* to the process of interpretation. More important is the reference to the assumption of the speaker's truthfulness as a chief principle for communication. A very much-quoted example to clarify this point is the Prophet's saying:

> (2) "Error and forgetfulness have been removed from my community".

In order to preserve the Prophet's truthfulness and make his message clear and informative, the assumed missing element 'the blame for' *(ithm)* has to be supplied so that the utterance reads as follows: the blame for error and forgetfulness has been removed from my community. Without retrieving the missing element, the utterance would not be taken to be true, given the actual occurrence of error and forgetfulness in the everyday life of the members of his community.[95]

The final definition to be discussed here is ᶜAbd al-Shakūr's definition. As he defines it, requirement *(iqtiḍāʾ)* is a state in which a stated meaning signifies that which constitutes a necessary condition for its rationality or legal validity *(dalālatu l-manṭūqi ᶜalā mā yatwaqqafu ṣiḥḥatuhu ᶜalayhi ᶜaqlan wa-sharᶜan)*.[96] The first thing to be noticed about this definition is the fact that, unlike the above two, it is a definition of requirement *(iqtiḍāʾ)* rather than the required *(al-muqtaḍā)*. Some Ḥanafī legal theorists distinguish between the requiring *(al-muqtaḍī)*, the required *(al-muqtaḍā)* and requirement *(iqtiḍāʾ)* as follows: "the requiring is the text", according to some legal theorists,[97] and "the maintenance of communication", according to others,[98] the required is a condition without which the text does not make sense; and requirement is a relation between the requiring and the required.[99] In the light of this definition of requirement, ʿAbd al-Shakūr's definition can be reformulated in the following form: requirement is a relation by virtue of which a stated meaning signifies that which constitutes a necessary condition for its rationality or legal validity.

In any case, the important points in this definition are

i It makes the relation between the stated meaning and the assumed meaning of presupposition type.
ii It renders the text rather than any other communicative factors as the requiring for the presumably missing elements. However, some legal theorists say, as has just been pointed out, that the need for the missing elements arises to maintain a proper communication.[100]
iii It implies that the supply of the assumed object contributes to the rationality of a text as in (**A**) or to its legal validity as in (**B**).

(**A**) In the *Qur'ānic* passage (3), the text requires, according to the majority view, the assumption of the phrase *ahl* (the people of) before the phrase "*al-qaryata*" (the town) in order for the text to make sense since, as al-Shāfiʿī remarks, "the town and the caravan [by themselves] cannot tell what the truth was".[101]

> (3) "Ask the town where we have been, and the caravan with which we have come" *(wa-isʾali l-qaryata -allatī kunnā fīhā wa-l-ʿīra -allatī aqbalnā fīhā)*.[102]

However, some legal theorists, notably Ibn Taymiyyah and Ibn al-Qayyim, argue against this account. Following their strictly contextual approach, they say that the word *qaryah* (town) can be applied to the place or the people who live in that place, relying in this regard on the contextual evidence.[103] Incidentally, this seems to be the common practice in the most authoritative dictionaries of English.[104] There is no need, according to Ibn al-Qayyim, for the assumption of ellipsis since

i "the utterance is independent";
ii "what is assumed to be omitted is in fact implicated"; and
iii "expressions signify by implication as well as by their explicit meanings".[105]

This approach is applied also to cases such as the following:

> (4) "Prohibited to you are dead meat, blood, the flesh of swine, and that on which hath been invoked the name of other than *Allāh,* that which hath been killed by strangling, or by a violent blow, or by a headlong fall, or by being gored to death . . .".[106]
>
> (5) "Lawful unto you are all four-footed animals, with the exceptions named".[107]
>
> (6) "Prohibited to you are your mothers . . .".[108]

The speaker's intentions in all these *Qur'ānic* verses, Ibn al-Qayyim tells us, are recovered from the conventional meaning, the habitual use of the utterance and the way the utterance is constructed.[109] In other words, the grasp of the intended meaning dose not hinge on an assumption of ellipsis *(iḍmār)*, omission *(ḥadhf)*, reflection (*tafkīr*) or calculation *(taqdīr)*.[110] Thus, once the above verses are heard, the mind goes immediately to the prohibition of the consumption of the items listed in (4), the permissibility of the consumption of all four-footed animals in (5) and the prohibition of the marriage of mothers in (6). What makes these particular interpretations determinate is their relevance to the communicative situation (cf. 4.9).

(**B**) Consider the following talk-exchange in which an owner of a slave is asked by a magnanimous person who wants the slave to be freed to sell him the slave and liberate him on his behalf in a single transaction:

> (7) a- Set your slave free on my behalf for a thousand.
> b- I have set him free.

The utterance *aᶜtaqtu* (lit, I have set free) is seen institutionally as a performative utterance *(inshāʾiyyah)* and institutionally characterised by Muslim jurists as one of the so-called *ṣiyagh al-ᶜuqūd wa-l-fusūkh* (lit, forms of contracts and revocations) as by virtue of its use in the above manner the speaker commits himself to set a slave free. The point here, however, is that once (7b) is performed the slave is sold to the speaker of (7a) and simultaneously freed on his behalf.[111] Clearly, what we have here is a case of a pragmatic presupposition where the speaker performs one of *ṣiyagh al-ᶜuqūd* to produce two illocutionary forces at once: the conventional illocutionary force by virtue of which the slave has become free and the presupposed one by virtue of which the slave has been sold.

Finally, it should be pointed out that some scholars draw a distinction between 'requirement' and 'the assumption of ellipsis' *(iḍmār)*, or omission *(ḥadhf)* on the grounds that the former is governed by extra-linguistic factors, such as the preservation of the legal validity of the text, while the latter is motivated by purely linguistic considerations.[112] Others, on the other hand, make the distinction on different bases, but all the distinctions suggested are of little practical importance, not to mention their being questionable.[113]

To sum up, the legal theorists distinguish three types of required meaning:

i what is assumed to have been omitted for the preservation of the speaker's truthfulness;
ii what is assumed to have been omitted for the preservation of the rationality of the text *(al-ṣiḥḥah al-ᶜaqliyyah)*; and
iii what is assumed to have been omitted for the preservation of the legal validity of the text *(al-ṣiḥḥah al-sharᶜiyyah)*.[114]

5.3.2. The *Shāfiᶜī* method of dividing text-signification

Prior to commencing the discussion of the present proposal for the classification of signification, it should be born in mind that what we mean by the *Shāfiᶜī* method is the approach which is followed not only by the *Shāfiᶜīs*, but also by the *Mālikī*, *Ḥanbalī*, and *Muᶜtazilī* scholars. In so doing, we are conforming to the common practice in PF according to which the term *Shāfiᶜī* is applied in this context to those legal theorists whose approach to the issues of PF, unlike the *Ḥanafīʾs*, is dominated by speculative and theological trend.

Seeking to ascertain the valid inferences upon which to formulate the law, the *Shāfiᶜīs* (in the broad sense of the term) introduce a number of different versions of significational classification which are propounded by different scholars. Although Muḥammad b. Idrīs al-Shāfiᶜī (d. 204/ 820), the founder of the *Shāfiᶜī* school of law and arguably the real founder of PF, touches on some types of meaning in his influential *Risālah*,[115] his brief outline of these types cannot, nevertheless, be rendered as a properly classificatory proposal. In fact, a complex classification does not seem to have appeared before the tenth, or perhaps, the eleventh century. Among the figures who lay the foundation for the *Shāfiᶜī* significational classification scheme in the eleventh century are the *Muᶜtazilī* scholar Abū l-Ḥusayn al-Baṣrī,[116] the *Malikī* Abū l-Walīd al-Bājī (d. 474/1081),[117] and the *Shāfiᶜī* (in the narrow sense of the term) Imām al-Ḥaramayn al-Juwaynī.[118] I shall not discuss the first two in the present work, instead I will consider al-Juwaynī's proposal as it constitutes the basis for two more common and highly developed proposals which will be the focus of our discussion in this section, namely those put forward later in the thirteenth century by al-Āmidī and Ibn al-Ḥājib. Besides, I shall be discussing al-Ghazālī's classification, as it forms the connection link between al-Juwaynī's and al-Āmidī's proposals.

5.3.2.1. Al-Juwaynī's classification

The important thing to note in al-Juwaynī's proposal, and in most versions of the *Shāfiᶜī* classification, is the distinction between the meaning of 'what is said' and the meaning of 'what is implicated', or, more precisely, the signification of 'what is articulated or pronounced' *(dalālat al-manṭūq)* and the signification of 'what is understood' *(dalālat al-mafhūm)*. Unlike many other Muslim legal theorists and modern pragmatists who attempt similar distinctions,[119] al-Juwaynī has a clear, though not necessarily accurate, picture of the difference between stated and implicated propositions. Any inferred proposition which represents either the analogue or the opposite of what is said would be characterised, according to al-Juwaynī's classification, as an implicated proposition. Any other proposition would, in contrast, be seen as either an explicitly or implicitly stated meaning. Consider the following examples where each utterance given an odd number implicates the utterance that directly follows it. The group (A) of these examples is meant to illustrate congruent implicature (*mafhūm al-muwāfaqah*), while the group (B) is designed to illustrate counter implicature *(mafhūm al-mukhālafah)*.

(A)
(1) If you give him a single penny, he will not return it to you.
(2) If you give him two pence, he will, with stronger reason, not return them to you.
(B)
(3) Those who passed the exam will be rewarded.
(4) Those who did not pass the exam will not be rewarded.
(5) If Zayd passes the exam, he will be rewarded.

(6) If Zayd does not pass the exam, he will not be rewarded.
(7) The lecture will continue until midday.
(8) The lecture will not continue after midday.
(9) Zayd has two children.
(10) Zayd has not three children.

Since implicature, within the Gricean framework, covers all kinds of pragmatic inferences that are not truth-conditional,[120] a great number of implicatures in the Gricean sense will, therefore, fall within the scope of 'what is said' in al-Juwaynī's use of the term (compare figure (5.4) with (5.5)).

Among implicatures that are not captured by al-Juwaynī's use of 'implicature' are:

I Conventional implicatures: those which, in contrast to conversational ones, are inferred from particular expressions associated with them such as 'but', 'therefore', 'even' etc., without recourse to certain co-operative principles. The use of 'therefore' in the following example commits the speaker by virtue of its meaning "to its being the case that his being brave is a consequence of (follows from) his being an Englishman".[121]

(11) He is an Englishman, he is, therefore, brave.

In PF, the meanings of such expressions are commonly regarded as conventional and discussed under the heading of *maᶜānī l-ḥurūf* (the meanings of particles). However, there are some controversies concerning whether the implications derived from utterances containing some articles are conventionally assigned to them or derived from extra-linguistic considerations. For instance, there are some debates

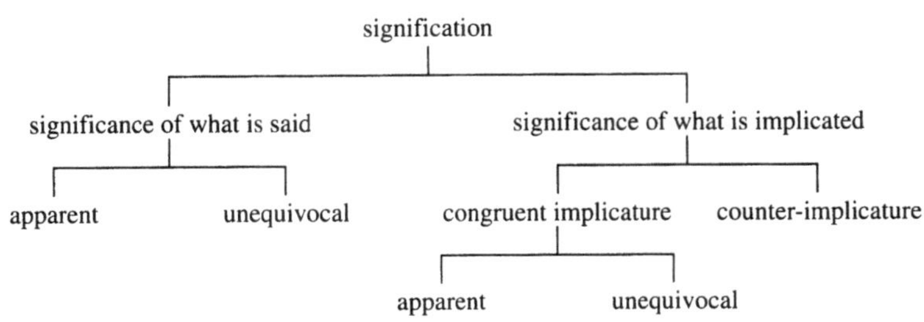

Figure 5.4 *al-Juwaynī's classification of signification*

concerning whether or not *wa* (and) can be interpreted as (and then), and other debates concerning how many and what kind of interpretations can be given to *aw* (or).[122]

II Particularised conversational implicatures: "cases in which an implicature is carried by saying that *p* on a particular occasion in virtue of special features of the context".[123] In modern pragmatics, it is generally accepted that "all implicatures that arise from the observing of Relevance are particularised, since utterances are relevant only with respect to the particular topic or issue at hand".[124] To take one of Grice's examples for particularised implicature:

(12) A: Smith doesn't seem to have a girlfriend these days.
B: He has been paying a lot of visits to New York lately.

According to Grice (who is regarded as the first to have developed a theory of what he coined 'implicature'), "B implicates that Smith has, or may have, a girlfriend in New York".[125] The type of implicature illustrated by the above example would probably be called in PF and Arabic rhetoric *taᶜrīḍ* (intimation) and subsumed under 'what is implicitly said'. *Taᶜrīḍ*, as defined by al-Sharīf al-Jurjānī, is "that by means of which the speaker implicitly makes his intention manifest to the hearer".[126] A good example of *taᶜrīḍ* is (13) where B, blaming A for harming another Muslim, implicitly indicates the falsehood of A's statement by citing a Prophetic saying:

(13) A: anā Muslim (I am a Muslim).
B: *"al-Muslimu man salima l-muslimūn min lisānihi wa-yadih"* (A Muslim is that who causes no harm to other Muslims either by tongue or by hand).[127]

However, most, if not all, of what Grice calls 'generalised conversational implicatures' are subsumable under the signification of 'what is understood' *(dalālat al-mafhūm)*. Generalised implicatures arise from observing the maxims of co-operation, particularly the Maxim of Quantity.[128] Grice illustrates his notion of generalised conversational implicature by the following example where (14) normally implicates (15):

(14) x is meeting a woman this evening.
(15) The woman is not his wife.[129]

Thus, the idea of implicature which al-Juwaynī and many other Muslim thinkers have in mind is much narrower than that of Grice.

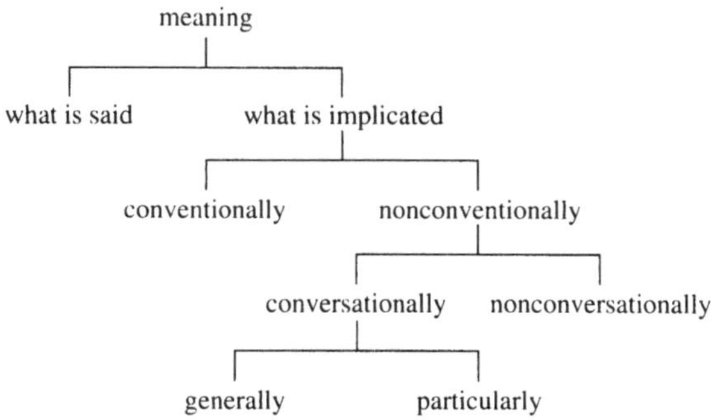

Figure 5.5 *Grice's classification of meaning.*[130]

5.3.2.2. Al-Ghazālī's classification

Al-Ghazālī[131] distinguishes three types of meaning: 'composed meaning' *(al-manẓūm)*, 'implied meaning' *(al-mafhūm)* and rationalised meaning *(al-ma^{c}qūl)*.[132] By 'composed meaning' al-Ghazālī means 'the *waḍ^{c}*-based meaning of the utterance', or to use modern linguistic terms, 'the semantic content of the utterance'. This meaning is derived, according to al-Ghazālī, from the primordial *waḍ^{c}* and the wording of the text *(al-ṣīghah)*.[133] 'Rationalised meaning' can roughly be defined as an unstated meaning arising from applying assertively or negatively the rule of the stated meaning to it on an analogical basis by virtue of a valid common feature between the two meanings.[134] As has already been explained, while some legal theorists view 'congruent implicature' (or 'inferred meaning' in the *Ḥanafī* model of classification) as a kind of analogical reasoning (or 'rationalised meaning' according to al-Ghazālī's classification), al-Ghazālī and others are careful not to confuse them (cf. 5.3.1.3). Congruent implicature, like any other implied meaning *(mafhūm)*, is engendered by applying certain communication principles over and above the consideration of the relevant contextual information. It is natural, therefore, that al-Ghazālī does not place 'rationalised meaning' – which requires special knowledge of Islamic law and a great deal of reflection much more than that usually needed for communicative purposes – under implied meaning.

Obviously, al-Ghazālī employs the term *(mafhūm)* in a sense similar to Grice's implicature, which is much broader than the standard sense of *(mafhūm)* in PF. But since al-Ghazālī sometimes uses *(mafhūm)* in its narrow sense, in order to avoid or at least minimise

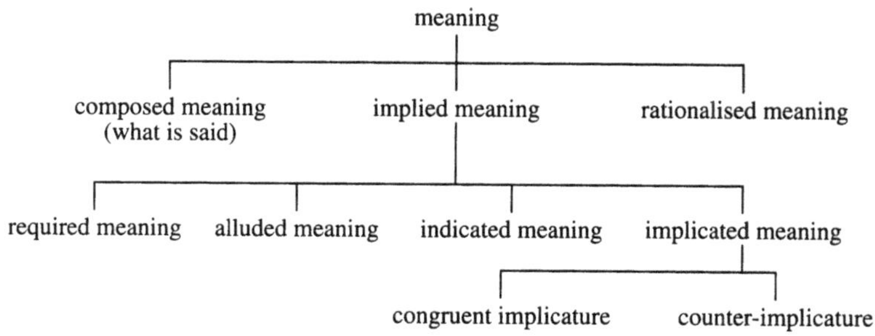

Figure 5.6 *al-Ghazālī's classification of signification*

terminological confusion, I will use 'implied meaning' for *(mafhūm)* in al-Ghazālī's wide sense and 'implicated meaning' for *(mafhūm)* in its standard confined sense which exclusively covers both congruent and counter implicature.

Required meaning *(iqtiḍāʾ)* and alluded meaning *(ishārah)* have already been dealt with in the discussion of the *Ḥanafī* model of classification (cf. 5.3.1.4 and 5.3.1.2), and there is nothing of importance that can be added to what was spelt out there. Implicated meaning, on the other hand, will be considered in the section devoted to the types of implicature (cf. 5.3.3.1). As for indicated meaning *(īmāʾ)*, it will be dealt with within the discussion of al-Āmidī's classification as his in-depth elaboration of this type of meaning will be crucial to our discussion (cf. 5.3.2.3).

5.3.2.3. Al-Āmidī's classification

Echoing al-Ghazālī, al-Āmidī divides signification into two types: composed *(dalālat al-manẓūm)* and non-composed *(dalālat ghayr al-manẓūm)*. Composed signification comes in two varieties: 'equivalence-signification' *(dalālat muṭābaqah)*, and 'incorporational signification' *(dalālat taḍammun)* (cf. 5.2.1.1). Non-composed signification could be unintended or intended. Under the former category, al-Āmidī places only one class of signification, namely 'alluded signification' *(dalālat al-ishārah)*. Under the latter, he subsumes three different classes: required signification (*dalālat al-iqtiḍāʾ*), indicated signification (*dalālat al-tanbīh wa-l-īmāʾ*); and implicated signification (*dalālat al-mafhūm*).[135] Al-Āmidī draws the distinction between the last three classes of signification as follows:

> "If [the signified] is integral to what the speaker is intending to get across, then either it is such that the truthfulness of the speaker and the correctness of his speech depend on it, in which case it is called [. . .] *dalālat al-iqtiḍā*ʾ or it is not. If the latter, then either the implication arises directly from the explicit meaning of the text, in which case it is called *dalālat al-tanbīh wa-l-īmā*ʾ, or it does not arise directly from the explicit meaning, in which case it is called *dalālat al-mafhūm*".[136]

As we have learnt from the above quotation, indicated signification is to be contrasted to implicated signification, which means that a large number of implicatures which do not represent the analogue or the opposite of what is said will be characterised as indicated significations. But, as we will shortly explain, the implications derived by *īmā*ʾ are, practically speaking, exclusively limited to a particular class of meaning. So, al-Āmidī's classification does not exhaust all the kinds of implicature linguistic utterances can bear.

Indicated signification is regarded as one of the valid methods for determining 'the cause' *(al-ᶜillah)*, which is specifically pertinent to the formulation of the law on the basis of analogy. Among the other methods is the explicit signification of the text, where the legislator either explicitly states that the cause behind a particular rule is such-and-such, or uses one of the particles 'establishmentally' designed to indicate the cause *(ḥurūf al-taᶜlīl)*, such as *li* (for the reason) in the following *Qur'ānic* example:

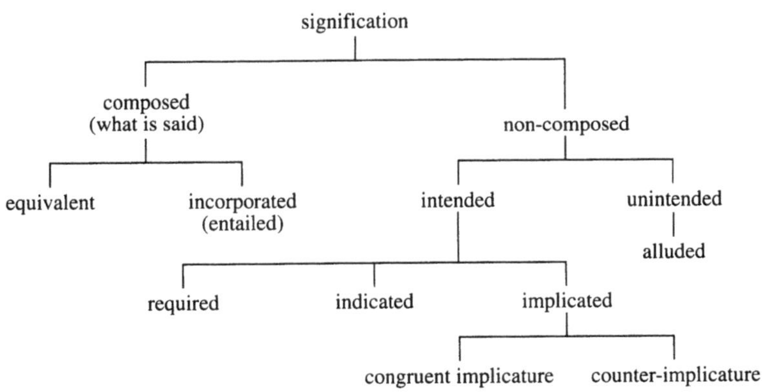

Figure 5.7 *al-Āmidī's classification of signification*

(1) *"wa-mā khalaqtu l-jinna wa-l-insa illā li-ya^cbudūn"* (I have created jinns and men only for the reason that they may worship Me).[137]

Clearly, the distinction made here between explicit and indicated signification is based on the distinction between composed and non-composed signification: while explicit signification pertains to composed signification, indicated signification relates to non-composed signification. Theoretically speaking, implicated causes are not the only implications that can be derived from indicated signification, but since the ascertaining of the cause is of paramount importance in PF – because it is essential for juridical analogy *(qiyās)*, by means of which a large number of legal rules are derivable – the legal theorists are fully preoccupied by it and pay no attention to other meanings that may be derived in the same manner.

According to the legal theorists, indicated meaning arises from implicitly connecting a particular rule with a particular quality in a way suggesting the involvement of a causal relationship, or as Ibn al-Ḥājib puts it, "in such a manner that the assumption of the involvement of any relationship other than causation *(al-ta^clīl)* as the purpose behind this association seems to be farfetched".[138] One of the many examples provided by al-Āmidī, for this type of meaning is the following:

(2) *"sahā rasūlu Allāhi (ṣallā Allāhu ^calayhi wa-sallam) fī l-ṣalāti fa-sajad"* (The Prophet neglected [to perform an integral part of the prayer] in his prayer and so he prostrated).

The Arabic conjunction *fa*, which is usually interpreted as (and so), implies in the above example that the prostration took place after, and as a result of, the Prophet's unintentional omission of some parts of the prayer. Similar examples are

(3) *"wa-l-sāriqu wa-l-sāriqatu fa-qṭa^cū aydiyahumā"* (As for the thief, male or female, [*fa*] cut off their hands).[139]
(4) The Prophet's saying, *"man aḥyā arḍan mayyitatan fa-hiya lah"*
"Whoever revives dead land, [*fa*] it is his."[140]

According to al-Āmidī, indicated signification is implicated by the '*waḍ^c*-based meaning' of the expression, rather than being 'establishmentally signified' by the expression. Accordingly, the causal relationship derived from *fa,* which conventionally indicates the involvement of temporal succession in examples of the above kind is not due to its being conventionally assigned to it but because it is implicationally associated with it. it seems to me that what we are dealing with here is a kind of what Grice calls 'conventional implicature' which has been outlined above (cf. 5.3.2.1). However, some of al-Āmidī's examples, because they are cancellable, do not lend themselves to Grice's conventional implicature. In fact, they are probably allied to conversational implicatures. Consider the following:

(5) A Bedouin who came to the Prophet said,
(a) I am doomed and have caused another to be doomed.
The Prophet said,
(b) What have you done?
He said,
(c) I had sexual intercourse with my wife intentionally in the daytime during Ramaḍān.
The Prophet said,
(d) Free a slave.[141]

The indicated signification in (5) is that the cause behind the Bedouin being required to free a slave is the fact that he had sexual intercourse. But in order for this signification to obtain, one has to assume that (d) is relevant to (c). In other words, the derivation of this signification is based on our knowledge that the Prophet's delivery of the rule was a response to the Bedouin's enquiry. So, in a situation in which a slave says to his master:

(6) (a) Has the sun arisen?
and the master replies,
(b) Give me some water to drink.

the slave will not, according to al-Āmidī, take (b) as an answer to, or as being stimulated by, (a). He will, rather, take it as a refusal to answer his question either because of absence of mind or because of an opt out from the conversation. This possibility is unlikely in the case of the Prophet for he, as prophet, is not usually distracted and does not delay necessary information.[142]

The difference between (5) and (2)–(4) has to do with the degree of the unequivocalness of the text: In al-Āmidī's view, the degree of probability attaching to the indicated signification in each one of (2)–(4) in which the *fa* is actually used is much greater than that attaching to the indicated signification in (5) where the *fa* is only assumed.[143] As a matter of fact, unlike that of (5), the indicated signification in each of (2)–(4) is certain. This can be proven by 'the cancellability test' (cf.

5.3.3.1.2.2) where the indicated signification in (5) in contrast to (2)–(4) can be cancelled. For example, in a hypothetical situation similar to that of (5) the Bedouin could be answered as follows:

(7) Free a slave, and remember it is not because you had sexual intercourse with your wife that you were asked to free a slave, but because you were rather impolite in your reporting of the incident.

The rest of al-Āmidī's examples seem to be best classified as presuppositions. Consider the following *Qur'ānic* verse,

(8) "Keep away from women
In their courses, and do not
Approach them until
They are clean."[144]

The indicated signification in (8) is that menstruation is the reason why women cannot be approached. There is no conventional element in the verse to which this signification can be assigned. So, this indicated signification is either conventionally or conversationally implicated. It is unlikely that it is conventionally implicated in the Gricean sense of the term, because the speakers of Arabic do not intuitively attach this signification to this kind of structure, that is, they do not feel that the speaker who says

(9) I fast until sunset.

commits himself to its being the case that the daytime is the reason behind his fasting in the same way the person who says (10) commits himself "to its being the case that his being brave is a consequence of (follows from) his being an Englishman".

(10) He is an Englishman, he is, therefore, brave.

And since the indicated signification in (8) is derivable irrespective of the context, it follows that it cannot be particularised conversational implicature. It is also unlikely that this type of signification is subsumable under generalised conversational implicature for the reason that it cannot be cancelled, that is, one cannot deny it without causing contradiction. Thus, one cannot say (11) without committing contradiction.

(11) Do not have sexual intercourse with your wife until she is clean, and the reason has nothing to do with menstruation.

The reason why classifying this type of example as presupposition is the best way to handle it relates to the fact that it survives negation, which is taken by most pragmatists to be the most workable test for identifying presupposition. Thus, the negation of (12) affects its truth-conditional content, while the presupposition that menstruation is the reason why women can/cannot be approached remains unaffected.

(12) He does not have sexual intercourse with his wife until she is clean.

To take two slightly different examples, (13) presupposes that anger is the cause behind the disallowance of passing judgement, and (14) presupposes that their being scholars is the cause behind their being honoured.

(13) The Prophet's saying, "A judge must not pass judgement when he is angry"
(14) The scholars should be honoured.

5.3.2.4. *Ibn al-Ḥājib's classification*

The essential difference between al-Āmidī's classification and Ibn al-Ḥājib's lies in their different conceptions of what is said. At the practical level, Ibn al-Ḥājib, unlike al-Āmidī, places most kinds of implied inferences – including alluded signification, required signification, and indicated signification – under the signification of 'what is said'. Following al-Juwaynī, Ibn al-Ḥājib applies the term *manṭūq* (what is said) in a very broad sense. According to his proposal of significational classification, with the exception of congruent and counter implicatures, all inferences drawn from linguistic utterances are either explicitly or implicitly stated. 'What is explicitly said' is meant to refer to conventional meaning. This includes both equivalence-signification and incorporational signification. By 'what is implicitly said', Ibn al-Ḥājib refers to the kind of inference which is conveyed by implicational signification. To put it Ibn al-Ḥājib's way, "that which is implied from the meaning to which the expression is assigned"[145] (i.e., the conventional meaning). However, since implicational signification is a very obscure and confusing idea, saying 'that 'what is implicitly said' refers to what is signified by implication would not be a great help to clarify the distinction between 'what is explicitly said' and 'what is implicitly said'. In fact, it raises doubt about the accuracy of the distinction between 'what is implicitly said' and 'what is implicated'. It is true that 'what is implicated' is employed exclusively to inferred propositions which represent either the analogue or the opposite of what is said, but what is the difference between what is implicated by way of congruence or opposition and what is implicated by any other way? Al-Taftāzānī, though he describes the distinction between 'what is implicitly said' and 'what is implicated' as questionable *(maḥallu naṭar)*, says that the difference lies in that in the case of *al-mafhūm* ('what is implicated' i.e., congruent implicature and counter implicature), the illocutionary force *(al-ḥukm)* is assigned to an unmentioned object, while in the case of 'what is implicitly said', "the illocutionary force, even if it is not stated, constitutes one of the affairs and rules of the mentioned object" *(fa-inna l-ḥukm fīhi wa-in lam yudhkar wa-lam yunṭaq bihi lākinnahu min aḥwāli l-madhkūri wa-aḥkāmihi).*[146] I find it difficult to understand what he exactly means by the affairs and rules of the mentioned object, but let us, nevertheless, take some examples to see whether there is any real difference between 'what is implicitly said' and 'what is implicated'.

(1) The Prophet's saying: "Alms-tax is due upon free-grazing sheep".

The counter implicature here is that alms-tax is not due upon sheep that are not free-grazing, that is, stall-fed sheep. The illocutionary

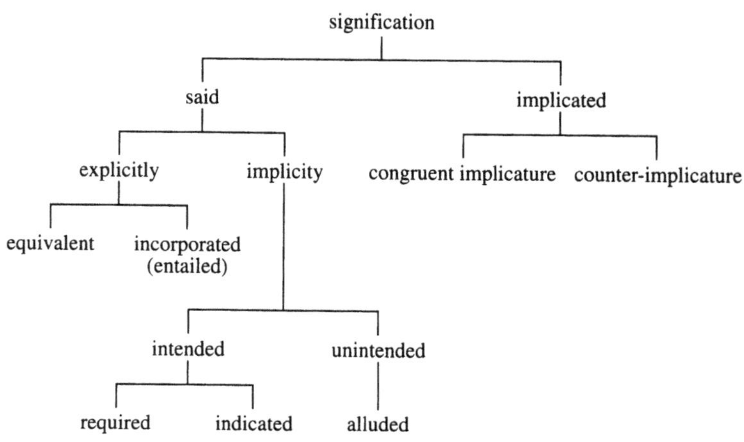

Figure 5.8 *al-Ibn al-Ḥājib's classification of signification*

force *(al-ḥukm)* in this implicature, which is the exemption from alms-tax, is assigned to an unmentioned object, that is, stall-fed sheep.

(2) If you give him a hundred pounds, he will return it to you.

This implicates that if you give him ten pounds, he will, with more reason, return it to you. The unmentioned object in this congruent implicature is 'ten pounds' and the illocutionary force is the implication that he will, with more reason, return to you.

(3) A- My car is out of petrol.

B- There is a garage round the corner.

According to Grice, "B would be infringing the maxim 'Be relevant' unless he thinks, or thinks it possible, that the garage is open, and has petrol to sell; so he implicates that the garage is, or at least may be open".[147] This is one of Grice's examples of implicature which is not viewed as an implicature in the Muslim legal theorists' narrow sense of the term. The reason behind this, according to al-Taftāzānī's account of the difference between 'what is implicitly said' and 'what is implicated', has to do with the fact that the illocutionary force, which is here the implication that the garage is open, even if not stated, constitutes one of the affairs and rules of the *mentioned* object, namely the garage. One of the other relevant affairs and rules of the garage could be that it has petrol to sell.

Thus, determining whether a given inference is implicitly stated or implicated depends on whether the illocutionary force is assigned to a mentioned or unmentioned object: in the former case the inference is regarded as implicitly stated, while in the latter it is regarded as implicated. In the following sections I will examine the two types of implicature, namely congruent implicature and counter implicature as well as the subclasses of counter implicatures.

5.3.3. Implicature

There are three senses in which the term *dalālat al-mafhūm* (implicature) is applied in PF:

i a very broad sense: 'the signification of what is implied' versus 'the signification of what is said';
ii a broad sense: 'the signification of what is implicated', which involves both (and only) congruent implicature and counter implicature.

iii a narrow sense: where it refers exclusively to counter implicature.

From now on, we will use the term *al-mafhūm* (implicature) in the sense (ii), but during the discussion of the types of counter implicature, we will use it in the sense (iii). So we will say, for example, the Implicature of a Condition, instead of the counter implicature of a condition. In doing so, we are, in fact, conforming to the common practice in the PF.

5.3.3.1. Types of implicature

5.3.3.1.1. Congruent implicature

Congruent implicature *(mafhūm al-muwāfaqah)* is the *Shāfiᶜī* equivalent of what the *Ḥanafīs* call 'inferred meaning' (cf. 5.3.1.3). Although the *Shāfiᶜīs'* treatment of this type of signification is similar for the most part to that of the *Ḥanafīs*, the *Shāfiᶜīs* still have something different to offer in terms of its definition, its relationship with other types of meaning and its manifestations.

A good definition is that which is capable of pinpointing the distinctive features which set the definiendum (the concept defined) apart from its partners involved in the same classification scheme. And one of the relatively good definitions of 'congruent implicature' is al-Juwaynī's definition, which is based on the following brief outline of the notion made by Muḥammad b. Idrīs al-Shāfiᶜī.[148] Rendering congruent implicature as the strongest kind of analogy, al-Shāfiᶜī says

> The strongest kind [is the deduction] from an order of prohibition by God or the Apostle involving a small quantity, which makes equally strong or stronger an order of prohibition involving a great quantity, owing to the [compelling] reason in the greater quantity. Similarly the commendation of a small act of piety implies the presumably stronger commendation of a greater act of piety; and similarly an order of permission involving a great quantity would render permissible something involving a smaller quantity.[149]

Putting this rough outline into a definition form, al-Juwaynī states that 'congruent implicature' is "that which indicates that the rule of the unstated meaning is congruent with the rule of the stated meaning with greater reason *(mā yadullu ᶜalā anna l-ḥukma fī l-maskūti ᶜanhu muwāfiqun li-l-ḥukmi fī l-manṭūqi bi-hi min jihati l-awlā).*[150] The main point in this definition is that 'congruent implicature' rests on equating the rule of the unstated meaning with the rule of the stated meaning. The qualification "with greater reason" is designed to stress the assumption that the common rule which the unstated and stated meaning share should be more appropriate to the unstated than to the stated meaning. However, this assumption is not always true, for there are some instances of 'congruent implicature' at least in one sense of this term in which this assumption does not seem to be applicable. Consider the following *Qur'ānic* verse:

(1) Those who unjustly
Eat up the property
Of orphans, eat up
A Fire into their own
Bodies: they will soon
Be enduring a blazing fire![151]

It seems sensible to infer from this verse that the destruction of the property of orphans in any way is also forbidden, but there is no evidence that setting fire, for example, to the property of orphans is more conducive to its destruction than eating it up. This is an instance in which the common rule ('the destruction' in this example) cannot be safely said to be more relevant to the unstated than to the stated meaning. Some legal theorists term this type of meaning *laḥn al-khiṭāb* (the implicit meaning of the discourse) distinguishing it from *faḥwā l-khiṭāb* (the import of the discourse), where the unstated meaning is stronger (or more relevant to the common rule) than the stated meaning. Both *laḥn al-khiṭāb* and *faḥwā l-khiṭāb*, according to this view, are included under 'congruent implicature'.[152] However, for others including al-Āmidī and Ibn al-Ḥājib, there is no way to subsume *laḥn al-khiṭāb* in the above sense[153] under 'congruent implicature', since they make as a necessary condition for 'congruent implicature' that the common rule must be more relevant to the unstated than to the stated meaning.[154] Thus, 'congruent implicature' in this narrow sense manifests itself exclusively into two forms:

i 'hinting at the higher by means of the lower' *(al-tanbīh bi-l-adnā ᶜalā l-aᶜlā)*; and
ii 'hinting at the lower by means of the higher' *(al-tanbīh bi-l-aᶜlā ᶜalā l-adnā)*.[155]

A very well-studied example of (i) is the following *Qur'ānic* verse:

(2) Then shall anyone who
Has done an atom's weight
Of good, see it!
And anyone who
Has done an atom's weight
Of evil, shall see it.[156]

It is understood from this verse that those who have done greater than an atom's weight of good or evil will *a fortiori* see it. Among the examples al-Āmidī provides to illustrate this type of meaning are the following: if a master tells his slave "do not give Zayd a grain", the slave would immediately understand that he is disallowed to give what exceeds a grain. In like manner, it is understood "from the Prophet's saying, "[Distribute] thread and needle," that one is to [distribute] baggage and money and the like, and from his saying, "whoever steals the stick of a Muslim must return it," that what exceeds a stick must also be returned".[157]

The form (ii) of congruent implicature, on the other hand, is commonly illustrated by the following *Qur'ānic* passage:

(3) Among the People of the Book
are some who, if entrusted
With a hoard of gold,
Will (readily) pay it back.[158]

The implicit meaning of this passage is that those who pay back a hoard of gold will, with a yet stronger reason, pay back what is less than that.

The legal theorists maintain that in order for one to generate this type of meaning in either of its two forms illustrated above, one has to go beyond the explicit meaning of the text. This, as has already been pointed out (cf. 5.3.3.1.1), involves a scrutiny of the relevant intended illocutionary import of the utterance *(al-maᶜnā l-munāsib al-maqṣūd mina l-ḥukm)*, which is always looked upon as the effective cause which promotes the attribution of the rule of the antecedent to the derivative. Thus, if one is to infer that those who have done greater than an atom's weight of good or evil will see it, one has to presume on the strength of the context that the illocutionary import at which the verse is driving is the determination to reward the well-doer and punish the evildoer. Similarly, the inference that those who pay back a hoard of gold will pay back what is less than that rests on the assumption that the illocutionary import of the utterance is the attribution of trustworthiness to some of the People of the Scripture.[159]

The point to be made here is that the illocutionary import is looked upon as one of a set of premises which should be combined together to generate a congruent implicature. The epistemological status of a congruent implicature is always determined by each premise in the set. Accordingly, there is a correlation between the definiteness of the relevant intended illocutionary import of an utterance and the determinacy of its congruent implicature: the more definite the illocutionary import, the more determinate the congruent implicature will be. On the other hand, any doubt raised about the illocutionary import will influence the congruent implicature. This being the case, in order for one to be certain of the conclusion (derived from the above verse concerning parents) that killing one's parents is forbidden, one has to be certain of the following:

i the illocutionary import of "do not say 'Fie' to them" is 'do not harm them' (contextual information);
ii killing one's parents causes harm to them (knowledge about the world).

With respect to this particular *Qur'ānic* verse, the legal theorists seem to be in agreement that both (i) and (ii) certainly hold and have no doubt, consequently, about the determinacy of the inference that killing one's parents is forbidden. But, as al-Āmidī remarks, there could be a situation in which a king commands his executioner to kill his father if he knows for sure that his father is to fight him over his kingship. And it is conceivable for the king in such a situation to ask his executioner not to say 'Fie' to his father while he is carrying out the order of the execution.[160] As al-Ghazālī points out, the difference between situations of the type illustrated by the *Qur'ānic* verse and this situation lies in that in the latter case, the king might well say to the executioner without contradicting himself; "do not say 'Fie' to my father, but kill him".[161] But in situations such as that of the *Qur'ānic* verse, it is not possible to say 'do not say 'Fie' to your parents, but kill them" without logical contradiction. This comparison between two different situations is designed to show:

a) that congruent implicature is not part of the explicit (or the stated) meaning of the utterance but is derivable from the context.[162]

b) that congruent implicature can be deterministic *(qaṭᶜī)* as is the case with the last two *Qur'ānic* examples quoted above, or probabilistic *(ẓannī)* as is the case with the above hypothetical situation.[163] Al-Juwaynī employs *naṣṣ* (unequivocal) and *ẓāhir* (apparent) instead of deterministic and probabilistic respectively.[164] If the context indicates that the congruent implicature is deterministic, the congruent implicature cannot be cancelled, but if the context indicates that the congruent implicature is probabilistic, the speaker will be able to deny it without creating a contradiction.[165] Al-Juwaynī reports that some scholars consider probabilistic congruent implicatures to be invalid inference for formulating the law.[166]

5.3.3.1.2. Counter implicature

The notion of counter implicature *(mafhūm al-mukhālafah)* is highly relevant to what is called in contemporary pragmatics 'scalar implicature'. In fact, the two ideas seem to be two faces of the same coin. Although the legal theorists' designation of the notion appears to be more precise, the fact that we have two different designations underlying different approaches is very advantageous since each designation stimulates great insights into the subject. Hopefully, the insights developed by Muslim legal theorists and their approach to the subject will contribute considerably to the development of 'scalar implicature'. In particular, they may, at least, lead to expanding the notion to cover all the types regarded by the legal theorists as types of counter implicature.

5.3.3.1.2.1. The pillars of counter implicature

Each instance of counter implicature consists of the following pillars:

i The mentioned case *(al-madhkūr)* e.g., 'free-grazing sheep' in (1).

(1) Alms-tax is due upon free-grazing sheep.

ii The rule of the mentioned case *(ḥukm al-madhkūr)* e.g., 'being taxable' in (1).

iii The qualification *(al-qayd)* which can be, for example, a condition, stated number, time limit, etc., e.g., 'free-grazing' in (1).

iv The unmentioned case *(ghayr al-madhkūr)* which represents the opposite of the mentioned case, e.g., 'sheep that are not free-grazing' in (1).

v The rule of the unmentioned case *(ḥukm ghayr al-madhkūr)* which represents the opposite of the rule of the mentioned case, e.g., 'being not taxable' in (1).[167]

5.3.3.1.2.2. The validity of counter implicature

One of the issues which Muslim legal theorists concern themselves with is whether or not counter implicature is a valid inference for the formulation of the law. While the majority of the *Shāfiᶜīs* rely on at least some types of counter implicature in their derivation of the rules from the *Qur'ānic* and Prophetic texts, most of the *Ḥanafīs* say that counter implicature is a weak source to rely on for the formulation of the law, though it can be used as a valid inference in non-legal discourse. Within the present section, I will discuss the most important arguments put forward by the two parties to the controversy and will begin with the *Ḥanafīs*' arguments against the validity of counter implicature. It should be pointed out here that the following arguments are applicable to all kinds of counter implicature, other arguments which concern certain types of counter implicature will be dealt with later when we discuss the types of counter implicature.

(**I**) There are three basic recognisable types of signification only, namely equivalence-signification, incorporational signification and implicational signification; each textual inference can be traced back to one of these types, but counter implicature does not fit in in any of the above three types of signification. Clearly, counter implicature cannot belong to the first two types since it represents the opposite, rather than the equivalent, or the partial, meaning of what is said. Furthermore, counter implicature cannot be regarded as implicational signification, for it is a necessary condition for a proposition to be regarded as an instance of implicational signification, to occur immediately to the mind once the expression is produced" *(li-anna sharṭahu sabqu l-dhihni mina l-musammā ilayh)*, but in the case of 'alms-tax is due upon free-grazing sheep' "the hearer may conceive the obligation of paying alms-tax for free-grazing sheep, while failing to conceive the rule of stall-fed sheep in any negative or assertive way, in fact, he may not think of stall-fed sheep at all".[168]

However, some of the *Shāfiᶜīs,* notably Ibn al-Ḥājib, seem to view counter implicature as a distinct kind of inference not pertaining to any of the three basic recognisable types of signification just mentioned;[169] others, on the other hand, state clearly that counter implicature belongs under implicational signification.[170] Among the arguments advanced to prove that counter implicature is of implicational type are:

a) The attribution of the rule to a qualified, rather than an unqualified, object implies a correlation between the rule and the qualification. So, it is reasonable that the absence of the qualification implies the negation of the rule. This argument is refuted on the grounds that the correlation between the rule and the qualification is not determinate since there could be other justifications for the qualification.[171] For example, there could be a situation in which (2) comes as an answer to (1).

   (1) Is alms-tax due upon free-grazing sheep?
   (2) Yes, alms-tax is due upon free-grazing sheep.
   (3) Alms-tax is not due upon sheep which are not free-grazing

Thus, (2) does not implicate (3), for the qualification 'free-grazing' is not made for the exclusion of stall-fed sheep, but because it was the subject of the question made in (1). However, the *Shāfiᶜīs* do not deny that the validity of counter implicature is constrained by certain conditions which will be dealt with later, and that the above example is nothing but an instance of invalid counter implicatures which are constrained by these conditions.

b) Implication is that which the mind switches to and is understood by means of calculation, irrespective of whether it is mental *(dhihnī)* or conventional *(ᶜurfī)*. In this extended sense of implication, counter implicature, which is conventional, can be covered by the term.[172] 'Conventional' should be understood here in its very broad sense such that it covers all kinds of non-logical inferences.

(**II**) The non-existence of the rule in the unmentioned is not derived from the attribution of the rule to the mentioned; it is rather due to the maintenance of the status quo before the statement is made.[173] This amounts to saying that the rule of the unmentioned is not affected in any way by the rule of the mentioned. So determining whether alms-tax is due or not due upon sheep which are not free-grazing rests upon the addressee's knowledge of the rule before the statement is made and the saying of what is said does not alter this knowledge. Should the addressee have no previous knowledge about the rule, he will, according to this view, presume the primordial non-existence *(al-ᶜadam al-aṣlī)*. To back up this argument, al-Āmidī points out that if a master says (4) to his servant, it would not be reasonable for the servant to buy a non-black slave.[174]

(4) Do not buy for me a black slave.

Similarly, (5), according to this view, does not implicate (6), for "the assertive rule does not follow from the primordial non-existence" *(al-ḥukmu al-thubūtī lā yumkinu an yathbuta binā'an ᶜalā l-ᶜadami al-aṣlī)*[175]

(5) Alms-tax is not due upon stall-fed camels.
(6) Alms-tax is due upon camels which are not stall-fed camels.

(**III**) If the attribution of the rule to the mentioned implicated its negation with respect to the unmentioned, making any statement indicating the attribution of the rule of the mentioned to the unmentioned after attributing it to the mentioned would be a contradiction, but since this is false, the attribution of the rule to the mentioned does not implicate its negation with respect to the unmentioned.[176] In other words, if (i) (i.e., saying that p implicated that *not-q*) was true, then (ii) (i.e., explicating that q after saying that p would be a contradiction) would be true, but since (ii) is false, then (i) is false. To give examples, if (7) implicated (8), (9) would be a contradiction to (7). Equally, if (10) implicated (11), (12) would be a contradiction to (10).[177]

(7) Alms-tax is due upon free-grazing sheep.
(8) Alms-tax is not due upon sheep which are not free-grazing.
(9) Alms-tax is due upon free-grazing sheep and sheep which are not free-grazing.
(10) Pay alms-tax for free-grazing sheep.
(11) You do not have to pay for sheep which are not free-grazing.
(12) Pay alms-tax for free-grazing sheep. Pay alms-tax for sheep which are not free-grazing.

This argument is refuted on the grounds that (i) does not necessarily produce (ii), for counter implicature, as any other apparent proposition *(ẓāhir)*, is so weak that it can be cancelled without contradiction. It is a property of probabilistic signifiers that they are cancelled without committing contradiction when they are in conflict with deterministic or more probabilistic ones.[178] In contrast, deterministic propositions cannot be cancelled without contradiction. So, (13), to take al-Baṣrī's examples, contradicts (14).

(13) I have beaten Zayd now in this place.
(14) I have not beaten Zayd now in this place.[179]

According to al-Juwaynī, "counter implicature is not self-dependent and not part of the discourse *(al-khiṭāb)* itself, but an implication from the expression, so if it is cancelled for some reason, the expression and its other implications will not be affected".[180] If, by contrast, the signification of what is said is cancelled, the implicature derived from it will consequently be cancelled.[181]

In modern pragmatics, Grice and his followers take cancellability as one of the defining properties of conversational implicatures. For some Muslim legal theorists, this is implausible since not only implicatures but all kinds of 'apparent propositions' *(ẓawāhir)* (cf. 4.9.1) are cancellable.[182] As has already been pointed out, presupposing a given interpretation to be apparent has a practical importance in the PF, for apparent meanings are taken to be the intended meanings unless they are cancelled by verbal or non-verbal contexts. In the case of 'what is said', it is very often to take one interpretation of an indeterminate utterance to be its apparent meaning. The immediacy test, which is highly intuitive, is commonly recognised as a practical method to check whether or not a given meaning is the apparent meaning of the utterance. According to this test, any interpretation which strikes the mind first will be regarded as the apparent meaning of the utterance. In the case of 'what is implicated', the implicature is taken to be apparent and intended meaning unless there is evidence to the contrary, which causes the implicature to be cancelled.

Another way of attacking the above argument is to say with Ibn Taymiyyah, that "it is not reasonable to consider a speaker's utterance before he is completely silent or a writer's work before he completely finishes".[183] Following his strict contextual approach, and emphasising his pragmatic dictum that "an expression can be regarded as a signifier if and only if it is complete and disconnected from what follows it"[184] *(wa-quṭiᶜa ᶜan mā baᶜdah)*, Ibn Taymiyyah argues that a part of an utterance (like 'alms-tax is due upon free-grazing sheep' in (9)) cannot be taken to be meaningful without its complementary clause (like 'and sheep which are not free-grazing'). So in cases like (9), it would be wrong to say that a part of an utterance contradicts another.[185]

(IV) It is typically appropriate for the hearer to ask the speaker about the rule of the unmentioned after hearing the rule of the mentioned. If counter implicature was a valid inference, enquiring about the rule of the unmentioned would not be appropriate.[186] To take al-Ghazālī's examples, if (15) implicated (16) why would it be appropriate for the hearer of (15) to say (17)?[187]

(15) If Zayd hits you intentionally, hit him back.
(16) If Zayd hits you unintentionally, do not hit him back.
(17) But if he hits me unintentionally, shall I hit him back?

In response to this argument the advocates of counter implicature raise several objections, of which I shall mention only two:

a) The reason why the enquiry in cases like (17) is appropriate relates to the fact that implicatures are probabilistic rather than deterministic.[188] So, it is similarly appropriate for the hearer of (18) to say (19) although the answer to his enquiry is explicitly said in (18), which means that the appropriateness of enquiry *(ḥusn al-istifhām)* in (17) is not due to the invalidity of counter implicature, but rather to its indeterminacy.

   (18) I saw the sultan entering the town.
   (19) Did you see the sultan himself or only his procession.[189]

b) Enquiry could be motivated by the search for new information or for seeking assurance for uncertain information already obtained by the enquirer;[190] (17) is one of the latter kind.

(V) It is possible to say

(20) Alms-tax is due upon free-grazing sheep, but not upon stall-fed sheep.

If (7) implicated (20), the clause 'but not upon stall-fed sheep' would be redundant.

One of the objections raised to this argument is that the validity of counter implicature does not conflict with the *waḍ*^{c} of a special expression to express the same meaning, since *waḍ*^{c}-based expressions are more informative and more appropriate for conveying communicative intentions.[191] Another objection is that the appropriateness of reinforcement *(ḥusn al-taʾkīd)* is not confined exclusively to implicatures, but can equally be applied to the signification of 'what is said'. Consider (21) where the word 'himself' is designed to confirm that Zayd, rather than anybody else, has come,[192] and (22) where the same word adds force to the word 'manager'.

(21) Zayd himself has come.
(22) I need to speak to the manager himself.

The notion of the appropriateness of reinforcement is similar to that of 'reinforceability' proposed by Sadock as an additional test, not mentioned by Grice, for identifying conversational implicatures. According to Sadock,

> Since conversational implicatures are not part of the conversational import of the utterances, it should be possible to make them explicit without being guilty of redundancy. Conversational implicatures, that is, ought to be reinforceable, whereas conventional implicatures should not. In the clear cases, this test accords well with intuition. Thus, the second clause of *It's odd that dogs eat cheese and they do* is redundant because it restates what is conventionally implicated by the first clause. But no redundancy shows up when a clearly conversational implicature is made explicit, as in *Maggie ate some, but not all, of the cheddar.*[193]

Coinciding with the Muslim legal theorists view, Sadock points out that reinforceability, like cancellability, does not "distinguish conversational additions from privative ambiguities".[194]

The advocates of counter implicature, on the other hand, advance a number of arguments to support their view, among which are the following:

i Speakers commonly infer (24) from (23) and (26) from (25).[195]

(23) Buy a small house for me.
(24) Do not buy a big one.
(25) If you enter the house, you will be divorced.
(26) If you do not enter the house, you will not be divorced.

As was explained in (II), the opponents of counter implicature reject that (24) and (26) are associated with the saying of (23) and (25) respectively, arguing that they had already been held before (23) and (25) were said since speakers, by virtue of the principle of *istiṣḥāb*, presume a past state to remain until a diverting indicator emerges.[196]

ii It would be very odd or/and funny to say (27), (29) or (31) when all people equally have the same properties attributed to the Sudanese in (27), the Jews in (29) and the tall in (31). If (27), (29) and (31) did not implicate (28), (30) and (32) respectively, why is this so?

(27) When the Sudanese feel thirsty, they will not be sated until they drink.[197]
(28) When other people feel thirsty, they will be sated without having drink.
(29) Dead Jews cannot see.[198]
(30) Other dead people can see.
(31) Tall men cannot fly.[199]
(32) Short men can fly.

In response to this argument al-Ghazālī says that the oddness of utterances like (29) is not due to singling out a particular person or group, but to staying a very self-evident fact. Thus, it would be similarly odd to say utterances like (33).[200]

(33) The dead cannot see.

Clearly, al-Ghazālī's response to the above argument is defective, for the oddness of (29), in contrast to that of (33), is certainly not fundamentally due to its being self-evident, but because it gives rise to a false implicature (30).

iii The saying of (34) would annoy the *Ḥanafīs*. Were it not for that the *Ḥanafīs* infer (35) from (34), they would not be annoyed.

(34) The *Shāfiᶜī* jurists are righteous.
(35) The *Ḥanafī* jurists are not righteous.

The opponents of counter implicature admit that the *Ḥanafīs* may be annoyed at (34), but they say that the annoyance is not because that (34) gives rise to (35), but because the saying of (34) leaves the hearer wondering whether the *Ḥanafī* jurists are also righteous or not.[201] But the question that should be raised here is why is it that the hearer wonders whether the *Ḥanafī* jurists are also righteous or not? Is it not because that (34) is one possible implication of (35) regardless of its degree of probability? In any case, nobody claims that counter implicature is deterministic.[202] In fact, it is generally accepted that the derivation of a counter implicature is probabilistic rather than deterministic.[203] And this is the only reason why cancellability, the appropriateness of reinforcement and the appropriateness of enquiry are taken to be its defining properties.[204]

iv Since speakers are assumed to be rational and their contributions are taken to be informative, and since a rational speaker must have a reason for connecting a rule with a particular attribute, in saying (Alms-tax is due upon free-grazing sheep) the speaker, therefore, must have some purpose for qualifying 'sheep' by mentioning the attribute 'free-grazing', instead of using 'sheep' in an unqualified way. The purpose can only be that he intends to exclude sheep that are not free-grazing.[205]

The problem with this line of reasoning, say the opponents of counter implicature, is that it could be applied to counter implicature derived from a designation *(mafhūm al-laqab)*,[206] which is rejected by the vast majority of the legal theorists, although it is believed by a small minority to be the weakest type of counter implicature. According to the advocates of this type of counter implicature, (36) implicates (37), (38) etc.

(36) Alms-tax is due upon sheep.
(37) Alms-tax is not due upon cattle.
(38) Alms-tax is not due upon camels.

Al-Shīrāzī responds to the above rejection by distinguishing between counter implicature derived from a designation and counter implicature derived from a restrictive attribute. He mentions three differences between them, but only one is important here. In the case of counter implicature derived from a designation, the speaker does not 'descend' from a general concept to a specific one *(lam yanzil ᶜan ismin ᶜāmmin ilā ismin khāṣ)*, while in the case of counter implicature derived from a restrictive attribute he does. So, unlike the latter case, there is no intention of 'indicating contrast' *(al-mukhālafah)* involved in the former.[207] However, if there is contextual evidence indicating a departure from a general concept to a specific one, counter implicature will be irresistible no matter whether the implicature-bearing expression is a name or otherwise. Thus, according to al-Shīrāzī's account, in (39) the Prophet was in a position to say (41) but he departed from it to (39) in order to implicate (40), though the implicature-bearing expression is a name.[208]

(39) All land has been ordained for us to be a place for prayers and its sand as a substitute cultic purifier *(wa-juᶜilat*

lanā l-arḍu masjidan wa-turābuhā lanā ṭahūrā).
(40) Not all the land (but only its sand) has been ordained for us to be a substitute cultic purifier.
(41) The land has been ordained for us to be a place for prayers and a substitute cultic purifier.

5.3.3.1.2.3. The bases for counter implicature

The ultimate conclusion that a hearer seeks when he is involved in the process of working out a counter implicature is to see whether or not the propositional converse of the speaker's utterance is an integral part of his message. In this section, we will examine how this type of inference has been generated and the assumptions on which it is based. A large portion of the discussion to be introduced here can be looked upon as a continuation of the arguments for the validity of counter implicature outlined in the preceding section.

Before proceeding, it is important to point out that counter implicature is not, strictly speaking, a logical inference. It is rather a communicative (or conversational) implicature *(mafhūm khiṭābī)*[209] constrained by, and based on, 'the principles of communication' *(qānūn al-khiṭābiyyāt)* rather than 'the principles of demonstration' *(qānūn al-istidlāl)*, to use al-Taftāzānī's terms.[210] It might be helpful at this point to say that modern pragmatists do share the Muslim legal theorists' view that implicatures are not logical inferences.[211] The difference between conversational implicatures and demonstrative deductions are drawn in the following manner: communicative implicatures are informal inferences which derive from specific communicative assumptions shared by the participants, while demonstrative deductions are formal inferences obtained by applying logical rules to given premises. Considering how the actual examples of counter implicature are accounted for and the way scalar-implicature, which, I assume, is the closest modern notion to counter implicatures, is treated, the Maxim of Quantity, among Grice's co-operative maxims, seems to play the essential role in generating counter implicatures. In PF, this generally seems to be true to a considerable extent. However, other principles, such as the Principle of Relevance and the Principle of the Speaker's Disposition to Make his Intention Manifest are also important. Furthermore, different scholars, as we shall see, place emphasis on different principles.

(i) The Principle of the Speaker's Disposition to Make his Intention Manifest and the Principle of *Iᶜmāl*.

The speaker is rational and has interest in making his intention manifest (the Principle of the Speaker's Disposition to Make his Intention Manifest),[212] so the hearer will take the utterance to be as informative as possible (the Principle of *Iᶜmāl*), assuming that 'increasing the communicative import' *(takthīr al-fāʾidah)* is consistent with the very essence of communication and the intentions of rational communicators.[213] Furthermore, the hearer will take any qualification made by the speaker to be operative, since ignoring it will amount to the assumption that the speaker's qualification is based on a random choice *(tarjīḥan min ghayri murajjiḥ)*,[214] which means that the speaker behaves arbitrarily. The *iᶜmāl* of ('making sense of') the expression in this case, the argument continues, can be made only if the hearer takes counter implicature to obtain, since it is the sole communicative import *(al-fāʾidah)* derived from the qualification.[215]

At this point, we should say something about the notion of *fāʾidah* in PF, which can roughly be translated as (communicative import). According to this notion, which is motivated by the Principle of the Speaker's Disposition to Make his Intention Manifest and the Principle of *Iᶜmāl*, any utterance in the actual communicative situation involves a communicative import (e.g., assertion, negation, questioning, congruent implicature, counter implicature). Communicative imports vary in terms of their importance. Assertion and negation, for example, are said to be essential communicative imports to any declarative sentence, while *al-mukhālafah* (contrasting or, technically speaking, counter implicature) is the weakest communicative import. So, when there is a conflict between a counter implicature and another communicative import, preference must be given to the other communicative import.[216]

However, grammatical construction is not the only way by means of which a communicative import is imparted; there are also pragmatic ways such as

- The departure *(al-ᶜudūl)* from a common construction or grammatical order, where the addressee understands from the addresser's transgression of the common order, for example, a particular implicature.[217]
- Setting a context *(naṣb qarīnah)*.

- Silence *(sukūt al-mutakallim)*, where the relevant silence of the speaker during the conversation is treated by some scholars as an informative process and is, consequently, given a certain communicative function. (cf. 4.7)

It should be noted, however, that the term *fāʾidah* is occasionally employed, especially in the discussion of counter implicature, in an extended sense where it refers to the purpose or the motive behind the speaker's qualification. In this extended sense of *fāʾidah*, extra-linguistic purposes and motives such as fear of the consequences of the use of an unqualified statement are captured by this term.[218]

(ii) The Principle of Quantity.

It is a general principle that speakers are taken to speak as much as is required. Consequently, it is normally wise to take all the speaker's words to be meaningful.[219] Thus, when someone says (1), he usually means (2), for if the rule of free-grazing camels was the same as that of camels which are not free-grazing, the speaker would be taken to be talking too much with a little meaning, or to use Ibn Taymiyyah's terms "he would be taken to lengthen the form and reduce the content" *(la-kāna qad ṭawwala l-lafẓa wa-naqqaṣa l-maᶜnā)*.[220]

(1) Alms-tax is due upon free-grazing camels.
(2) Alms-tax is not due upon camels which are not free-grazing.

Similarly, in utterances like (3), it is self-evident, says Ibn Taymiyyah, that the rule would be taken to be applicable exclusively to Muslims. In contrast, in the Prophet's saying (4), and if somebody initially says (5), counter implicature is perhaps invalid, for the speaker, in singling out Muslims rather than others, is taken to comply with the common practice by virtue of which people talk about Muslims rather than others owing to the fact that they live in a Muslim community.[221] This and similar constraints on counter implicature will be discussed later.

(3) People are of two kinds: Muslims and unbelievers, as for Muslims you have to be very kind to them.
(4) "Unlawful to a Muslim is every thing belonging to another Muslim: his blood, his property and his honour".
(5) You must be kind to Muslims.

Taking a similar position, Grice holds that implicatures attaching utterances like (3) are derived as a result of a flouting of the first

Maxim of Quantity;: "Make your contribution as informative as is required (for the current purpose of the exchange)".[222] His typical example of this kind of implicature is the following:

> [6] A is writing a testimonial about a pupil who is a candidate for a philosophy job, and his letter reads as follows: 'Dear Sir, Mr. X's command of English is excellent, and his attendance at tutorials has been regular. Yours, etc.' (Gloss: A cannot be opting out, since if he wished to be uncooperative, why write at all? He cannot be unable, through ignorance, to say more, since the man is his pupil; moreover, he knows that more information than this is wanted. He must, therefore, be wishing to impart information that he is reluctant to write down. This supposition is tenable only if he thinks Mr. X is no good at philosophy. This, then, what he is implicating.).[223]

Since first introduced by Grice, the Maxim of Quantity has been revised. I shall be introducing Harnish's revised version and Gazdar's account of this maxim in order to cast light on its role in generating counter implicatures. Combining it with the Maxim of Quality "(Have evidence of what you say)" and the Maxim of Relevance "(Be relevant)", Harnish proposes what he calls 'the Maxim of Quantity-Quality: "Make the strongest relevant claim justifiable by your evidence".[224] In a more straightforward account, Gazdar states that

> anyone uttering an a-sentence who was in a position to utter a d-sentence would be being less informative than he could be since the d-sentence makes a stronger claim about the world than the a-sentence. Thus, if the speaker is being cooperative and observing the Maxim of Quantity, it follows that in uttering a he is implicating the negation of d. The negation of d is simply b, so b is an implicature of the utterance of a.[225]

As Leech points out, "'strength' here refers to the amount of information communicated [. . .]: 'If *P* entails *Q* and *Q* does not entail *P*, then *P* is stronger than *Q*".[226] To put it the legal theorists' way, the general is stronger than the specific. Thus, descending *(nuzūl)* or switching *(intiqāl)*, as al-Shīrāzī subtly formulates it, from a general concept to a specific one *(ʿan ismin ʿāmmin ilā ismin khāṣ)*, would be the basis for generating this kind of implicatures.[227] In other words, if the speaker descends from a general proposition to a specific one, he will be taken to implicate the negation of the general proposition. Leech provides the formulation of this rule this way: "THE WEAKER

PROPOSITION IMPLICATES THAT S BELIEVES THE NEGATIVE OF THE STRONGER PROPOSITION".[228] So, (7) implicates (8).

(7) Jill ate some of the biscuits.
(8) Jill did not eat all the biscuits.
(9) Jill ate all the biscuits.

Leech explains how implicatures like (8) are generated in the following formula:

a) *s* has uttered a weaker proposition *Q* [(7)] where *s* could just as easily and relevantly have uttered a stronger proposition *P* [(9)].
b) By the Maxim of Quantity-Quality, this, in the absence of contrary information, means that the evidence *s* has does not justify the assertion of *P* [(9)], but does justify the assertion of Q [(7)].
c) This leads to the implicature that *s* believes *P* [(9)] to be false, *i.e.,:* *s* believes that *not-P* [(8)].[229]

(iii) The Principle of Relevance.

Among Muslim legal theorists, al-Juwaynī holds that relevance *(al-munāsabah)* is essential to generate a valid counter implicature. By relevance al-Juwaynī means the connection between the rule and the mentioned case. According to him, the reason why counter implicature is obtainable in (10) has to do with the fact that the property of being free-grazing is a relevant cause to being taxable since free-grazing sheep are far less costly than stall-fed sheep. Similarly, delaying an overdue debt for a person who is capable of payment in (11) is a relevant cause to being unjust, since he has no excuse for procrastination.

(10) Alms-tax is due upon free-grazing sheep.
(11) "It is unjust for a finder (a person who is able to pay) to procrastinate an overdue payment" *(layyu l-wājidi ẓulm)*. (A Prophetic saying).

Obviously, there is no connection between whiteness and becoming full in (12), since all people become full if they eat. So, (12), in al-Juwaynī's view, does not implicate (13).[230]

(12) White man becomes full if he eats.
(13) Non-white man does not become full if he eats.

However, as pointed out in the discussion of the second argument of the advocates of counter implicature, the oddness of utterances like (14) and (12) is due to the fact that they give rise to false implicatures such as (15) and (13). If this is true, it will, then, be wrong to subscribe to al-Juwaynī's view that (12) does not implicate (13).

(14) Dead Jews cannot see.
(15) Other dead people can see.

5.3.3.1.2.4. The conditions for the validity of counter implicature

We have already seen that counter implicature is a weak inference and can, therefore, easily be cancelled. In this section we shall be discussing the conditions of the validity of counter implicature, the lack of each of which represents a constraint on its validity and causes it to be cancelled. These conditions are as follows:

i the unmentioned is neither more fitting to the rule than the mentioned nor equal to it.[231] So in the *Qur'ānic* verse (1) where the rule (the prohibition of killing children) is more relevant to the unmentioned (killing children without fearing poverty) than the mentioned (killing them for fear of poverty), counter implicature (2) is invalid.[232]

(1) "Kill not your children for fear of poverty".[233]
(2) It is permissible to kill your children if you do not fear poverty.

The cancellation of counter implicature here is governed by a well-established rule by virtue of which: when a stronger signifier is in conflict with a weaker signifier, the weaker must be overruled by the stronger.[234] And since the counter implicature here is in conflict with a stronger implicature, that is, the congruent implicature in (3), it must be cancelled.

(3) With a yet stronger reason, do not kill your children if you do not fear poverty.

A similar example would be (4) which does not give rise to (5).

(4) If you fail the exam, you will not be punished.
(5) If you pass the exam, you will be punished.

ii The qualification is not due to a dominant custom, otherwise it will be regarded as a description rather than a condition. Thus, the qualification (under your guardianship) ***(allātī fī ḥujūrikum)*** in the *Qur'ānic* verse (6) is said to be made not to exclude step-daughters that are not under guardianship but to describe the common custom according to which step-daughters live with their mothers and their step-fathers.[235]

(6) "Prohibited to you are your mothers, [. . .], your step-daughters under your guardianship, born of your wives to whom you have gone in".[236]

In an attempt to account for the invalidity of counter implicature in such a situation, al-Qarāfī says that this is

> because of the fact that the dominant property of an entity is associated with it in the mind [. . .]. So, if the speaker recalls the entity in order to attribute something to it, the entity conjures the property up. The speaker, therefore, mentions the property not to indicate the negation of the rule with respect to the unmentioned case but because of its association in his mind with that entity.[237]

To take another example, the clause 'in my pocket' in (7) is not said to exclude the money deposited in the bank, simply because it is very common to express oneself in this way in such situations.

(7) a- Are you going abroad this summer?

b- It depends on how much money I have in my pocket.

iii The text containing the qualification is not uttered in response to a particular question or event.[238] So, (8), as already pointed out, does not implicate (9), for the qualification 'free-grazing' is not made to exclude stall-fed sheep, but because it was the subject of the question made in (8).

(8) Is alms-tax due upon free-grazing sheep?
(9) Yes, alms-tax is due upon free-grazing sheep.

A similar example may be quoted from Levinson:

> Suppose that in order to get the lavish subsidy under the EEC Cow Subsidy Scheme one must have three cows, and the inspector asks John's neighbour the following question:
>
> (10) I: Has John really got the requisite number of cows?
>
> N: Oh sure, he's got three cows all right.[239]

In such a situation, (10) does not implicate (11) "because it is clear from the context that all the information that is required is whether John's herd passes the threshold for subsidy payment, not the exact number of cows he might in fact have".[240]

(11) John has only three cows and no more.

iv There is no supposition that the speaker is ignorant of the rule of the unmentioned, otherwise the hearer may think that the speaker has left the unmentioned out because of his ignorance of its rule.[241]

It may be helpful here to adopt Leech's distinction between the 'positive version' and the 'neutral version' of an implicature.

> "The neutral version is: '*S* does not believe that *P* is true, nor does s believe that *P* is false'. This would be the conclusion if *s* simply did not have enough evidence to decide, as in:
>
> (12) Jill ate SOME of the biscuits (but I don't know whether she ate all of them).[242]

According to Leech, determining whether an implicature is positive or neutral depends on contextual information. "One context will suggest that *s* has withheld the information because of lack of knowledge, and another that *s* has withheld it because of a definite belief to the contrary".[243]

These are some of the conditions mentioned by Muslim legal theorists for the validity of counter implicatures. Both the proponents and opponents of counter implicature agree that counter implicature is invalid when any of the constraints obtains, but the proponents say that they are definite in number and that the hearer will be able to detect them. So, if there is no contextual evidence that any of them exists, the hearer will take the counter implicature to be valid. The opponents of counter implicatures, on the other hand, hold that the constraints are indefinite and it is not in the capacity of the addressee to come to the conclusion that none of them exists. Therefore, he will not be able to infer whether or not a particular counter implicature is an integral part of the speaker's message. This view is rejected on the grounds that counter implicature is calculable and probabilistic, and based on the addressee's supposition that there is no evidence to the contrary.[244]

5.3.3.1.2.5. Types of counter implicature

Although Muslim legal theorists distinguish several types of counter implicature, there is no general agreement among them on the number of these types. However, it is generally accepted that each of these types can be looked upon as an inference arising from the use of one of different kinds of premodifiers and post-modifiers such as conditions, qualifiers and quantifiers. In this section, I will sketch out the most distinctive types of this kind of implicature:

(I) *Mafhūm al-laqab* (The implicature of a Designation). This is an implicature derived from the attribution of a particular rule to a proper name or a common noun. Only a handful of Muslim scholars, notably Abū Bakr al-Daqqāq (d. 392/1001), assume the validity of this type of counter implicature for the formulation of the law, while the overwhelming majority strongly controvert that.[245] Those who assume the validity of the implicature of a Designation say that (1) gives rise to implicatures like (2) and (3). Moreover, they argue that if one says (4) to his adversary, he will be implicating (5), and this is the only reason why great jurists like Mālik Ibn Anas (d. 179/795) and Aḥmad Ibn Ḥanbal (d. 241/855) hold that anyone who says an utterance like (4) should be charged with *qadhf* (defamation) for accusing his adversary's mother of fornication.

(1) Alms-tax is due upon sheep.
(2) Alms-tax is not due upon cattle.
(3) Alms-tax is not due upon camels.
(4) My mother is not a fornicator.
(5) Your mother is a fornicator.

The opponents of this kind of implicature say that (5) does not follow from the saying of (4) alone but with the help of the situational contexts (the fact that the participants are being engaged in a quarrel with the presumption that people do intend to insult each other in such situations). So it cannot be subsumed under the type of counter implicature which arises from the linguistically apparent meaning of the expression *(alladhī yakūnu l-lafẓu ẓāhiran fīhi lughatan)*.[246] To put it in modern terms, this is a particularised rather than generalised implicature since its generation is sensitive to context and dependent on observing the maxim of relevance. Genuine examples of counter implicature, in contrast, are valid irrespective of the context in which they are uttered and are worked out with recourse to the Maxim of Quantity. And the reason why this particular example does not lend itself to the Maxim of Quantity relates, as indicated earlier, to the fact that there is no presumption that the speaker has 'descended' from a general concept to a specific one, and consequently no intention of 'indicating contrast' *(mukhālafah)* is involved.[247] However, there are some borderline cases where it is hard, for the lack of evidence, to judge whether or not the speaker has departed from a general concept to a specific one, and since it is not clear whether or not the saying of (1) involves a descent (in al-Shīrāzī's sense of the term) from the general concept *naʿam* (livestock) to the specific *ghanam* (sheep), it follows that (1) could be one of these borderline cases.

(**II**) *Mafhūm al-ṣifah* (The implicature of a Restrictive Attribute). The term 'Restrictive Attribute' is extended here to cover more categorises than is covered by *ṣifah* or *naʿt* (adjective) in Arabic Grammar. It covers such grammatical categories as adverbs of time ((6) +> (i.e., implicates) (7)), adverbs of place ((8) +> (9)), adverbs of manner ((10) +> (11)), as well as post-adjectives ((12) +> (13) and (14) +> (15)), pre-adjectives ((16) +> (17) and (18) +> (19)) and controversially adjectives without nouns ((20) +> (21)).[248]

(6) Travel on Friday.
(7) Do not travel on any day other than Friday.
(8) Sit in front of him.
(9) Do not sit behind him (or in anyplace other than the one specified).
(10) He has read the story quickly.
(11) He has not read it slowly.
(12) *fī l-ghanami l-sāʾimati zakāh.*
(13) *laysa fī ghayri l-ghanami l-sāʾimati zakāh.*
(14) Send all the cars available.
(15) You do not have to send cars which are not available.
(16) *fī sāʾimati l-ghanami zakāh.*
(17) *laysa fī sāʾimati l-ghanami zakāh.*
(18) Alms-tax is due upon free-grazing sheep.
(19) Alms-tax is not due upon sheep which are not free-grazing.
(20) Alms-tax is due upon the free-ranging (al-*sāʾimah*).
(21) Alms-tax is not due upon the non-free-ranging.

However, not any attribute is relevant here but only those which are intended to restrict and identify the noun *(al-waṣfu -alladhī yakūnu li-l-takhṣīsi ay naqṣi l-shuyūʿi wa-taqlīli l-ishtirāk)* (i.e., restrictive attributes and defining relative clauses). So the mentioning of attributes which have no restrictive function but are mentioned for other purposes such as 'praise' *(thanāʾ)* in (22), 'condemn' *(dhamm)* in (23), emphasis *(taʾkīd)* in (24) does not give rise to counter implicatures.[249]

(22) "In the name of God, Most Gracious, Most Merciful".[250]

(23) "We have guarded them from every evil spirit accursed".[251]

(24) *amsi l-dābiru lā yaʿūd* (Yesterday gone by will not come again).

Another kind of attribute which is not regarded as restrictive, and consequently not indicative of counter implicature, is what is called *ṣifāt ittifāqiyyah* (accidental attribute) such as *ḥabashī aswad* (a black Negro), the relative clause "who bowed (as in Islam) to God's Will" in the *Qur'ānic* verse (25) and the relative clause "that flies on its wings" in the *Qur'ānic* verse (26).[252]

(25) "It was We who revealed
The Law (to Moses): therein
Was guidance and light.
By its standard have been judged
The Jews, by the Prophets
Who bowed (as In Islam)
To God's Will, By the Rabbis
And the Doctors of Law".[253]

(26) "There is not an animal (that lives) on the earth, nor a bird that flies on its wings, but (forms part of) communities like you".[254]

(III) *Mafhūm al-sharṭ* (The Implicature of a Condition). By this kind of implicature, a conditional statement "if *p*, then *q*" is interpreted as a biconditional one, which is typically represented in English by "if and only if *p*, then *q*". The Implicature of a Condition is a subject of considerable controversy in PF. Before we commence our discussion of this controversy, it is important to point out that conditionals come in two varieties: causal and real. By a causal conditional, I mean a conditional formula which expresses a causal connection between two clauses, no matter whether the antecedent *(al-muqaddam)* (or the first clause) is the cause and the consequent *(al-tālī)* (or the second clause) is the effect like (27) or *vice versa* as in (28).[255]

(27) If the sun is shining, it is a daytime.
(28) If it is a daytime, the sun is shining.

'Cause' is defined here as "that whose existence implies the existence of something else and non-existence implies the non-existence of that thing" *(mā yalzamu min wujūdihi l-wujūd wa-min ᶜadamihi l-ᶜadam)*.[256] In other words, *p* is a cause for *q* if and only if (i) when *p* occurs *q* necessarily follows and (ii) *q* does not occur when there is no *p*. So, 'cause' is interpreted here as a 'sufficient condition' or, as al-Jurjānī calls it, 'the complete cause' *(al-sabab al-tāmm)*.[257]

By a real conditional, I mean a conditional formula which expresses no causal connection between the antecedent and the consequent. What I am trying to suggest by the term 'real', therefore, is that real conditions are compatible with the very nature of conditions as defined by Muslim legal theorists. According to al-Qarāfī, condition *(al-sharṭ)* is "that whose non-existence implies the non-existence of something else but its existence does not imply the existence nor the non-existence of that thing"[258] That is to say, *p* is a condition for *q* if and only if when there is no *p* there is no *q* no matter whether *q* occurs or does not occur when there is *p*. So, 'condition' is interpreted here as 'necessary condition' or, as al-Jurjānī calls it, 'the incomplete cause' *(al-sabab al-ghayr al-tāmm)*.[259]

It should not be understood from the word 'real' in this context that real conditionals are more common or more frequent in communication than causal conditionals. In fact, the converse is true, 'linguistic conditions *(al-shurūṭ al-lughawiyyah)*, according to al-Qarāfī, are of the causal type.[260] Some legal theorists, however, prefer to say most, rather than all, of linguistic conditions are of the causal type in order, I assume, to include utterances such as (29) where there is no causal relationship in the above sense of the term between the antecedent (being human) and the consequent (being an animal).[261]

(29) If Zayd is a human, he is an animal.

'Linguistic conditions' are usually contrasted with 'non-linguistic conditions'. By the former, (also called syntactic conditions *(al-shurūṭ al-naḥwiyyah)* are meant conditional statements expressed in the language by the syntactic form "if *p*, then *q*" (or similar forms). By the latter are meant "rational conditions like living for learning, legal conditions, like purification for performing prayer, and normal conditions like nutrition for remaining alive".[262] On the surface, the distinction between linguistic and non-linguistic conditions are implausible since each of the so-called non-linguistic conditions can be expressed by the syntactic form "if *p*, then *q*", but what the legal theorists seem to mean is this: a non-linguistic condition in its nature, and before being expressed by the language, can be a sufficient or necessary one, but once it is put in the syntactic form "if *p*, then *q*" by a given speaker in a given communicative situation, the addressee will understand that the speaker implies that *p* is a sufficient condition, and consequently the syntactic form "if *p*, then *q*" will be interpreted as "if and only if *p*, then *q*".[263] The addressee will probably reason as follows: if there had been any other condition, the speaker would have said so, but since he did not mention any other condition, it follows that there is probably no other condition.[264] However, there could be situations where the speaker sets two or more conditions in one conditional statement either by disjunction as in (30), or by conjunction as in (31), but such cases still fall under causal conditions.[265]

(30) If you open the window or switch the light on, you can read the book.
(31) If you open the window and switch the light on, you can read the book.

Thus, there is no doubt that the basis for the generation of 'The Implicature of a Condition' is not logical but conversational, but the question is which maxim gives rise to it? According to Levinson, this kind of implicature

> is working in the opposite direction from ordinary Quantity inferences: normally by Quantity if I say a weaker statement where a stronger one would have been relevant, I implicate that I am not in a position to make the stronger one. Here on the other hand by making the weaker statement [34] I implicate the stronger one [35].[266]

This, however, does not seem to be a plausible account. In fact, 'The Implicature of a Condition' is an ordinary Quantity inference, where the speaker is assumed, by virtue of the Maxim of Quantity, to have descended from the general (because he believes it to be false) to the specific. For example, the *Qur'ānic* verse in (32), which concerns divorced women, gives rise to (33) because the general (i.e., (36)) has deliberately been left out to indicate (33).

(32) "And if they carry (life
In their wombs), then
Spend (your substance) on them
Until they deliver".[267]
(33) If they are not pregnant, you do not have to spend for them.
(34) Spend for them if they are pregnant.
(35) Spend for them if and only if they are pregnant.
(36) Spend for them whether they are pregnant or not.

However, the opponents of the Implicature of a Condition advance few arguments against its validity, only one of which appears to be powerful. I will discuss this powerful argument soon, but before that I should point out that part of the confusion about the validity of the Implicature of a Condition seems to come from the use of improper examples, which is in turn due to the fact that the term 'condition' in Arabic grammar is misleading. Most, if not all, of the traditional Arab grammarians consider utterances such as (37), (38), (39) and (40) as conditional statements. Some legal theorists take this view for granted and use such utterances, accordingly, as counter-examples to the notion of the Implicature of a Condition. Al-Bājī, for instance, says that if someone says (37), it is understood that he clearly states that 'whoever comes must be given a Dirham', but he says nothing about the non-coming.[268]

(37) *man jāʾaka fa-aʿṭihi* dirhaman
(Whoever comes to you, give him a Dirham).
(38) *aynamā tadhhab adhhab maʿak*
(Wherever you go, I'll go with you).
(39) *matā tadhhab adhhab maʿak*
(Whenever you go, I'll go with you.
(40) *mahmā tafʿal fī l-dunyā fa-Sa-sa-tarāhu fī l-ākhirah*
(Whatever you do in this life, you will see it in the hereafter).

Although one may be tempted to include such utterances under counter implicature, possibly under the implicature of a Designation, this, however, does not seem to be as strong an inference as the advocates of the Implicature of a Condition would think it to be.

However, the most serious objection directed to the Implicature of a Condition is that in utterances like (41) where the antecedent is more general than (i.e., entails) the consequent, it would be paradoxical to infer counter implicature.[269] Thus, (41) does not implicate (42), because (42) contradicts the very self-evident fact that not all animals are human.

(41) If Zayd is a human, he is an animal.
(42) If Zayd is not a human, he is not an animal.

One possible escape from this objection is to say that (42) is invalid because, as already stated, the connection between the antecedent (Zayd is a human) and the consequent (he is an animal) is not of a causal nature. Granted that (41) is not a causal conditional, the question arises here as to whether it is true that this kind of implicature is based, as mentioned above, on the assumption that the speaker in saying an utterance like (41), with this particular form "if *p*, then *q*", is assuming a causal connection between the antecedent and the consequent. In dealing with this issue, I would point out the following: it is essential here to recognise that we are dealing with two separate issues: (i) whether (41) fails to give rise to (42); and (ii) whether (42) is a valid logical inference. It is arguable that both (i) and (ii) are false, but their falsehood is due to different reasons. With respect to (i), it is false because (41) by virtue of the Maxim of Quantity and its underlying principle, that is, the Principle of Co-operation, the speaker in saying (41) is implicating (42), otherwise he will be regarded as uncooperative and misleading. As for (ii), it is false because it conflicts with the logical fact that some animals are not human. Accordingly, it is reasonable to say that the speaker of (41) is implicating (42) but the hearer would not take (42) to be an intended communicative intention of the speaker, owing to a diverting context, which is the fact that not all animals are human. In my discussion of the circumstances in which diverting contexts eliminate irrelevant interpretations (cf. 3.5.1.4), I pointed out that an interpretation is discarded if it contradicts logical or customary facts.[270] In the case of the signification of 'what is said', when the literal interpretation is recognised to be nonsense, unlikely or impossible, the addressee eliminates it and searches for an ulterior one (cf. 3.5). In the case of implicature, there is no literal or non -literal interpretation; instead, there are two possibilities: either to take the implicature to be valid (when there is no diverting context) or to take it to be invalid (when it is cancelled by a diverting context as in (42)). The difference between the two cases has to do with the Principle of *Iᶜmāl*, which stipulates that, in the case of the signification of 'what is said', if there is evidence that expressions are not being used in their literal meanings "they must be interpreted figuratively in order to avoid the cancellation of the utterance and leaving the expression without intention"[271] (cf.

3.5.1.3). This is obviously inapplicable to implicatures since they can easily be cancelled in communication. However, modern logicians, semanticians and pragmatists distinguish between what they call 'material implication', which is represented by "if *p*, then *q*" from that called 'equivalence', which is represented by "if and only if *p*, then *q*" in terms of their truth-conditions.[272] In the case of material implication, the conditional sentence must be false only if the antecedent is true and the consequent is false. So, from a strictly logical viewpoint, the saying of (43) commits the speaker to the falsity of (46) only (as it contradicts the propositional content of what he explicitly stated) but not to that of (44) and (45).[273]

(43) If you fail the exam, you will be punished.
(44) If you do not fail the exam, you will be punished.
(45) If you do not fail the exam, you will not be punished.
(46) If you fail the exam, you will not be punished.

The saying of (47), in contrast, commits the speaker not only to the falsity of (50) but also to the falsity of (48), and consequently to the truth of (49).

(47) If and only if you fail the exam, you will be punished.
(48) If you do not fail the exam, you will be punished.
(49) If you do not fail the exam, you will not be punished.
(50) If you fail the exam, you will not be punished.

Compare the following two tables:[274]

Truth table for material implication

p (the antecedent)	q (the consequent)	$p \rightarrow q$	examples
true	true	true	(43)
true	false	false	(46)
false	true	true	(44)
false	false	true	(45)

Truth table for equivalence

p (the actecedent)	q (the consequent)	$p \rightarrow q$	examples
true	true	true	(47)
true	false	false	(50)
false	true	false	(48)
false	false	true	(49)

(IV) *Mafhūm al-ghāyah* (The implicature of a Time Limit). When the speaker connects the rule with a time limit, he will be taken, according to the advocates of counter implicature, to be (i) explicitly stating that the rule is confined to that limit, and (ii) implicating that the rule of the unmentioned (i.e., the time beyond the limit) is opposite to the rule of the unmentioned. The opponents of the implicature of a Time Limit, on the other hand accept (i) but reject (ii).[275] Thus, (51a), according to the advocates of counter implicature, implicates (52), and (53) implicates (54).

(51a) "Keep away from women
In their courses, and do not
Approach them until
They are clean."[276]
(52) You may (or it is permissible for you to) approach women when they are clean.
(53) The lecture will continue till midday.
(54) The lecture will not continue after midday.

The proponents of the Implicature of a Time Limit say that the mentioning of a time limit is a proclamation on the part of the speaker that the rule will lapse when the time limit is reached. If the time after that limit was given the same rule, there would be no point of setting that limit and the speaker' utterance would be deemed nonsense *(laghw)*, something which is avoidable in communication.[277] Furthermore, it is inappropriate for the hearer of the utterance (53) to ask the question in (55) since the answer is already available in (53).[278]

(55) Will the lecture continue after midday?

As we saw earlier, the appropriateness of enquiry is one of the widely recognised tests applied in the PF (as in the above example) to check whether or not an utterance gives rise to a particular inference; it is used by some legal theorists, with objections from others, to ascertain whether a given inference is derived from what is said or by implication.

The opponents of this kind of implicature, on the other hand, say that in utterances like (53), the speaker is, in actual fact, silent about the situation after the time limit.[279] For example, the speaker of (53) said nothing about whether or not the lecture will continue after midday. It is only for this reason, continues the argument, that there are many *Qur'ānic* and non-*Qur'ānic* texts in which the rule of the unmentioned is clearly not meant to be contrasted to the rule of the mentioned. To take one example, the *Qur'ānic* verse (51a) does not implicate (52), for there is another condition that should be fulfilled before men can approach their wives, that is, 'women should purify themselves'.[280] This condition is understood from the rest of the verse (51b):

(51b) "But when they have
Purified themselves,
Ye may approach them
In any manner, time, or place
Ordained for you by
God"[281]

The simple answer to such an argument is to say that this is an instance in which an implicature is cancelled by a stronger indicator. In other words, (51a) implicates (52) but this inference is cancelled by the context (i.e., the rest of the verse cited above).

(V) *Mafhūm al-ʿadad* (the Implicature of a Stated Numeral). The controversy concerning the validity of counter implicature here takes the form of whether or not specifying a particular number implies that the rule of the higher and lower numbers is different from that of the stated number. Before we begin our discussion of this controversy, it should be remarked that it is quite relevant to this discussion to realise that there is a difference between the relation between a general (or universal) and specific (or particular) concept on the one hand, and the relation between a higher and lower number on the other, in terms of the effect of the assertion of any of the two pairs to its assertion to its partner, and the negation of any of the two pairs to its negation with respect to its partner.

In the case of the former, as explained earlier, logically speaking,

i the assertion of the specific entails the assertion of the general (e.g., (56) entails (57)).[282]
ii the negation of the general entails the negation of the specific (e.g., (58) entails (59)).[283]
iii the assertion of the general does not necessarily entail the assertion of the specific (e.g., (57) does not entail (56)).[284]
iv the negation of the specific does not entail the negation of the general (e.g., (59) does not entail (58)).[285]

(56) There is a 'man' in the house.
(57) There is a human in the house.
(58) There is no human in the house.
(59) There is no man in the house.

In the case of the latter, the rules, at least in some examples, are different:

i the assertion of a rule to the lower may or may not entail its assertion to the higher, so (60) entails (61), but (62) does not entail (63).

(60) Three thousand pounds are enough (or too much) for the car.
(61) Four thousand pounds are enough (or too much) for the car.
(62) Zayd has three children.
(63) Zayd has four children.

ii the negation of a rule with respect to the higher may or may not entail its negation with respect to the lower, so (64) entails (65), but (66) does not entail (67).

(64) Four thousand pounds are not enough (or too much) for the car.
(65) Three thousand pounds are not enough (or too much) for the car.
(66) Zayd has not four children.
(67) Zayd has not three children.

iii the assertion of a rule to the higher may or may not entail its assertion to the lower, so (63) entails (62), but (61) does not entail (60).

iv the negation of a rule with respect to the lower may or may not entail its negation with respect to the higher, so (67) entails (66), but (65) does not entail (64).

According to al-Baṣrī, whether the assertion of a given rule to a particular number entails or does not entail its assertion to the *higher* number depends on whether the utterance is obligation, prohibition or permission.

i In the case of obligation, the lower does not entail the higher, so (69) does not entail (68).

(68) Give him a hundred pounds.
(69) Give him fifty pounds.

ii In the case of permission, the lower may entail the higher, thus (73) entails (72), and may not entail it, so (71) does not entail (70).

(70) You may give him a hundred pounds.
(71) You may give him fifty pounds.
(72) You may base your judgement on the testimony of two witnesses.
(73) You may base your judgement on the testimony of one witness.

iii In the case of prohibition, the lower, according to al-Baṣrī, entails the higher, so (75) entails (74), but, I would argue, there are some cases in which the lower may not entail the higher, so (77) does not entail (76).[286]

(74) Do not give him a hundred pounds.
(75) Do not give him fifty pounds.
(76) Do not base your judgement on the testimony of two witnesses.
(77) Do not base your judgement on the testimony of one witness.

Similarly, whether the assertion of a given rule to a particular number entails or does not entail its assertion to the *lower* number depends on whether the utterance is obligation, prohibition or permission.

i In the case of obligation, the higher, according to Abū l-Ḥusayn al-Baṣrī, entails the lower, so (68) entails (69), but again, I would assume, there are some cases in which the higher may not entail the lower, so (78) does not entail (79). In fact, utterances like (78) implies (77) which represents the falsity of (79), and this is one of three cases which are admitted by ᶜAbd Allāh al-Baṣrī to be instances of counter implicatures.[287]

(78) Base your judgement on the testimony of two witnesses.
(79) Base your judgement on the testimony of one witness.

ii In the case of permission, the higher may entail the lower, thus (70) entails (71), and may not entail it, so (72) does not entail (73).

iii In the case of prohibition, the higher does not entail the lower, so (74) does not entail (75).[288]

However, as far as counter implicature is concerned, the advocates of this kind of implicature hold that the saying of (80) implicates that (81) and (82) are true, while the opponents deny that.[289]

(80) Zayd has three children.
(81) Zayd has not only (or exactly) two children.
(82) Zayd has not four children.

To explain this, we should point out that, for the proponents of the implicature of a Stated Numeral, there are three possible interpretations for specifying a certain number in terms of counter implicature:

i at least (i.e., no less than) *p*, which requires that the rule of the lower number must be the opposite (e.g., the Prophetic saying in (83));

(83) Five sucks makes the sucker an unmarriageable person *(khamsu raḍaᶜātin yuḥarrimnn).*

ii at most (i.e., no more than) *p*, which requires that the rule of the higher number must be the opposite (e.g., the *Qur'ānic* verse in (84);[290] and

(84) "If thou ask seventy times
For their forgiveness, God
Will not forgive them".[291]

iii exactly (i.e., no less or more than) *p*, which requires that the rule of both the lower and the higher number must be the opposite (e.g., the *Qur'ānic* verse in (85)). All the above interpretations are rejected by the opponents of the Implicature of a Stated Numeral.

(85) "And those who launch
A charge against chaste women,
And produce not four witnesses
(to support their allegations),_
Flog them with eighty stripes;
And reject their evidence".[292]

With respect to (83) the advocates of counter implicature argue that if four (or less) sucks were enough to make the sucker an unmarriageable person, then it would imply that the fifth suck is not the decisive one and is consequently dispensable. For if the prohibition already obtained before the fifth, it would be impossible to obtain by the fifth, a conclusion which leads to the cancellation of what is said.[293]

With respect to (84), the advocates say that when this verse was revealed, the Prophet said *"la-azīdanna ᶜalā l-sabᶜīn"* (I will exceed seventy), which means that what exceeds seventy would make a difference.[294]

Among the counter-arguments developed by the opponents of the implicature of a Stated Numeral to reject this conclusion are the following: the mentioning of 'seventy' in the above verse is intended not to be taken in its literal sense, but to express exaggeration.[295] And the reason why the Prophet said 'I will exceed seventy' could be just to express good intention towards them in order to attract them to the religion.[296]

As to (85), the opponents say that the negation of the higher number is not due to counter implicature, but to the absence of evidence. And when there is no evidence to the contrary, a past state should be maintained.[297]

Finally, it should be pointed out that all the above cases in which a higher number entails a lower number (as between (68)–(69), (70)–(71)) or *vice versa* (as between (75)–(74)) can be regarded as instances of congruent implicature at least in one of the two senses of the term.

(**VI**) *Mafhūm al-istithnāʾ* (the Implicature of an Exception). According to this type of implicature, (86) gives rise to (87).

(86) Nobody is generous except Zayd.
(87) Zayd is generous.

This kind of inference differs from the typical types of counter implicature which have been dealt with so far in that it is not so clear whether the implicit inference (i.e., (87)) is an integral part of the conventional propositional content of the utterance (i.e., (86)) or implicated by it. Al-Qarāfī, who wrote a book of more than six hundred pages on 'exception', holds that an inference indicating the rule of the thing excepted (e.g., (87)) is derived from the implicational rather than equivalent signification of an utterance containing the exception (e.g., (86)). He argues that 'exception particles' are 'established' exclusively for the exclusion from the general term. Giving the thing excepted a rule opposite to that of the general term, on the other hand, is not a conventional, but rational, issue. It is an issue based on the theorem that contradiction involves only two parties, the exclusion from either of which necessarily implies the inclusion in the other, which represents the exact opposite. So, supposing that contradiction involved more than two parties, the exclusion from one party would not necessitate the inclusion in the opposite.[298] Therefore, what we are dealing with here is a special kind of counter implicature which, for being determinate, cannot be cancelled without contradiction.

(VII) *Mafhūm al-ḥaṣr* (the Implicature of Confinement). This kind of implicatures is said to arise in utterances in which the subject is intensionally more general than the predicate. In other words, when the subject potentially denotes more individuals than the predicate does.[299] For example, when there is no evidence that the phrase 'the scholar' is being used referentially, (88) gives rise to (89).

(88) The scholar in the town is Zayd.
(89) There is only one scholar in the town.

There is, however, a considerable amount of controversy about whether this kind of reference is derived from 'what is said, drawn by counter implicature or drawn by the departure from the natural order usually used for predication.[300]

There are three possibilities of dealing with (89): either

i to take it to have been asserted (by the speaker of (88)), or
ii to take it to have been presupposed, or
iii to take it to have been implicated.

To put it another way, we may either equate, roughly speaking, (89) with (89a), (89b) or (89c).

(89a) I assert that there is only one scholar in the town.
(89b) I presuppose that there is only one scholar in the town.
(89c) I implicate that there is only one scholar in the town.

Obviously, it is very unlikely, if at all, that (89a) is an accurate interpretation of (88), because if (89) was asserted by (88), the truth-condition of both propositions would have the same effect if (88) is negated, but it is very clear that the negation of (88) (which is expressed in (90)) will have no effect on the truth-condition of (89). That is to say, (90) still engenders (89).

(90) The scholar in the town is not Zayd.

So, there remain two valid possibilities: (89b) and (89c). The advocates of the Implicature of Confinement opt for (89c),[301] but, I would argue that (89b) is more plausible on account of two reasons: first, counter implicature like any other conversational implicature is cancellable without contradiction, but (89) is not; and second, as explained earlier (cf. 5.2.1.1), it is a characteristic feature of presuppositions that if an utterance p presupposes q, and p is false, presupposition requires that q must be true, and this is exactly the case with the relationship between (88) and (89).

Those who say that the inference (92), to take another example, is engendered by flouting the natural order; hold that it is more natural to say 'Zayd is my friend' than to say (91), but if the speaker reverses, this order by saying (91), he would probably be taken to indicate (92).[302]

(91) My friend is Zayd.
(92) I have no friend other than Zayd.

The rationale behind the belief that 'Zayd is my friend' is the natural order, for predication has to do with the widely held rule that predicates must be either as general as or more general than subjects,[303] which means that (93) is an acceptable utterance, but (94) is not. In order to maintain this rule, the subject is always interpreted as either equal or less general than the predicate, thus, since 'Zayd' is particular, then 'friend' must be so; that is, the speaker of (91) must have only one friend, namely Zayd.

(93) Zayd is a human being.
(94) A human being is Zayd.

NOTES

1 Al-Sharīf al-Jurjānī, *al-Taᶜrīfāt*, p. 55; see also al-Subkīs, *al-Ibhāj*, 1/203; al-Asnawī, 2/31; al-Tahānawī, 1/486.
2 Al-Tahānawī, 1/486; see Fākhūrī, *ᶜIlm al-Dalālah . . .*, p. 39.
3 Saussure, *Course in Général Linguistics*, pp. 13–15.
4 Al-Sharīf al-Jurjānī, *Ḥāshiyah ᶜalā Sharḥ al-ᶜAḍud*, 1/120–121; see also, al-Asnawī, 2/31.
5 Al-Āmidī (1986), 1/36–37; Ibn al-Ḥājib, 1/120; al-Sharīf al-Jurjānī, *Ḥāshiyah ᶜalā Sharḥ al-ᶜAḍud*, 1/121.
6 Al-Tahānawī, 1/488; see Fākhūrī, *op. cit.*, p. 27.
7 Al-Harawī, 1/121.
8 Al-Tahānawī, 1/488.
9 Al-Sharīf al-Jurjānī, *Ḥāshiyah ᶜalā Sharḥ al-ᶜAḍud*, 1/120.
10 *Dhirāᶜ* differs as we pass from one Arab country to another: in Syria, for example, it equals (.68 m); in Egypt, there is *baladī dhirāᶜ* which equals (.58) and *istanbūlī dhirāᶜ* which equals (665m) etc.; see Cowan (ed.), *Arabic-English Dictionary . . .*, (*dhirāᶜ*).
11 Al-Asnawī, 2/31.
12 See Mullākhusrū, 1/198.
13 Al-Qarāfī, *Sharḥ Tanqīḥ*, p. 23; see also, al-Asnawī, 2/31–32.
14 See al-Qarāfī, *Sharḥ Tanqīḥ*, p.23.
15 Al-Subkīs, *al-Ibhāj*, 1/204.
16 Ibn Ḥazm, *al-Iḥkām*, 1/41.

17 Al-Mawṣilī, 2/68. Ibn al-Qayyim remarks that it is common to devote *dilālah (bi-kasri l-dāl)* to the former sense and *dalālah (bi-fatḥi l-dāl)* to the latter (2/68).
18 Al-Fanārī, *Ḥāshiyah*, 1/163.
19 See al-Tahānawī, 1/489.
20 Al-Subkīs, *al-Ibhāj*, 1/192.
21 *Ibid.*, 1/191–192.
22 Al-Tahānawī, 1/492.
23 *Ibid.*
24 In PF, one may find some statements which indicate that Muslim legal theorists adopt the linguists' rather than the logicians' view, Mullākhusrū, for example, points out that "signification, according to legal theorists, [..] is regarded if and only if it is joined with intention" Mullākhusrū, 1/227. However, this is not unqualifiedly true.
25 Al-Sharbīnī, 1/236.
26 Ibn al-Ḥalabī, p. 370; see also Ibn al-Malik, p. 369.
27 See al-Qarāfī, *Sharḥ Tanqīḥ*, p. 24; al-Anṣārī, 1/181–182.
28 See al-Qarāfī, *Sharḥ Tanqīḥ*, pp. 96–97.
29 See *ibid.*
30 See *ibid.*
31 See *ibid.*
32 *Ibid.*, p. 25.
33 For definitions of 'entailment' see Lyons, *Linguistic Semantics . . .*, P. 117; *idem*, *Semantics*, 1/165; Kempson, *Semantic Theory*, p. 39; Crystal, *A Dictionary of Linguistics . . .*, p. 122 (entailment); Levinson, *Pragmatics*, pp. 174–175; Bussmann, *Routledge Dictionary*, p. 220–221 (implication).
34 See Kempson, *op. cit.*, pp. 3–4; Crystal, *op. cit.*, (entailment) p. 122; Levinson, *Pragmatics*, pp. 174–175.
35 See Crystal, *op. cit.*, (entailment) p. 122.
36 See al-Rāzī, 1/82–83.
37 To put these utterances into context, it should be noted that this constitutes a part of policy to curb slavery and liberate as many slaves as possible.
38 Al-Asnawī, 2/32.
39 *Ibid.*
40 Al-Sharīf al-Jurjānī, *al-Ta*ᶜ*rīfāt*, p. 56 *(al-dalālah al-lafẓiyyah al-waḍ*ᶜ*iyyah)*.
41 Al-Rāzī, P.1/76.
42 Al-Asnawī, 2/32.
43 See Mullākhusrū, 1/303; al-Muṭīᶜī, *Sullam* 2/35.
44 See al-Muṭīᶜī, *Sullam*, 2/34.
45 Al-Marjānī, *Ḥāshiyah* ᶜ*alā Sharḥ al-Tawḍīḥ* ᶜ*alā l-Tanqīḥ*, 2/29.
46 Al-Qarāfī, *Sharḥ Tanqīḥ*, p. 26.
47 Al-Āmidī (1986), 1/36–37; ᶜAḍud, 1/120; al-Sharīf al-Jurjānī, *Ḥāshiyah* ᶜ*alā Sharḥ al-*ᶜ*Aḍud*, 1/121
48 See al-Rāzī, 1/58; al-Subkī, *Matn Jam*ᶜ *al-Jawāmi*ᶜ, 1/238; al-Subkīs, *al-Ibhāj*, 1/203; al-Maḥallī, 1/238; al-Bannānī, 1/238–239.
49 See al-Subkīs, *al-Ibhāj*, 1/203.
50 See al-Bannānī, 1/239; al-Muṭīᶜī, *op. cit.*, 2/31.
51 Al-Qarāfī, *Sharḥ Tanqīḥ*, pp. 12–13.

52 *Ibid.*, p. 13.
53 See Lyons, *Linguistic Semantics,* p. 108.
54 Simpson and Weiner, *The Oxford English Dictionary*, XI/20.
55 See Lyons, *Linguistic Semantics,* pp. 114–116.
56 See Ibn Taymiyyah, *al-Radd,* 1/64.
57 This term is frequently used in the PF, see for instance, al-Ruhāwī, p 516.
58 The last three terms have been adopted from Kamali, but for methodological reasons I would prefer to use 'the express meaning' instead of 'the explicit meaning' which he applies for *(ᶜibārat al-naṣṣ)*; see Kamali, *Principles . . .*, p. 124.
59 Al-Sharīf al-Jurjānī, *al-Taᶜrīfāt,* p. 79.
60 See Ibn al-Malik, p 522.
61 Ali's Translation of *THE HOLY QURᵓĀN,* 2/275.
62 See al-Tahānawī, 2/1407 *(naṣṣ)*.
63 See Muḥibb Allāh, 1/407; Ṣadr al-Sharīᶜah, 2/1–2; al-Taftāzānī, *Ḥāshiyat al-Talwīḥ,* 2/2–4; al-Ruhāwī, p 522; al-Muṭīᶜī, *op. cit.*, 2/195.
64 see Lyons, *Semantics,* 2/503.
65 Al-Nasafī, *Matn al-Manār,* pp. 521–522.
66 Al-Sharīf al-Jurjānī, *al-Taᶜrīfāt,* p. 16; see also, al-Bazdawī, pp. 174–175; al-Bukhārī, pp. 174–175.
67 *THE HOLY QURᵓĀN,* 2/233; see Ali's Translation, 2/233.
68 See al-Sarakhsī, 1/237; al-Bukhārī, pp. 178–179; Ibn al-Malik, p 523; al-Ruhāwī, p 523; Ibn al-Ḥalabī, pp. 523–524; al-Nasafī, *Tafsīr al-Nasafī* 1/117–118.
69 This inference is very frequently supported by the Prophet' saying: "you and your property belong to your father". See al-Sarakhsī, 1/237; al-Bazdawī, pp. 178–179; Ibn al-Malik, p 523; al-Ruhāwī, p 523; Ibn al-Ḥalabī, pp. 523–524; Kamali, *op. cit.*, p. 125.
70 Al-Sharīf al-Jurjānī, *al-Taᶜrīfāt,* p. 126 *(naẓm)*.
71 *THE HOLY QURᵓĀN,* 59/8; see Ali's Translation, 59/8.
72 Al-Nasafī, *Matn al-Manār,* pp. 521–522; al-Sharīf al-Jurjānī, *al-Taᶜrīfāt,* p. 16; see also al-Bazdawī, pp. 174–175; al-Samarqandī, 1/567; ᶜMuḥibb Allāh, 1/407; Ṣadr al-Sharīᶜah, 2/1.
73 Al-Nasafī, *Matn al-Manār,* pp. 521–522; al-Sharīf al-Jurjānī, *al-Taᶜrīfāt,* p. 16; see also al-Bazdawī, pp. 174–175; Ṣadr al-Sharīᶜah, 2/1.
74 Al-Sarakhsī, 1/236; Ibn al-Malik, p 522; al-Samarqandī, 1/567.
75 Al-Samarqandī, 1/567.
76 Al-Bukhārī, p. 184.
77 Al-Ghazālī defines this type of meaning as "the understanding of an unstated meaning from the stated meaning by an indication from the context and the illocutionary import of the utterance" *(fahmu ghayri l-manṭūqi mina l-manṭūqi bi-dalālati siyāqi l-kalāmi wa-maqṣūdih)*. Al-Ghazālī, *al-Mustaṣfā,* 2/190.
78 *THE HOLY QURᵓĀN,* 17/23; see Ali's Translation, 17/23.
79 Muḥibb Allāh, 1/408.
80 Al-Bājī, 2/440; al-Sarakhsī, 1/241; al-Samarqandī, 1/570; Ibn al-Malik, p. 528, al-Ruhāwī, p. 526; Zādah, p. 528.
81 Al-Bājī, 2/440; al-Samarqandī, 1/570;
82 Weiss, *The Search,* p. 490.

83 Al-Āmidī (1986), 3/77; see Weiss, *The Search*, p. 490.
84 Al-Āmidī (1986), 3/77; see Weiss, *The Search*, p. 490; Ibn al-Ḥājib, 2/173, ᶜAḍud, 2/173; al-Āmidī (1986), 3/77; see Weiss, *The Search*, p. 490.
85 Al-Āmidī (1986), 3/77; see Weiss, *The Search*, p. 490.
86 Al-Bukhārī, p. 185.
87 Al-Shīrāzī, *Sharḥ al-Lumaᶜ*, 1/425; al-Shīrāzī, *al-Tabṣirah*, pp. 227–228.
88 Al-Maḥallī, 1/244.
89 Al-Sharbīnī, 1/244.
90 See al-Ghazālī, *al-Mustaṣfā*, 2/191.
91 Al-Bukhārī, p. 189; al-Tahānawī, 2/1239 *(al-muqtaḍā)*.
92 The Arabic text reads as follows: "*huwa ᶜibāratun ᶜan ziyādatin ᶜalā l-manṣūṣi ᶜalayhi yushtaraṭu taqdīmuhu li-yaṣīra l-manẓūmu mufīdan aw mūjiban li-lḥukmi, wa-bi-dūnihi lā yumkinu iᶜmālu l-manẓūm*". Al-Sarakhsī, 1/248
93 *THE HOLY QURᵓĀN*, 4/23.
94 Al-Bukhārī, p. 188.
95 Al-Sarakhsī, 1/251; al-Ghazālī, *al-Mustaṣfā*, 1/347–348; al-Āmidī (1986), 3/72; see Weiss, *The Search*, p. 483; al-Qarāfī, *Sharḥ Tanqīḥ*, p. 55.
96 Muḥibb Allāh, 1/411.
97 Ibn al-Malik, p. 534.
98 Al-Bukhārī, p. 189.
99 Ibn al-Malik, p. 534.
100 Al-Bukhārī, p. 189.
101 Al-Shāfiᶜī, *Treatise*, p. 103.
102 *THE HOLY QURᵓĀN*, 12/82.
103 See Ibn Taymiyyah, *Fatāwā*, 20/463; al-Mawṣilī, 2/98–99.
104 See, e.g., Simpson and Weiner, *The Oxford English Dictionary*, (town); Summers and others, *Longman Dictionary . . .*, (town); Hanks and others, *Collins Dictionary . . .*, (town).
105 Al-Mawṣilī, 2/100.
106 *THE HOLY QURᵓĀN*, 5/3; see Ali's Translation, 5/3.
107 *THE HOLY QURᵓĀN*, 5/2; see Ali's Translation, 5/2.
108 *THE HOLY QURᵓĀN*, 4/23; see Ali's Translation, 4/23.
109 Al-Mawṣilī, 2/103.
110 *Ibid.*, 2/104.
111 Al-Sarakhsī, 1/249–250; al-Samarqandī, 1/5734; al-Taftāzānī, *Ḥāshiyat al-Talwīḥ*, 1/23–24; Ibn al-Malik, pp. 538–541; al-Ruhāwī, pp. 538–540; al-Anṣārī, 1/412.
112 Al-Sarakhsī, 1/251–53; al-Bazdawī, pp. 188–194; al-Samarqandī, 1/573–576.
113 For a discussion of these distinctions, see Ibn al-Malik, pp. 535–538; al-Ruhāwī, pp. 536–538; Ibn al-Ḥalabī, pp. 535–538.
114 Al-Bukhārī, pp. 191–192; al-Maḥallī, 1/239; al-Bannānī, 1/239.
115 Al Shāfiᶜī, *al-Risālah*, ed. Shākir, pp. 512–517; al Shāfiᶜī, *Treatise*, pp. 102–103, 308–309.
116 See al-Baṣrī, 1/296–299.
117 See al-Bājī, pp. 438–441.
118 See al-Juwaynī, 1/448–453.

119 For profound discussions of the distinction between 'what is said' and 'what is implicated' in modern pragmatics, see, e.g., Grice (1991), pp. 305–315; Harnish, "Logical Form and Implicature", pp. 316–364; Sadock, "On Testing for Conversational Implicature", pp. 365–376; Recanati, "The Pragmatics of What Is Said", pp. 106–107.

120 See Levinson, *Pragmatics*, p. 127.

121 Grice (1991), p. 307.

122 For an extended discussion of *wa*-conjunction, see al-Āmidī (1986), 1/96–102; Ibn al-Ḥājib, 1/189–192, ᶜAḍud, 1/189–192; al-Taftāzānī, *Ḥāshiyah ᶜalā Sharḥ al-ᶜAḍud,* 1/190–192; al-Sharīf al-Jurjānī, *Ḥāshiyah ᶜalā Sharḥ al-ᶜAḍud,* 1/190–192. And for a discussion of (the meanings of particles) in general, see al-Āmidī (1986), 1/94–105; al-Subkī, *Matn Jamᶜ al-Jawāmiᶜ*, 1/335–365; al-Maḥallī, 1/335–365; al-Bannānī, 1/335–365; al-Sharbīnī, 1/336–365.

123 Grice (1975), p. 56; Grice (1991), p. 314.

124 Levinson, *Pragmatics*, p. 127.

125 Grice (1991), p. 311.

126 Al-Sharīf al-Jurjānī, *al-Taᶜrīfāt*, p. 33 *(al-taᶜrīḍ)*; al-Tahānawī, 2/1287 *(al-Kināyah)*.

127 Al-Tahānawī, 1/216.

128 See Grundy, Doing Pragmatics, p. 45.

129 See Grice (1975), p. 56; Grice (1991), p. 314.

130 See Grice (1975), pp. 43–58; Grice (1991), pp. 306–315; Sadock, "On Testing for Conversational Implicature", pp. 365–367; Levinson, *Pragmatics*, p. 131, Groundy, Doing Pragmatics, 48.

131 Abū Ḥāmid Muḥammad b. Muḥammad al-Ṭūsī al-Ghazālī was a Muslim philosopher, an Ashᶜarī theologian and a Shāfiᶜī jurist (450/1058–505/1111). In his early thirties, he began a deep private study of logic and philosophy. He wrote two profound philosophical books: *Maqāṣid al-Falāsifah* in which he elucidated the philosophy of al-Fārābī and Ibn Sīnā and *Tahāfut al-Falāsifah* in which he showed how the doctrines of these two philosophers were incompatible with Islamic religion. In the science of the principles of *fiqh,* al-Ghazālī's main contribution was *al-Mustaṣfā* which is a clear manifestation of the influence of Greek philosophy on his approach to this field where he managed to incorporate logic into religion.

(See Lewis, Pellat and Schacht, *Encyclopaedia of Islam,* (1038–1041).

132 Al-Ghazālī, *al-Mustaṣfā*, 1/316.

133 *Ibid.*, 1/317, 2/186.

134 See *ibid.*, 2/228.

135 Al-Āmidī (1986), 3/71.

136 Weiss, *The Search*, p. 482; al-Āmidī (1986), 3/71.

137 *THE HOLY QURᵓĀN,* 51/56, see Ali's Translation, 51/56.

138 See Ibn al-Ḥājib, 2/171, ᶜAḍud, 2/172, al-Taftāzānī, *Ḥāshiyah ᶜalā Sharḥ al-ᶜAḍud,* 2/172.

139 *THE HOLY QURᵓĀN,* 5/41, see Ali's Translation, 5/41.

140 Weiss, *The Search*, p. 600; al-Āmidī (1986), 3/279.

141 Weiss, *The Search*, p. 601; al-Āmidī (1986), 3/280.

142 Al-Āmidī (1986), 3/280–281.

143 *Ibid.*, 3/281; Weiss, *The Search*, p. 601.
144 Ali's Translation of *THE HOLY QURʾĀN*, 2/222.
145 Ibn al-Ḥājib, 2/171, ʿAḍud, 2/171–172, al-Taftāzānī, *Ḥāshiyah ʿalā Sharḥ al-ʿAḍud*, 2/171.
146 Al-Taftāzānī, *Ḥāshiyah ʿalā Sharḥ al-ʿAḍud*, 2/171; see also ʿAḍud, 2/171.
147 Grice (1991), p. 311.
148 Al-Shāfiʿī, *al-Risālah*, ed. Shākir, pp. 512–517; al-Shāfiʿī, *Treatise*, pp. 308–309.
149 Al-Shāfiʿī, *Treatise*, p. 308.
150 Al-Juwaynī, 1/449.
151 Ali's Translation of *THE HOLY QURʾĀN*, 4/10.
152 Al-Subkī, *Matn Jamʿ al-Jawāmiʿ*, 1/240–241; al-Subkīs, *al-Ibhāj*, 1/368–369; al-Maḥallī, 1/240–242; al-Bannānī, 1/241–242; al-Anṣārī, 1/409. See al-Subkīs, *al-Ibhāj*, 1/203.
153 Some legal theorists employ *laḥn al-khiṭāb* to refer to 'congruent-implicature', (al-Āmidī (1986), 3/74; Ibn al-Ḥājib, 2/172), others, on the other hand, use it as synonymous with 'counter-implicature' (al-Asnawī, 2/205).
154 Al-Āmidī (1986), 3/77; see Weiss, *The Search*, p. 490; Ibn al-Ḥājib, 2/173, ʿAḍud, 2/172–173, al-Taftāzānī, *Ḥāshiyah ʿalā Sharḥ al-ʿAḍud*, 2/173.
155 Hallaq employs '*a minori ad maius*' for (i) and '*a maiori ad minus*' for (ii). See Hallaq, "Non-analogical Arguments . . .", p. 289; see also Weiss, *The Search*, p. 486.
156 Ali's Translation of *THE HOLY QURʾĀN*, 99/7–8.
157 Weiss, *The Search*, p. 488; Āmidī (1986), 3/76.
158 Ali's Translation of *THE HOLY QURʾĀN*, 3/75.
159 See ʿAḍud, 2/173.
160 Al-Āmidī (1986), 3/75; see Weiss, *The Search*, p. 487.
161 Al-Ghazālī, *al-Mustaṣfā*, 2/190
162 Al-Juwaynī, 1/451–452; al-Ghazālī, *al-Mustaṣfā*, 2/190; al-Āmidī (1986), 3/75; see also, al-Maḥallī, 1/243–244; al-Bannānī, 1/243–244; al-Sharbīnī, 1/244.
163 See al-Āmidī (1986), 3/77–78; Ibn al-Ḥājib, 2/173, ʿAḍud, 2/173.
164 See al-Juwaynī, 1/451–452.
165 See al-Samarqandī, 1/444–445.
166 Al-Juwaynī, 1/451–452.
167 See al-Darīnī, *al-Manāhij* . . ., p. 403.
168 Al-Subkīs, *al-Ibhāj*, 1/375–376; al-Asnawī, 2/215; see al-Anṣārī, 1/417.
169 Ibn al-Ḥājib, 2/171, ʿAḍud, 2/171–172, al-Taftāzānī, *Ḥāshiyah ʿalā Sharḥ al-ʿAḍud*, 2/171.
170 See, e.g., al-Qarāfī, *Sharḥ Tanqīḥ*, p. 56; al-Asnawī, 2/215.
171 See al-Subkīs, *al-Ibhāj*, 1/376; al-Asnawī, 2/215–216.
172 See al-Anṣārī, 1/417.
173 See al-Ghazālī, *al-Mustaṣfā*, 2/208–209; al-Maḥallī, 1/255; Ibn al-Malik, p. 552.
174 See al-Āmidī (1986), 3/85.
175 See Ṣadr al-Sharīʿah, 2/35.

176 See al-Shīrāzī, *al-Tabṣirah;* p. 223; al-Shīrāzī, *Sharḥ al-Luma*[c], 1/437; Ibn al-Ḥājib, 2/179, [c]Aḍud, 2/179–180, al-Taftāzānī, *Ḥāshiyah* [c]*alā Sharḥ al-*[c]*Aḍud,* 2/179–180.
177 See al-Āmidī (1986), 3/91–92; Ibn al-Ḥājib, 2/179; [c]Aḍud, 2/179–180; al-Taftāzānī, *Ḥāshiyah* [c]*alā Sharḥ al-*[c]*Aḍud,* 2/179–180; al-Anṣārī, 1/416.
178 See al-Shīrāzī, *al-Tabṣirah;* p. 223; al-Shīrāzī, Sharḥ al-Luma[c], 1/437–438, al-Āmidī (1986), 3/92; Ibn al-Ḥājib, 2/179, [c]Aḍud, 2/180, al-Taftāzānī, *Ḥāshiyah* [c]*alā Sharḥ al-*[c]*Aḍud,* 2/180; al-Anṣārī, 1/416.
179 See al-Baṣrī, 1/155–156.
180 Al-Juwaynī, 1/473–474.
181 See al-Shīrāzī, *Sharḥ al-Luma*[c], 1/442.
182 See, e.g., *ibid.,* 1/438; al-Juwaynī, 1/473.
183 Ibn Taymiyyah, *Fatāwā*, 31/114.
184 *Ibid.*, 31/140.
185 See *ibid.*, 31/113–114, 117–118, 140; see also al-Āmidī (1986), 3/91.
186 Al-Shīrāzī, *al-Tabṣirah;* p. 225; al-Shīrāzī, Sharḥ al-Luma[c], 1/438.
187 See al-Ghazālī, *al-Mustaṣfā*, 2/192–193.
188 See al-Shīrāzī, *Sharḥ al-Luma*[c], 1/438–439; al-Āmidī (1986), 3/90.
189 See al-Āmidī (1986), 3/90.
190 See al-Baṣrī, 1/216–217; see also, al-Āmidī (1986), 3/90.
191 See al-Āmidī (1986), 3/92–93.
192 See al-Baṣrī, 1/218–219. It should be pointed out here that al-Baṣrī did not raise this objection to the above particular argument but to a similar one, but is quoted here because it is equally applicable.
193 Sadock, "On Testing for Conversational Implicature", p. 374; see Barton, *Nonsentential Constituents . . .*, p. 148.
194 Sadock, "On Testing for Conversational Implicature", p. 374.
195 For this argument and similar examples, see al-Shīrāzī, *al-Tabṣirah;* p. 222; al-Shīrāzī, *Sharḥ al-Luma*[c], 1/432–433; al-Juwaynī, 1/461–462; al-Ghazālī, *al-Mustaṣfā*, 2/199; al-Āmidī (1986), 3/84–85.
196 See al-Juwaynī, 1/462; al-Ghazālī, *al-Mustaṣfā*, 2/199; al-Āmidī (1986), 3/85.
197 See al-Juwaynī, 1/463.
198 See al-Ghazālī, *al-Mustaṣfā*, 2/211; al-Subkīs, *al-Ibhāj*, 1/374.
199 Ṣadr al-Sharī[c]ah, 2/31; al-Taftāzānī, *Ḥāshiyat al-Talwīḥ*, 2/31.
200 See al-Ghazālī, *al-Mustaṣfā*, 2/211–212.
201 See Ibn al-Ḥājib, 2/176, [c]Aḍud, 2/177; al-Marjānī, *Ḥāshiyah* [c]*alā Sharḥ al-Tawḍīḥ* [c]*alā l-Tanqīḥ*, 2/2213; Muḥibb Allāh, 1/420; al-Anṣārī, 1/420.
202 Al-Ruhāwī, p. 564.
203 See, e.g., al-Shīrāzī, *Sharḥ al-Luma*[c], 1/438; al-Juwaynī, 1/473; [c]Aḍud, 2/180; al-Taftāzānī, *Ḥāshiyah* [c]*alā Sharḥ al-*[c]*Aḍud,* 2/182; Muḥibb Allāh, 1/416; al-Anṣārī, 1/416.
204 See al-Āmidī (1986), 3/90–91.
205 See al-Baṣrī, 1/158; al-Āmidī (1986), 3/85–86, Weiss, *The Search*, p. 497; [c]Aḍud, 2/175; al-Sharbīnī, 1/249; Ibn Taymiyyah, *Fatāwā*, 31/182.
206 See al-Bājī, 2/449; al-Juwaynī, 1/463; al-Ghazālī, *al-Mustaṣfā*, 2/200–201; al-Taftāzānī, *Ḥāshiyat al-Talwīḥ*, 2/31–32.
207 See al-Shīrāzī, *Sharḥ al-Luma*[c], 1/436; al-Shīrāzī, *al-Tabṣirah;* pp. 222–223.

208 See al-Shīrāzī, *Sharḥ al-Luma*[c], 1/436.
209 Al-Sharbīnī, 1/257.
210 Al-Taftāzānī, *Ḥāshiyah* [c]*alā Sharḥ al-*[c]*Aḍud,* 2/183.
211 See, e.g., Leech, *Principles of Pragmatics*, p. 85; Mey, *Pragmatics* . . ., 102.
212 See al-Ghazālī, *al-Mustaṣfā*, 2/200; al-Āmidī (1986), 3/85. For the involvement of the Principle of the Speaker's Making of his Intention Manifest in such inferences, see also Ibn Taymiyyah, *Fatāwā*, 1/135, 138.
213 See Ibn al-Ḥājib, 2/174, 176, [c]Aḍud, 2/175–176; al-Taftāzānī, *Ḥāshiyat al-Talwīḥ*, 2/31–32.
214 See al-Taftāzānī, *Ḥāshiyat al-Talwīḥ*, 2/31–32.
215 See al-Ghazālī, *al-Mustaṣfā*, 2/200–201; [c]Aḍud, 2/175; al-Taftāzānī, *Ḥāshiyat al-Talwīḥ*, 2/31–32; al-Subkīs, *al-Ibhāj*, 1/375.
216 See Ibn al-Ḥājib, 2/173; [c]Aḍud, 2/174; al-Qarāfī, *Sharḥ Tanqīḥ*, p. 174; al-Taftāzānī, *Ḥāshiyat al-Talwīḥ*, 2/ 28, 33–35; al-Maḥallī, 1/246–247; al-Anṣārī, 1/414.
217 See al-Sharbīnī, 1/257.
218 See Ibn al-Ḥājib, 2/173, [c]Aḍud, 2/174; al-Maḥallī, 1/245; al-Bannānī, 1/ 245.
219 See Ibn Taymiyyah, *Fatāwā*, 31/117.
220 *Ibid.*, 31/137.
221 See *ibid.*
222 Grice (1975), p. 45; Grice (1991), p. 308.
223 Grice (1975), p. 52; Grice (1991), p. 311.
224 Robert M. Harnish, "Logical Form and Implicature", p. 340.
225 Gazdar, *Pragmatics* . . ., p. 51.
226 Leech, *Principles of Pragmatics*, p. 85.
227 See al-Shīrāzī, *Sharḥ al-Luma*[c], 1/436; al-Shīrāzī, *al-Tabṣirah;* pp. 222–223.
228 Leech, *Principles of Pragmatics*, p. 85.
229 *Ibid.*, p. 85–86.
230 See al-Juwaynī, 1/466–469.
231 Ibn al-Ḥājib, 2/173, [c]Aḍud, 2/174; al-Qarāfī, *Sharḥ Tanqīḥ*, p. 174; Ibn Taymiyyah, *Fatāwā*, 31/138; Ibn al-Malik, pp. 547–548; Ibn al-Ḥalabī, p. 547; al-Anṣārī, 1/414.
232 Al-Āmidī (1986), 3/94.
233 *THE HOLY QUR*[ɔ]*ĀN*, 17/31.
234 See al-Juwaynī, 1/512–513; Weiss, *The Search*, p. 495.
235 Ibn al-Ḥājib, 2/173, [c]Aḍud, 2/174; al-Qarāfī, *Sharḥ Tanqīḥ*, p. 174; Ibn Taymiyyah, *Fatāwā*, 31/138; al-Taftāzānī, *Ḥāshiyat al-Talwīḥ*, 2/34; al-Maḥallī, 1/246; Ibn al-Malik, p. 548; al-Anṣārī, 1/414.
236 *THE HOLY QUR*[ɔ]*ĀN*, 4/23; see Ali's Translation, 4/23.
237 Al-Qarāfī, *Sharḥ Tanqīḥ*, p. 272; al-Subkīs, *al-Ibhāj*, 1/273.
238 Ibn al-Ḥājib, 2/173, [c]Aḍud, 2/174; al-Qarāfī, *Sharḥ Tanqīḥ*, p. 174; Ibn Taymiyyah, *Fatāwā*, 31/138; al-Taftāzānī, *Ḥāshiyat al-Talwīḥ*, 2/34; al-Maḥallī, 1/246; Ibn al-Malik, p. 548; al-Anṣārī, 1/414; Kamali, *Principles* . . . p. 134.
239 Levinson, *Pragmatics*, p. 115–116.
240 *Ibid.*, p. 116.

241 Ibn al-Ḥājib, 2/173, ᶜAḍud, 2/174; al-Qarāfī, *Sharḥ Tanqīḥ*, p. 174; al-Taftāzānī, *Ḥāshiyat al-Talwīḥ*, 2/34; al-Maḥallī, 1/246; al-Anṣārī, 1/414; Kamali, *Principles . . .*, p. 133.
242 Leech, *Principles of Pragmatics*, p. 86.
243 *Ibid.*
244 See al-Fanārī, *Ḥāshiyah*, 2/38; al-Bannānī, 1/247; al-Sharbīnī, 1/246.
245 For arguments against this kind of counter-implicature, see al-Baṣrī, 1/148–149; al-Bājī, 2/448; al-Shīrāzī, *Sharḥ al-Lumaᶜ*, 1/435–437; al-Shīrāzī, *al-Tabṣirah;* pp. 222–223; al-Juwaynī, 1/471–472; al-Ghazālī, *al-Mustaṣfā*, 2/193; Ibn al-Ḥalabī, p. 549.
246 Ibn al-Ḥājib, 2/182, ᶜAḍud, 2/182.
247 See al-Shīrāzī, *Sharḥ al-Lumaᶜ*, 1/436; al-Shīrāzī, *al-Tabṣirah;* pp. 222–223.
248 See al-Subkī, *Matn Jamᶜ al-Jawāmiᶜ*, 1/250–251; al-Subkīs, *al-Ibhāj*, 1/203; al-Maḥallī, 1/250–251; al-Bannānī, 1/250–251; al-Fanārī, *Ḥāshiyah*, 2/31.
249 See Ṣadr al-Sharīᶜah, 2/32–33; al-Taftāzānī, *Ḥāshiyah ᶜalā Sharḥ al-ᶜAḍud*, 2/174; al-Taftāzānī, *Ḥāshiyat al-Talwīḥ*, 2/34–35; al-Subkīs, *al-Ibhāj*, 1/378; al-Bannānī, 1/250–251.
250 Ali's Translation of *THE HOLY QURᵓĀN*, 1/1.
251 *Ibid.*, 15/17.
252 Ibn al-Malik, p 563; al-Ruhāwī, p 563.
253 Ali's Translation of *THE HOLY QURᵓĀN*, 5/47.
254 *THE HOLY QURᵓĀN*, 6/38; see Ali's Translation, 6/38.
255 See al-Ruhāwī, pp 563–564.
256 Al-Qarāfī, *Sharḥ Tanqīḥ*, p. 81.
257 Al-Sharīf al-Jurjānī, *al-Taᶜrīfāt*, p. 62
258 Al-Qarāfī, *Sharḥ Tanqīḥ*, p. 82.
259 Al-Sharīf al-Jurjānī, *al-Taᶜrīfāt*, p. 62
260 Al-Qarāfī, *Sharḥ Tanqīḥ*, p. 85.
261 See, e.g., ᶜAḍud, 2/181.
262 Al-Qarāfī, *Sharḥ Tanqīḥ*, p. 85.
263 See *ibid.* It should be noted, however, that the opponents of this kind of implicature deny that the syntactic condition is interpreted as "if and only if *p*, then *q*". See al-Āmidī (1986), 3/100; Ibn al-Malik, pp. 563–564.
264 See al-Baṣrī, 1/144–145; ᶜAḍud, 2/181; al-Taftāzānī, *Ḥāshiyah ᶜalā Sharḥ al-ᶜAḍud*, 2/181; al-Ruhāwī, p. 564.
265 See al-Baṣrī, 1/141.
266 Levinson, *Pragmatics*, p. 146.
267 Ali's Translation of *THE HOLY QURᵓĀN*, 65/6.
268 Al-Bājī, 2/452.
269 See al-Anṣārī, 1/422; al-Muṭīᶜī, *Sullam*, 2/217.
270 See al-Anṣārī, 1/221.
271 *Al-Taftāzānī*, *Ḥāshiyat al-Talwīḥ*, P.1/322.
272 See Lyons, *Semantics*, 1/144–145.
273 See Lyons, *Linguistic Semantics . . .*, p 167.
274 See Cann, *Formal Semantics . . .*, pp. 70–74.
275 See al-Bājī, 2/453–455, al-Baṣrī, 1/145–146.
276 Ali's Translation of *THE HOLY QURᵓĀN*, 2/222.

277 See al-Bājī, 2/454, 456; al-Ghazālī, *al-Mustaṣfā*, 2/208; Ibn al-Ḥājib, 2/181, ʿAḍud, 2/181.
278 See al-Bājī, 2/455; al-Ghazālī, *al-Mustaṣfā*, 2/208.
279 See al-Bājī, 2/454–455; al-Ghazālī, *al-Mustaṣfā*, 2/208.
280 See al-Bājī, 2/454–455.
281 Ali's Translation of *THE HOLY QURʾĀN*, 2/222.
282 See al-Qarāfī, *Sharḥ Tanqīḥ*, pp. 96–97.
283 See *ibid.*, pp. 96–97.
284 See *ibid.*
285 See *ibid.*
286 See al-Baṣrī, 1/146.
287 See al-Āmidī (1986), 3/80–81; ʿAḍud, 2/175.
288 See al-Baṣrī, 1/146–147; al-Asnawī, 2/222–223.
289 See al-Baṣrī, 1/146–148; al-Āmidī (1986), 3/103–104; al-Asnawī, 2/221–223.
290 Modern semanticists and pragmatists hold that 'The Browns have two daughters' "will normally implicate that the Browns have only (i.e., no more than) two daughters". Lyons, *Linguistic Semantics . . .*, P. 288; Harnish, "Logical Form and Implicature", p. 341; Recanati, "The Pragmatics of What Is Said", p. 115; Carston, "Implicature, Explicature . . .", p. 46; Levinson, *Pragmatics*, p. 106; Leech, *Principles of Pragmatics*, p. 88.
291 Ali's Translation of *THE HOLY QURʾĀN*, 9/80.
292 *Ibid.*, 24/4.
293 See al-Āmidī (1986), 3/88–89; ʿAḍud, 2/179; al-Shīrāzī, *Sharḥ al-Lumaʿ*, 1/433–434.
294 See al-Bājī, 2/450; al-Ghazālī, *al-Mustaṣfā*, 2/195; al-Āmidī (1986), 3/82; Ibn al-Ḥājib, 2/176; ʿAḍud, 2/177–178.
295 See Ibn al-Ḥājib, 2/176; ʿAḍud, 2/178.
296 See al-Āmidī (1986), 3/82.
297 See al-Muṭīʿī, *op. cit.*, 2/221–222.
298 See al-Qarāfī, *al-Istighnāʾ fī l-Istithnāʾ*, pp. 472–473; al-Qarāfī, *Sharḥ Tanqīḥ*, p. 56.
299 See al-Taftāzānī, *Ḥāshiyah ʿalā Sharḥ al-ʿAḍud*, 2/183.
300 Ibn al-Ḥājib, 2/183, ʿAḍud, 2/183–185.
301 See al-Taftāzānī, *Ḥāshiyah ʿalā Sharḥ al-ʿAḍud*, 2/183.
302 Al-Juwaynī, 1/479–481; al-Ghazālī, *al-Mustaṣfā*, 2/207; Ibn al-Ḥājib, 2/183, ʿAḍud, 2/183–185.
303 See al-Ghazālī, *al-Mustaṣfā*, 2/207; Ibn al-Ḥājib, 2/183, ʿAḍud, 2/183–185. For a similar notion, see Cooper, *Philosophy . . .*, pp. 95, 98.

Conclusion

There is a common belief among researchers in communication and pragmatics that only recently has verbal communication been viewed as involving both coding and inferential processes. According to Sperber and Wilson, "from Aristotle through to modern semiotics, all theories of communication were based on a single model which [they] call the *code model*".[1] They claim that in recent years "several philosophers, noticeably Paul Grice and David Lewis, have proposed a quite different model" which Sperber and Wilson call *"the inferential model"*, according to which "communication is achieved by producing and interpreting evidence".[2] The present study has shown this to be untrue. The Sunni Muslim legal theorists developed at least two pragmatic models of textual communication centuries ago. These are the mainstream model and the *Salafī* one. Both presuppose that successful communication cannot be achieved by merely "encoding and decoding messages".

Within the mainstream framework, there is a controversy concerning whether expressions are designations for extra-mental entities or for the mental representations of these entities. Both views assume that the language of the late generations are established and determined by the early generations. However, the two views differ as to how a particular utterance produced by a given speaker relates to *waḍ*ᶜ. The former view assumes that each produced utterance is based by way of analogy on a similar utterance used by the establisher. The latter view, on the other hand, assumes that the establisher has 'established' the lexicon and the grammatical systems of the language in a universal manner. This includes the derivational rules of word formation and the syntactic rules of sentence-generation. So each utterance used by a speaker is taken to be a realisation of a set of pre-established universal rules, patterns and facts. Since speakers do not always speak literally and because of the problematic features inherent in the language, the recovery of intention of the speaker depends on the context. Thus, literal meanings are determined and understood by reference to *waḍ*ᶜ, whereas the intentions of the speakers are recoverable by the context. One of the fundamental assumptions of this conceptual view, which is far more dominant in Islamic thought than its rival, is the tacit claim that knowledge of the subsumptive *waḍ*ᶜ can enable the speaker to generate an infinite number of utterances from each abstract construction. Each generated utterance is viewed as a manifestation of a primordially established pattern. The peculiarity of a particular generated utterance derives from its being selected to express the speaker's intention. So each utterance used in a given communicative situation pertains partly to *waḍ*ᶜ and partly to use. What belongs to *waḍ*ᶜ is the lexical items and the grammatical patterns being used in the utterance. What pertains to use, on the other hand, is the speaker's selection of the very particular lexical items as well as the selection of the very particular grammatical patterns, and the way the lexical and grammatical units are constructed, organised and related to the communicative situation. Thus, the judgement that an utterance is not well-formed is ascribed to its being incompatible with the common constructional patterns of the language, whereas the judgement that an utterance is true or false, conceivable or inconceivable, is ascribed to the speakers' proposition encapsulated in the selected sentence.

As for *personal pronouns* and definite nouns in general, which have received a special treatment by the legal theorists, we may conclude from our discussion of al-Qarāfī that their universal signification is determined by virtue of *waḍ*ᶜ while their particular reference is governed by use.

The third component of the mainstream communication model (the first two being *waḍ*ᶜ and use) is *al-ḥaml* (interpretation), which is defined as the hearer's own understanding of the speaker's intention. Muslim legal theorists presume that interlocutors follow certain norms in communication processes. Their model of communication involves a set of *uṣūl*. I have distinguished between two kinds of *aṣl*. The first, which I call bases are designed to describe discourse in its ideal form (which is in conformity with *waḍ*ᶜ). The second, which I call principles are intended to describe the behaviour of the interlocutors during the communicative process. The violation of the bases may generate some rhetorical goals. The violation of the principles, on the other hand, leads to problems in communication. For example, if the speaker flouts the 'literalness' base; (i.e., 'the base' is the literal use), his utterance will be taken as figurative in nature, but if he infringes the principle of truthfulness, his utterance will be taken to be false, leading to the breakdown of communication. The reason is that in violating *the base,* the speaker sets up a context which indicates the violation, thus making his intention manifest. In the case of violating *the principle,* the speaker, by contrast, intends to mislead the addressee. Five principles govern successful communication:

i The Principle of *Istiṣḥāb* (i.e., the presumption of the status *quo)*, by virtue of which each base is maintained until evidence to the contrary is made manifest.

ii The Principle of the Speaker's Disposition to Make his Intention Manifest. In order for the speaker to be said to have applied this principle, he ought to intend his discourse to be taken in its ostensive interpretation, otherwise the speaker would be intending something which his discourse does not signify. Thus, the speaker has either to use his utterance in accordance with *waḍ*ᶜ or to indicate his departure from it by contextual evidence. In other words, he ought to conform to the bases or to introduce a valid context to show the addressee that he has violated one or more bases. So, in the case of violating the literalness base, the speaker has to provide the hearer with two kinds of context:
   a) diverting context to indicate his departure from the original meaning; and
   b) guiding context to pinpoint the intended meaning.

iii The Principle of the Speaker's Truthfulness. The Muslim legal theorists point out that in the case of apparently false statement if it is known or presumed that the speaker is not telling a lie, it will be known that the utterance is intended to be taken non-literally. Conversely, if the hearer presumes that the speaker is lying, he will halt the process of *i*ᶜ*māl* (i.e., making sense of the expressions). Thus, in order for language to function properly, we have to take the speaker's statement to be true unless there is evidence to the contrary.

iv The Principle of *I*ᶜ*māl*. According to this principle, which is based on the assumption that interlocutors have mutual interest in communicating with each other, the hearer tends to make the received discourse and the relevant contexts operate by exploiting them to their maximum capability as they are the clue to the speaker's intention. If there is evidence that the expressions are not being used in their literal meanings, they must be interpreted figuratively in order to avoid the cancellation of the utterance and leaving the expressions without intention.

v The Principle of Immediacy. Immediacy *(tabādur)* is regarded as the primary criterion on which the addressee bases himself in his selection of the proper interpretation. It is commonly held that the first interpretation that occurs to the hearer is the one which is most likely to represent the speaker's intention. The immediate interpretation is usually
   a) the one in accordance with bases;
   b) the one in accordance with *waḍ*[c];
   c) the most expected one; and/or
   d) the literal or the nearest to the literal meaning.

Within the *Salafī* framework, Ibn Taymiyyah advances some scattered, but powerful, arguments against what can be called atomism and foundationalism as developed by the adherents of the notion *waḍ*[c], in favour of a well-developed version of compositionalism and contextualism. Ibn Taymiyyah argues that since language is used as a means to express the contents of the external world, there must be a correspondence between the structure of reality and the use of language in a way that the structure of reality is reflected in the language. Consequently, since there is no abstract thing in the external world but all entities are conceived to be qualified in some way, it follows that there would be no unqualified expressions in the language to signify it. There is no such thing as an unqualified expression or an unqualified meaning other than the mental representations of real expressions and meanings, which are in effect nothing but abstract constructs having no reality in the external world. So a plausible inquiry can be achieved only by an empirical approach which takes the overall communicative situation into account. His opponents' misconception, says Ibn Taymiyyah, is due to a confusion between the world *per se* and their assumptions about the world. They incorrectly think that what they construct in their minds represents the external reality, although their mental representations are decontextualised and divested of the individual variations of the external entities which are generated by their individuation and which, he believes, is the sign of their real existence in the physical world. Ibn Taymiyyah holds the view that actual utterances have a chronologically prior existence to the unobservable and abstracted structure of utterances (i.e., sentences). This position contrasts with the Platonic realist's doctrine according to which sentences as universals exist prior to utterances as particulars. It is also in contrast with the mainstream conceptual view of *waḍ*ᶜ which presupposes that expressions are 'established' for the mental representations of the external entities.

Ibn Taymiyyah distinguishes quite clearly between mentioning a word without the intention of communicating a certain proposition and the process in which the user intends to convey a particular message to the hearer. It is only the latter case that can, in his view, be said to pertain to the use of language. This distinction is very useful for understanding his conception of meaningfulness and his rejection of the distinction between *ḥaqīqah* (literal meaning) and *majāz* (non-literal meaning), where he claims that words such as 'lion' taken in isolation from every context would never be meaningful, let alone characterised as *ḥaqīqah*. It should be noted, however, that Ibn Taymiyyah does not deny the existence of relationships holding between literal and figurative meanings or the possibility that one meaning is chronologically prior to the other(s), but what he disputes is the possibility of finding reliable tests by which one can judge that a particular meaning is *ḥaqīqah* or *majāz*. Ibn Taymiyyah argues that the fact that a particular meaning of a multi-meaning expression tends to occur to the mind prior to the others does not justify the distinction between *ḥaqīqah* and *majāz*. For the meanings of some *ḥaqīqah*-expressions may also tend to occur to the mind prior to others. There is no constant immediate meaning attached to each word in the language, but the context in which the word is processed determines which interpretation is most likely to be the first to occur to the hearer's mind. The essence of his argument is that the etymological and diachronic account of *majāz* is invalid since it is founded upon non-demonstrable assumptions. According to Ibn Taymiyyah's account of *majāz*, each pair of the so-called *ḥaqīqah*-expression and *majāz*-expression represents two variants of a wider unqualified expression. Thus, instead of saying that 'the bird's wing' is a *ḥaqīqah*-expression, and 'the wing of humility' is a *majāz*-expression, the *Salafīs* would say that both 'the bird's wing' and the wing of humility' are two different variants of 'wing', which only has mental, not actual, existence. In other words, just as the *mushakkik*-expression 'white', given the appropriate context, is capable of referring to the whiteness of ice and the whiteness of milk, the *mutawāṭī*ᵓ-expression 'man' refers equally to Zayd and 'Umar, and the *mushtarak*-expression '*al-mushtarī*' is applicable to a 'buyer' and 'Jupiter', in the same way that the personal pronoun 'I' can refer to different speakers in different situations; thus the expression 'wing' can be applied equally to 'a bird's wing' and 'the wing of humility', subject to the condition that identifying which one of them is the intended meaning will depend on context.

There is a consistent correlation, in his view, between qualification and meaningfulness, i.e., the more restricted the expression the more meaningful it is, and *vice versa*. The absolute is, thus, nothing but a mental image that has no existence in the external world. In order to maintain consistency in his claim that expressions cannot be used without contextual qualifications, Ibn Taymiyyah introduces the notion 'non-existential signification'.

His rejection of the notion *waḍ*ᶜ in its folk sense according to which expressions are 'established' in isolation from context leads to the neutralisation of the differentiation between meaning and intention. One consequence of conflating the two ideas, i.e., meaning and intention is to entail that conventional meaning is trivialised to the advantage of contextual meaning.

Compared with the mainstream model, the *Salafīs*' model of interpretation appears to be more straightforward. The *Salafīs* appeal to the Principle of Immediacy rather than that of *Istiṣḥāb*, because it is consistent with their belief that valid interpretations are not obtainable in isolation from communicative situations. Furthermore, the *Salafīs* believe that the Principle of *Istiṣḥāb* is incompatible with the Principle of the Speaker's Disposition to Make his Intention Manifest, which forms with the Principle of Immediacy the cardinal postulates in their model of interpretation. They defend this position in this regard by pointing out that in recovering the signification of an utterance the hearer does not have to move from a literal-base meaning to a non-literal subsidiary or derivative one. In fact, the intended meaning strikes the hearer directly by virtue of the Principle of the Speaker's Disposition to Make his Intention Manifest and the Principle of Immediacy. In other words, the hearer's mind goes directly to the intention of the speaker without the need for mediating meanings, simply because it is the appropriate context, not the context-independent meaning, of the expression which provides the effective guide to the speaker's intention.

The main difference between the mainstream model and Ibn Taymiyyah's model of interpretation is that the mainstream model presupposes that the hearer examines the first interpretation in accordance with *uṣūl*. If the first interpretation is ruled out by a diverting context the hearer will look for other interpretations until a proper one is found. Ibn Taymiyyah's model, by contrast, presupposes that the hearer goes directly to the contextually relevant interpretation. As a result, the mainstream model can be characterised as indeterminate since it leaves the way open for other possible interpretations whereas Ibn Taymiyyah's model is determinate.

It is widely accepted that an act of *taʾwīl* involves a departure from the most immediate interpretation to the hearer's mind, which presupposes the assumption that the speaker is not co-operating sufficiently in communication. This assumption attracts strong criticism from the *Salafī*s on the grounds that it is not in harmony with the Principle of the Speaker's Disposition to Make his Intention Manifest, which is regarded by all parties as the primary principle behind any process of successful communication.

Moreover, the *Salafīs* and the PF mainstream disagree concerning what kind of expression is liable to *taʾwīl*. The PF mainstream hold that *taʾwīl* is applicable to any *ẓāhir*-expression, provided that there is a contextual indicator that the apparent meaning is not the meaning intended by the speaker. For the *Salafī*s, this is not necessarily true. They confine *taʾwīl* to those *ẓāhir*-expressions whose signification in a particular context appears, as Ibn al-Qayyim puts it, to be different from its equivalents *(khārijan ʿan naẓāʾirih)*. To put it another way, if the hearer notices that the apparent meaning of the utterance is not in conformity with what the speaker habitually means by such an utterance in such a situation, then he has to interpret it in line with the speaker's own lexicon and his consistent habit. Thus, the *Salafī*s' main contention is that if the hearer knows that the speaker is able and willing to make his intention manifest, it would be wise to think that he intends his utterance to be taken in its apparent meaning.

The fourth component of the mainstream model of communication is signification. Muslim legal theorists discuss two different models of significational classification: the first is semiotic; the other is a text-based one. Within the semiotic classification, they distinguish two types of signification: verbal and non-verbal. Each type is subdivided into further types: verbal signification is classified into *waḍʿ*-based *(waḍʿiyyah)*, rational *(ʿaqliyyah)* and natural *(ṭabīʿiyyah)*. Non-verbal signification, on the other hand, is classified into *waḍʿ*-based and rational types. For the linguists and legal theorists *waḍʿ*-based verbal signification (or linguistic signification) is the most important type of signification.

The meaning of an utterance is not determined by the *waḍʿ*-based signification of that utterance alone, since non-*waḍʿ*-based components such as the context, are ultimately the determining factor for recovering the intention of the speaker. However, there is a disagreement among Muslim thinkers as to whether or not signification can operate without intention. Generally speaking, linguists tend to make intention as a necessary condition for signification, since signification, in their view, is the understanding of intention, not meaning in its unqualified sense. Logicians, on the other hand, believe that signification is the understanding of meaning whether it is intended by the speaker or not. As for the legal theorists, the *Salafīs* strongly deny that signification is obtainable in isolation of a particular communicative situation, while most scholars hold that there are some meanings which can be abstracted from actual utterances and identified as *waḍ^c*-based.

Following Muslim logicians, the legal theorists distinguish between three types of the *waḍ^c*-based signification: 'equivalence-signification' *(dalālat muṭābaqah)*, 'incorporational signification' *(dalālat taḍammun)* and 'implicational signification' *(dalālat iltizām)*. If the expression *rajul* (man), for example, is used to refer to an 'adult human male', the expression is said to be used to signify its equivalent meaning, since this is the meaning to which the expression is assigned. In addition to this meaning, the legal theorists say that the word *rajul* 'incorporationally signifies' each one of the following features: 'adult', 'male' and 'human'. Incorporational signification' is widely seen as a relationship between the specific and the general, where the specific word incorporates *(tataḍamman)* the general one. Implicational signification, on the other hand, is loosely defined as the process in which an expression signifies its implication *(dalālatu l-lafẓi ^{c}alā lāzimih)*. The notion of implication *(iltizām)* is intended to cover all that which is excluded from equivalence and incorporational signification.

In PF, there are two common proposals for what I have called 'text-based classification of signification': the majority proposal known as the *Shāfi^{c}ī* method of dividing signification and the *Ḥanafī* one.

The *Ḥanafī* scholars distinguish four types of meaning at the textual level:

i the express meaning *(^{c}ibārat al-naṣṣ)*. Broadly speaking, this is the meaning which is taken to be the main import the speaker intends to convey by his utterance. To put it more literally, the meaning "at which the utterance is driven" *(al-masūqu lahu l-kalām)*.

ii the alluded meaning *(ishārat al-naṣṣ)*. This term is used to refer to the meaning conveyed by the linguistic construction of the utterance, but does not represent the intention of the speaker at which the text is driven.

iii the inferred meaning *(dalālat al-naṣṣ)*. Inferred meaning is a special case of analogical reasoning in which an unstated meaning is derived on 'all-the-more-reason basis' from a stated meaning by virtue of the consideration of the context and the speaker's illocutionary import.

iv the required meaning *(iqtiḍāʾ al-naṣṣ)*. This term is commonly used to refer to the semantic content of ellipted parts of an utterance which is believed to be essential to the meaningfulness of the whole utterance. The legal theorists distinguish three types of required meaning:

   a) what is assumed to have been omitted for the preservation of the speaker's truthfulness;
   b) what is assumed to have been omitted for the preservation of the rationality of the text *(al-ṣiḥḥah al-ʿaqliyyah)*; and
   c) what is assumed to have been omitted for the preservation of the legal validity of the text *(al-ṣiḥḥah al-sharʿiyyah)*.

Compared with the *Ḥanafī*, the *Shāfiʿī* classification involves the following types:

i the signification of 'what is said' *(dalālat al-manṭūq)* (the equivalent of (i) in the *Ḥanafī* classification);

ii 'alluded signification' *(dalālat al-ishārah)* (the equivalent of (ii) in the *Ḥanafī* classification);

iii required signification (*dalālat al-iqtiḍāʾ*) (the equivalent of (iv) in the *Ḥanafī* classification);

iv indicated signification (*dalālat al-tanbīh wa-l-īmāʾ*). This type of signification, which has no equivalent in the *Ḥanafī* classification arises from implicitly connecting a particular rule with a particular quality in a way suggesting the involvement of a causal relationship; and

v implicated signification (*dalālat al-mafhūm)*, which is divided into:

   a) congruent implicature (*mafhūm al-muwāfaqah)* (the equivalent of (iii) in the *Ḥanafī* classification); and
   b) counter implicature (*mafhūm al-mukhālafah)*. Most of the *Hanafīs* say that counter implicature is a weak source to rely

on for the formulation of the law, though it can be used as a valid inference in non-legal discourse.

The important thing to note in most versions of the *Shāfiʿī* classification, is the distinction between the meaning of 'what is said' and the meaning of 'what is implicated'. Unlike many other Muslim legal theorists and modern pragmatists who attempt similar distinctions, al-Juwaynī has a clear, though not necessarily accurate, picture of the difference between stated and implicated propositions. Any inferred proposition which represents either the analogue or the opposite of what is said would be characterised, according to al-Juwaynī's classification, as an implicated proposition. Any other proposition would, in contrast, be seen as either an explicitly or implicitly stated meaning.

The notion of counter implicature is highly relevant to what is called in contemporary pragmatics 'scalar implicature'. The insights developed by Muslim legal theorists and their approach to the subject may contribute considerably to the development of 'scalar implicature'. In particular, they may, at least, lead to expanding the notion to cover all the types regarded by the legal theorists as types of 'counter implicature'.

The Maxim of Quantity, among Grice's co-operative maxims, seems to play the essential role in generating counter-implicatures. However, other principles, such as the Principle of Relevance and the Principle of the Speaker's Disposition to Make his Intention Manifest are also important. Furthermore, different scholars place emphasis on different principles.

Muslim legal theorists distinguish several types of counter implicature. Some of these types are

I *Mafhūm al-laqab* (The Implicature of a Designation).
II *Mafhūm al-ṣifah* (The Implicature of a Restrictive Attribute).
III *Mafhūm al-sharṭ* (The Implicature of a Condition).
IV *Mafhūm al-ghāyah* (The Implicature of a Time Limit).
V *Mafhūm al-ʿadad* (the Implicature of a Stated Numeral).
VI *Mafhūm al-istithnāʾ* (the Implicature of an Exception).
VII *Mafhūm al-ḥaṣr* (the Implicature of Confinement).

Finally, there remains a great deal of work to be done so as to reach a precise account of the Muslim legal theorists' pragmatic models of textual communication. In particular, the principles and bases of communication, and both the semiotic and the text-based classification of signification need to be examined in more detail. This work is but a start in that direction.

Notes

1 Sperber and Wilson, *Relevance . . .*, p. 2; see also Akmajian, Demers, and Harnish, *Linguistics . . .*, pp. 392–400.
2 *Ibid.*

Bibliography

1. ARABIC TITLES

1.1. Primary sources

ʿAḍud al-Millah wa-l-Dīn, *Sharḥ Mukhtaṣar al-Muntahā l-Uṣūlī li-Ibn al-Ḥājib,* 2nd edn. (Beirut: Dār al-Kutub al-ʿIlmiyyah, 1983).

Al-Āmidī, Sayf al-Dīn ʿAlī b. Muḥammad, *al-Iḥkām fī Uṣūl al-Aḥkām* (Beirut: Dār al-Kutub al-ʿIlmiyyah, 1983).

——, *al-Iḥkām fī Uṣūl al-Aḥkām,* ed. Sayyid al-Jumaylī, 2nd edn. (Beirut: Dār al-Kitāb al-ʿArabī, 1986).

Al-Anṣārī, ʿAbd al-ʿAlī, *Fawātīḥ al-Raḥamūt bi-Sharḥ Musallam al-Thubūt,* 2nd edn. (Qum, Iran: Dār al-Dhakhāʾir, 1368).

Al-Asnawī, Jamāl al-Dīn ʿAbd al-Raḥīm b. al-Ḥasan, *Nihāyat al-Sūl fī Sharḥ Minhāj al-Uṣūl* (Beirut: ʿĀlam al-Kutub, n.d.).

Al-Bājī, Abū al-Walīd Sulaymān b, Khalaf, *Iḥkām al-Fuṣūl fī Aḥkām al-Uṣūl,* ed. ʿAbd Allāh Muḥammad al-Jabūrī (Beirut: Muʾassasat al-Risālah, 1989).

Al-Bannānī, ʿAbd al-Raḥmān, *Ḥāshiyah ʿalā Sharḥ al-Jalāl al-Maḥallī ʿalā Matn Jamʿ al-Jawāmiʿ* (Beirut: Dār al-Fikr, 1982).

Al-Baṣrī, Abū l-Ḥusayn Muḥammad b. ʿAlī b. al-Ṭayyib, *al-Muʿtamad fī Uṣūl al-Fiqh,* ed. Khalīl al-Mays (Beirut: Dār al-Kutub al-ʿIlmiyyah, 1983).

Al-Bayḍāwī, Nāṣir al-Dīn ʿAbd Allāh b. ʿUmar, *Minhāj al-Uṣūl bi Sharḥ al-Asnawī* (Beirut: ʿĀlam al-Kutub).

Al-Bazdawī, Fakhr al-Islām, *Uṣūl al-Bazdawī* (bi-Kashf al-Asrār li-l-Bukhārī), 2nd edn. (Beirut: Dār al-Kitāb al-ʿArabī, 1994).

Al-Bukhārī, ʿAlāʾ al-Dīn ʿAbd al-ʿAzīz b. Aḥmad, *Kashf al-Asrār ʿan Uṣūl Fakhr al-Islām al-Bazdawī,* ed. Muḥammad al-Muʿtaṣim Bi-Allāh al-Baghdādī, 2nd edn. (Beirut: Dār al-Kitāb al-ʿArabī, 1994).

Al-Fanārī, Ḥasan, *Ḥāshiyah ʿalā Ḥāshiyat al-Talwīḥ ʿalā Sharḥ al-Tawḍīḥ ʿalā l-Tanqīḥ* (Cairo: al-Maktabah al-Khayriyyah, 1306 A.H).

Al-Ghazālī, Abū Ḥāmid, *Kitāb Miḥakk al-Naẓar fī l-Manṭiq* (Beirut: Dār al-Nahḍah al-Ḥadīthah, 1966).

——, *Miʿyār al-ʿIlm fī Fann al-Manṭiq,* 4th edn. (Beirut: Dār al-Andalus, 1983).

——, *al-Mustaṣfā min ʿIlm al-Uṣūl,* 2nd edn. (Qum, Iran: Dār al-Dhakhāʾir, 1368).

Al-Harawī, Ḥasan, *Ḥāshiyah ᶜalā Ḥāshiyat al-Sharīf al-Jurjānī ᶜalā Sharḥ al-ᶜAḍud,* 2nd edn. (Beirut: Dār al-Kutub al-ᶜIlmiyyah, 1983).
Ibn al-Ḥājib al-Mālikī, *Mukhtaṣar al-Muntahā l-Uṣūlī,* 2nd edn. (Beirut: Dār al-Kutub al-ᶜIlmiyyah, 1983).
Ibn al-Ḥalabī, Raḍī al-Dīn Muḥammad b. Ibrāhīm, *Ḥāshiyat Anwār al-Ḥuluk ᶜalā Sharḥ al-Manār* (n.p. al-Maṭbaᶜah al-ᶜUthmāniyyah, 1319 A.H.).
Ibn. Ḥalūl, Abū l-ᶜAbbās Aḥmad b. ᶜAbd al-Raḥmān al-Qayrawānī, *Ḥāshiyah ᶜalā Sharḥ Tanqīḥ al-Fuṣūl* (Tunis: al-Maṭbaᶜah al-Tunusiyyah, 1910).
Ibn Ḥazm, Abū Muḥammad ᶜAlī al-Ẓāhirī, *al-Iḥkām fī Uṣūl al-Aḥkām* (Cairo: Dār al-Ḥadīth, 1984).
Ibn al-Malik, Muᶜizz al-Dīn ᶜAbd al-Laṭīf b. ᶜAbd al-ᶜAzīz, *Sharḥ al-Manār* (n.p. al-Maṭbaᶜah al-ᶜUthmāniyyah, 1319 A.H.).
Ibn Qayyim al-Jawziyyah, *Iᶜlām al-Muwaqqiᶜīn ᶜan Rabb al-ᶜĀlamīn,* ed. ᶜAbd al-Raḥmān al-Wakīl (Cairo: Dār al-Kutub al-Ḥadīthah, 1969).
Ibn al-Shāṭ, *Idrār al-Shurūq ᶜalā Anwār al-Burūq fī Anwāʾ al-Furūq: Ḥāshiyah ᶜalā l-Qarāfī's Furūq* (Cairo: Dār Iḥyāʾ al-Kutub al-ᶜArabiyyah, 1344.AH).
Ibn Taymiyyah, Aḥmad, *Bayān Talbīs al-Jahmiyyah fī Taʾsīs Bidaᶜihim al-Kalāmiyyah aw Naqḍ Taʾsīs al-Jahmiyyah,* ed. Muḥammad b. ᶜAbd al-Raḥmān b. Qāsim (Mecca: Maṭbaᶜat al-Ḥukūmah, 1391 AH).
——, *Darʾ Taᶜāruḍ al-ᶜAql wa-l-Naql,* ed. Muḥammad Rashād Sālim (Riyadh: Jāmiᶜat al-Imām Muḥammad Ibn Saᶜūd al-Islāmiyyah, 1979).
——, *al-Imān,* ed. Muḥammad Nāṣir al-Dīn al-Albānī and Zuhayr al-Shāwīsh (Beirut: al-Maktab al-Islāmī, 1986).
——, *Kitāb al-Ṣafdiyyah,* ed. Muḥammad Rashād Sālim, 2nd edn. (n.p., 1406 AH).
——, *Majmūᶜ Fatāwā,* ed. ᶜAbd al-Raḥmān b. Qāsim and Muḥammad ᶜAbd al-Raḥmān b. Qāsim (Rabāṭ: Maktabat al-Maᶜārif, n.d.).
——, *al-Radd ᶜalā l-Manṭiqiyyīn,* ed. Muḥammad ᶜAbd al-Sattār Naṣṣār and ᶜImād Khafājī (Cairo: Maktabat al-Azhar, 1977).
Al-Jurjānī, al-Sharīf, *Sharḥ al-Mawāqif fī ᶜIlm al-Kalām,* ed. Aḥmad al-Mahdī (Cairo: Maktabat al-Azhar, 1976).
——, *Ḥāshiyah ᶜalā Sharḥ ᶜAḍud al-Millah wa-l-Dīn li-Mukhtaṣar al-Muntahā l-Uṣūlī,* 2nd edn. (Beirut: Dār al-Kutub al-ᶜIlmiyyah, 1983).
——, *al-Taᶜrīfāt* (Tunis: al-Dār al-Tūnusiyyah li-l-Nashr, 1971).
Al-Juwaynī, Imām al-Ḥaramayn Abū l-Maᶜālī, *al-Burhān fī Uṣūl al-Fiqh,* ed. ᶜAbd al-ᶜAẓīm al-Dīb (Qaṭar: 1399, A.H.).
Al-Kafawī, Abū-l-Baqāʾ, *al-Kulliyāt,* ed. ᶜAdnān Darwīsh and Muḥammad al-Maṣrī (Damascus: Manshūrāt Wazārat al-Thaqāfah wa-l-Irshād al-Qawmī, 1981).
Al-Maḥallī, Shams al-Dīn Muḥammad, *Sharḥ Matn Jamᶜ al-Jawāmiᶜ* (Beirut: Dār al-Fikr, 1982).
Al-Marjānī, Hārūn, *Ḥāshiyah ᶜalā Sharḥ al-Tawḍīḥ ᶜalā l-Tanqīḥ* (Cairo: al-Maktabah al-Khayriyyah, 1306 A.H).
Al-Mawṣilī, Muḥammad, *Mukhtaṣar al-Ṣawāᶜiq al-Mursalah ᶜalā l-Jahmiyyah wa-l-Muᶜaṭṭilah li-Ibn Qayyim al-Jawziyyah* (Mecca: al-Maktabah al-Salafiyyah, 1349 A.H.).
Muḥibb Allāh. b. ᶜAbd al-Shakūr, *Sharḥ Musallam al-Thubūt,* 2nd edn. (Qum, Iran: Dār al-Dhakhāʾir, 1368).

Mullākhusrū, *Ḥāshiyah ᶜalā Ḥāshiyat al-Talwīḥ ᶜalā Sharḥ al-Tawḍīḥ ᶜalā l-Tanqīḥ* (Cairo: al-Maktabah al-Khayriyyah, 1306 A.H).

Al-Nasafī, Abū l-Barakāt Ḥāfiẓ al-Dīn, *Matn al-Manār* (n.p. al-Maṭbaᶜah al-ᶜUthmāniyyah, 1319 A.H.).

——, *Tafsīr al-Nasafī* (Beirut: Dār al-Kitāb al-ᶜArabī, 1982).

Al-Qarāfī, Shihāb al-Dīn Aḥmad b. Idrīs, *Anwār al-Burūq fī Anwāʾ al-Furūq* (Cairo: Dār Iḥyāʾ al-Kutub al-ᶜArabiyyah, 1344.AH).

——, *al-Iḥkām fī Tamyīz al-Fatāwā ᶜan al-Aḥkām wa-Taṣarrufāt al-Qāḍī wa-l-Imām,* ed. ᶜAbd al-Fattāḥ Abū Ghaddah (Ḥalab, Syria: Maktab al-Maṭbūᶜāt al-Islāmiyyah, 1967).

——, *al-Istighnāʾ fī l-Istithnāʾ,* ed. Muḥammad ᶜAbd al-Qādir ᶜAṭā (Beirut: Dār al-Kutub al-ᶜIlmiyyah, 1986).

——, *Sharḥ Tanqīḥ al-Fuṣūl fī Ikhtiṣār al-Maḥṣūl fī l-Uṣūl,* ed. Ṭaha ᶜAbd al-Raʾūf Saᶜd (Cairo: maktabat al-kulliyyāt al-Azhariyyah, 1973).

Al-Rāzī, Fakhr al-Dīn, *al-Maḥṣūl fī ᶜIlm Uṣūl al-Fiqh* (Beirut: Dār al-Kutub al-ᶜIlmiyyah, 1988).

Al-Ruhāwī, Yaḥyā, *Ḥāshiyah ᶜalā Sharḥ al-Manār* (n.p. al-Maṭbaᶜah al-ᶜUthmāniyyah, 1319 A.H.).

Ṣadr al-Sharīᶜah ᶜUbayd Allāh b. Masᶜūd, *Sharḥ al-Tawḍīḥ ᶜalā l-Tanqīḥ* (Cairo: al-Maktabah al-Khayriyyah, 1306 A.H).

Al-Samarqandī, ᶜAlāʾ al-Dīn Shams al-Naẓar Abū Bakr Muḥammad b. Aḥmad, *Mīzān al-Uṣūl fī Natāʾij al-ᶜUqūl fī Uṣūl al-Fiqh,* ed. ᶜAbd al-Malik ᶜAbd al-Raḥmān al-Saᶜdī (Baghdad: Maṭbaᶜat al-Khulūd, 1987).

Al-Sarakhsī, Abū Bakr Muḥammad b. Aḥmad, *Uṣūl al- Sarakhsī,* ed. Abū l-Wafāʾ al-Afghānī (Beirut: Dār al-Kutub al-ᶜIlmiyyah, 1993).

Al-Shāfiᶜī, Muḥammad b. Idrīs, *al-Risālah,* ed. Aḥmad Muḥammad Shākir, 2nd edn. (Cairo: Dār al-Turāth, 1979).

Al-Sharbīnī, ᶜAbd al-Raḥmān, *Taqrīrāt ᶜalā Ḥāshiyat al-Bannānī ᶜalā Sharḥ al-Jalāl al-Maḥallī ᶜalā Matn Jamᶜ al-Jawāmiᶜ* (Beirut: Dār al-Fikr, 1982).

Al-Shāṭibī, Abū Isḥāq, *al-Muwāfaqāt fī Uṣūl al-Sharīᶜah,* ed. ᶜAbd Allāh Drrāz and Muḥammad ᶜAbd Allāh Drrāz, 2nd edn (Beirut: Dār al-Maᶜrifah, 1975).

Al-Shīrāzī, Abū Isḥāq Ibrāhīm, *Sharḥ al-Lumaᶜ,* ed. ᶜAbd al-Majīd Turkī (Beirut: Dār al-Gharb al-Islāmī, 1988).

——, *al-Tabṣirah fī Uṣūl al-Fiqh,* ed. Muḥammad Ḥasan Haytū (Damascus: Dār al-Fikr, 1980).

Al-Subkī, ᶜAlī b. ᶜAbd al-Kāfī and al-Subkī, Tāj al-Dīn ᶜAbd al-Wahhāb b.ᶜAlī b. ᶜAbd al-Kāfī, *al-Ibhāj fī Sharḥ al-Minhāj ᶜalā Minhāj al-Wuṣūl ilā ᶜIlm al-Uṣūl,* ed. Shaᶜbān Muḥammad Ismāᶜīl (Cairo: Maktabat al-Kulliyāt al-Azhariyyah, 1981).

Al-Subkī, Tāj al-Dīn ᶜAbd al-Wahhāb, *Matn Jamᶜ al-Jawāmiᶜ* (Beirut: Dār al-Fikr, 1982).

Al-Suyūṭī, Jalāl al-Dīn, *al-Muzhir fī ᶜUlūm al-Lughah wa-Anwāᶜihā,* ed. Muḥammad Aḥmad Jād al-Mawlā, ᶜAlī Muḥammad al-Bijāwī and Muḥammad al-Faḍl Ibrāhīm (Beirut: Dār al-Fikr, n.d.).

——, *al-Rawḍ al-Unuf fī Tafsīr al-Sīrah al-Nabawiyyah li-Ibn Hishām* (Beirut: Dār al-Maᶜrifah, 1978).

——, *al-ʾShbāh wa-l-Naẓāʾir fī Qawāᶜid wa-Furūᶜ Fiqh al-Shāfiᶜiyyah* (Dār al-Shām li-l-Turāth "n.p." "n.d.").

Al-Taftāzānī, Saʿd al-Dīn, *Ḥāshiyah ʿalā Sharḥ ʿAḍud al-Millah wa-l-Dīn li-Mukhtaṣar al-Muntahā l-Uṣūlī*, 2nd edn. (Beirut: Dār al-Kutub al-ʿIlmiyyah, 1983).

——, *Ḥāshiyat al-Talwīḥ ʿalā Sharḥ al-Tawḍīḥ ʿalā l-Tanqīḥ* (Cairo: al-Maktabah al-Khayriyyah, 1306 A.H).

Al-Tahānawī, Muḥammad Aʿlā b. ʿAli, *Kashshāf Iṣḥilāḥāt al-Funūn*, ed. Muḥammad Wajīh and others. (Calcutta: The Asiatic Society of Bengal, 1862).

Ṭāshkubrizādah, *Miftāḥ al-Saʿādah*, ed. Kāmil Kāmil Bakrī and ʿAbd al-Wahhāb Abū l-Nūr (Cairo: Dār al-Kutub al-Ḥadīthah, 1968).

Al-Zarkashī, Badr al-Dīn Muḥammad b. ʿAbd Allāh, *al-Burhān fī ʿUlūm al-Qurʾān*, ed. Muḥammad Abū al-Faḍl. Ibrāhīm, 2nd edn. (Beirut: Dār al-Maʿrifah li-l-Ṭibāʿah wa-l-Nashr, n.d.).

Zādah, ʿAzmī, *Ḥāshiyah ʿalā Sharḥ al-Manār* (n.p. al-Maṭbaʿah al-ʿUthmāniyyah, 1319 A.H.).

1.2. Secondary sources

Aḥmad, ʿAbd al-Jabbār, *Sharḥ al-Uṣūl al-Khamsah*, ed. ʿAbd al-Karīm ʿUthmān, 2nd edn. (Cairo: Maktabat Wahbah, 1988).

Ali, A. Yusuf, *THE HOLY QURʾAN: Text, Translation and Commentary* (Brentwood, USA: Amana Corp, 1983).

Ali, Mohamed Mohamed Y., *Waṣf al-Lughah al-ʿArabiyyah Dilāliyyan fī Ḍawʾ Mafhūm al-Dalālah al-Markaziyyah: Dirāsah Ḥawla l-Maʿnā wa-Ẓilāl al-Maʿnā* (Tripoli, Libya: Manshūrāt Jāmiʿat al-Fātiḥ, 1993).

Astarābādhī, Raḍī l-Dīn, *Sharḥ al-Raḍī ʿalā l-Kāfiyah*, ed. Yūsuf Ḥasan ʿUmar (Banghāzī, Libya: Manshūrāt Jāmiʿat Banghāzī 1978).

Al-Bukhārī, Abū ʿAbd Allāh Muḥammad b. Ismāʿīl, *Ṣaḥīḥ al-Bukhārī* (Cairo: Maṭbaʿat al-Bābī al-Ḥalabī, 1345 A.H.).

Al-Darīnī, Fatḥī, *al-Manāhij al-Uṣūliyyah fī l-Ijtihād bi-l-Raʾy fī l-Tashrīʿ al-Islāmī* (Damascus: Dār al-Rashīd, 1976).

Fākhūrī, ʿĀdil, *ʿIlm al-Dalālah ʿind al-ʿArab: Dirāsah Muqārinah maʿa l-Sīmyāʾ al-Ḥadīthah* (Beirut: Dār al-Ṭalīʿah, 1985).

Ibn Khaldūn, *al-Muqaddimah* (Cairo: Maktabat al-Taqaddum, 1322 A.H.).

Ibn Yaʿīsh, Muwaffaq al-Dīn Yaʿīsh b. ʿAlī, *Sharḥ al-Mufaṣṣal* (Beirut: ʿĀlam al-Kutub, n.d.).

Kaḥḥālah, ʿUmar Riḍā, *Muʿjam al-Muʾallifīn: Tarājim Muṣannifī l-Kutub al-ʿArabiyyah* (Beirut: Maktabat al-Muthannā and Dār Iḥyāʾ al-Turāth al-ʿArabī, 1957).

Al-Jawhrī, Ismāʿīl Ibn Ḥammād, *al-Ṣiḥāḥ: Tāj al-lughah wa-Ṣiḥāḥ al-ʿArabiyyah*, ed. Aḥmad ʿAbd al-Ghafūr ʿAṭṭār, 4th edn. (Beirut: Dār al-ʿIlm li-l-Malāyīn, 1987).3

Al-Jurjānī, ʿAbd al-Qāhir, *Asrār al-Balāghah*, ed. H., Ritter, 3rd edn. (Beirut: Dār al-Masīrah, 1983).

——, *Dalāʾil al-Iʿjāz*, ed. Muḥammad Ruḍwān al-Dāyah and Muḥammad Fāyiz al-Dāyah (Dār Qutaybah, n.p., 1983).

Al-Jurjānī, Muḥammad b. ʿAlī b. Muḥammad, *al-Ishārāt wa-l-Tanbīhāt fī ʿIlm al-Balāghah*, ed. ʿAbd al-Qādir Ḥusayn (Cairo: Dār Nahḍat Miṣir, 1982).

Al-Muṭīʿī, Muḥammad Bakhīt, *Sullam al-Wuṣūl li-Sharḥ Nihāyat al-Sūl* (Beirut: ʿĀlam al-Kutub, n.d.).

Al-Ṭarūdī, Aḥmad Muṣṭafā l-Tunusī, *Kitāb Jāmiʿ l-ʿIbārāt fī Taḥqīq al-Istiʿārāt,* ed. Muḥammad Ramaḍān al-Jirbī (Miṣrātah, Libya: Dār al-Jamāhīriyyah, 1986).

Turkī, ʿAbd al-Majīd, *Munāẓarāt fī Uṣūl al-Sharīʿah al-Islāmiyyah bayn Ibn Ḥazm wa-l-Bājī,* trans and ed. ʿAbd al-Ṣabūr Shāhīn, revised by Muḥammad Maḥmūd (Beirut: Dār al-Gharb al-Islāmī, 1986).

Al-Zahrāwī, ʿAbd al-Ḥamīd, "ʿIlm al-Waḍʿ", ed. ʿAbd al-Ilāh Nabhān, Majallat Majmaʿ Dimashq, 70 (1995), 3/451–472.

Zaydān, ʿAbd al-Karīm, *al-Wajīz fī Uṣūl al-Fiqh* (Beirut: Muʾassasat al-Risālah, 1987).

Al-Ziriklī, Khayr al-Dīn, *al-Aʿlām: Qāmūs Tarājim li-Ashhar al-Rijāl wa-l-Nisāʾ mina l-ʿArab wa-l-Mustaʿribīn wa-l-Mustashriqīn* (Beirut: Dār al-ʿIlm li-l-Malāyīn, 1980).

2. ENGLISH TITLES

Akmajian, Adrian, Demers, Richard A., and Harnish, Robert M., *Linguistics: An Introduction to Language and Communication,* 2nd edn. (Cambridge: the MIT press, 1984).

Barton, Ellen L., *Nonsentential Constituents: A Theory of Grammatical Structure and Pragmatic Interpretation* (Amsterdam: John Benjamins Publishing Company, 1990).

Blakemore, Diane, *Understanding Utterances: An Introduction to Pragmatics* (Oxford: Blackwell Publishers, 1992).

Bosch, Peter, "Context Dependence and Metaphor", in Wolf Paprotte and Rene Dirven (eds.), *The Ubiquity of Metaphor: Metaphor in Language and Thought (*Amsterdam Studies in The Theory and History of Linguistic Science IV; Current Issues in Linguistic Theory Volume 29), (Amsterdam: John Benjamins Publishing company, 1985).

Brown, Gillian and Yule, George, *Discourse Analysis* (London: Cambridge University Press, 1983).

Bussmann, Hadumond, Routledge *Dictionary of Language and Linguistics,* trans and ed. Gregory P. Trauth and Kerstin Kazzazi (London and New York: Routledge, 1996).

Cann, Ronnie, *Formal Semantics: An Introduction* (Cambridge: Cambridge University Press, 1993).

Carston, Robyan, "Implicature, Explicature, and Truth-Theoretic Semantics", in Steven Davis (ed), *Pragmatics/ A Reader,* pp. 33–51.

Cooper, David, *Philosophy and the Nature of Language,* (London: Longman, 1973).

Cowan, J M. (ed.), *Arabic-English Dictionary: The Hans Wehr Dictionary of Modern Written Arabic* (Ithaca, New York: Spoken Language Services, Inc. 1976).

Crystal, David, *A Dictionary of Linguistics and Phonetics,* 3rd edn. (Oxford: Blackwell, 1991).

Dascal, Marcelo, "On the Pragmatic Structure of Conversation", in J. R. Searle (ed.) (compiled and introduced by Herman Parret and Jef Verschueren), *(On) Searle on Conversation* (Amsterdam: John Benjamins Publishing Company, 1992), P. 77–90.

Davidson, Donald, "What Metaphors Mean", in Steven Davis (ed.) *Pragmatics*, pp. 495–506.

Davis, Steven (ed.) *Pragmatics* (New York: Oxford University Press, 1991).

Gazdar, G, *Pragmatics: Implicature, Presupposition and Logical Form* (New York: Academic Press, 1979).

Grice, H. P., "Logic and Conversation" in Peter Cole and Jerry L. Morgan (eds.), *Syntax and Semantics, 3: Speech Acts* (New York: Academic Press, 1975), pp. 41–58.

——, "Logic and Conversation", in Steven Davis (ed.), *Pragmatics: A Reader* (New York: Oxford University Press, 1991), pp. 305–315.

——, "Meaning", in Danny D. Steinberg and Leon A. Jakobovits (eds.), *Semantics: An Interdisciplinary Reader in Philosophy, Linguistics and Psychology* (London: Cambridge University Press, 1971), pp. 53–59.

——, "Utterer's Meaning, sentence-meaning, and word-meaning", in J. R. Searle (ed.), *the Philosophy of Language* (Oxford: Oxford University Press, 1971), pp. 54–70.

Grundy, Peter, *Doing Pragmatics* (London: Edward Arnold, 1995).

Gully, Adrian, *Grammar and Semantics in Medieval Arabic: A study of Ibn-Hisham's 'Mughni l-Labib'* (Richmond, Curzon Press, 1994).

Hallaq, Wael, "Brief Communications: Notes on the Term *qarīnah* in Islamic legal discourse", *Journal of the American Oriental Society*, 108.3 (1988), 475–480.

——, "Non-analogical Arguments in Sunni Juridical Qiyās", *Arabica*, 36 (1989), pp. 286–306.

Hanks, Patrick and others, *Collins Dictionary of the English Language*, 2nd edn. (London: Collins, 1986).

Harnish, Robert M., "Logical Form and Implicature", in Steven Davis (ed.), *Pragmatics: A Reader*, pp. 316–364.

Heer, Nicholas, "al-Jāmī's Treatise on Existence", in Parviz Morewedge (ed.), *Islamic Philosophical Theology* (Albany: State University of New York, 1979).

Heinrichs, Wolfhart, "On the Genesis of the *Ḥaqīqa* and *Majāz* Dichotomy", *Studia Islamica*, 59 (1984).

Ibn Khaldūn, *The Muqaddimah: An Introduction to History*, 2nd ed, trans. Franz Rosenthal (U.S.A: Princeton University Press, 1980).

Kamali, Muhammad. Hashim, *Principles of Islamic Jurisprudence* (Cambridge: Islamic Texts society, 1991).

Katz, Jerrold J., *Language and Other Abstract Objects* (Oxford: Basil Blakwell, 1981).

——, Linguistic Philosophy: the Underlying Reality of Language and its Philosophical Import (London: Allen and Unwin, 1972).

——, *Semantic Theory* (New York: Harper & Row, 1972).

Kempson, Ruth M., *Semantic Theory* (Cambridge: Cambridge University Press, 1977).

Leech, Geoffrey N., *Principles of Pragmatics* (London: Longman, 1983).
Levinson, Stephen C., *Pragmatics* (Cambridge: Cambridge University Press, 1983).
Lewis, B. L., Pellat Ch. and Schacht, J., *Encyclopaedia of Islam* vol 2. (Leiden: E.J.Brill, 1965).
——, *Encyclopaedia of Islam* vol 3. (Leiden: E.J.Brill, 1971).
Lyons, John, *Language and Linguistics: An Introduction* (Cambridge: Cambridge University Press, 1981).
——, *Linguistic Semantics: An Introduction* (Cambridge: Cambridge University Press, 1995).
——, *Semantics* (Cambridge: Cambridge University Press, 1977).
Maclean, Ian, *Interpretation and Meaning in the Renaissance: The Case of Law* (Cambridge: Cambridge University Press, 1992).
Majid, Nurcholish, "Ibn Taymiyya on *Kalām* and *Falsafa:* A Problem of Reason and Revelation in Islam", unpublished PhD thesis (Faculty of the Division of the Humanities; Dept of Near Eastern Languages and Civilisations, 1984).
Marmor, Andrei, *Interpretation and Legal Theory* (Oxford: Clarendon Press, 1992).
Martinet, A., *A Functional View of Language* (Oxford: Clarendon Press, 1962).
——, *Elements of General Linguistics,* trans. E Palmer (London: Faber, 1964).
Mey, Jacob L., *Pragmatics: An Introduction* (Oxford: Blackweel, 1993).
Netton, Ian Richard, *A Popular Dictionary of Islam* (London: Curzon Press, 1992).
——, *Allāh Transcendent: Studies in the Structure and Semiotics of Islamic Philosophy, Theology and Cosmology* (London: Routledge, 1989).
——, *Muslim Neoplatonists: An Introduction to the Thought of the Brethren of Purity* (Ikhwān al-Ṣafā᾽) (London: George Allen and Unwin, 1982).
Platts, Mark de Bretton, *Ways of Meaning: An Introduction to Philosophy of Language* (London: Routledge & Regan Paul, 1975).
Recanati, Francois, "The Pragmatics of What Is Said", in Steven Davis (ed.), *Pragmatics: A Reader,* pp. 97–120.
Runes, Dagobert D., *Dictionary of Philosophy,* 16th edn. (New York: Philosophical Library, n.d.).
Sadock, Jerrold M., "On Testing for Conversational Implicature", in Steven Davis (ed.), *Pragmatics: A Reader,* pp. 365–376.
Saussure, F.D, *Cours de Linguistique général* (Paris: Payot, 1968).
——, *Course in General Linguistics,* ed. Charles Bally, Albert Sechehaye and Albert Riendlinger, trans. Roy Harris (London: Duckworth, 1983).
Searle, J.R., Speech Acts: An Essay in the Philosophy of Language (London: Cambridge University Press, 1969).
——, "Metaphor", in Steven Davis (ed.), *Pragmatics: A Reader* (New York: Oxford University Press, 1991), pp. 519–539.
Serajul Haque, *Imām Ibn Taimīya and his Projects of Reform* (Islamic Foundation Bangladesh).
Al-Shāfiᶜī, Muḥammad b. Idrīs, *al-Risāla fī Uṣūl al-Fiqh: Treatise on the Foundations of Islamic Jurisprudence,* trans. Majid Khadduri, 2nd edn. (Cambridge: the Islamic Texts Society, 1987).

Simpson, J.A. and Weiner, E.S.C., *The Oxford English dictionary* (Oxford: Larendon, 1989).
Sperber, Dan and Wilson, Deirdre, "Irony and the Use-Mention Distinction", in Steven Davis (ed.) *Pragmatics: A Reader* (New York: Oxford University Press, 1991), pp. 550–564.
——, *Relevance: Communication and Cognition* (Oxford: Blackwell, 1986).
Summers, Della and others, *Longman Dictionary of Contemporary English,* 2nd edn. (Essex: Longman Group UK Limited, 1987).
Weiss, B.G., "Language in Orthodox Muslim Thought: A Study of 'waḍ^{c} al-lughah' and its Development", unpublished PhD thesis (Faculty of Princeton University; Dept of Oriental Studies, 1966).
——, *The Search for God's Law: Islamic Jurisprudence in the Writings of Sayf al-Dīn al-Āmidī* (Salt Lake City: University of Utah Press, 1992).
Wunderlich, Dieter, *Foundations of Linguistics,* trans. Roger Lass (Cambridge: Cambridge University Press, 1979).

Index

'Abd al-Shakūr 167–8, 170, 172
absolute 89, 91, 239 *see* expression, meaning, *al-muṭlaq*
abstinence 104
accessible *(qarīb)* 132 *see ta'wīl*
'ādah see habit
'Aḍud 27
adverbs; — of manner 210; — of place 210; — of time 210
al-aghrāḍ al-balāghiyyah (rhetorical goals or intentions) 48–9, 59, 235; *ta'addub* (politeness) 49; *(taḥqīr)* degradation 49, 63; *(ta'ẓīm)* (glorification) 49, 63;
'ahd 35–6, 55, 57
'alāqah (relation) 32, 36, 51, 62, 72, 74–5; — *dhātiyyah* (intrinsic relationship) 144
al-alfāẓ al-muhmalah (lit, disregarded expressions) 42
all-the-more-reason basis 170
ambiguity 7, 29; rationally-based — 29; *waḍ'*-based — 29
al-Āmidī 11, 42, 144, 156, 168, 176, 180–5, 189–91, 195
analogical 23, 168–70, 179, 242 *see* expression; — reasoning 168–70, 179, 242; Sharī'ah-related — reasoning *(al-qiyās al-shar'ī)* 168; *Sharī'ah*-related — deduction *(al-qiyās al-shar'ī)* 168
analogy 20–1, 168–9, 181–2, 188, 234 see *qiyās*; manifest — *(qiyās jalī)* 168
al-Anṣārī 6
antecedent *(al-muqaddam)* 168–9, 190, 211–12, 214–16
anti-taqlīd 87
apparent *(al-ẓāhir)* 66, 71, 75, 127–8, 130–5, 161, 169, 170–1, 192, 195–6, 209, 240 *see* expression, interpretation, meaning, *ta'wīl, ẓāhir*
appropriate 69, 74–5, 189, 197
appropriateness 32, 197–8, 200; — of enquiry *(ḥusn al-istifhām)* 197, 200, 217; — of reinforcement *(ḥusn al-ta'kīd)* 197, 200
'aql 1, 8, 22, 45
Arabic logic sources 11
Arabic philology 12
Arabic rhetorical sources 11
Aristotelian 88, 97
Aristotle 105, 234
asbāb al-nuzūl 5
Ash'arīs 7, 30, 45, 87, 132
assertion 150, 154, 202, 205, 218–20
aṣl (base or principle) 4, 58–9, 77–80, 107, 118, 124, 130, 169, 235 *see* base, principle; *al-— and al-far'* (base-subsidiary notion) 77, 118
assumption; — of the legal plausibility of the utterance 56; — of the speaker's rationality 56; — of the speaker's sincerity 56; — of the speaker's truthfulness 172
Astarābādhī 11, 23
atomism 88, 237
attribution 165

al-Bājī 176, 214
base 4, 43, 50, 58–60, 63, 65, 68–71,

80, 107, 118. 125–6, 135, 152, 164, 201, 235–7, 243 see *aṣl*; — for counter implicature *see* counter implicature; literalness — 125, 164, 235–6; flouts the — 235; violating the — *see* violation
al-Baṣrī 11, 64, 106, 176, 196, 219–20
bayān al-mutakallim (the speaker's disposition to make his intention manifest) 64, 125, 131 *see* principle
al-Bayḍāwī 11
biconditional 211
bisāṭ (the carpet) 55, 57
Bosch 103
al-Bukhārī 166–7, 170, 172
burhāniyyah (evidential) 95

calculable 166, 208
cancellability 196, 198–9; — test 183
cancellable 183, 196, 223
cancellation of counter implicature *see* counter implicature
causation *(al-ta'līl)* 182
cause 147, 152, 167–9, 181, 185; — *(al-'illah)* 168, 181; — *(mūjib)* 152; complete — *(al-sabab al-tāmm)* 212; effective — *(al-manāṭ)* 167–9, 190; incomplete — *(al-sabab al-ghayr al-tāmm)* 212; relevant — 205
Chomsky 22, 91
co-operation 42–3, 63–4, 66, 68, 215; — maxims 164; maxims of — 178; principle of — *see* principle
co-operative 201 *see* co-operation; — principles 177
co-text 35
coding 144, 234
cognition 88, 92, 141–2
communication; — principles 3, 10, 13, 74, 164–5, 171, 179; constitutive factors of — 15; maintenance of — *(ṣiyānat al-kalām)* 171, 173; models of — 8, 12–13, 240; models of textual — 10; pragmatic models of textual — 234; principles govern successful — 234; principles of — 73, 170, 201, 243; textual — 7, 13; theories of — 234; traditional message-model of — 15
communicative; — habits 99; — import *(al-fā'idah)* 166, 202; — intention 25, 30, 63, 126, 160, 171, 197, 215; — situations *(al-maqāmāt al-khiṭābiyyah)* 8, 15, 23, 30, 51–2, 59, 97, 99, 102, 109, 118, 125, 135, 148–9, 159, 170, 174, 202, 213, 235, 237, 239, 241
component; defining — 151, 157; non-defining — 157; non-*waḍ'*-based — 240; sense— specific to a particular language 157; universal sense— 157–8
compositionalism 88, 237
concept 18, 20, 28, 87, 95, 157–8, 188, 200, 204, 210, 218
conceptual view 21–2, 87–8, 235, 238
conceptualisation 18, 91, 95, 141–2
conceptualism 91
condition *(al-sharṭ)* 76, 78, 152, 192, 206, 209, 212–14; — in Arabic grammar 214; causal — 212; implicature of a — *(mafhūm al-sharṭ) see* implicature; legal — 212; linguistic — (al-shurūṭ al-lughawiyyah) 212–13; necessary — 212; non-linguistic — 213; normal — 212; rational — 212; real — 212; sufficient — 212–13; syntactic — *(al-shurūṭ al-naḥwiyyah)* 212
conditional 73, 177, 185, 211–13; causal — 213; real — 212
congruent implicature *(mafhūm al-muwāfaqah)* 14, 168–9, 176, 179–80, 185–92, 202, 206, 222, 242
conjunction 182–3; — *li* (for the reason) 181
consequent *(al-tālī)* 211–12, 214–16 *see* antecedent
constancy test 108
construction *see naẓm*

context 3, 5–6, 8–9, 12–13, 31–5, 43, 45, 48–9, 52–7, 60, 62, 66, 68, 70, 73, 76–7, 88, 96–103, 105, 110–11, 113, 115, 117–20, 122, 124–6, 129, 131–3, 147–8, 152–3, 159–60, 166–7, 170, 172, 178, 184, 190, 192, 202, 205, 208–9, 218, 235–6, 238–42; — of situation 31; available and actually considered — 54; cognitive— 61; definition of — 53; diverting — *(qarīnah ṣārifah)* 35–6, 50, 62–3, 73–4, 126–7, 135, 169, 171, 215–16, 236, 239; extra-linguistic — 9, 131; external — 5; guiding — *(qarīnah hādiyah)* 36, 62, 73–4, 77, 126–8, 171, 236; immediate — 55, 170; internal — 5; kinds of — 35, 62, 236; misleading — 50; non-linguistic — 163; non-verbal — 8, 55, 196, possible — 54; preventing — 62; rational — *(qarīnah 'aqliyyah)* 35, 60; situational — *(qarīnah ḥāliyyah)* 35, 55, 73, 110, 118, 209; types of — 35, 55, verbal — *(qarīnah lafẓiyyah)* 8, 35, 53, 55, 73, 110
context-dependency 88
context-dependent 111, 115, 121, 126, 153, 158, 161
context-independent 103
contextual; — approach 88–9, 134, 158, 173, 196; — framework 105, 147; — meaning 102, 239; — qualifications 104; — theory 90–1, 94; — theory of definition 95; — theory of interpretation 13, 88
contextualised 100, 116 *see* decontextualised
contextualism 88, 237
contradiction 65, 129, 184, 191–2, 195–6, 222–3
conversational 178, 183–4, 196, 198, 201, 223 *see* implicature
counter implicature *(mafhūm al-mukhālafah)* 14, 49, 176, 180, 185–8, 192–208, 211, 214, 216, 220–3, 242–3; bases for — 201; cancellation of — 206; conditions for the validity of — 206; invalid — 194; invalidity of — 197, 207; pillars of — 192; types of — 188, 192–3, 200, 209, 222, 243; valid — 205; validity of — 193–4, 197, 201, 206, 208, 218
createdness of the Holy *Qur'ān* 30
cultural practices 57
culture, — language specific 6
custom 55, 57, 111, 158, 206–7

dalālah (or *dalālat*) 7–8, 12, 95, 102–4, 113, 141, 148 *see* signification; — *'adamiyyah* (non-existential signification) 104, 117; — *bi-l-lafẓ* (SBE) 46; — *ghayr lafẓiyya* 143; — *ghayr al-manẓūm* 180; — *iltizām* (implicational signification) 14, 48, 76, 143, 149, 241; — *al-iqtiḍā'* 14, 180–1, 242; — *al-ishārah* (alluded signification) 14, 180, 242; — *al-lafẓ* 46, 49, 150–1, 241; — *lafẓiyyah* (verbal signification) 143; — *al-mafhūm* 14, 176, 178, 180–1, 187, 242 *see* implicature, implicated, implied signification; — *al-manṭūq* 172, 176, 242; — *al-manẓūm* 180; — *muṭābaqah* (equivalence-signification) 13, 48, 143, 149, 180, 241; — *al-naṣṣ* (inferred signification) 14, 159, 242; — *qaṭ'iyyah* (deterministic signification) 5; — *taḍammun* (incorporational signification) 13, 48, 143, 149, 180, 241; — *al-tanbīh wa-l-īmā'* (indicated signification) 14, 180–1, 242; — *wujūdiyyah* (existential signification) 104, 117; — *ẓanniyyah* (probabilistic signification) 5; non-*waḍ'*-based — 7; *ṭuruq al-—* (ways of signification) 141; *waḍ'*-based — 8
dalīl (sign) 148 *see* signifier
al-Daqqāq 209
Davidson 105
decoding 8, 234

decontextualised 89, 99–100, 237 *see* contextualised
definiendum 95, 98, 188
defining *see* component, feature, relative clause
definite article 57
definition 87–8, 95–8, 101, 157–8, 188 *see ḥadd;* Aristotelian — 97; descriptive — 98; logical — 95; nominal — 96–7; pragmatic — 98; scientific — 97; successful — 96; theory of — 88, 90, 95
departure *(al-ʻudūl)* 32, 60, 62, 65, 70, 162, 200, 202, 223, 236, 240; — from the most immediate interpretation 240
dependency 53, 88
derivative *see far'*
descending *(nuzūl)* 204; descend 200, 204; descended 210, 213; descent 210
determinacy 80, 191, 197
determinate 61, 127–8, 130, 174, 191, 194, 222, 240
deterministic *(qaṭʻī)* 5, 192, 196–7, 199 *see* signification
dhātī (contingent) 92–3, 101
disambiguation 163
discourse *(al-khiṭāb)* 7, 18, 42, 49, 59–62, 65, 68–9, 133, 154, 170, 189, 196, 236; conventionalised — 62–3; ideal — 7, 62; non-legal — 193, 243; properties of spoken — 42; *waḍ'*-based — 61–2
discursive 94
disjunction 213
driven at *(masūq ilayh)* 160–1, 163, 166, 169, 241–2
driven to 160
driving *(al-sawq)* 161, 167, 190

ellipsis 4, 79–80, 173–5
empirical 75, 95, 103, 115, 118; — approach 89, 237
encoding 8, 234
entail 149–50, 155, 204, 214, 218–20, 222
entailment 146, 150–1, 156
ephemerality 43
epistemological 13, 88, 90, 191
equivalence 13, 48, 143–4, 149, 151–7, 180, 185, 193, 216, 241
equivalent 96–7, 149, 153–4, 193, 222, 241 *see* meaning, *mukāfī,* signification
essence 92–3
establisher 7–8, 20–1, 23, 25–6, 93, 103, 106, 114, 234
establishment 4, 12–13, 15, 17, 21, 51, 63–4, 68 see *waḍ'*
eternal 30–1, 116–17
eternality 30
etymological 110, 238 *see majāz*
exception 222; — particles 222; implicature of an — see implicature
existence *(wujūd)*, 89–93, 100–1, 116–17, 237–9; eternal and everlasting — 116–17; external — *(al-wujūd al-khārijī)* 18–19, 89, 100–1, 116; mental — 93, 124, 238; metaphysical — 116–17; objective — 93; prior — 77, 93, 237
existential 104, 118–19 *see* signification
express meaning *see* meaning
expression; absolute — 99; abstract — 115, 120; abstracted — *(al-lafẓ al-muṭlaq al-mujarrad)* 99; analogical — 23; assumed — *(alfāẓ muqaddarah)* 100; *ḥaqīqah*- — 108, 112, 118, 120, 124, 238; indexical — 121; *majāz*— 108, 112, 117, 120–1, 124, 238; multi-meaning — 106–7, 109–11, 238; *mushakkik*— 116, 119, 124, 238; *mushtarak*— 124, 238; *mutawāṭī*— 124, 238; performative — 6; qualified — 100, 118, 238; single — *(al-lafẓ al-mufrad)* 95, 114–15; unqualified — 89, 114, 118, 121, 124–5, 237; *waḍ'*-based — 31, 197; *ẓāhir*— 131–3, 240
extension 144, 155
extensional; — method 12; — translation 1, 12
extensionally 145

fahm 4, 46–7, 64 *see* understanding
faḥwā l-khiṭāb (the import of the discourse) 189
fā'idah 69, 202–3 *see* communicative import
falsafah 6 *see* philosophy
falsehood 67–8, 178, 215
far' 4, 60, 77, 118, 169 *see* subsidiary
al-Fārābī 20, 87, 92
feature; defining — *(dākhil)* 152, 157–8, 165; non-defining — *(khārij* 157–8
figurative 4, 17, 27, 29, 31–2, 48, 56, 59, 61, 71–2, 74, 88, 105, 109–10, 112, 117–19, 153–4, 169, 235, 238 *see majāz*
fiqh 1–3, 13, 44–6, 51, 61; *uṣūl al*— 1
foundationalism 88, 237

Gazdar 204
general *(al-'āmm)* 120 *see* meaning, pragmatics, *waḍ'*
al-Ghazālī 11, 18, 20, 35, 62, 106–7, 128, 166, 176, 179–80, 191, 197, 199; —'s classification of signification *see* significational classification
grammar 2, 11, 16, 33, 57, 91, 210, 214
grammarians 6–7, 21–2, 27, 67, 77, Arab — 20, 27, 214
grammatical 16, 18, 20–1, 23–4, 62, 129, 162–3, 202, 210, 234–5
Grice 43, 59–60, 102, 178–9, 183, 187, 196, 198, 201, 203–4, 234, 243
Gricean 60, 73, 177, 184; — framework 10, 60, 177; — maxims 60, 73

habit 56–7, 65, 68, 71, 99, 111, 114–5, 126, 134; — of the speaker in the use of language 45; consistent — *('ādatihi al-muṭṭaridah)* 133, 240; speaker's — 43, 55–6, 111, 115, 126, 133–4
habitual; — use of the utterance 9, 134, 174; speaker's — use of language 45, 158

ḥadd (definition) 87, 98 *see* definition
ḥaml 4, 7–8, 12–13, 30, 41, 45–6, 69, 235 *see* interpretation
Ḥanafī 14, 128, 130–2, 159, 161–2, 173, 175, 179–80, 199, 241–2; — classification of signification *see* significational classification
Ḥanafīs 7, 14, 129–31, 152, 159, 161, 163–4, 166, 168, 171, 188, 193, 199, 242
Ḥanbalī 87, 94, 175
Ḥanbalīs 7, 30, 45
ḥaqīqah 27, 31, 59, 70, 74–5, 79–80, 99, 101, 106, 108, 110–13, 115, 118, 120, 122–5, 128, 149, 238 *see* expression, literal, meaning, use; — and *majāz* 94, 99, 105–6, 108–9, 111, 113, 115, 170, 238
al-Harawī 145
Harnish 204
'hinting at the higher by means of the lower' *(al-tanbīh bi-l-adnā 'alā l-a'lā)* 189
'hinting at the lower by means of the higher' *(al-tanbīh bi-l-a'lā 'alā l-adnā)* 189
al-ḥiss see sense
ḥissiyyah (perceptible) 95
homonym *(mushtarak)* 106–7, 116, 128
homonymous 29
homonymy *(ishtirāk)* 4, 108
huwiyyah (identity) 101

'ibārah (utterance) 30
'ibārat al-naṣṣ see express meaning
Ibn al-Ḥājib 11, 26, 75, 144, 156, 176, 182, 185, 189, 194
Ibn Ḥalūl al-Qayrawānī 46
Ibn Ḥanbal 87, 209
Ibn Ḥazm 11, 131, 147
Ibn Khaldūn 24
Ibn al-Malik 34
Ibn Mālik 22
Ibn al-Qayyim (Ibn Qayyim al-Jawziyyah) 7–8, 44, 56, 64–5, 89, 94, 99–100, 102–3, 109, 111, 113–14, 118, 123, 132–4, 147, 173–4, 240

Ibn Sīnā 20, 87, 89, 92, 146
Ibn Taymiyyah 1, 3, 7, 11, 13, 55, 61, 87–106, 109–12, 114–22, 124–7, 133–4, 158, 173, 196, 203, 237–40
Ibn Ya'īsh 11, 21
iḍāfah (annexation) 99
iḍmār 4
idrāk (cognition) 141 *see* cognition
al-Ījī 10
'illah 68 *see* cause and effective cause
illocutionary force *(al-ḥukm)* 171–2, 174–5, 186–7
illocutionary import 167, 169–70, 190–1; — of the utterance *(maqṣūd al-kalām)* 166–7, 190–1; speaker's — 242
īmā' see meaning, signification
i'māl (making sense of the expression) 64, 68–9, 171, 202, 236; principle of — *see* principle
immediacy *(tabādur)* 55, 64, 70, 111–12, 163, 237; — test 196, principle of — *see* principle
immediate 69–71, 74, 135, 163, 166, 169 *see* context, interpretation, meaning
implicate 176, 178, 187, 194–5, 199, 200, 204–8, 210, 213, 215, 217–18, 220, 223
implicated 162, 173, 182, 184, 187, 195, 197–8, 222–3 *see* meaning, signification; — causes 182; — proposition 176, 243; what is — *(mafhūm)* 159, 166, 176, 186–7, 196, 243
implicating 204, 209, 215–16
implication 33, 44, 76–7, 141, 146, 151, 157, 162–3, 174, 177, 181–2, 185, 187, 194, 196, 199, 217; material — 216
implicational 153, 156, 194, 222 *see* meaning, signification; — association *(al-luzūm, al-lawāzim)* 152; external — association 152; mental — associations 152
implicationally signifies 153
implicature 43, 51, 59–60, 73, 77, 177–81, 187–8, 196–8, 200–9, 211, 213, 215–18, 220, 222–3; — of a condition *(mafhūm al-sharṭ)* 188, 211, 213–14, 243; — of confinement *(mafhūm al-ḥaṣr)* 223, 243; — of a designation *(mafhūm al-laqab)* 209, 214, 243; — of an exception *(mafhūm al-istithnā')* 222, 243; — of a restrictive attribute *(mafhūm al-ṣifah)* 210, 243; — of a stated numeral *(mafhūm al-'adad)* 218, 221–2, 243; — of a time limit *(mafhūm al-ghāyah)* 216, 243; congruent — *(mafhūm al-muwāfaqah) see* congruent; conventional — 177, 183, 198; conversational — *(mafhūm khiṭābī)* 183, 196, 198, 201, 223; counter — *see* counter; false — 199, 206; generalised — 178, 209; generalised conversational — 178, 184; neutral version of an — 208; particularised — 178; particularised conversational — 178, 184; positive version of an — 208; scalar — 192, 201, 243
impossible *(muta'adhdhir)* for *ta'wīl* 132
inappropriate 217
incalculable 163
incorporational 144, 152–3, 156–7 *see* signification
incorporationally signifies 153, 241
indeterminacy 46, 79–80, 197
indeterminate 127–8, 132, 163, 196, 240
intended *(murād or maqṣūd)* 160 *see* meaning, referent; primarily — 160; subordinately — 160
intensional 11; — imports 1; — method 11
intensionally 155, 223
intention *(murād, qaṣd)* 13, 30–2, 34, 36, 43–6, 48, 51–2, 54–6, 60, 64–5, 68–9, 70–3, 75–7, 91, 96–9, 101–2, 105, 107, 114, 116, 125–6, 128, 131–4, 143, 148–9, 152–3, 160, 171, 178, 200–2, 210, 236–7, 239–41, 243 *see*

communicative; — of *Allāh* 1, 3, 5–6, 41, 43; — of the speaker *(murād al-mutakallim)* 4, 7, 18, 31–5, 41–2, 44–5, 48–54, 62, 64–5, 68–72, 77, 96, 98, 126, 131, 148, 153, 161, 215, 234–5, 241–2; — of the *Sharī'ah* 45; further — 45; rhetorical — 59; speaker's — 1, 3, 5, 31–6, 45, 49, 54, 56, 71–2, 74, 96, 99, 126–9, 131–4, 154, 158–9, 169, 172, 174, 235–7, 239; ulterior — 3, 71
intentionality 33–4, 42, 47, 160
interpretation 3–4, 7–9, 12–13, 15, 29–30, 41–6, 51, 53–9, 61–3, 66–7, 69–75, 80, 87–8, 103, 112, 118, 124–8, 131, 134–5, 143, 145–7, 162, 164, 172, 174, 177, 196, 215, 221, 223, 235–40 *see ḥaml*; apparent — *(ẓāhir)* 66; contextual theory of — 13, 87–8; dominant — 80; immediate — 63, 66, 70, 131, 237, 240; legal — 80; non-apparent — 94, 127 *see ta'wīl*; ostensive — 65, 70, 236; pragmatic — 73; preponderant, probable — 127, 162; proper — 43, 53, 69–70, 237
interpreter 7, 43, 45, 52, 130, 132–3, 143
invalid counter implicatures *see* counter implicature
invalidity of counter implicature *see* counter implicature
iqtiḍā' 151, 172–3, 180 *see dalālat al-iqtiḍā'*, signification; — *al-naṣṣ* (required meaning) *see* meaning
ishtirāk see homonymy
ishārat al-naṣṣ see alluded meaning
isti'māl 4, 8, 9, 12, 15, 17, 29, 75, 78, 147, 149 *see* use
istiṣḥāb (the presumption of the continuity) 64, 77, 80, 125, 239; principle of — *see* principle

al-Jawharī 120
al-Jawnafūrī 33–4
jurisprudence 1; Islamic — 1; science of — 46 *see fiqh*
al-Jurjānī ('Abd al-Qāhir) 11, 25, 61, 76, 156
al-Jurjānī (Muḥammad) 36
al-Jurjānī (al-Sharīf) 21, 29, 34, 145, 161, 164, 178, 212
al-Juwaynī 2, 11, 31, 176–8, 185, 188, 192, 196, 205–6, 243
juz'ī 18 *see* particular

al-kalām al-Nafsī (mental speech) *see* speech
Katz 91, 103
al-Khalīl Ibn Aḥmad 119
knowledge 4, 6, 8, 10–11, 16–18, 23–4, 32, 34–6, 43, 45, 54–7, 65, 71, 73, 87–8, 92–5, 97, 110, 115, 119, 133–4, 158, 162, 168, 179, 183, 195, 208, 235; — about the world 155, 191; — of *waḍ'* 16, 18, 22, 33, 61–2, 92; acquisition of — 94; background — 155, 164–5, 170
kullī 18 *see* universal

laḥn al-khiṭāb (the implicit meaning of the discourse) 189 *see* implicit meaning
language; — acquisition 102; — and speech 15, 17; abstract — 8, 114; creator of — 18; philosophy of — 15; structures of — 15
langue 15–16
lāzim 76, 92–3, 101, 146, 151, 241
Leech 204–5, 208
Levinson 207, 213
Lewis 234
lexical 18, 20–1, 23–4, 129, 162–3, 235; — and grammatical 23, 163
lexicographers 61, 111, 115, 119–20
lexicon 16, 20, 22, 42, 131, 234, 240
linguistics 9–10, 15, 22, 142–3
linguist(s) 6, 15, 67, 92, 100, 103, 105, 142–3, 148, 157, 161, 240–1
literal 13, 27, 29, 31–2, 45, 48, 51–2, 62–3, 67, 69–71, 73, 75, 87, 105, 110, 117, 126, 128, 135, 169–70, 215, 222, 237–9 *see* meaning, use
literalists *see Ẓāhirī*
logicians 87, 100, 149, 152, 155, 158–9, 241

Maclean 44
madlūl see signified
mafhūm see concept, implicature
māhiyyah (essence) 92–3, (quiddity) 101
mainstream 7–9, 12–13, 45, 51, 58, 92, 100–1, 106, 114, 116–17, 119–20, 124, 125–8, 130–3, 135, 147, 234–5, 238–40
majāz (figurative use, non-literal meaning, non-literal use) 4, 8, 59, 67, 71–5, 79–80, 88, 90, 94, 99, 105–24, 129, 149, 152, 169–70, 238 *see* expression, figurative; — *al-ta'qīd* (complex figurative use) 74; diachronic account of — 110, 238; etymological account of — 238; Ibn Taymiyyah's account of — 106, 114–16, 119–20, 124, 238; mainstream account of — 114, 119; synchronic account of — 110; theory of — 105
Mālik 209
Mālikī 57, 175
Mālikīs 58
ma'nā ḥaqīqī see ḥaqīqah, literal meaning
ma'nā see meaning; — *majāzī see* figurative, non-literal meaning, *majāz*
al-manṭūq (stated meaning) *see* meaning; *manṭūq* (what is said) 159, 167, 185, 189, *dalālat* — *see* signification; *ghayr* — *see* meaning
al-Marjānī 11, 152–3
Martinet 23
Māturīdīs 45
maxim 60, 187, 213 *see* co-operation; — of quantity 178, 201, 204, 209–10, 213, 215, 243; — of quantity-quality 204–5; — of relevance 73, 204, 209; Gricean — of quality 204
meaning *(ma'nā)* 3–10, 13, 15–18, 20–3, 26–9, 31–4, 36, 42–4, 46, 48, 54–6, 61–3, 67, 69, 71–2, 76–9, 88–92, 95–107, 109–20, 122, 124, 126–35, 141, 146–9, 151–57, 159–64, 166–77, 179–82, 185, 188–91, 193, 196–8, 203, 235–43; — and intention 13, 31, 33, 44, 73, 76, 102, 128, 239 — established for *(al-ma'nā l-mawḍū' lahu)* 32; — of — *(ma'nā l-ma'nā)* 76; — of particles *(ma'ānī l-ḥurūf)* 178; — of 'what is implicated 176, 180, 243; — of 'what is said' 176, 193; — used for 32; abstract — 117, 243; alluded — *(ishārat al-naṣṣ)* 14, 159, 161–4, 166, 180, 242; apparent — 71, 127–8, 130–5, 161, 170–1, 196, 209, 240; *see ẓāhir;* composed — *(dalālat al-manẓūm)* 179; contextual — 102, 239; conventional — 32–4, 76–7, 102, 162, 164, 174, 185, 239; equivalent — 149, 153–4, 241; explicit — 174, 181, 190; express — *('ibārat al-naṣṣ)* 14, 159, 161–4, 241; face-value — 170; figurative — 48, 105, 109–10, 112, 117–19, 153, 169, 238; general — 25–6, 28, 76, 122; grammatical — 163; Ibn Taymiyyah's account of — 98; immediate — 111–12, 238; implicated — 180; implicational — 153; implicit — 189–90; implied — *(mafhūm)* 179–80; indicated — *(īmā')* 180, 182; inferred — *(dalālat al-naṣṣ)* 14, 33, 159, 162, 166–70, 179, 188, 242; intended — *(al-ma'nā l-maqṣūd)* 5, 32, 34, 36, 49–50, 98, 112–13, 118, 120, 124, 126, 128, 132, 171, 174, 196, 236, 239; interpreted — 49–50; lexical — 23, 129; linguistic — 17, 29, 51, 62, 74, 105, 128–9, 131, 133, 142, 157, 163; literal — 1, 5–6, 17, 29, 33, 36, 43–4, 53, 62, 69–70, 75, 105, 107, 109–10, 112, 114, 117–19, 128–9, 135, 154, 169, 216, 235–8 *see ḥaqīqah*; literal — and intended — 62; literal and non literal — 13, 32, 51–2, 170; most probable intended — 128; non-apparent — 88–9, 127, 132; non literal — 152, 238 *see*

majāz; pragmatic — 67; proper — 109, 112; qualified — 100, 117–19; rationalised — 179; relatedness of — 106; relationship between expression and — 102; required — *(iqtiḍā' al-naṣṣ)* 14, 159, 162, 170–2, 175, 180, 242; sentence — 91, 103, 105; sentence — and utterance — 32, 73; single — 115, 117–18; speaker's — 111; specific — 122, 131; stated — *(al-manṭūq)* 166–7, 169–70, 172–3, 176, 179, 188–9, 191, 242–3 *see* stated, *manṭūq;* surface — 5, 44, 52, 54, 56; ulterior — 44, 127; unequivocal — 161 *see naṣṣ;* universal — 21, 116; unqualified — 89, 111, 117–18; unstated — *(ghayr al-manṭūq)* 166–7, 169–70, 179, 188–9, 242; utterance — 103, 105, 162; utterance — and the speaker's —. 32; *waḍ*'-based — 32, 34, 49–51, 91, 113, 179, 182
meaningfulness 13, 99, 170, 238–9, 242
mental; — image 19–20, 100–1, 103, 239; — worlds 93
mentioned 186–7, 192–5, 197, 205–6, 217
metaphor 7, 61, 105–8, 116–17 *see majāz*, meaning, *musta'ār;* theory of — 105
middle term *(al-ḥadd al-awsaṭ) 95*
model 7, 12–13, 15, 58, 61, 103, 125–7, 141, 179–80, 234–5, 239–40; — of communication 8, 13, 235; — of significational classification *see* significational classification; — of textual communication 10; code — 45, 234; inferential — 45, 234; mainstream — 8, 12–13, 125–7, 234, 239–40; pragmatic — of textual communication *see* communication; Salafite — 9, 12–13, 239; traditional message — of communication *see* communication
Morris 15
mufassar 128–30
mufradāt 19–23 *see* expression,
muḥkam 128
mujarrabah see empirical
mukāfī (equivalent) 96
munāsabah 32, 51, 205 *see* relevance
muqayyad see qualified
muqtaḍī 171, 173 *see iqtiḍā',* required, requiring for,
murādif (synonym) 96 *see* synonymous
musammā 95, 101 *see* nominatum
mushakkik 116–17, 124 *see* expression
mushtarak 106, 116, 124 *see* expression, homonym
musta'ār 106–7 *see* metaphor
mutawāṭi' (lit, concurrent or accordant) 116, 124 *see* expression
mutawātirah 95
Mu'tazilī 175–6
Mu'tazilīs 7, 30–1, 45, 87, 132
al-muṭlaq see unqualified; — *lā bi-sharṭ* (the unconditionally absolute universal) 91; — *al-maḥḍ* (the pure absolute) 90

name 54, 95–6, 98–103, 105, 156; common — 21; proper — *(al-asmā' al-a'lām)* 18, 20–1, 26, 28, 121; *waḍ*' of proper — *see waḍ'*
naql (transmission of knowledge) 8 *see* polysemy
al-Nasafī 161
naṣṣ (text) 159; — (unequivocal) 128–32, 161, 192 *see* unequivocal, meaning
natural 13, 141, 144–6 *see* universal, signification; — order 223–4; — signifier *see* signifier; flouting the — order 224
naẓm 164
negation 150, 154, 185, 194–5, 202, 204, 207, 218–19, 222, 204. 207, 218–19, 222–3
neutral; — version of an implicature *see* implicature

neutralisation; — of the distinction between *ḥaqīqah* and *majāz* 105; — of the distinction between sentences and utterances 91; — of the distinction between *waḍʿ* and use 135
nominatum 95–6, 98, 101, 109, 150, 156–7
non-existential 104, 117–18, 143 *see* signification
non-figurative *see majāz,* use
non-literal 36, 51, 67, 74, 107, 110, 126, 154, 170, 239 *see* interpretation, *majāz,* meaning, use
non-verbal 55, 144–6, 240 *see* context, signification
non-*waḍʿ*-based 7, *see* component
noun 210; common — 209; definite — 26–8, 57, 121, 235; demonstrative — 26, 29, 121

obligation 193, 220
omission 174–5
ontological 13, 88, 90–1, 93–4

paradigmatic relationships 48
parole 15–16, 143
participants 29, 31, 35–6, 88, 142, 148, 171, 201, 209
particular18–28, 31, 67, 75–6, 80, 90–4, 97, 103, 224, 238 *see juz'ī*; universal and particular *waḍʿ see waḍʿ*
particularised 178, 209 *see* implicature
pattern; abstract — 24, 26; constructional — 21–3, 25
performative *see* expression, utterance
permission 188, 220
PF 2–3, 5–6, 9–11, 15–16, 20, 26, 29, 32, 34, 36, 41, 43–5, 49–56, 59, 61, 64, 68–9, 73–5, 77–8, 92, 100–1, 107, 116, 128, 130, 132–3, 146–7, 149, 151, 159–60, 168, 175, 177–9, 182, 187–8, 196, 201–2, 211, 217, 240–1, — literature 10, 18, 34; — works 3, 5; —'s pragmatic theories 10; —'s terminology 5, 160; —'s works 11; real founder of — 175
philosopher 20, 87, 89–90, 93, 100–1, 105, 141–2, 234
philosophical 13, 90–1, 94–5
philosophy 6, 93, 204; — of language *see* language; Greek — 6, 87–8
pillars of counter implicature *see* counter implicature
Platonic 91–2; — realist 237
Platonist 91
politeness *see al-aghrāḍ al-balāghiyyah*
polysem *(manqūl)* 106–7
polysemy *(naql),* 4, 107
positive version of an implicature *see* implicature
post-adjectives 210
post-modifiers 209
pragmatic 1–3, 5–6, 9–13, 15, 30, 43, 48, 50, 52, 62, 88–9, 94, 141, 158–9, 196, 202, 234; — approach 7, 88, 94, 98, 103, 105; — definition *see* definition; — inferences 177; — models of textual communication *see* communication; — interpretation *see* interpretation; — meaning *see meaning;* — paradigm 88; — presupposition 174; — principles and strategies 51; — significational classification *see* significational classification; — theory 3, 10, 73, 88, 109
pragmatics 2–3, 5, 9–11, 15, 32, 45, 75, 88, 103, 150, 178, 192, 196, 234, 243; culture specific — 6; general — 5–6; language-specific — 6; medieval Islamic — 12
pragmatists 3, 7, 60, 105, 176, 185, 201, 243
pre-adjectives 210
predicate 142, 223
predication 99, 116, 223–4
premodifiers 209
preposing and postposing 79–80
presuppose 151, 185, 223

presupposed 160–1, 166, 171, 175, 223
presupposition 150–1, 173–4, 184–5, 223
principle 1, 3, 7, 10, 13, 41, 43, 45, 51–2, 57–60, 63–70, 72, 74, 77, 80, 87, 115, 125, 131, 177, 201, 203, 215, 235–6, 240, 243; — of co-operation 215; — of *fiqh* 1–3; — of *i'māl* 13, 63, 66, 68–9, 125–6, 165, 170–2, 202, 216, 236; — of immediacy (*tabādur*) 13, 63, 69, 80, 125–7, 135, 237, 239; — of *istiṣḥāb* 13, 77, 80, 125–6, 198, 236, 239; — of quantity 203; — of relevance 201, 205, 243; — of the speaker's disposition to make his intention manifest 13, 64–5, 72, 125–6, 131, 171, 201–2, 236, 239–40, 243 *see bayān al-mutakallim;* — of the speaker's truthfulness 13, 66, 68, 170, 236; — of truthfulness (*ṣidq al-mutakallim*) 59, 73, 125–6, 171, 236; — of unknown reference 165
principles of communication *see* communication
principles of demonstration (*qānūn al-istidlāl*) 201
principles-bases dichotomy 60
probabilistic (*ẓannī*) 5, 192, 196–7, 199, 208 *see* signification, signifier
prohibition 30, 206, 219–21
pronoun; personal — 26–9, 121, 124, 235, 238; relative — *see* relative
Pythagorean 92

qadhf (defamation) 209
al-Qarāfī 11, 16–17, 21, 27–31, 43, 46–9, 51, 66–7, 70, 72, 80, 116, 153–5, 157–8, 170, 207, 212, 222, 235
qarīnah see context
qawā'id al-tarjīḥ (rules of preference) *see* rules
qiyās 20, 168–9, 182 *see* analogy; *qiyās* (syllogism) 87
qiyāsiyyah; al-mufradāt al- — 23; *al-murakkabāt al-*— 23
qualification 79–80, 89, 99–101, 104, 108, 111, 114–15, 118, 192, 194, 202–3, 206–7, 239 *see* contextual; external — 101; intentional — 104; specific — 104; *waḍ'*-based verbal — 110–11
qualified 76, 114–15, 120–5, 129, 194, 237 *see* expression, meaning
qualifiers 209
quantifiers 209
quantity 213; maxim of — *see* maxim; principle of — *see* principle

al-Raḍī 23
rational 13, 80, 143, 145, 156–7, 240 — condition *see* condition; — context *see* context; — inference 33; — meaning *see* meaning, — sign 143; — signification *see* signification
rationality 56, 143, 168, 170, 172–3, 175, 242; assumption of the speaker's — *see* assumption; preservation of the — of the text (*al-ṣiḥḥah al-'aqliyyah*) 242
al-Rāzī 4, 11, 19–20, 46, 56–7, 66, 68, 73–6, 89, 152, 156
reference 28–9, 32, 44, 95–6, 98, 155, 163–5, 223, 235; — assignment 163
referent 19, 26–9, 57, 95, 97–8, 116, 121–2, 127; extra-mental — 95; intended — 121
reinforceability 198
reinforceable 198
relationship *see 'alāqah*, paradigmatic, syntagmatic
relative; — clause 211; defining — clause 211; — pronouns 121
relevance 51, 73, 161, 174, 178, 205; maxim of — *see* maxim; principle of — *see* principle; theory of — 74
required (*al-muqtaḍā*) 173, *see* meaning, signification
requiring for (*al-muqtaḍī*) 171, 173
rhetorical goals *see al-aghrāḍ al-balāghiyyah*
rhetoricians 62, 74, 77

rules; — of inference 7, — of preference *(qawā'id al-tarjīḥ)* 78; derivational — 23, 234, inflectional — 23, pre-established universal — 234

Sadock 198
Ṣadr al-Sharī'ah 11, 161
Salafī 87, 94, 127, 130, 234; — framework 103, 237
Salafīs 8, 10, 75, 100, 102, 106, 117–18, 122, 124–6, 131–3, 147, 149, 238–41; —' approach 119; —' framework 135
Salafite 9, 12–13, 147; — approach 7; — model *see* model
sam' 1, 45
samā' 33
al-Sarakhsī 11, 171–2
Saussure 48, 143
Saussurean 15–16
SBE (signifying by expressions) 47–9, 51, 153, 170
SE 47–9, 51, 153, 170 see signification
Searle 102, 105
segmentability 43
self-evident 95
semantic 158–9, 170, 179, 242 — significational classification *see* significational classification
semanticians, semanticists 7, 156
semantics 9, 15, 105, 150
semiotic 15, 142, 239, 243; — significational classification *see* significational classification
semiotics 142, 234
sense; — and force 32; — component *see* component; exterior — *(al-ḥiss al-ẓāhir)* 92; inner — *(al-ḥiss al-bāṭin)* 92; interior — *(al-ḥiss al-bāṭin)* 92; making — of the expression *see i'māl*
sentence 3, 5, 22–5, 67, 73, 90–4, 96, 103–5, 115, 148, 150–1, 159, 164, 204, 216, 235, 237–8; — meaning *see* meaning; —utterance dichotomy 91; declarative — 67, 112, 202; interrogative — 3, 112
Shāfi'ī 11, 14, 131, 168, 173, 175–6, 188, 199; — method of dividing signification 159, 166, 175, 241–3; — significational classification *see* significational classification
Shāfi'īs 131–2, 168–9, 175, 188, 193–4
shāhid 20
al-Shāṭibī 45, 52, 57
al-Shīrāzī 11, 19, 169, 200, 204, 210
ṣifāt ittifāqiyyah (accidental attribute) 211
sign 142–3, 145–6, 148 *see dalīl*; rational — *see* rational; system of — 143
signification *(dalālah)* 1, 5, 7, 12–13, 15, 30–1, 48, 51, 53, 95, 102–4, 111, 113, 122, 126, 133–4, 141–3, 146–59, 162, 164, 166, 180–4, 188, 193–4, 196, 239–242, *see dalālah;* — of expressions 31, 46–7, 49, 55, 153 *see* SE; — of 'what is articulated or pronounced' *(dalālat al-manṭūq)* 176; — of 'what is implicated' 187; — of 'what is implied' 187; — of 'what is said' *(dalālat al-manṭūq)* 185, 187, 196, 198, 215–6, 242; — of 'what is understood' *(dalālat al-mafhūm)* 176, 178; alluded — *(dalālat al-ishārah)* 14, 180, 185, 242; composed — *(dalālat al-manẓūm)* 180, 182; deterministic — *(dalālah qaṭ'iyyah)* 5; equivalence— *(dalālat muṭābaqah)* 13, 48, 143–4, 149, 151–7, 180, 185, 193, 222, 241; existential and non-existential — 104, 117–19; explicit and indicated — 182; generic — 25; implicated — *(dalālat al-mafhūm)* 14, 180–1, 242; implicational — *(dalālat iltizām)* 13, 48, 74, 76, 143–4, 149, 151–6, 185, 193–4, 241; inclusional — 150, 155–7; incorporational — *(dalālat taḍammun)* 13, 48, 143–4, 149–51, 155–7, 180, 185, 193, 241; indicated — *(dalālat al-tanbīh*

wa-l-īmā') 14, 180–5, 242; linguistic — 143, 240; natural — *(dalālah ṭabī'iyyah)* 144–5; non-composed — *(dalālat ghayr al-manẓūm)* 180; non-existential — 104, 117, 143, 239; non-verbal — *(dalālah ghayr lafẓiyyah)* 143–5, 240; probabilistic — 5; rational — 143–5; required — *(dalālat al-iqtiḍā')* 14, 180, 185, 242; system of — 143; types of — 104, 143–4, 149, 152, 155–6, 193–4, 240; universal — 29, 235; verbal — 143–5, 240; *waḍ'*-based — 8, 13, 32, 145–8, 151–7, 240–1; *waḍ'*-based verbal — 143, 146–7, 149, 240
significational classification, classification of signification 13, 141, 153–5, 158–9, 170, 175–6, 185, 240; common — 144; al-Ghazālī's — 176, 179; Ḥanafī — 159, 162, 242; pragmatic — 158; semantic — 158; semiotic — 13, 142, 144, 158, 240; Shāfi'ī — 176, 242–3; text-based — 13, 159, 241–3
signified *(madlūl)* 31, 34, 69, 101, 107, 113, 142, 144, 148, 151–2, 156–8, 181
signifier *(dalīl)* 31, 34, 53, 69, 103, 113, 142, 144–5, 148, 156, 196, 206 *see* sign; natural — 145; probabilistic — 196
signifying by expressions 31 *see* SBE
silence *(sukūt al-mutakallim)* 104, 203; relevant — 104, 111, 203
ṣiyagh al-'uqūd (forms of contract) 6, 41, 174
siyāq 35 *see* co-text, context, *qarīnah*
specific *(al-khāṣṣ)* 120
speech; — acts 30, 41; — habit *('ādat khiṭāb)* 114; mental — 30; types of — 30
Sperber 105, 234
stated 170, 185–7, 216 *see* meaning, *manṭūq;* — and implicated propositions 176; implicature of a — numeral *see* implicature
subject 142, 223–4
subsidiary 4, 60, 63, 77–9, 126, 239 *see far'*
Sunnī 10–11, 31, 89, 131, 234
al-Suyūṭī 12, 19, 106
switching *(intiqāl)* 128, 204
synonymous 96, 101, 141, 154
syntactic 16, 61, 148–9, 212–13; — condition *see* condition
syntagmatic relationship 48, 99
syntax 15

ta'āwun see co-operation
tabādur (immediacy) 55, 63–4, 70, 111–12, 125, 163, 237; principle of — *see* principle
al-Taftāzānī 21, 25–7, 75, 186–7, 201
al-Tahānawī 34, 141–2, 145, 160
takhṣīṣ (restriction) 58
ta'mīm (generalisation) 58
taqyīd see qualification
ta'rīḍ (intimation) 178
taṣawwur (conceptualisation, forming concepts, non-propositional apprehension) 87, 141–2
taṣdīq (judgement, making judgements, propositional apprehension) 87, 141–2
Ṭāshkubrīzādah 10
ta'wīl (diverting to non-apparent meaning) 88–9, 94, 127–33, 135, 240; — conditions 132; accessible — 132; conditions of the proper — 130; far-fetched — 132; liable to — 129–30, 133, 240; limitations of — 130; misapplication of — 133; types of — 132
theological 2, 13, 17, 30, 45, 88–9, 175
theory; — of cognitive relativism 13, 88, 90, 94; — of communication *see* communication; — of definition *see* definition; — of *majāz see majāz;* — of metaphor *see* metaphor; — of relevance *see* relevance

transgression 202
truth 150, 169, 216; — -condition 223; — -conditional 177, 185; — table 216; — -value 154
truthfulness 60, 66–8, 172, 181; assumption of the speaker's — *see* assumption; preservation of the speaker's — 175, 242; principle of the speaker's — *see* principle; the speaker's — *(ṣidq al-mutakallim)* 64, 66

understanding 87, 141–2; *see fahm, fiqh*
unequivocal 128, 161, 192 *see naṣṣ*
universal 18–19, 21–2, 24, 26–8, 87, 90, 92, 94, 109, 122, 218 *see* meaning, signification, *waḍ'*; — versus particular 25, 90; the natural — *(al-kullī l-ṭabī'ī)* 91
unmentioned 171, 186–7, 193–5, 197, 206–8, 217
unqualification (*iṭlāq*) 79–80, 118
unqualified *(muṭlaq)* 53, 76, 88, 99, 101, 118–20, 123, 129, 194, 200, 203, 237, 241 *see* expression, meaning
unstated *see* meaning
'urf (custom) 56
use 4, 8–9, 13, 16–18, 24–6, 29–32, 34, 41, 43–48, 53, 56, 59–61, 63, 65, 68, 71–2, 75, 90–1, 97, 99–100, 102–3, 105–6, 108–9, 111–15, 118, 124–6, 134–5, 147–9, 153, 158, 170, 174, 235, 237–8 *see isti'māl*; figurative — 4, 74, 88; literal — 17, 59, 61, 67, 71, 74, 80, 235 *see ḥaqīqah*; non-figurative — 154; non-literal — 51, 59, 67, 74–5, 80 *see majāz;* science of — 9; single — 17
uṣūl 50, 58–9, 63, 125, 127, 235, 239 *see* principle; — *al-fiqh see fiqh*

valid; — counter implicature *see* counter implicature
validity; — of counter implicature *see* counter implicature; legal — 160, 170, 172–3, 175; preservation of the legal — of the text *(al-ṣiḥḥah al-shar'iyyah)* 175, 242
verbal 4, 44, 55–6, 110, 143–6, 155–6, 196, 234, 240 *see* context, qualification, signification
violation, — of the base 59–60, 63, 69, 78–80, 235; — of the grammar 33; — of the principle 59–60, 72, 235; — of the principle of the speaker's disposition to make his intention manifest 72
vocative 121

waḍ' 4, 7–10, 12–13, 15–34, 42, 44–6, 49, 51, 53, 56, 59–62, 64–5, 67, 70–1, 76, 88, 90–3, 95, 100, 102–3, 106, 108–10, 113, 116–17, 135, 143, 148–9, 156, 197, 234–9; — and use 15–16, 90–1, 100, 135; — of proper names 28; conventional — *(al-waḍ' al-'urfī)* 108; general and special conventional — 108, 143; general and specific — 13, 18, 25; general conventional — *(al-waḍ' al-'urfī l-'āmm)* 16–17, 108; individual — *(al-waḍ' al-shakhṣī)* 23–4, 108, 149; isolative — 33, 62; isolative and subsumptive — 23–4; legal *(al-shar'ī)* — 16–17; linguistic — 16–17, 26, 29, 108; non-linguistic — 16; original — 108; science of — 10; *Sharī'ah*-based — *(al-waḍ' al-shar'ī)* 108; special conventional or technical *('urfī khāṣṣ)* — 16–17, 108; subsumptive — *(al-waḍ' al-naw'ī)* 62, 108, 149, 235; universal — 24; universal and particular — 13, 18
waḍ'-based 32, 46, 50, 110–11, 143, 145–9, 156–7, 179, 240–1 *see* ambiguity, component, *dalālah*, discourse, expression, meaning, qualification, signification
Weiss 10, 16, 23
well-formedness 32–3
'what is explicitly said' 185
'what is implicitly said' 178, 185–7

'what is presupposed' and 'what is in focus' 161
'what is said' *see mantūq*
Wilson 105, 234
word formation 23, 234
wujūd see existence
Wunderlich 102
Zādah 35
ẓāhir 66, 127–33, 161, 192, 196, 240, *see* apparent
Ẓāhirī 131, 133
Ẓāhirīs 9, 44–5, 131
al-Zarkashī 22, 33, 67